NEITHER CONFIRM
NOR DENY

GLOBAL AMERICA

GLOBAL AMERICA

Edited by Jay Sexton and Sarah B. Snyder

Columbia University Press's Global America series pushes the history
of U.S. foreign relations in new directions, sharpening and diversifying
our understanding of the global dimensions of American history from
the colonial era to the twenty-first century. Books in the series explore
America's global encounters, including how external forces have shaped
the development of the United States and vice versa; why American
encounters with the wider world have produced volatility, ruptures, and
crises; the shifting contours of U.S. power over time; and the impact of
hierarchical attitudes regarding identity in shaping U.S. foreign
relations. Taken together, the series analyzes the global history of the
United States; its authors employ a diverse range of methodological,
chronological, disciplinary, geographical, and ideological perspectives.

M. TODD BENNETT

NEITHER CONFIRM NOR DENY

How the Glomar Mission Shielded the CIA
from Transparency

Columbia University Press / *New York*

Columbia University Press
Publishers Since 1893
New York   Chichester, West Sussex
cup.columbia.edu
Copyright © 2023 Columbia University Press
All rights reserved

Library of Congress Cataloging-in-Publication Data
Names: Bennett, M. Todd, author.
Title: Neither confirm nor deny : how the Glomar mission shielded the CIA
from transparency / Todd Bennett.
Description: New York : Columbia University Press, [2022] | Series: Global
America | Includes bibliographical references and index.
Identifiers: LCCN 2022012916 (print) | LCCN 2022012917 (ebook) |
ISBN 9780231193467 (hardback) | ISBN 9780231193474 (trade paperback) |
ISBN 9780231550321 (ebook)
Subjects: LCSH: United States. Central Intelligence Agency—History—
20th century. | Glomar Explorer (Ship) | Espionage, American—Soviet
Union—History—20th century. | Intelligence service—United States—
History—20th century. | Cold War.
Classification: LCC JK468.I6 B46 2022 (print) | LCC JK468.I6 (ebook) |
DDC 327.1273009—dc23/eng/20220623
LC record available at https://lccn.loc.gov/2022012916
LC ebook record available at https://lccn.loc.gov/2022012917

Cover design: Chang Jae Lee
Cover image: *Hughes Glomar Explorer* at sea.

CONTENTS

List of Abbreviations vii

Introduction 1

1 The Old Lines 15

2 The Hughes Connection 41

3 The Rules of the Game 69

4 Inside Job 105

5 Fish or Cut Bait? 131

6 Colby's Dike 157

7 Neither Confirm nor Deny 185

8 Shivering from Overexposure 213

9 Hold the Line 241

Conclusion 271

Acknowledgments 293

Notes 297

Selected Bibliography 347

Index 361

ABBREVIATIONS

ABM	antiballistic missile
ACLU	American Civil Liberties Union
AGI	auxiliary, general intelligence
CIA	Central Intelligence Agency
CNO	chief of naval operations
DA	district attorney
DCI	director of central intelligence
DEFCON	defense readiness condition
DIA	Defense Intelligence Agency
DNC	Democratic National Committee
DoD	Department of Defense
DS&T	Directorate of Science and Technology
DSSP	Deep Submergence Systems Project
EO	executive order
EXCOM	Executive Committee
FBI	Federal Bureau of Investigation
FOIA	Freedom of Information Act
FY	fiscal year

HGE	*Hughes Glomar Explorer*
HSCI	House Select Committee on Intelligence
ICBM	intercontinental ballistic missile
IRS	Internal Revenue Service
JCS	Joint Chiefs of Staff
KGB	Komitet Gosudarstvennoy Bezopasnosti, or the Committee for State Security
LAPD	Los Angeles Police Department
MIRV	multiple independently targetable reentry vehicle
MRV	multiple reentry vehicle
NATO	North Atlantic Treaty Organization
NCDC	neither confirm nor deny
NRO	National Reconnaissance Office
NSA	National Security Agency
NSC	National Security Council
NURO	National Underwater Reconnaissance Office
OMB	Office of Management and Budget
OPEC	Organization of the Petroleum Exporting Countries
PDB	President's Daily Brief
RCFP	Reporters Committee for Freedom of the Press
SALT	Strategic Arms Limitation Talks
SAP	Special Access Program(s)
SEC	Securities and Exchange Commission
SSCI	Senate Select Committee on Intelligence
UPI	United Press International
USIB	United States Intelligence Board
USSR	Union of Soviet Socialist Republics
VP	vice president
WCPO	West Coast Program Office (CIA)

NEITHER CONFIRM
NOR DENY

INTRODUCTION

Y ou must be crazy," CIA director Richard Helms declared when his deputy, Carl Duckett, laid it out. In March 1968, a nuclear-armed Golf-class Soviet submarine suffered an accident and sank to the bottom of the Pacific Ocean, tragically killing all ninety-eight hands aboard. This fact did not faze Helms in the least. U.S. intelligence had pinpointed the sub's remains months later near the geographic coordinates of 40° north, 180° west, approximately 1,560 nautical miles northwest of Pearl Harbor, Hawaii. Reconnaissance showed the wreckage split into sections resting some 16,500 feet—more than three miles—below the water's surface.

What did faze Helms was the recovery plan Duckett proposed. Duckett ran the CIA's Directorate of Science and Technology, or DS&T. This was the home of the so-called wizards of Langley, engineers and scientists renowned for innovations such as the U-2 spy plane, which flew at a record-breaking altitude of seventy thousand feet, high above the reach of Soviet air defenses when it was introduced in the mid-1950s. Their ambitious plan basically called for the construction of an enormous surface ship equipped with a claw-like capture vehicle capable of reaching the submarine in the depths of the Pacific. To prevent the Soviet Union from becoming aware of, and possibly interfering with, the clandestine intelligence-gathering activity, they proposed hiding it in plain sight under commercial cover as a deep ocean mining initiative, a speculative enterprise that hardly existed at the time. "He damn near threw me out the window," Duckett said of Helms's reaction.[1]

No one could accuse Helms of being risk averse. He had participated in many of the most forward-leaning operations in CIA history, including some that would come back to haunt the agency. But this proposal sounded like science fiction. Never before in history had anyone come close to raising something as heavy as a waterlogged submarine (estimated at nearly four million pounds) from such a great depth—much less in secret. Navy experts did not think it could be done, let alone by the CIA, an agency without significant marine experience. DS&T's aerospace wizards seemed out of their element. "We knew more about the backside of the moon than the bottom of the ocean," one later confessed.[2]

The plan's visibility was concerning. Cool, controlled, and exacting—the type of man who cleared his desk at the end of each workday, no matter how eventful the day had been—Helms was known even among fellow intelligence professionals for the premium he placed on discretion. "When Helms said secret he meant *secret*," CIA inspector general Lyman Kirkpatrick recalled, "secret from inception to eternity." In the aptly titled *The Man Who Kept the Secrets*, biographer Thomas Powers observed that the spymaster preferred to operate in the shadows. "Let's do it right, let's do it quietly, let's do it correctly," he advised.[3]

The "boat project," as DS&T officials called it, was anything but discreet. It would take years to design, build, and test the prototypical hardware needed to lift the target. That hardware included the capture vehicle, which stood up to nine stories high; a submersible barge the size of an aircraft hangar in which to assemble and maneuver the claw into the cavernous well of the lift ship; and the ship itself. Oversized to accommodate the targeted section of the submarine, it grew to measure more than 618 feet long and 115 feet wide—too wide, it turned out, to pass through the Panama Canal. Unmissable at that size, the surface ship would operate out in the open all that time, raising the possibility that someone, somewhere might see through the charade.

Plus, there were all the people to worry about. Hundreds of U.S. government officials and private contractors already knew about some aspect of the sub-raising plan by the time it landed on Helms's desk. Thousands more would become witting before the ship was ready to sail. And they would leave a paper trail of memos and studies and reports.

Tight security could mitigate the risk. But size was the program's "biggest weakness," according to cover staff director Walter Lloyd, the official charged with keeping it under wraps. "Too many people" knew, he said, and the "potential for leakage was enormous." Even a scrap of paper left by one careless or disgruntled individual could sink the entire operation—and waste all the resources poured into it.[4]

CIA initially estimated the probability of success at just 10 percent. Research and development raised expectations as time went on. But 10 percent was "a not very assuring number," one participant recalled. And agency calculations were strictly technical. They did not consider security or what effect the disclosure of the sub-raising mission might have on America's foreign policy or defense interests. Such "political judgments," Helms sniffed, should be made closer to the time of the actual recovery mission, which was scheduled for 1974.[5]

Intelligence was Helms's chief concern. In his view, the benefits of acquiring the submarine, designated *K-129* by the Soviet Navy, outweighed the costs, considerable though they were. The section of the submarine officials had targeted contained unique intelligence available nowhere else. There was a nuclear warhead and ballistic missile system but also code materials and cryptographic gear. If the United States could secretly acquire these, it stood to gain a major intelligence victory and an edge in the underwater Cold War, a hidden but important battleground where each superpower raced to develop countermeasures against the other's ever quieter, ever deadlier submarines. In 1970, Helms chaired a meeting of U.S. intelligence agency heads that placed "highest priority" on recovering the target.[6]

Helms's word wasn't the last. Major programs were subject to review by the National Security Council (NSC). And the White House would eventually weigh in. But his green light took the project, code-named AZORIAN, off the drawing board and onto a course that would prove difficult to reverse. Government contracts totaling an estimated $350 million—the exact figure remains classified—flowed to private firms. DS&T staff invited billionaire Howard Hughes, secluded in a Las Vegas penthouse, to front the "mining" program. Shipbuilders busied themselves preparing the *Hughes Glomar Explorer* for its 1974 voyage.

* * *

Underwater espionage. Impossible technology. A reclusive industrialist. Outside the CIA, critics assailed a plan that read like a Jules Verne novel with an Ian Fleming twist. The CIA had allowed its imagination to run wild. Senior military officials called the mission "crazy and impossible." Some suggested that limits needed to be placed on the agency.[7]

Inside the CIA, the view was different. Sure, AZORIAN pushed the envelope. But it took imagination—and the freedom to give it flight—to accomplish the agency's core mission of collecting foreign intelligence, whether that took its members to the heavens or the bottom of the sea. DS&T enjoyed a stellar reputation because it had gone where few others dared—to space. Helms was confident in its ability to perform an underwater moonshot. Duckett "is running an imaginative shop in a difficult area," he boasted.[8]

CIA officers wore their pursuit of a seemingly impossible mission as a badge of honor—and a shield against the slings and arrows that came their way. "AZORIAN ranks in the forefront of imaginative and bold operations undertaken in the long history of intelligence collection," an internal history declared. Any intelligence "organization too timid to undertake calculable risks in pursuit of a proper objective would not be true to itself or to the people it serves." AZORIAN proved that CIA professionals had the right stuff. Pursuing "tradecraft in a most imaginative manner," they applied rapid advances in science and technology in search of military-grade data beneficial to national security.[9]

They wear that badge still. Today, a portrait of the *Hughes Glomar Explorer* hauling up part of the submarine hangs inside CIA headquarters in Langley, Virginia. Titled *We Are Only Limited by Our Imagination*, it is one of a collection of artworks celebrating great moments in American intelligence history, from U-2 overflights of the Soviet Union in the 1950s to the introduction of Stinger antiaircraft missiles into Afghanistan in the 1980s. According to a spokesperson, the collection's aim is didactic, to instill pride and show the CIA's current workforce "where we've come from as an agency so they can lead us to where we will go."[10]

To one AZORIAN veteran, the image serves as a reminder of a time when the agency's ambition was not limited by political, intellectual, or other barriers, and it carried the CIA to the ends of the earth. There were "no limitations—none," he said, proudly pointing to a framed print that hangs in his suburban Washington, DC, home. The initiative's "scope was unimaginable, and we allowed nothing to get in our way."[11]

Published accounts paint a similar picture. Several books have appeared since the CIA declassified the history of Project AZORIAN in 2010. Each book has taken a deeper dive than the last into the technology and tradecraft that went into not only raising the sub from such a great depth but keeping the colossal undertaking secret for years. All praise the operation, ranking it among the greatest in CIA history, despite the fact that AZORIAN's ambition ultimately exceeded its grasp. The *Explorer*'s claw failed during the 1974 lift attempt, allowing part (the most valuable part, declassified records confirm) of the sub to fall back to the seabed. And the mission's cover was blown in 1975 after Hughes's Los Angeles headquarters was burglarized, ending plans for a return mission and leaving the agency in the headlines, where Helms didn't want it to be.[12]

AZORIAN or MATADOR, its final codename, surely ranks among the most audacious collection efforts in CIA history, and getting to the bottom of it is important for that reason alone. Yet celebrations of high-tech gadgetry and of how Langley's wizards employed it to conquer nature, appealing though such tales may be, distract attention from other matters of equal or greater importance to students of intelligence history. This book situates *Glomar* in its historical context to explore these and a host of related matters, including CIA public affairs, the agency's attempts to shape popular understanding of intelligence work, and its relationship with the media more generally; intelligence outsourcing; foreign relations, national security, and international law, and their uneasy coexistence with intelligence activities; intelligence budgeting practices and procedures; intelligence oversight, or the lack thereof; bureaucratic politics and the role they played in intelligence decision making; and the dramatic expansion of collection initiatives that occurred in the 1960s and 1970s, not only technologically but locationally and organizationally as well.

Glomar's main through line was government secrecy, which rose and fell (and rose again) over the program's seven-plus-year history, a span of the Cold War that stretched from 1968 to 1975, the "Year of Intelligence," and beyond. By "secrecy," I mean not just the type of operational security that defines every clandestine activity, though it did require an inordinate amount of deception to hide the true purpose of the hulking, 63,300-ton *Glomar Explorer* in plain sight. Rather, I mean the opacity that, in an age of intelligence unaccountability, left the CIA's imagination unchecked, free to dream up a bold scheme to steal a Soviet submarine; the plausible deniability that enabled the espionage plan even as Washington pursued détente with Moscow; and the classified data still protected by the *Glomar* response ("We can neither confirm nor deny the existence of the information requested, but hypothetically, if such data were to exist, the subject would be classified and could not be disclosed."). By stressing these and other matters, this book seeks to contribute to a small but growing body of literature investigating how governments keep national security secrets, and why.[13]

Scholars say that intelligence activities like AZORIAN/MATADOR illustrate the tension between national security and civil liberty that runs throughout American history. To effectively protect the nation against adversaries, U.S. intelligence agencies often must act covertly. Yet secrecy frustrates oversight, and without accountability the American people cannot be certain that spy agencies function well and in accord with stated national principles. Secrecy is essential, but so, too, is openness. Americans have struggled to find the right balance between the two, a point of equilibrium that has moved as circumstances dictate.[14]

During the early Cold War, the balance tilted heavily in favor of secrecy. The year 1968, when U.S. intelligence located the wreckage of the *K-129*, marked the tail end of an era in which Congress exercised oversight of the CIA so minimal as to constitute "undersight," according to historian Richard Immerman. To be sure, some limits were in place. But executive branch controls were "anemic," Loch Johnson notes, and congressional watchdogs were toothless. Controlled by powerful committee chairs like Senator Richard Russell (D-Georgia), cold warriors who trusted America's silent service to do whatever was necessary to combat communism, they asked few questions and held even fewer hearings. Combined, the four House and Senate intelligence subcommittees that existed in lieu of standing committees met just twice in all of 1971. "You have to make up your mind that you are going to have an intelligence agency and protect it as such and shut your eyes some and take what is coming," Russell's protégé, John Stennis (D-Mississippi), said of his own management style.[15]

That kind of "oversight," such as it was, "positively invited the CIA not to be squeamish," observes Helms's biographer, Thomas Powers. Or, as intelligence studies pioneer Harry Howe Ransom put it, the permissive climate that prevailed during the so-called era of trust gave the agency almost complete freedom to do as it wished.[16]

Had the CIA been more answerable, one DS&T veteran speculates that AZORIAN might never have gotten off the drawing board. But the agency was not accountable, not in any real way. And so it embarked on a plan involving a giant claw, an experimental ship, and a "naked madman," as one biographer characterized Hughes—a plan Helms once dismissed as too crazy to believe; a plan that, by the CIA's own reckoning, had little chance of succeeding.[17]

* * *

Could the CIA raise the *K-129*? Maybe, Helms determined. Should it? Nobody really addressed that question until President Richard Nixon stepped off a helicopter in June 1972 to proclaim that he and Soviet leader Leonid Brezhnev had established the basis for a new era of peace at their historic Moscow Summit.

Détente did not always live up to the hype. But it did introduce an element of uncertainty for the CIA, a Cold War creature that had become accustomed to watching the Kremlin. AZORIAN put the agency in the crosshairs. What if a failure of some sort occurred? Would negative publicity scuttle the president's plans and embarrass him in the eyes of the world, as the U-2 incident had flustered Dwight Eisenhower? Was the sub-raising mission really in America's interest?

Senior officials asked these questions for two reasons. The first was because the Golf was a historical relic. Launched in 1959, the diesel-powered model had since been superseded by two (going on three) generations of Yankee- and Delta-class nuclear-powered subs carrying missiles with far greater ranges. The second reason was because AZORIAN was highly provocative. Taking a sunken warship that not only remained the legal property of the USSR but contained the bodies of some of the dozens of Soviet submariners who went down with their ship virtually guaranteed that the Kremlin would retaliate if it found out. Soviet leaders could order a replay of 1968's *Pueblo* incident, in which North Korean forces seized the USS *Pueblo*—an intelligence ship, like the *Explorer*—killing one American and holding dozens of crewmembers hostage. Or, more likely, they could take a page from the playbook of ex-premier Nikita Khrushchev, who in 1960 torpedoed a détente-like thaw in the Cold War by making a spectacle of the fact that Soviet air defenses had downed an American spy plane.[18]

Either way, AZORIAN risked provoking a confrontation on the high seas that, tit for tat, could spiral out of control. In the eyes of opponents—of which there were many throughout the highest reaches of the U.S. government—the mission's anticipated intelligence gains, however great, were not worth the geopolitical risk. The mission raised fundamental questions about intelligence operations and their place in foreign policy. What role, if any, would espionage play in détente? Did greater Soviet-American cooperation raise the political threshold to the point of reducing or even eliminating competitive Cold War–style spying? Would the president, in the words of Henry Kissinger, his national security advisor (and, for a time, also secretary of state), "want to risk relations with the Soviet Union for the sake of an intelligence coup?"[19]

Surely not, historians of American foreign relations have long presumed. Despite its importance, intelligence remains the "missing dimension" of U.S. diplomatic history forty years after Christopher Andrew and David Dilks noted the subject's absence from the academic literature. There are exceptions, of course, and the field of intelligence history is expanding. Yet the extent to which the superpowers carried their competitive, Cold War habit of spying on one another into the more cooperative era of détente goes underappreciated.[20]

Intelligence goes underappreciated, I would add, in part *because* of détente and *Glomar*, a combination that produced the aforementioned *Glomar* response: "We can neither confirm nor deny the existence of the information requested . . ." Commonplace today, that legalese originated in 1975 in response to requests for data about the *Explorer*'s mission, including those filed under the Freedom of Information Act, strengthened by Congress in 1974. Arguably *Glomar*'s most durable legacy, the response has since worked to frustrate transparency efforts by scholars, journalists, and watchdogs, denying public access to the kind of U.S. government records on which intelligence history depends.

Writing a policy history of the *Glomar* expedition only became possible with the release of *National Security Policy, 1973–1976*, a volume of the *Foreign Relations of the United States* (*FRUS*) series, the official documentary record of U.S. foreign policy published by the Department of State. Published in 2014 after extensive declassification review, the volume contains a cache of program records available nowhere else. They include files of the 40 Committee, the high-level NSC panel that reviewed major covert initiatives during the Nixon and Ford administrations.[21]

Full disclosure: I edited that *FRUS* volume in my former capacity as a State Department historian, in which role I was required by law to produce a "thorough, accurate, and reliable" record of U.S. foreign policy decisions.[22] To be clear, this book is based solely on publicly available materials. It does not contain classified information. (The CIA ensured that by subjecting the manuscript to prepublication review, because I once had access to agency materials.) The experience of researching that *FRUS* volume, though, of rifling through White House intelligence files, CIA archives, and other collections that remain inaccessible to the general public, gives me unique insight into *Glomar*'s recorded history. And this book pairs *FRUS* with recently declassified material, research in multiple archives, and interviews with participants to go behind Washington's closed doors to a vantage point that yields fresh geopolitical perspective on a project hitherto known solely for its remarkable operational history.

Time and again, the historical record shows that the CIA's ambitious plan received the go-ahead despite the risks—and was backed, surprisingly enough, by Kissinger, one of détente's foremost architects. Why and how the project went forward speaks to the history of not just détente but intelligence, and the uneasy coexistence of diplomacy and espionage, generally speaking.[23] A central figure, Kissinger acted as Nixon's intelligence chief due to the president's well-documented distrust of the East Coast sophisticates who he believed controlled the CIA. Kissinger understood better than most that détente's spirit of bilateral cooperation did not foreclose great power competition. The Cold War soldiered on, and the superpowers continued to do what states routinely do: vie for political influence, arm themselves with deadly weapons, and spy on one another.[24]

Kissinger also understood how secrecy operated behind the scenes to downplay—and sometimes encourage, though that was not the intent—potentially destabilizing competition. Kissinger and Nixon, scholars know, had a penchant for conducting foreign relations in secret, including through private back channels.[25] Kissinger used his confidential contacts with Soviet ambassador Anatoly Dobrynin, for example, to mitigate any ill effects Soviet-American intelligence battles might have on the two countries' bilateral relations. As this book will show, their conspiracy of silence helps explain why Kissinger backed AZORIAN so forcefully from the start, and how *Glomar*, unlike the U-2, avoided becoming "the subject of international acrimony," in the words of William Colby, who inherited the sub-raising mission when he succeeded Helms as CIA director in 1973.[26]

Intelligence gathering and international relations may coexist uneasily. But *Glomar*'s history demonstrates that intelligence—from dueling covert actions to competitive analyses—was integral to détente and the unfolding of superpower relations over the 1970s. The same goes for secrecy, insofar as nondisclosure prevented the superpowers from becoming embroiled in the sort of public posturing that doomed previous fence-mending efforts. Official silence enabled the appearance of good Soviet-American relations to continue, despite the Cold War competition that existed (literally, in *Glomar*'s case) just below the surface.

* * *

Over the program's life span, U.S. government efforts to shield certain facts from the public in the name of national security received closer scrutiny. *Glomar*'s disclosure by journalists such as Jack Anderson and Seymour Hersh helped inaugurate the "Year of Intelligence," as the *New York Times* dubbed 1975. The incident exemplified the changes that had occurred within the news media, and in its relationship with the U.S. government since the program's inception. Disillusioned by official lies regarding Vietnam, reporters, now more skeptical of the powers that be, routinely investigated Washington's official accounts. Such investigations exposed scandals like Watergate and further elevated the stature of the Fourth Estate, widely seen as a defender of the public interest against official malfeasance.[27]

Disclosure of the CIA's underwater "boondoggle," as critics called it, also boosted efforts on Capitol Hill to restrain the intelligence community as part of a wider congressional "revolution" against the outsized authority of the imperial presidency. "If the CIA can spend $350 million with which to pay Howard Hughes to raise obsolete eighteen-year-old submarines," remarked Senator Frank Church, chair of a select committee empaneled to investigate U.S. intelligence activities, then it is "no wonder we are going broke." "I think the agency needs a cost-to-benefit ratio," added Church, who pledged to look into underwater espionage as part of his committee's probe.[28]

Together, Congress and the news media served as the cornerstones of a culture of transparency that dawned in the late sixties and early seventies. Predicated on the "unprecedented openness of institutions to critical view and correction," writes political scientist Hugh Heclo, the sunshine era took a dim view of official secrecy.[29] The security balance swung suddenly toward openness, and some of the deepest, darkest practices of the U.S. intelligence community were exposed, from domestic spying schemes and botched assassination attempts to dirty tricks, secret wars, and covert actions. In that climate, the disclosure of a less-than-fully-successful attempt to raise an elderly Soviet sub—and to do so, no less, in cahoots with Hughes, a shadowy figure whose under-the-table dealings with disgraced former president Nixon were then spilling into view—struck critics as yet another misstep that made the CIA appear inept, even sinister. Some called for the dissolution of the spy agency, which faced the severest existential crisis in its history to that point.

Assaults on the U.S. intelligence community remain fixed in historical memory. They exemplify the "great shift" in American culture and politics that historians say occurred in the seventies.[30] Yet *Glomar*'s unmasking also bolstered efforts to protect the CIA from overexposure, an under-studied but important development that calls into question just how transformative the 1970s really were when it came to matters of national security. Unauthorized disclosure of the still active operation provoked a backlash by foreign policy hawks concerned that transparency was moving too far, too fast, and resulting in the indiscriminate release of sensitive information. Excessive congressional regulation, they warned, would "cripple" the CIA's ability to perform cutting-edge initiatives such as "the Great Submarine Snatch" in the future.[31]

That backlash restrained the congressional and journalistic revolutions before they could expose more intelligence secrets, and, I argue, was among the reasons *Glomar* played a pivotal but underappreciated role in saving the CIA from the clutches of transparency. Other developments contributed, certainly. But news of the underwater mission changed the conversation. Widely hailed as one of the most "imaginative, energetic and ingenious" operations in memory, on par with the U-2 spy plane or Berlin tunnel, the sub-raising effort provided a rallying point for CIA supporters—and a timely reminder that the agency served an important national purpose. "The CIA Was Doing Its Job," opined the *Washington Star*, voicing a widely held view. "It wasn't shadowing U.S. dissidents around Washington or New York; it was out on the high seas performing a function that was legitimate and potentially of high intelligence value."[32]

Glomar worked to establish new limits on the post-Vietnam, post-Watergate culture of disclosure. That was the conclusion reached by one Washington insider, the columnist Joseph Kraft. The affair served to "right the balance," he wrote. As we will see, this was a balance that left the CIA's imagination relatively free to dream up new schemes—not as free as it had been prior to 1975, certainly, but freer than seemed likely at the start of the year, and free enough to earn a place of honor in CIA halls.[33]

* * *

What is the proper balance between the public's right to know and the government's duty to protect national security information? Under what limits must the U.S. intelligence community operate? Where should the line be drawn?

These questions are as vital today as they were decades ago. The pages that follow address them by providing the history of a rebalancing act. They tell Glomar's story both to weigh in on America's ever-present tension between the demands of democracy and the need for secrecy in national security and foreign policy, and to offer an alternative perspective on the 1970s, a decade known for expansive openness.

1

THE OLD LINES

Without secrecy the CIA was "not worth a plugged nickel," Senator Richard Russell (D-Georgia) drawled in response to calls to strengthen congressional oversight of intelligence, which at the time was limited to small, informal subcommittees of each chamber's Appropriations and Armed Services Committees. Russell, a staunch segregationist, was on the wrong side of civil rights history. But he remained a formidable presence on Capitol Hill when the submarine project entered the pipeline. A member of Congress since 1933, he continued to exert a great deal of influence, especially behind the scenes, in matters of defense policy, national security, and intelligence. The Senate's CIA subcommittees jointly acted as one under his chairmanship, as they had for years. He also used his position to protect the agency from scrutiny. According to his biographer, "Russell had almost a phobia for military security and for a high degree of independence by the Central Intelligence Agency."[1]

America could not afford closer accountability, Russell insisted—not when it was battling the Soviet Union, a ruthless adversary whose security services were not known for following rules of fair play. To keep Americans safe, the CIA had to operate in the shadows, be they in the halls of

Congress or the streets of Moscow. The smallest indiscretion could compromise U.S. assets, a possibility that required Russell to take every security precaution, from convening subcommittees unannounced in executive session, to keeping minimal records, to leaving the annual CIA outlay unpublished. "No," he answered those who insisted that American taxpayers—and their duly elected representatives—had a right to know more. "We have not told the country, and I do not propose to tell the country in the future, because if there is anything in the United States which should be held sacred behind the curtain of classified matter, it is information regarding the activities of this agency."[2]

Russell practiced what he preached throughout his tenure as the CIA's foremost ally on the Hill. His archived papers, which run into the thousands of boxes, contain only a smattering of intelligence-related files. But by the late 1960s, the septuagenarian, a lifelong smoker, suffered from severe emphysema. He was growing forgetful. So, his staff tucked little index cards inside his breast pocket, each bearing typewritten notes reminding him to take his medicine, call his doctor, or convene a meeting. Some cards include handwritten notes on which Russell specified additional details, like the subject of a certain discussion or the title of a recommended book, like Jessica Mitford's *The American Way of Death*. Most simply list his daily schedule: "10:30 CIA Subcmte," one reads; "3:00 Richard Helms," reads another.[3]

As inscrutable as they are, the cards can be paired with other sources to track the path the submarine project took through Russell's system of intelligence oversight, such as it was. Generally paperless to deter outside scrutiny, that system of closed-door meetings, smoke-filled rooms, and handshake deals remains difficult for historians to document. Rapidly decaying, it would soon succumb to the weight of the very intelligence abuses that reformers always claimed it enabled. For better or worse, though, Russell's was the system in place at the time the sub-raising mission got underway, and it effectively empowered a small network of senior lawmakers to appropriate millions of taxpayer dollars for a scheme involving a giant claw, without anyone seriously questioning whether it was a wise investment.

* * *

Richard Helms did not share many confidences with lawmakers. Charged with protecting the nation's intelligence secrets, he said as little as possible so as to avoid leaks. He once misled Congress to protect a particularly controversial covert activity, thereby earning himself a criminal charge, but also the respect of the supporters who lionized him as "the man who kept the secrets."[4]

Besides, at no point during his tenure as director of central intelligence (DCI), which lasted from 1966 to 1973, was he under any legal obligation to keep lawmakers in the loop. The CIA's founding statute, the National Security Act of 1947, made DCIs (and the agency generally) answerable only to the National Security Council, the White House body also created by the act to coordinate the interagency process of foreign policymaking and to advise the president on national security issues. Other than acknowledging the Senate's role in confirming nominees to serve as DCI, the act included no language requiring any administration official to notify Congress about agency activity.[5]

Helms did sometimes discuss sensitive matters, though. Not with Congress as a whole, or even each chamber's intelligence subcommittees, but their chairs and, perhaps, ranking minority members. Helms held these discussions, he explained, when a proposed operation was especially "dicey, tricky, or might fail" and he wanted to "hold hands" with Congress. A DCI sounded out lawmakers to determine "how far he may go" in questionable activities. Without obtaining preapproval, and the political cover that came with it, a DCI was left out on a limb, where he felt "very lonely indeed" if something went wrong.[6]

With its estimated 10 percent chance of success, the submarine operation certainly qualified as dicey. Legislative files show that Helms reached out to hold hands with House Appropriations chair George Mahon (D-Texas), among other key lawmakers, during the operation's early days. But he cultivated Russell in particular because Russell was singularly influential. With the exception of a two-year stint during the Eisenhower administration, when Republicans briefly formed a majority, Russell chaired the Armed Services Committee from 1951 to 1969, a seat he gave up that year only to chair Appropriations, the Senate's other standing committee

FIGURE 1.1 Senator Richard Russell and Richard Helms chat on June 23, 1966, as the Senate held hearings to confirm Helms's appointment as director of central intelligence.

Source: Associated Press.

with intelligence oversight responsibilities. Throughout much of that time, the two committees' CIA subcommittees jointly acted as one under his leadership, an arrangement that gave him unmatched authority over intelligence. "Generally speaking," recalled the chief of naval operations, Admiral Thomas H. Moorer, "it was sufficient simply to tell Senator Russell that you were doing it, and no one else, and it never leaked."[7]

Perhaps Helms pulled Russell aside after the CIA subcommittee met on July 16, 1968, to brief him about the sub-raising effort.[8] By that time U.S. naval intelligence—alerted by a massive but failed Soviet search conducted by dozens of ships and aircraft over a two-month period—had determined that a Soviet Golf II–class ballistic missile submarine had gone down in March in the central North Pacific.[9] Designated *K-129* by the Soviets, the Golf was one of four subs that disappeared that year, still the deadliest for submariners since World War II. Incidents at sea occurred all too frequently at the time, fueling speculation that the *K-129* had collided with another ship, an American sub perhaps. Or maybe it simply suffered a battery explosion, snorkel failure, missile accident, or other such catastrophic malfunction. The cause remains disputed today.[10]

American officers may not have known for sure what downed the G-722 (they identified the Golf by its hull number, 722). Unlike the Soviets, though, they knew exactly where its wreckage was located. Using a network of hydrophone arrays and acoustic sensors maintained by the U.S. Navy and Air Force to track Soviet submarines and missile tests, analysts geolocated the Golf near the coordinates of 40° north, 180° west some 1,560 nautical miles northwest of Pearl Harbor.[11]

According to *Blind Man's Bluff*, journalists Sherry Sontag and Christopher Drew's account of American underwater espionage, a U.S. spy submarine, the USS *Halibut*, set out to surveil the site in July. It reportedly returned with photographs—twenty-two thousand top-secret photos that officially do not exist and that have never been released by the U.S. government—showing the wreckage damaged and split into sections. They showed "a hole blown nearly ten feet wide, just behind the Golf's conning tower." One of the sub's three missiles had been reduced to "twisted pipe." Another was missing altogether. But the "third silo was intact."

Lying on its starboard side, some 16,500 feet below water on a relatively flat surface, the G-722 appeared to be in surprisingly good condition, given everything it had been through. The "submarine looked basically intact," Sontag and Drew's sources said. Officials targeted the sub's forwardmost section extending from the sail to the bow, because it was most valuable from the intelligence standpoint. According to an engineer who had access to photos and video recordings of the wreckage, the section measured approximately 160 feet long, 64 feet wide, and 55 feet high, and weighed almost two thousand tons.[12]

Or perhaps Helms briefed Russell when they met privately in the senator's office on November 17, 1969.[13] By that time the CIA had taken over following a bitter dispute with the navy over whether and how to recover the submarine. Launched in 1959, the G-722 underwent a major upgrade in the mid-sixties. Converted to a Golf II configuration, it carried the SS-N-5 missile, significant as the first in the Soviet arsenal that could be launched from a submerged submarine. Yet the sub itself was neither fast (its maximum submerged speed was just thirteen knots) nor quiet by contemporary standards. Superseded by two classes of nuclear-powered subs (Hotel and Yankee) since its launch, the diesel-powered G-722 was a historical artifact in some respects. Many of its components had only "modest value, due to obsolescence," experts agreed. Metallurgical analysis of its steel hull might reveal some additional details. But naval intelligence had been tracking Golfs for over a decade. And they did not think it was worth spending hundreds of millions of dollars to haul up tons of mostly antiquated gear. Those resources, they believed, could be better spent developing other intelligence priorities.[14]

By contrast, the sub's contents held *"unique intelligence value"* in the eyes of the United States Intelligence Board (USIB), the panel of senior officials that set requirements for the entire U.S. intelligence community. That is, the target included information obtainable from no other source, on subjects of great importance to national defense. This material included the SS-N-5. In service since 1963, the SS-N-5 was no longer the Soviet fleet's most advanced submarine-launched ballistic missile. Liquid-fueled, its maximum range was just 750 nautical miles. So far as is known, however, the CIA had never before acquired a strategic Soviet missile. The SS-N-5's acquisition, along with that of its nuclear warhead and any associated documentation found aboard the Golf, promised to *"provide important new insight into Soviet nuclear technology, weapon design concepts, and related operational procedures."* This insight, in turn, could establish *"a much improved baseline for estimates of the current and future Soviet strategic threat,"* including the follow-on SS-N-8 system, with a range of 4,000 nautical miles.

As important as those items were, the Golf's cryptographic machines and materials were the real prizes. Their recovery and exploitation would represent "*a major milestone*," the USIB determined. Soviet codes were highly advanced, and authorities probably changed them as soon as they realized the Golf was gone. But obtaining a working cipher machine, along with information specifying how it functioned, could allow American cryptan-alysts to break encrypted Soviet traffic, something they had yet to do, despite their years of trying. Reading the Soviet Navy's mail, as it were, could help American watchers track Soviet submarines, monitor Soviet naval procedures, and predict Soviet military behavior more generally.

"Crypto" was "the driving factor" behind the sub-raising effort, said for-mer National Security Agency director Admiral Bobby Ray Inman. Acquiring the Golf's code room would represent a major achievement—comparable, he said, to British and American successes breaking German and Japanese codes during World War II.[15]

What military capabilities did the Soviet Union have? How could they be used against the United States? The Golf contained answers to *the* ques-tions facing American intelligence agencies at the time. Its secrets prom-ised to give the United States an edge in the underwater Cold War, a hidden but important battlespace that witnessed a dramatic escalation in the late 1960s, as the Soviet Navy rapidly expanded to challenge the U.S. Navy for maritime supremacy.[16]

Naval officials targeted those items and only those items for recovery. Captain James F. Bradley Jr., undersea warfare director of the Office of Naval Intelligence, and Dr. John Piña Craven, chief scientist of the Special Projects Office, spearheaded the navy's underwater intelligence program. Their submarine, the *Halibut*, had photographed the G-722's remains. And they proposed to send a small drone, or unmanned underwater vehicle, equipped with television cameras, propellers, and robotic arms to surgically open holes in the 722's sail with explosives. Using its remote-controlled arms, the minisub, as officials described it, would then reach in and grab selected items, including the Golf's surviving missile and nuclear warhead, and codebooks and cipher machines.[17]

Relatively modest, Bradley and Craven's plan was well within their reach. Led by Craven, the U.S. Navy's Deep Submergence Systems Project (DSSP) did exploratory work that would make Jacques Cousteau blush. Instituted in the wake of the deadliest American submarine incident on record—1963's downing of the USS *Thresher*, which killed all 129 aboard—DSSP operated SEALAB, an underwater experiment testing the ability of aquanauts to withstand extreme environments. DSSP also developed a proven ability to perform deepwater search, rescue, and recovery missions. In 1964, a navy bathyscaphe recovered a small part of the *Thresher* from a depth of eighty-four hundred feet. And in 1966, the world breathed a little easier when a cable-controlled underwater recovery vehicle secured a hydrogen bomb from the bed of the Mediterranean Sea.[18]

DSSP initiatives made submarining safer. Some also provided cover for the navy's growing suite of clandestine programs. (According to Craven, SEALAB prepared deep-sea divers for underwater collection missions.) Directed by Bradley, these black programs went deeper than ever before to gather intelligence treasure buried on the bottom of the sea, treasure that was vulnerable to collection, Bradley reasoned, because nobody (the Soviets included) thought it could be taken. In an operation code-named IVY BELLS, for instance, specially equipped American subs tapped Soviet off-shore communication cables. In SAND DOLLAR, they collected reentry vehicles and other fragments of Soviet missiles from the bottom of the Pacific, where they lay, unattended, after being test-fired from launch sites located deep within the Soviet interior.[19]

Bradley and Craven's breakthroughs gave the US clearer insight into Soviet capabilities and intentions. But their Golf plan was killed before it left the navy. Despite evidence to the contrary, Admiral Moorer doubted that explosives could open penetrable holes in the sub's sail without destroying the priceless objects inside—or that, if they did survive the blast unharmed, items as delicate as a code machine or nuclear warhead could be secured by a remote-controlled submersible operating more than three miles below water. Besides, photos showed that the targeted section of the G-722 was substantially intact. Why not get the whole thing? "If we were going to do anything, we might as well go all the way," he reasoned.[20]

The Pentagon turned to the CIA. In an April 1969 letter, Deputy Secretary of Defense David Packard, cofounder of the computer firm Hewlett-Packard, invited Helms to study the submarine problem. Helms tasked

Deputy Director for Science and Technology Carl Duckett with devising an acquisition plan.[21]

Duckett's shop, the Directorate of Science and Technology, was the arm of the CIA responsible for developing technical means of collecting and evaluating intelligence. DS&T's products included not just the high-flying U-2 spy plane but also the U-2's successors, the supersonic A-12 and SR-71 aircraft, and CORONA, the world's first photoreconnaissance satellite system. These achievements earned the directorate's aerospace engineers and scientists, the "wizards of Langley," stellar reputations within the intelligence community for delivering highly complex, highly technical projects on time, on budget, and on spec.[22]

However, none of Langley's wizards had much experience working in marine environments. To them, the deep was "an unstudied abyss." "We all shared the common credential of zero experience in ocean engineering," one task force member recalled. Early lift concepts betrayed their aeronautical roots: amateurish schemes to use rocket boosters, flotation devices, or pentane-filled platforms to blast, float, or otherwise bring the target to the surface were all quickly discarded as impractical, dangerous, or both. "Looking back, we were an unlikely group to be taking on a marine engineering task that the chief of naval operations had declared 'probably impossible.' "[23]

Yet they were confident. Many would remember this era fondly as the apogee of the agency's golden age. Not as golden, certainly, as the Allen Dulles years, when CIA-backed coups toppled foreign governments with impunity. Several setbacks—from the shooting down in 1960 of the U-2 to *Ramparts* magazine's 1967 exposé of the CIA's political action network—had since trimmed the agency's sails somewhat. But this was nonetheless a time before Vietnam's final chapter was written; before Watergate exposed official misdeeds; before Congress imposed strictures that "shackled a once imaginative and aggressive" agency, a former officer complained, preventing agents from taking the sort of bold action that the adventurous men under Helms had once took.[24]

The crisis of confidence that would beset the nation was nowhere to be found inside DS&T. Not in 1969. Not with the Apollo 11 spacecraft poised for its historic July flight, and America on the verge of meeting President Kennedy's challenge to put a man on the moon, a feat that once seemed impossible. "Those were the days," a DS&T engineer recalled, when "it was assumed American technology could solve any problem."[25]

DS&T's wizards conquered the heavens. Reconnaissance satellites revolutionized intelligence collection, overflying previously denied areas behind the Iron Curtain to vastly increase the volume of information available to American analysts. (After 1960, more than 90 percent of U.S. intelligence on the Soviet Bloc came from satellites.) Numbers alone did not tell the full story about foreign intentions. But technical intelligence took much of the guesswork out of estimating Soviet military strength. "Because of satellites," President Johnson crowed in 1967, "I *know* how many missiles the enemy has."[26]

DS&T's almost uninterrupted string of space-age successes gave task force members the "technical hubris," one recalled, to believe they could do what the navy dared not.[27] They proposed to reach down more than three miles to collect the entire target, all 3.9 million pounds of the G-722's forwardmost section. No one had ever succeeded in raising an object of comparable weight from such a great depth—much less in secret. *Trieste II*, the navy bathyscaphe that retrieved part of the *Thresher*, would come close in 1972, going 16,400 feet below water to retrieve a wayward film capsule dropped by an American satellite. At several hundred pounds, however, the capsule weighed only a fraction of the estimated weight of the Golf. The record for the deepest salvage of a submarine stood at just 643 feet, set in 1969 when the Soviets raised one of their own subs, the *S-80*, from the friendly waters of the Barents Sea.[28]

Covertly retrieving a foreign sub from the depths of the Pacific posed a far greater challenge. The technical hurdles alone rivaled those faced by America's space program. According to the CIA's own guesswork, DS&T's underwater moonshot, as some called it, hardly stood a chance.[29]

Navy officers reacted to the plan with disbelief. A "pipe dream," Bradley called it. The CIA "turned loose some guys who as far as the ocean was concerned were a bunch of amateurs," groused Craven, who categorically dismissed DS&T's proposal as a "lamebrained project put together by a bunch of land-based engineers who couldn't tell the seabed from a flower bed."[30]

Helms reacted similarly. Details still needed ironing out, Duckett cautioned when he presented the plan. But DS&T called for the construction of a prototypical surface ship equipped with a claw-like capture vehicle capable of reaching down 16,500 feet to lift the 160-foot-long, 64-foot-wide section from the ocean bottom and into the well of the ship. Oversized to accommodate the target, the ship itself measured over 618 feet long and 115 feet wide. Plans also called for an aircraft-hangar-sized submersible barge in which to secretly build and then maneuver the claw into and out of the ship's cavernous well.

It would take many years, hundreds of millions of dollars, and thousands of people to design, build, and operate all that hardware. Everything but the capture vehicle—which operated entirely below water, and whose exact specifications remain classified even today—would exist out in the open throughout that time. Specialists were busy devising a cover story to hide

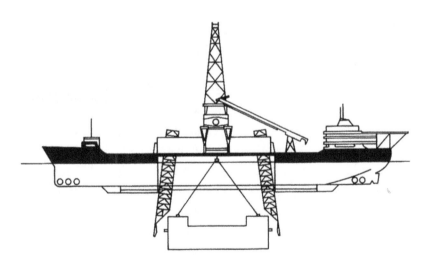

FIGURE 1.2 Diagram of the *Hughes Glomar Explorer*'s lift system, including the docking/undocking of the capture vehicle.

Source: Victorddt, Wikipedia Commons, accessed May 23, 2022, https://commons .wikimedia.org/wiki/File:Glomar_Explorer_(T-AG-193).jpg.

the true purpose of the clandestine operation from the Soviets, who did not know that the Americans had located the G-722, and who would certainly oppose any attempt to steal its secrets. But approximately five hundred U.S. government officials—CIA but also members of the navy, air force, and Department of Defense—already knew about some aspect of the sub-raising plan by the time it landed on Helms's desk. Thousands more government employees and private contractors—a grand total of eighteen hundred by one count, four thousand by another—spread from coast to coast would know by the time the lift ship was ready to set sail. A breach was bound to occur somewhere along the way.[31]

Evidently, it was all too much for the man who kept the secrets, the spymaster who preferred to operate quietly, in the shadows. Cool, calm, and collected, Helms sat silent for a moment before threatening to defenestrate Duckett. The plan seemed unrealistic.[32]

That said, the idea of pulling off a big score appealed to Helms, a former clandestine operative who supervised the digging of the Berlin Tunnel in the 1950s. He trusted his staff. ("Helms was a fellow who by and large gave the people who worked with him his confidence," a colleague recalled. "His instinct was to trust them."[33]) And he cultivated a forward-leaning, mission-centric organizational culture that rewarded risk taking, sometimes to a fault. Helms encouraged DS&T's wizards "to push the envelope of what was possible," one recalls. He praised Duckett's "imaginative shop."[34]

Besides, extraordinary security measures were already being taken to keep the undertaking secret. U.S. government officials routinely limit access to national security information by classifying it as confidential, secret, or top secret. But the sub-raising effort was among a category of highly sensitive programs that received additional safeguards. Known as Special Access Programs (SAP), they include black operations, covert actions, and secret weapons systems, in addition to clandestine collection activities. Information about each individual SAP is compartmentalized, segregated even from other top-secret activities. That is, access is strictly limited to those persons who have a demonstrated "need to know," and who possess the requisite sub-clearance, designated by a specific code word—initially AZORIAN in the case of the submarine project.[35]

AZORIAN's dedicated security system even had its own code name: JENNIFER. Early published accounts often misidentified the sub-raising mission as the "JENNIFER Project." The confusion is understandable, for AZORIAN and JENNIFER were almost indistinguishable, a reflection of the emphasis agency leaders from the top down placed on security. According to a CIA security officer, AZORIAN's program manager, John Parangosky, believed that security should "be involved in every aspect of the program, including planning, from the very first. Security was not to be used just to clean up a mess or tamp down flaps after they developed. It was to be part of all program deliberations. The imprimatur of security was to be obtained before any action was taken. In this way many potential problems were avoided."[36]

Tight security came at a price. According to a 1971 Office of Management and Budget (OMB) review, compartmentalization "served to hide or obscure competitive [intelligence-gathering] capabilities from evaluation, comparison, and tradeoff analysis."[37] But JENNIFER sought to "leak-proof" AZORIAN. Expanding upon previous systems used to defend the U-2, the A-12/SR-71, and the CORONA programs from unauthorized disclosure, JENNIFER provided 360-degree protection, from information management to physical security, communication controls and personnel surveillance. Some credit JENNIFER for sealing off AZORIAN from John Anthony Walker Jr., the navy chief warrant officer whose spy ring gave the Soviets almost unlimited access to classified navy documents for decades starting in 1968, the year naval intelligence located the Golf.[38]

Intelligence professionals regarded JENNIFER as a model. "It was a good security system," recalled Deputy Assistant Secretary of State for Intelligence and Research William McAfee, who cited JENNIFER's principles of "briefing fully as few as possible, putting as little down on paper as you have to, [and] not leaving papers where they can be worked over [by outsiders]." When air force officials planned the B-2 stealth bomber, he said, "they went to CIA to talk security procedures because they wanted to know how [the submarine project], which had so many people involved, had been kept so secret" for so long.[39]

JENNIFER's existence reassured Helms, for whom compartmentalization was an article of faith. "In the secret operations canon it is axiomatic that the probability of leaks escalates exponentially each time a classified document is exposed to another person—be it an agency employee, a member of Congress, a senior official, a typist, or a file clerk," he explained. "Effective compartmentation is fundamental to all secret activity."[40]

AZORIAN boiled down to a judgment call. The mission entailed some "very close judgements," Helms wrote. Certain that the program would remain secret, he decided to proceed. In July 1969, he notified Packard that the CIA had made considerable progress. Impressed, the deputy secretary extended the agency's remit, effectively handing AZORIAN to the CIA.[41]

Given an opportunity to grow the agency's portfolio, Helms next pushed for the establishment of a "new organization" to manage not only the Golf recovery effort, but underwater reconnaissance full stop. Little is known about this organization, other than the fact that the White House approved it in 1969. Its very existence remains unacknowledged by the U.S. government. According to unofficial sources, it was the National Underwater Reconnaissance Office (NURO), patterned after the National Reconnaissance Office (NRO), established in 1961 to coordinate overheard reconnaissance efforts by the air force, navy, and CIA, each of which had been developing its own satellite capabilities independently.

NURO was supposed to be a joint navy-CIA enterprise. Under Secretary of the Navy John Warner initially headed the office, and the navy's assistant secretary for research and development served as staff director. But naval officers complained that the CIA dominated from the outset. They saw NURO much as air force officers had seen NRO a decade earlier: as a thinly veiled attempt by the CIA to expand its intelligence empire, fish in their waters, and encroach on acquisition programs they had been running for years. In the navy's case, these extended well beyond AZORIAN to include SAND DOLLAR, IVY BELLS, and other underwater initiatives.[42]

Helms then chaired a critical 1970 meeting at which the USIB established the G-722 as "the highest priority target."[43] Helms wore three hats at the meeting—those of DCI, CIA director, and chair of the board charged with reviewing his agency's intelligence proposal. Such an arrangement effectively meant that Helms, a competitor for resources owing to his responsibilities as director of the CIA, which had a large collection program of its own on the table, could not "be wholly objective in providing guidance for community-wide collection," in the words of the 1971 OMB review, which rebuked Helms's management of the community generally.[44] Nevertheless, the board's decision forever established the Golf's recovery as a national intelligence requirement of which the CIA would be left in command.

* * *

Or perhaps Helms pulled Russell aside after the CIA subcommittee wrapped up a hearing on January 30, 1970, by which time DS&T had refined its lift concept. The index cards Senator Russell carried in his breast pocket don't say for sure.[45] At some point, though, Helms needed money—lots of it—to fund the operation. And at that point, he would have gone to Russell. There was no other option.

Intelligence spending figures, even historical ones, are closely guarded. At no point during AZORIAN's multiyear life span, for example, did the federal budget include a single line item specifying the nation's annual intelligence budget, much less that of the CIA. More information is available today. Yet from beginning to end, much of AZORIAN's money trail remains obscured, and any attempt to follow it requires educated guesswork. Careful examination of the clues that do exist can bring intelligence spending into sharper focus, though, yielding a clearer picture of what budgetary practices existed when AZORIAN got underway, and how they underwrote such an expensive undertaking.

AZORIAN's cost remains officially uncounted. According to legislative files, Congress obligated $259.9 million for the project from fiscal year (FY) 1970 through March 1975. However, that figure only covers congressionally authorized funds; it includes neither monies expended after March 1975, nor those expended before FY 1970, from Congress or other sources, on efforts to locate, surveil, or plan the recovery of the Golf. Including those expenditures raises the overall cost closer to $350 million, the figure cited by many credible estimates. If accurate, that price point—equivalent to at least $1.9 billion in 2022—places AZORIAN among the costlier known collection efforts in CIA history.[46]

Start-up money probably came from the director's reserve fund. Authorized by the Central Intelligence Agency Act of 1949, it permitted expenditures "for objects of a confidential, extraordinary, or emergency nature, [with] such expenditures to be accounted for solely on the certificate of the Director and every such certificate shall be deemed a sufficient voucher for the amount therein certified." These "unvouchered funds" enabled the DCI to act quickly in the face of contingencies—political crises, certainly, but also unforeseen collection opportunities. Seed money for the U-2 program came from the director's reserve fund.[47] Nothing suggests that Helms departed from established practice when the Golf project came along.

AZORIAN quickly exhausted those funds, forcing Helms to seek an appropriation from Congress. According to available records, this occurred sometime during FY 1970, which began October 1, 1969.[48] He could be reasonably certain of receiving a favorable hearing for at least two reasons. First, because he enjoyed a great deal of spending flexibility—more, in fact, than a DCI would have again for almost a generation. To be sure, there were indicators suggesting that the "long boom," the U.S. economy's extended period of mostly uninterrupted growth since World War II, might be ending. Inflation was inching up. Consumer spending and housing starts had both dipped a bit. Most signs pointed to good times ahead, though. Fueled by cheap energy, the American economic engine continued to chug along quite nicely. Despite increased foreign competition, the country still managed to run an annual trade surplus, as it had each year since the 1890s. Unemployment declined in 1969 to just 3.5 percent, a near record low. Gross national product rose. And the federal government operated in the black, enjoying a $3.2 billion budget surplus. Government red ink, trade deficits, deindustrialization, the dispiriting combination of double-digit inflation, sluggish growth, and joblessness known as "stagflation"—all those markers of the gloomy 1970s lay in the future when CIA accountants forecasted AZORIAN's costs.[49]

Intelligence funding remained high as well. According to declassified numbers, the United States spent $6 billion on intelligence in 1970.[50] That figure represented a drop from FY 1968, when intelligence spending peaked with the intensification of the American war effort in Vietnam. Six billion dollars, though, represented more funding than would be available for the remainder of the 1970s, a decade of austerity in which post-Vietnam defense cutbacks steadily reduced annual intelligence outlays. It wasn't until 1983 that the United States again lavished as much money on intelligence.[51]

The second reason Helms felt he could expect a sympathetic hearing from lawmakers was because AZORIAN entered the pipeline at the tail end of an era of minimal intelligence oversight. The liberty-security balance swung heavily in favor of secrecy during the early Cold War, when fear of Soviet attack overrode any worries that a permanent intelligence establishment might metastasize into a repressive "American Gestapo." Passed at the dawn of the superpower conflict, the aforementioned National Security Act of 1947 made the CIA answerable to the NSC. Congress, ordinarily a check on presidential power, played almost no role. As a result, "the growth and operation of the Intelligence Community was wholly an executive branch affair," historian Clayton Laurie writes.[52]

Having surrendered authority to the White House, members of Congress sat back and did little for the next quarter century. True, intelligence subcommittees of each chamber's Appropriations and Armed Services Committees provided some direction. However, they operated under the thumbs of committee chairs, who wielded outsized power thanks to the seniority system that prevailed in Congress. With Democrats generally controlling both chambers by wide margins, little turnover occurred among these chairs, who retained their seats as they kept getting reelected, which incumbents almost always did, especially in a one-party region like the South, then a Democratic stronghold.

Congressional oversight of the CIA, then, rested mostly in the hands of a small group of southern Democrats who comprised a "good old boy network," according to Laurie. Over the course of AZORIAN's life span, seven of ten committee chairs with CIA oversight responsibilities represented former Confederate states. Representatives L. Mendel Rivers (South Carolina), F. Edward Hébert (Louisiana), and George Mahon (Texas), and Senators Allen Ellender (Louisiana), John McClellan (Arkansas), John Stennis (Mississippi), and Richard Russell (Georgia) were conservative defense hawks who trusted America's silent service to do whatever was necessary to combat international communism.[53] Though generally protective of congressional prerogative, they deferred to presidential leadership of foreign affairs, and they gave the CIA considerable leeway out of a belief that intelligence agencies deserved "unique freedom from restrictive oversight arrangements because of the inevitable secrecy in which much of their work had to be conducted if it was to be successful," in the words of a CIA deputy director.[54]

By all accounts, Richard Brevard Russell Jr. lorded over the network. A self-described "loyal soldier" to the commander in chief, Russell insisted that increased scrutiny would harm the performance of U.S. intelligence.[55] He beat back numerous attempts to strengthen oversight procedures during his lengthy tenure as the Senate's foremost protector of the CIA. The latest attempt had come in 1966 from Senate Foreign Relations Committee chair J. William Fulbright. A leading opponent of the Vietnam War, Fulbright claimed that the CIA, the "freest of all agencies to advocate its projects and press home its views," according to a *New York Times* investigation, had misled the United States into the quagmire. Congressional inattention spurred poor decision making, waste, and overreach by the agency. He urged the Senate to establish a standing intelligence committee to curb the CIA's overactive "imagination."[56]

"Poppycock," Russell replied. Secrecy was essential: without it, the CIA couldn't operate effectively. Congress was leaky. Every additional person who received classified information increased the likelihood of an unauthorized disclosure. "I am frank," Russell wrote Majority Leader Mike Mansfield, a longtime advocate of closer congressional management of intelligence, "to say that my principal objection has been to avoid discussing our intelligence operations in an open forum before the eye of the entire world."[57]

Besides, Russell saw Fulbright's resolution as an attempt to muscle in on his territory. Raising a point of order, Russell insisted that any move to modify intelligence oversight procedures must come from Armed Services, the standing committee under whose jurisdiction the CIA fell, and which he then chaired. The Senate agreed, voting 61–28 to refer the matter to Armed Services, where it quietly died, joining hundreds of other reform proposals that suffered a similar fate on Russell's watch.[58]

His victory over heavyweights Fulbright and Mansfield reconfirmed Russell as "the uncrowned king of the Senate's inner Establishment," the leader of "the Club," the informal clique of powerbrokers who wielded tremendous influence behind the scenes, in cloakrooms, private offices, and unofficial hideaways, out of earshot of the press.[59] Russell, who, Robert Caro observed, took great "pains to cloak his Senate work in anonymity," continued to act as a one-man intelligence committee of his own when AZORIAN came along. As chair, he established CIA subcommittee ground rules, set calendars, and restricted membership to a select number of trustworthy lawmakers, aided by a small professional staff. Like other chairs, he asked CIA officials few questions and held even fewer hearings. On average, the Senate CIA subcommittee met just 2.6 times per year between 1966 and 1975, available records show. It did not convene once in 1971, the year Congress's three intelligence subcommittees (two on the House side) combined to meet just twice. "You have to make up your mind that you are going to have an intelligence agency and protect it as such, and shut your eyes some and take what is coming," said Russell's protégé, Senator Stennis, whom Russell handpicked to succeed him as Armed Services chair in 1969, when he moved over to head Appropriations.[60]

To prevent leaks, record keeping was kept to a minimum. On those rare occasions when they did convene, subcommittee members met unannounced in executive session. Rules prevented them from sharing data, even with other members of the Armed Forces or Appropriations Committees, not to mention the 535-person Congress. As a result, only a tiny minority of the nation's duly elected legislators could claim to have firsthand knowledge of U.S. intelligence operations. "No one knows anything about the

CIA," Senator Daniel Inouye (D-Hawaii), a decorated World War II veteran who would go on to chair the Senate's first Select Committee on Intelligence, complained in 1969.[61]

* * *

"No Money shall be drawn from the Treasury, but in Consequence of Appropriations made by Law; and a regular Statement and Account of the Receipts and Expenditures of all public Money shall be published from time to time." The framers inserted the so-called Appropriations Clause (article I, section 9, clause 7) into the U.S. Constitution to ensure that the legislature could check the executive by controlling the government purse. Self-proclaimed fiscal conservatives, Russell and House Appropriations chair George Mahon diligently exercised the power of the purse against many forms of discretionary spending. And Russell sometimes threatened to trim the CIA's budget "just to let you know that Congress is around."[62]

But he seldom followed through on such threats. "Russell was a friend of the agency," author John Ranelagh explains, and the senator defined his role as the "protector of the security and position of the CIA," rather than its overseer. Spies usually got what they wanted *if* they had Russell's support, and having his support was enough at a time when a cohort of senior members like Russell ruled Capitol Hill. Generally speaking, Admiral Moorer recalled, it was enough to tell Senator Russell and no one else.[63]

Russell gave America's spies blank-check authority to fight the Cold War. He and Mahon routinely rubber-stamped CIA budget requests, often without bothering to closely examine the figures, much less hold hearings. According to one student of Congress, "intelligence was the only area where . . . Appropriations was an advocate and proponent of increased spending rather than an avid budget cutter." When intelligence officials appeared on the Hill to make pitches—often before just the committee chair and maybe a trusted aide or colleague or two, depending on the sensitivity of the matter involved—appropriators typically asked not "Why do you need all this money?" but "Do you have enough?" Their main concern was "to make sure we had what we needed to do our job," recalled CIA legislative counsel John Maury.[64]

Exactly what Helms told Russell remains unclear. The CIA has kept mum on the subject. An internal history of AZORIAN says only that key members of Congress were "kept informed of project progress and reviewed budget requests for the project."[65]

But we know that Russell was in the loop. North Dakota's Milton Young, the ranking Republican on the Senate Appropriations Committee, confirmed as much. In an interview published years after Russell's death, Young said that he and the late senator had been briefed at an early stage.[66]

He probably wasn't told much, both because Helms volunteered few details, and because Russell seldom pressed for more. Age may have had something to do with it. "The older members," Maury reported, "occasionally suffer from a decreasing attention span, and particularly in afternoon sessions are prone to intermittent dozing." Some struggled to master basic facts. Maury recalled an incident in which an "elderly chairman," when shown a chart displaying various categories of covert actions, demanded to know "what the hell are you doing in covert parliamentary operations?" When the briefer explained that the chart displayed *paramilitary* operations" the member was much reassured, remarking, "the more of these the better—just don't go fooling around with parliamentary stuff—you don't know enough about it."

Mainly, though, Russell didn't ask questions because he wanted to maintain plausible deniability. "Part of the desire not to know, particularly to have prior knowledge, was based upon a practical political reason," a *New York Times* reporter explained. "If a senator or a congressman knows about a covert operation ahead of time, does not protest it and it fails, he shares some of the responsibility."[67]

In other words, it was politically safer not to know. "It almost chills the marrow of a man to hear about" certain CIA activities, Russell once declared. He asked Helms to tell him no more than was absolutely necessary.[68] Without identifying AZORIAN's target or revealing the program's cover, Helms may have thus told him nothing more than that the CIA had embarked upon an unusually sensitive, highly technical underwater collection effort to gain unique Cold War intelligence.

Russell must have approved in principle, for no major CIA program received funding without his support. Helms, who characterized Russell as "reliable and ultra-discreet," described how their private sessions usually went: "I would go down with all the documents and I would say, 'Senator, we are contemplating such and such a thing,' and I wouldn't get very far into it and he'd say, 'Dick, do you really think we ought to do this?' And I would say, 'Yes, Senator, I do.' And the senator would say, 'Well, that's good enough for me.' "[69]

With that, AZORIAN passed Russell's "oversight," such as it was. He and Mahon then applied the coup de grâce. Working with little, if any, input from other subcommittee members, they tucked program funds, unidentified as such, inside the Pentagon's FY 1970 budget. The proposed spending measure went to the Appropriations Committees and the full House and Senate, the vast majority of whose members voted on the bill without knowing whether it included millions of dollars to support a risky operation or where the funds were located. Once Congress approved, the chairs quietly notified OMB of the amount and true location of appropriated funds (under the navy's Research, Development, Test, and Evaluation line item, congressional files show). OMB officials then transferred monies as needed, pursuant to the Central Intelligence Agency Act of 1949.[70]

Unpublished, the annual intelligence budget remained unknown to all but a select few. Appropriations chairs took these measures for security reasons, they said. Without them, Russell claimed, the Soviets might obtain a budgetary "blueprint" of America's clandestine programs. A big, costly program like AZORIAN made opacity all the more important. Any sign of a "conspicuous bump" in CIA spending might alert Moscow to the fact that the United States was developing an expensive new high-tech collection system aimed against them. Forewarned, Soviet spies could get a jump start on deploying countermeasures.[71]

But of course, burying intelligence funds in the defense budget also hid AZORIAN's "conspicuous bump" from American legislators, not to mention American taxpayers. However large this bump may have been, appropriators knew it was less noticeable—and politically objectionable—buried in the Pentagon's $69.6 billion FY 1970 allocation than it would have been in a smaller appropriation given, say, to the State Department. CIA expenditures represented only a "very, very small percentage of the amount of tax money spent each year by the Armed Forces for research and development of new weapons," Russell said. Surely members of Congress could not object to directing a tiny portion of the military's budget to aid the CIA in its "effort to keep up with the activities of those arrayed against us in [the intelligence] field."[72]

Keeping up with the Ivanovs. That rationale kept even high officials like Dean Rusk, secretary of state at the time the Golf was discovered, outside the loop. "I never saw a budget of the CIA," averred Rusk, who also said that Russell would "lose the CIA budget in the defense budget, and he wouldn't let anybody question it. There were no public hearings on it. So again, his judgment, his word on that was the last word."[73]

* * *

Russell succumbed to emphysema in January 1971. His death weakened the CIA's support system, leaving Representatives Hébert (age seventy-one), Mahon (seventy-two), Stennis (seventy-one), and Ellender (eighty-one) atop the committees with intelligence responsibilities. Able but less commanding than Russell, those elder lawmakers struggled to stave off reformers, as Congress reemerged in the wake of Vietnam as a check against executive action. "The congressional power structure, which has for a quarter of a century served to shield the Agency from intrusion or attack by the rank-and-file membership, is in a state of flux," Maury's year-end report noted:

> One need not go far down the seniority lists of the committees over which [the senior leaders] preside to find members of substantially different temperament and outlook. They include men who have over the years become increasingly suspicious or jealous of the secretive manner in which the Agency oversight committees have exercised their responsibilities. And their ranks are being periodically reinforced by newly elected

younger members . . . , some of [whom] appear to have been infected by the anti-establishment and anti-Agency campaigns of the "New Left." Faced with the resulting pressures, our aging and harassed protectors on the Hill can no longer be expected to hold the old lines.[74]

Indeed, those lines would collapse in 1975 under the weight of reports disclosing that the CIA had exceeded its charter for years by spying on American citizens, plotting to assassinate foreign leaders, and much else besides. Many retroactively faulted Russell's generation for failing to curb the agency. And Congress introduced reforms that heralded a new age of intelligence oversight.

But the old lines, as Maury called them, held long enough to launch an ambitious plan to wrest a sunken submarine from the bottom of the sea. It was a 10 percent activity that proved, despite DS&T's confidence, to be beyond the reach of even Langley's wizards. A multimillion-dollar endeavor that, when it came to light in 1975, prompted questions about the CIA's performance. An impossible mission that was the predictable outcome, critics said, of the CIA having easy access to too much money.

To be sure, the White House had yet to sign off. And Helms and Russell were always quick to point out that the president had final say. But their actions—Helms's show of support, Russell's provision of funds, each taken without much in the way of external review—had already put AZORIAN on a course that would prove difficult to reverse. With the CIA's congressional overseers rubber-stamping the DCI's checks, DS&T's wizards could afford to build the collection platform of their dreams—a Rube Goldberg–like system involving a prototypical ship, a maneuverable claw, and an enormous submersible barge, all designed to accomplish a submarine mission navy experts dismissed as too unlikely for serious consideration. Using congressionally appropriated funds, DS&T's Special Projects Staff began awarding government contracts worth hundreds of millions of dollars years before the plan reached the president's desk. By the time it got there, most of the money had already been spent. And Helms could argue that canceling the program at that late stage would only harm the CIA's relationships with the contractors who had put other projects aside to build the hardware—a serious matter in intelligence operations, he said, where trust between government agencies and private enterprise was key.

Had the CIA been more answerable, the plan might never have gotten off the drawing board. But the CIA was not accountable, not in any real way, not yet. And AZORIAN received the green light even though it stood, by the CIA's own reckoning, only a small chance of succeeding. Full steam ahead.

2

THE HUGHES CONNECTION

From a distance, Howard Hughes appeared to be the ideal front man. Granted, he no longer resembled his former self, that dashing young man of black-and-white yesterday who decamped from his native Houston shortly after inheriting his father's drill bit firm, Hughes Tool Company, to find fame and more fortune as a Hollywood movie mogul, record-setting aviator, and celebrated playboy. No, 1970 found the sixty-four-year-old secluded in the darkened penthouse atop Las Vegas's Desert Inn, curtains drawn, windows sealed, armed with paper towels, tissue paper, and other "insulation" from germs. Wracked by undiagnosed mental illness—severe obsessive-compulsive disorder, some psychologists speculate—he had not stepped outside the suite in four years, not since abruptly moving there in 1966 from a Beverly Hills bungalow, his on-and-off hideaway since dropping out of sight a decade earlier.[1]

Heavy security shielded him from the outside world. Other than a loyal circle of personal attendants, no one—not even his top business executives, with whom he corresponded exclusively by phone or in writing—laid eyes on him. "To describe the security arrangements in Mr. Hughes's quarters here as elaborate would be an understatement," a Las Vegas correspondent confirmed.[2]

Rumor had it that Hughes was in sharp mental and physical decline. Those of his attendants who later broke ranks described his appearance as "horrifying." Refusing to bathe or groom himself for long periods, he allowed his straggly beard to hang to his chest, his hair to reach halfway down his back, and his fingernails to grow so long they corkscrewed. Sometimes he wore underpants. More often he went naked, revealing that his six-foot, two-inch frame had become cadaverously thin. (He weighed ninety-three pounds at the time of death, his 1976 autopsy showed.) To dull his pain, he consumed "vast amounts" of codeine, Valium, and other drugs, sometimes intravenously, which left him "drowsy and incoherent."[3]

But Hughes's spokespersons insisted that he remained in good health. And he checked all of the CIA's boxes. Reputed to be among the richest living Americans, he presided over a business empire estimated to be worth as much as $2 billion, with holdings in oil-drilling equipment, aerospace, electronics, airlines, communications, and real estate. Hughes Tool Company (a.k.a. Toolco), the company at the center of his fortune, was a major supplier of drill bits to companies involved in offshore oil exploration.

As such, the company was among a select few organizations qualified to plausibly pose as the driving force behind a deep ocean mining program, which was the cover CIA staff selected to hide the sub-raising effort in plain sight. The Golf rested in the vicinity of a known concentration of manganese nodules. Containing valuable minerals, these potato-sized masses littered the seabed, and commercial interest in harvesting them was growing worldwide. But the industry was in its infancy. Technique had yet to evolve to the point where anyone possessed a widely accepted industry standard by which to measure the credibility of whatever method or approach DS&T might employ. Deep ocean mining, CIA staff agreed, was an ideal disguise for the mission.

Better yet, Toolco was a private company, solely owned by Hughes. As such, it was not required to submit reports to the Securities and Exchange Commission. Without shareholders to answer to, Hughes was accountable to no one. His company could serve as a black box in which to conceal the movement of hundreds of millions of dollars behind the clandestine operation.[4]

Hughes's "personal eccentricities," as a CIA cover evaluation called them, also worked in his favor. His passion for secrecy shrouded both his business operations and his personal life. Everything about him was so mysterious—the "phantom financier," the *Las Vegas Sun* noted, had not been photographed in years—"that news media reporting and speculation about his activities frequently range[d] from truth to utter fiction."[5]

The CIA reasoned that any news of Hughes bankrolling an ambitious deep ocean mining scheme would seem entirely within character: a crazy man pursuing a crazy scheme. After all, he was widely "recognized as a pioneering entrepreneur," a maverick businessman willing, eager even, to invest in speculative ventures. The Hughes H-4 Hercules, the gigantic, World War II–era wooden seaplane developed by the Hughes Aircraft Company, may have once led to a congressional investigation in which senators famously asked why he had spent tens of millions of government dollars only to deliver a useless product that stayed aloft for just seconds after barely achieving liftoff during its lone test flight in 1947. But the "Spruce Goose," as the experimental aircraft was known, lived on in the minds of CIA officers. "He'd been associated with sort of far-out ideas in the past, with the [Spruce] Goose and some other things of that nature, so he's absolutely perfect," William Colby once said of Hughes. "Hughes gravitated into areas that other people refused to go into or didn't believe in," a top-ranking intelligence official told *Newsweek*.[6]

Plus, Hughes had an established track record of working with U.S. intelligence agencies. The full extent of that record remains undisclosed.[7] Declassified files, though, show that it began with "straightforward commercial arrangements."[8] According to published reports, these included government contracts for Hughes Aircraft to supply eavesdropping equipment, reconnaissance satellites, and other spy gear. Besides employing former CIA officers, including the first CIA deputy director for science and technology, Hughes Aircraft reportedly provided commercial cover for CIA agents working overseas.[9]

All told, Hughes was a "perfect match," program cover staff director Walter Lloyd recalled. "The whole mystique of Howard we couldn't have bought."[10] CIA officers wanted him to front AZORIAN.

The only problem was that CIA officers couldn't contact him, secluded as he was atop the Desert Inn. They didn't trust their lone contact in his inner circle, Hughes's Nevada operations chief Robert Maheu.

Finding another go-between was not easy. Other Hughes lieutenants were similarly "tainted by their association with Las Vegas gaming interests." Eventually, CIA officers settled on Houston-based Hughes Tool executive vice president Raymond Holliday. Holliday did not have direct physical access to Hughes. He had not actually seen him in years. But Holliday, a Toolco accountant since 1938, was concerned about reports that Maheu was skimming profits from Hughes's casinos in league with organized crime. Like other executives, he was worried about the influence Maheu had come to exert over Hughes and his affairs.[11] So, he agreed to write a memorandum.

We don't know exactly what Holliday's memo said; police never recovered it after it was reported stolen from a Hughes-owned warehouse some years later. Despite repeated requests, the CIA has yet to disclose a version known to exist in the agency's archive—a product, perhaps, of efforts by security officers to reconstruct events. Officially, the agency has said only that "it was thought that among the stolen documents there might be a memorandum from a senior Hughes official to Howard Hughes describing a proposed CIA attempt to recover a sunken Soviet submarine and requesting Hughes' approval for Hughes Company participation."[12]

Nor do we know Hughes's reaction, whether he saw the memo, or if he was even competent to make decisions. For his part, Holliday, who in 1972 would succeed Hughes as the head of Toolco, insisted that Hughes remained in full control. Hughes "never left any doubt with any of us that he was always in charge," Holliday said of his fellow executives. "We never made any major decisions without Mr. Hughes' approval."[13]

Be we do know two things. First, that Holliday signed a letter agreement on November 13, 1970, establishing Hughes Tool as AZORIAN's outward face. "Due to necessity for cover purposes to operate the mission

FIGURE 2.1 Patch worn by crew members of the *Hughes Glomar Explorer* to enhance AZORIAN's commercial cover.

Source: CIA Museum, accessed May 23, 2022, https://www.cia.gov/legacy/museum /artifact/glomar-explorer-crew-patch/.

under the guise of an overt commercial deep sea mining project," read the black contract, partially declassified as a result of a legal proceeding, "the Sponsor [identified only as an arm of the U.S. government] desires to enter into a contract with the Agent [Hughes Tool] who shall represent and act in the stead of the Sponsor, who shall at all times remain an unidentified principal." In other words, Hughes Tool agreed to act as the customer of record for deals with private contractors, starting with Global Marine Inc., the California-based offshore drilling firm selected to design, deliver, and operate a dynamically positioned deep-sea "mining" ship, named the *Hughes Glomar Explorer*. Weeks later, the firms held a joint press conference (stage-managed behind the scenes by CIA specialists to promote the commercial cover) to announce they were embarking on an ambitious deep ocean mining project.[14] And the second thing we know is that the CIA-Hughes deal drove a split in the Hughes organization that reached all the way to Washington.

* * *

Although Robert Maheu may not be a household name, he was once at the center of the action. A onetime agent of the Federal Bureau of Investigation (FBI), Maheu began working for Hughes as a private detective in the mid-1950s. As the tycoon retreated from view, Maheu muscled others aside to become Hughes's public face. It was Maheu who fixed Hughes's problems, including with politicians; Maheu who oversaw his 1966 move to Las Vegas; and Maheu who, as chief executive of Hughes's Nevada operations, led a four-year spending spree that saw the tycoon purchase six casinos, five hotels, an airport, a television station, and most of the undeveloped land on the Strip to become Nevada's third-largest landowner (trailing only the federal government and the state's leading power company) by 1970.[15]

Maheu doubled as a CIA contractor throughout his tenure with Hughes. Declassified records show that the CIA recruited him in 1954. Over the next sixteen years, his private security firm, Robert A. Maheu and Associates, provided nonofficial cover for CIA agents operating around the world, at the same time that it represented Hughes's interests in Washington.[16]

A self-described "problem solver," Maheu also acted as a cutout, an intermediary who performed highly sensitive assignments but who could not be easily connected to the CIA. Acting in this capacity, Maheu participated in some of the more notorious episodes in CIA history. His name appears no fewer than thirty-three times in the "Family Jewels," the catalog of illegal or inappropriate actions that the CIA compiled in 1973 in response to media accounts of the agency's involvement in the Watergate scandal. He conducted a campaign of wiretaps and dirty tricks to scuttle a deal that would have given Greek shipping magnate Aristotle Onassis exclusive control over Saudi petroleum exports—and excessive power over world oil supplies, some U.S. officials feared. In other instances, he procured women to lure foreign leaders into compromising honey traps. When one trap failed to snare Indonesian president Sukarno, Maheu, at the CIA's direction, produced a pornographic film designed to leverage Sukarno by showing a Sukarno look-alike in bed with a Soviet agent.[17]

Maheu even played a central role in a failed CIA plot to assassinate Cuban leader Fidel Castro with help from members of the Mafia. Organized crime figures were motivated to eliminate Castro, or so the thinking went in 1960, because he had shuttered their lucrative casino holdings upon seizing power in Cuba the previous year. Due to his familiarity with "gangster elements," the agency recruited Maheu to serve as the go-between with a rogues' gallery, including John Roselli, West Coast representative of the Chicago-based organized crime syndicate known as the Outfit. Roselli, whose territory included Hollywood and Las Vegas, and who reportedly held stakes in Hughes-owned properties along the Strip, introduced Maheu to his boss, Sam Giancana, Al Capone's successor as chief of the Outfit. Giancana had the stature necessary to reach out to a fellow godfather, Florida-based Santo Trafficante Jr., reputedly the most powerful mobster in pre-Castro Cuba. Together, they hatched a plan to slip poison pills into Castro's food or drink.[18]

The plan failed, and the CIA pulled the plug after the 1961 Bay of Pigs fiasco. Still, the fact that the CIA once plotted with members of the FBI's ten-most-wanted list to kill a foreign leader remained closely held. Maheu, a key link connecting the CIA to the plot, was a living, breathing skeleton that Richard Helms wanted desperately to keep in the closet. Early in his directorship, declassified files show, Helms personally terminated the agency's cover arrangement with Maheu and Associates and ruled that Maheu himself was never again to be used in any capacity. He reinforced that ruling when AZORIAN project staff sought out Hughes. "At the outset Director Helms specified that Robert Maheu was to have no connection with or knowledge of the AZORIAN program," Lloyd, the cover chief, said.[19]

* * *

Cutting Maheu loose made sense. He had ties to organized crime and to some of the most infamous schemes in CIA history, and Helms considered him a security risk. According to Lloyd, the Hughes people with whom project staff worked—including Holliday, New York attorney Chester Davis, and Los Angeles Toolco executive Frank William "Bill" Gay— proved to be quite tight-lipped. CIA officers spent years congratulating themselves for having the foresight to avoid a potential problem. In 1974, Colby told a roomful of officials that they "could all thank the wisdom of Dick Helms that Robert Maheu did not know anything about Howard Hughes' connection with this project because if Maheu did, it would be all out now."[20]

However, the decision to approach Hughes—a gambit widely hailed as perhaps the most audacious part of an already audacious plan to raise a Soviet sub from a depth of three miles—had disastrous consequences. For it triggered a nasty corporate power struggle that cracked the thick shell of secrecy surrounding the "Invisible Billionaire," shattering one of Hughes's chief qualifications for spy work.[21] Closely held secrets—good ones, certainly, but bad ones too—came spilling out. They ended up jeopardizing not just *Glomar* but the president himself.

"I told [the White House] that the breakup of the Hughes empire in Nevada was going to sink Nixon," a Maheu ally, *Las Vegas Sun* publisher Hank Greenspun, later told a Watergate investigator. "Dramatic organizational changes" occurred within Hughes's orbit in 1970, President Nixon's friend, Charles G. "Bebe" Rebozo, was to testify. "When you get family squabbles sometimes, they shoot from the hip in every direction and I thought that I just didn't want anything, even remotely, to reflect on the [president's 1972 reelection] campaign," Rebozo said in an attempt to explain why he later returned a supposed campaign donation that he originally squirreled away in a safe-deposit box. "Unfortunately, the Hughes name had almost become a stigma with respect to campaign contributions because of [a] previous issue."[22]

* * *

The dangers of entrusting a "naked madman," as one of Hughes's biographers once called him, became evident before the ink was dry on the November 13, 1970, agreement. Twenty-four hours later, Hughes's signature appeared on a November 14 proxy granting Holliday, Davis, and Gay exclusive management powers over Hughes's Nevada operations, the portion of his business empire previously overseen by Maheu. Then, on Thanksgiving Eve, Hughes abruptly exited his Desert Inn penthouse for the first time in four years and left Las Vegas, flying to a new hideaway in the Bahamas, never to return to the United States. Some of his papers and personal effects traveled with him; others, possibly including Holliday's memo, went to a building he owned in Los Angeles for safekeeping.[23]

The sudden disappearance of the world's most newsworthy recluse did not go unnoticed. "HOWARD HUGHES VANISHES!" blared the *Las Vegas Sun*. Correspondents flocked to Las Vegas to cover the "Shootout at the Hughes Corral," as *Time* dubbed the internal struggle that accompanied the financier's flight. Accused of corruption and financial mismanagement, Maheu was fired from his $500,000-a-year job, stripped of his status as Hughes's right-hand man, and evicted from "Little Caesar's Palace," the opulent Hughes-owned property he and his family called home.[24]

If CIA agents figured that Maheu, a Mafia-connected Las Vegas power broker, would quietly slink away in defeat, they badly miscalculated. Maheu was angry, and he resolved "to make those bastards pay." Maheu learned of Hughes's departure while dining with his colleague, Democratic political operative Lawrence O'Brien, who then served as Hughes's Washington lobbyist. "The battle lines were drawn and I came out swinging," Maheu recalled.[25]

A loose cannon, he began by taking legal action. In December, he obtained a restraining order from a Nevada court temporarily preventing the Holliday-Davis-Gay takeover. Hughes's health came under the microscope, as Maheu's lawyers challenged the authenticity of the November 14 proxy. Hughes could not have competently signed the instrument because he was of unsound mind and body, according to medical evidence they introduced. As *Newsweek* observed, the case "illuminated a good deal more of Hughes's obscure way of life than the celebrated recluse would have wished."[26]

When the court lifted the restraining order after Hughes's lawyer, Davis, produced evidence authenticating Hughes's signature, Maheu filed

FIGURE 2.2 Hughes attorney Chester Davis (front center) and Hughes Tool executive Frank William "Bill" Gay (back) exit a Las Vegas courthouse on December 8, 1970, following a day of legal maneuvering in their power struggle against former Hughes aide Robert Maheu.

Source: Editorial photo #515292342, Bettmann Collection, Getty Images.

a second lawsuit alleging breach of contract. When he lost that case as well, he filed a third in February 1972 in response to comments Hughes made during a January teleconference held to disavow a bogus autobiography, one of several books written about the businessman following his Las Vegas departure. Asked why he had fired Maheu, Hughes shot back: "Because he's a no-good, dishonest son of a bitch, and he stole me blind."[27]

Alleging slander and libel and seeking $17.5 million in damages, Maheu's defamation would play out in a Los Angeles court for years. When the case reached trial in 1974, Maheu would tell all. In the meantime, he began talking to the media, to lawyers, to anyone who would listen, really, about what he knew.

FIGURE 2.3 Robert Maheu (center) leaves the same Las Vegas court-house on December 5, 1970. Days later, the court would reject his legal challenge to his November dismissal. "The battle lines were drawn and I came out swinging," he recalled.

Source: Editorial photo #515292328, Bettmann Collection, Getty Images.

Did he know about AZORIAN? Probably not in detail, though he knew enough to call the CIA deputy director of security within days of his dismissal to complain "that the Agency had embarked on a new project with the Howard Hughes organization and had not gone through him." He evidently put two and two together from the press conferences and cover stories issued by CIA officers to promote the fiction that his former boss was bankrolling a speculative deep-sea mining venture. "Look into the *Hughes Glomar Explorer*, Jim, I'm sure it's a CIA operation," he told investigative journalist James Phelan, a veteran Hughes watcher. Newly declassified records show that CIA security officers identified Maheu as the probable source of several unauthorized leaks that threatened to blow *Glomar's* cover at one point.[28]

Maheu—profiled by *60 Minutes* as an insider privy to all Hughes's secrets and whose main interest was to spill them—certainly knew a great deal, which is what made him dangerous. Headlined "6 Attempts to Kill Castro Laid to CIA," Jack Anderson's syndicated Washington Merry-Go-Round column of January 18, 1971, indicated as much. This was not the first Anderson column to expose the agency's plans to assassinate the Cuban dictator in league with organized crime. He had been hearing rumors for years. But it provided additional details based on new information Anderson said he had recently received from key people involved.[29]

Anderson did not name his sources. And Maheu insisted he kept quiet. The CIA suspected otherwise. Days after Anderson's column appeared, Helms received a memo from his security chief, who recommended revoking Maheu's security clearance. His reasons went beyond the Castro matter: "Maheu's financial manipulations in Las Vegas are currently under investigation by executives of the Hughes Tool Company. He, in turn, has filed suit for damages against the Company. Because of this, I recommend that we cancel all existing clearances with Maheu and Associates." Helms signed his approval the next day, formally ending the agency's seventeen-year relationship with Maheu.[30]

Severing ties did not stop more secrets from leaking out. On August 6, 1971, Anderson published the first of several columns revealing that Nixon's associate, Bebe Rebozo, had recently accepted $100,000 from Hughes in cash. In return, Hughes allegedly received government favors, including from Attorney General John Mitchell, who in 1970 overruled the Justice Department Antitrust Division, clearing the way for Hughes to purchase yet another Las Vegas hotel and casino, the Dunes.[31]

Here again, Anderson did not reveal his sources. His FBI file, though, indicates that they included Maheu. Federal agents routinely tailed Anderson to identify the whistle-blowers who fed the muckraking journalist inside information, some of it classified. Declassified decades later, his file incudes an August 7 telegram that FBI director J. Edgar Hoover received from the special agent in charge of the bureau's Las Vegas Field Office. According to the telegram, a confidential informant told FBI agents that Anderson had recently traveled to Las Vegas, where he met Maheu.

Apparently, Anderson planned to "run a series of articles on the Hughes–Maheu situation which would be unfavorable to Hughes and the current faction [Holliday et al.] controlling his Nevada operations."[32]

And Maheu knew about the $100,000 because it was he who, as Hughes's then fixer, had arranged payment to Rebozo on Hughes's behalf. The money (equal to almost $730,000 today) represented a contribution to Nixon's reelection bid, Rebozo later told the Senate Watergate Committee, which investigated as part of its mandate to examine possible illegal, improper, or unethical conduct associated with the 1972 campaign. However, Nixon's reelection committee did not yet exist at the time of the supposed campaign contribution, which was transmitted in two $50,000 cash payments, the last coming as late as October 30, 1970—just weeks before Toolco's letter agreement with the CIA, it bears mentioning. Rebozo, a Florida banker known for handling private matters for Nixon, did not disclose his receipt of the donation, as required by law. Nor did he use the funds for campaign purposes. Instead, Rebozo placed the cash in a safe-deposit box, where he claimed the money remained undisturbed. In truth, the contents of "Bebe's 'tin box,' " as Nixon's chief of staff, H. R. "Bob" Haldeman, called it, became a slush fund that Rebozo maintained on Nixon's behalf. Rebozo disbursed monies from the account to purchase jewelry for First Lady Pat Nixon and to furnish and make improvements to Nixon-owned properties in Key Biscayne, Florida. Funds reportedly also went toward the legal fees of Watergate defendants and, as gifts, to the president's brothers and his longtime secretary, Rose Mary Woods.[33]

* * *

Nixon's aides may not have known what was behind the Hughes shake-up. But they immediately recognized the hazard it posed to the president. They knew this because Nixon had been burned by his relationship with Hughes before. In October 1960, columnists Drew Pearson and Jack Anderson reported that Nixon had secretly pocketed $205,000 (worth over $2.15 million today) from Hughes in 1956. Hughes nominally loaned the money to Nixon's younger brother, Donald, to finance Donald's Los Angeles–area drive-in restaurant, home of the "Nixonburger." In fact, however, the money amounted to a carefully concealed gift to then vice president Nixon, Pearson and Anderson claimed. As collateral, Nixon's family offered only a small plot of land valued at just $13,000—a fraction of the value of the "loan," which Donald never repaid because the terms did not require him to do so. Instead, the funds went through intermediaries before apparently ending up in the hands of Richard Nixon, who personally reached out to Hughes to request the money. Soon after Hughes approved the payment, the vice president purchased an elegant, nine-thousand-square-foot Tudor-style home in Washington, DC, complete with eight bedrooms, six bathrooms, a library, a butler's pantry, and a solarium.

In exchange, Hughes reportedly received favorable decisions from federal agencies. These included the Internal Revenue Service (IRS), which reversed a previous ruling to give the Howard Hughes Medical Institute tax-exempt status, saving Hughes millions of dollars in current or back taxes. The IRS reversal, a White House review noted, came three months after the loan.

Nixon's camp issued denials. And Pearson and Anderson found no hard evidence proving he had influenced agency decisions. Yet their October surprise cost him crucial votes, or so Nixon believed, and he forever blamed the columnists—and the news media generally—for his narrow loss to John Kennedy.[34]

Nixon overcame that setback to one day occupy the Oval Office. But his closest aides knew that he remained sensitive about the topic. "On matters pertaining to Hughes," Haldeman recalled, "Nixon sometimes seemed to lose touch with reality." And they knew that he was touchy because he continued to accept gifts from the billionaire.[35]

Within weeks of the Hughes split, Haldeman, on January 18, 1971, sent White House counsel John Dean a memo requesting a situation report. "Bebe," he noted, cryptically, due to the sensitive nature of the subject matter, "has some information on this although it is, of course, not solid."[36]

Dean dispatched Jack Caulfield, a former New York City police officer employed by the administration as a security operative, to investigate. Caulfield quickly discovered that the "Mahew [sic] disaster," as he called it, reverberated all the way to Washington. "As one gets closer to Mayhew's dealings," Caulfield warned, "it becomes evident that his tentacles touch many extremely sensitive areas of government, each one of which is frought [sic] with potential for Jack Anderson type exposure." Caulfield may not have known the whole story. But he pieced together enough information to identify Maheu as the individual who "forwarded Hughes' political contributions, personally," and to connect Maheu to Rebozo and Rebozo to the president.[37]

Maheu, he also learned, was close friends with Larry O'Brien, a notorious name among Nixon aides. An experienced Democratic operative, O'Brien directed John Kennedy's 1960 presidential campaign before serving as postmaster general during the Lyndon Johnson administration and advising Robert Kennedy in 1968. Sometime after RFK's death, Maheu arranged for O'Brien to work as Hughes's Washington representative. But he, too, was fired in the 1970 housecleaning.

Now O'Brien chaired the Democratic National Committee (DNC). Nixon advisors considered him to be a formidable, and dangerous, foe heading into the next election cycle. "The presence of Lawrence O'Brien as Chairman of the Democratic National Committee unquestionably suggests that the Democratic nominee will have a strong, covert intelligence effort counted against us in 1972," Caulfield wrote.[38]

Thanks to Maheu, Caulfield reported, O'Brien was possibly in possession of information about the $100,000 Hughes contribution. Moreover, he was certain to use that information against Nixon at some point during the 1972 campaign. Dean reached out to Rebozo before relaying this alarming news to Haldeman on January 26, 1971. "Bebe is under the impression that Maheu had a good bit of freedom with Hughes' money when running the Nevada operation," Dean added. Before any action was taken, Rebozo asked to be notified "because of his familiarity with the delicacy of the relationships as a result of his own dealings with the Hughes people."

Rebozo and Robert Bennett, another figure with whom Dean spoke, sought to neutralize O'Brien by revealing his ties to Hughes. Bennett, son of Utah senator Wallace F. Bennett (and a future senator himself), owned the Robert R. Mullen Company, a Washington public relations firm that maintained a documented relationship with the CIA. In January 1971, for instance, it employed E. Howard Hunt, a retired CIA agent recruited to join the White House Special Investigations Unit, the leak-plugging group known as the Plumbers. The company also took over Hughes's account from O'Brien. ("I'm sure I need not explain the political implications of having Hughes' affairs handled here in Washington by a close friend," wrote Nixon's "hatchet man," White House special counsel Charles Colson.) Bennett maintained good contacts with the faction now running Hughes's affairs. And he believed he could help. According to Dean, Bennett said

> that he will be going to the West Coast to talk about the specifics of his Hughes relationship with Mr. Gay (the man who is responsible for releasing Maheu). Bennett also indicated that he felt confident that if it was necessary to document the retainer with O'Brien that he could get the necessary information through the Hughes people, but it would be with the understanding that the documentation would not be used in a manner that might embarrass Hughes.[39]

Haldeman liked the idea of discrediting O'Brien. He tasked Dean with developing a plan, in consultation with Colson, to leak the information once Bennett returned from Los Angeles. "Frankly," Haldeman wrote, "I can't see any way to handle this without involving Hughes so the problem of 'embarrassing' him seems to be a matter of degree. However, we should keep Bob Bennett and Bebe out of it at all costs."[40]

Caulfield discouraged these efforts. Citing Maheu's associations with the Mafia and the CIA, connections that were only vaguely known at the time, Caulfield characterized Maheu as a skilled covert operator who could be counted on to fight dirty. A "consumate [sic] namedropper," he also possessed an extensive Rolodex that included Democratic and Republican politicians who had accepted Hughes's money over the years. If the White House attempted to smear O'Brien, Maheu could simply name—or threaten to name—some of them, perhaps to Jack Anderson. His doing so, Caulfield warned, in a thinly veiled reference to Rebozo and Nixon, "might well shake loose Republican skeletons from the closet."

Under oath, Caulfield later decoded his language in testimony before the Senate Watergate Committee:

Caulfield: Well, specifically what I meant by it was . . . the Maheu-Hughes blowup had occurred by then, [and] the whole situation out there in Nevada was getting very sticky and very ugly. I was attempting to convey . . . that there was an interrelationship, apparently, based on Maheu's activities over the years with people of the Republican stripe, and it may well have come back and proved embarrassing to the people in the administration.

Committee Counsel: In other words, if you began an investigation into O'Brien's getting money from Hughes, it might very likely turn up that Hughes was also involved, and Maheu was involved with Republicans in a comparable—

Caulfield: That's precisely what I meant.[41]

White House attempts to discredit O'Brien largely stopped at that point. But the "goddamned Hughes thing," as President Nixon called the controversy that forever swirled around his relationship with the financier, flared up again in 1972. In January, Jack Anderson published a second column detailing the Hughes-Rebozo payments. This time, Anderson noted that he had "documentary evidence" to substantiate his claims, including handwritten exchanges between Hughes and Maheu. He quoted a 1968 memo instructing Maheu to go "every inch of the way" in supporting Nixon and bringing him "under our sponsorship and supervision."[42]

Anderson's election-year piece sent Nixon aides into a panic because it not only revisited the Hughes controversy but also indicated that corroborating records—Maheu's correspondence with Hughes—existed somewhere. On February 3, they discovered one possible location. The *New York Times* reported that Hughes's personal papers were circulating in Las Vegas. Hank Greenspun, the Maheu ally who published the *Las Vegas Sun*, maintained a large collection. Speaking from his office, Greenspun said he had "about 200 individual items," including memos in Hughes's own handwriting and notes from Hughes employees in response to various assignments.[43]

Nixon's aides were particularly worried about Greenspun because he was an associate of Jack Anderson, who owned a small piece of the *Sun*. On February 4, the day after the *Times* report, Attorney General Mitchell, White House Counsel Dean, Committee to Reelect the President general counsel G. Gordon Liddy, and deputy campaign chief Jeb Stuart Magruder met in Mitchell's Justice Department office to discuss Operation Gemstone. It was Liddy's plan for, among other things, electronic surveillance of and illegal break-ins at various targets. According to the final report of the Senate Watergate Committee, Mitchell suggested many targets at this meeting, including "DNC chairman Larry O'Brien and Las Vegas publisher Hank Greenspun, who allegedly has explosive material . . . in his office safe."[44]

White House Plumbers Liddy and Hunt prepared to burglarize Greenspun's office. Hunt's employer, Robert Mullen head Bob Bennett, hosted a meeting at the firm's offices introducing them to Hughes's security chief, Ralph Winte. According to Hunt's testimony, they discussed "the Nevada political situation, the litigation then in progress between Robert Maheu and Mr. Hughes, the position politically speaking vis-à-vis Mr. Greenspun and Mr. Hughes." The meeting reached a point, Hunt recalled, where Bennett suggested "that there was a commonality of interest between the Hughes Tool Co. and Mr. Liddy and myself." Hunt and Winte then withdrew to Hunt's office, where the Hughes official agreed to provide Hunt with a diagram of Greenspun's office and to furnish him with local support, including hotel rooms, automobiles, and so forth.[45]

The Greenspun plan never reached completion. But investigators determined that Liddy's Gemstone proposal led to the break-ins at the DNC's headquarters in the Watergate Office Building. Sometime after the February 4 meeting, Magruder received a call from Colson, who told him to "get on the stick and get the Liddy project approved so we can get the information from O'Brien." (Dean later said that Colson's call "helped get the thing off the dime.") After gaining approval, Liddy and Hunt cased the building. And on the night of May 27, the burglary team went to the sixth-floor offices of the DNC, where James McCord, a CIA veteran, like Hunt, placed electronic bugging devices in the telephones of DNC chairman O'Brien and another DNC official.[46]

However, the wiretap on O'Brien's phone malfunctioned. So, on June 17, the burglary team entered his office a second time to make repairs. "The second Watergate break-in was apparently made to correct the difficultly experienced with the wiretap device on Mr. O'Brien's telephone," the Senate committee concluded.[47]

* * *

The Hughes connection to Watergate got lost amid the discovery of the break-ins, and of the White House's attempts to cover up ties to them. Attention focused, as it should have, on determining what the president knew and when he knew it. But key participants said that the break-ins were motivated by the White House's desire to learn what O'Brien knew about Nixon's dealings with Hughes, and how the DNC chair planned to use that information during the upcoming presidential contest. The purpose "was to find out what O'Brien had of a derogatory nature about us," Liddy recalled. "As far as I know the primary purpose of the break-in was to deal with the information . . . about Howard Hughes and Larry O'Brien and what that meant as far as the cash that had supposedly been given to Bebe Rebozo and spent later by the President possibly," agreed Magruder, who joined Liddy, Hunt, Colson, Haldeman, and others in federal prison for their roles in the scandal.[48]

The lawyer who led the Senate's Hughes-Rebozo investigation reached the same conclusion. "My theory," recalled former assistant chief counsel Terry Lenzner, "was that the president and his senior advisors believed O'Brien had evidence that Hughes's $100,000 contribution was connected to administration favors, and they assumed that O'Brien was just waiting for the right time to put out that information. They feared the secret Hughes loan was going to ruin Nixon politically again, just as it had in 1960."[49]

Nixon, not the CIA, was chiefly responsible for the Watergate scandal. As Senate Watergate Committee member Howard Baker observed, though, there were an awful lot of animals crashing around in the forest.[50] Many were there as a result of the agency's outreach to Hughes, which opened a rift that swallowed the president of the United States, the very office the CIA, indeed the entire national security apparatus, was supposed to protect. That, by definition, is an intelligence failure. And it is the ugly truth behind the *Glomar* operation.

No one could have predicted the twists and turns the Hughes connection would take. By any measure, though, Hughes proved to be the mission's weakest link. In retrospect, it is clear that officials erred in selecting him, for it was he who brought unwanted attention and ill repute not just to the Oval Office but to AZORIAN, an otherwise justifiable—if ambitious—mission to collect foreign intelligence.

The most charitable thing that can be said is that a comedy of procedural and communication errors prevented officials from performing their due diligence—from reading press clippings, say, pointing to under-the-table Hughes-Nixon dealings. (Either that, or they did do their homework and went ahead anyway, perhaps on White House orders, which is worse.) The right hand did not know what the left was doing. Mostly, that was due to Nixon's furtiveness; it took Watergate investigators years to trace the Hughes connection, and even then many aspects remained undisclosed. But it was also due to a fundamental disconnect between the White House and the CIA.

"One department which particularly needs a housecleaning is the CIA," Nixon wrote Haldeman in May 1972. "The problem in the CIA is muscle-bound bureaucracy which has completely paralyzed its brain and the other is the fact that its personnel, just like the personnel in State, is primarily Ivy League and the Georgetown set," complained the president, using some of his favored terms to slur the liberal establishment. To remake the CIA, Nixon proposed reducing its executive-level workforce by as much as 50 percent. Publicly, he said, the administration would justify the decapitation on budgetary grounds; privately, trusted aides would "know the real reason."[51]

Practically no other president entered office with a lower opinion of the CIA than Nixon. His complaints dated from 1960. During that year's presidential campaign, top agency officials allegedly fed Democratic operatives misinformation suggesting that President Dwight Eisenhower—and Vice President Nixon, by extension—had allowed the Soviet Union to open a "missile gap" vis-à-vis the United States. In reality, it was the United States that enjoyed the advantage, and by a wide margin, a fact that administration officials knew from U-2 surveillance but could not reveal due to the sensitive nature of the intelligence involved. Nevertheless, the accusation helped tip the balance in the razor-thin election, insisted Nixon, who forever blamed the CIA and the news media for screwing him out of the presidency.[52]

Nixon went on to lose California's gubernatorial race in 1962 before staging a Lazarus-like political comeback to win the presidency in 1968. His victory capped a lengthy career in the national spotlight that began with his election to Congress two decades earlier. Yet Nixon—the grocer's son who worked his way out of little Whittier, California, to Duke University's law school, only to be rejected by Wall Street firms because he lacked the proper credentials—still considered himself an outsider. "I won the 1968 election as a Washington insider," he recalled, "but with an outsider's prejudices."[53]

As such, Nixon returned to Washington in 1969 "in the mood of a general occupying an enemy town," Richard Helms's biographer writes. The first Republican since Eisenhower to occupy the Oval Office, Nixon distrusted the political loyalties of top federal bureaucrats appointed by Democrats John Kennedy and Lyndon Johnson. In particular, he suspected the Department of State and the CIA—both of which did, by all accounts, lean left at the time—of being strongholds of the Georgetown Set, that collection of impeccably pedigreed, mostly liberal, and well-connected socialites, journalists, and officials who populated Georgetown, the tony Washington enclave that JFK once called home away from home. Deeply insecure, President Nixon regarded members of the Georgetown Set as the embodiment of the East Coast establishment that had attempted to exclude him. Conspiratorial and paranoid, he also regarded them as enemies. "Nixon considered the CIA a refuge of Ivy League intellectuals opposed to him," recalled Henry Kissinger, the president's assistant for national security affairs (and himself an Ivy Leaguer).[54]

The president's suspicions extended to Richard Helms. Nominated by LBJ in 1966, Helms tried to remain nonpartisan, and Nixon, despite misgivings, retained him as director of central intelligence. Yet the two men never established a rapport. Nixon "felt ill at ease with Helms personally, since he suspected that Helms was well-liked by the liberal Georgetown set," Kissinger averred. Helms did not live in Georgetown, and he avoided socializing there. Still, he was under no illusion as to how the president perceived him. Nixon associated "me with . . . the other East Coast, Ivy League, establishment figures whom he loathed and thought of as dominating the upper brackets of . . . CIA," Helms recalled.[55]

Distrustful of Helms's motives, dismissive of his views, the president entered office determined to exclude the CIA director from his innermost circle of foreign policy advisors. DCIs customarily opened National Security Council meetings with an intelligence briefing and remained in place to answer questions during the policy discussions that followed. Nixon, though, proposed to bar Helms from attending NSC meetings altogether. When that proposal met resistance—considering major foreign policy issues without input from the nation's intelligence chief would leave the president vulnerable to criticism, advisors warned—Nixon allowed Helms to attend NSC meetings, but only long enough to give his introductory briefing. Promptly after completing each briefing, Helms was supposed to gather his things, arise from his seat, and leave the room, an awkward ritual that served only to humiliate the DCI.[56]

Nixon eventually relented, allowing Helms to remain present throughout NSC meetings. Yet the CIA's performance during the president's first term did little to allay his concerns. Analysts inaccurately measured troop levels in Vietnam. They also, Nixon believed, consistently underestimated Soviet military strength. "Intelligence has been wrong on Soviet projections since 1962," he thundered, claiming that the CIA, for political reasons, underreported the extent of a Soviet military buildup that followed the Cuban Missile Crisis.[57]

In particular, Nixon pointed to the SS-9, a powerful new Soviet intercontinental ballistic missile (ICBM). Pentagon reports claimed that the missile's three warheads were multiple independently targetable reentry vehicles, or MIRVs, capable of separating from the ICBM to land in a precise footprint closely resembling the triangular arrangement of silos housing Minuteman missiles, the mainstay of the U.S. deterrent force. In 1969, the White House cited these reports in proposing Safeguard, a controversial antiballistic missile (ABM) system to counter the Soviet first-strike threat. But CIA analysts maintained that the SS-9 carried MRVs, multiple reentry vehicles that scattered less predictably, like buckshot. To be sure, the SS-9 marked a significant qualitative improvement, the agency acknowledged, but it did not pose a mortal danger to the Minuteman, as both the Pentagon and the White House claimed.

In light of CIA analysis, Safeguard looked less like a military necessity than a bargaining chip for upcoming strategic arms limitation talks with Moscow. And when a story appeared in the *New York Times* reporting that unnamed CIA officials had secretly briefed ABM opponents in Congress, Nixon went ballistic. "Give Helms unshirted hell for this!" ordered the president, who regarded it as an act of betrayal. "Tell him to crack down" on "his Georgetown underlings." He directed Kissinger "to call Helms and tell him he has fifteen minutes to decide which side he is on."[58]

Pressured to get on board, Helms revised a national intelligence estimate to downplay the intelligence split. But the SS-9 controversy only confirmed Nixon's poor impression. He generally ignored the CIA's advice, seldom reading written products, including the President's Daily Brief, traditionally the agency's primary vehicle for keeping the commander in chief abreast of day-to-day intelligence and analysis, as well as late-breaking reports. Nor did he often speak with Helms by phone or face-to-face outside of NSC meetings. In that regard, too, Nixon broke with past presidential practice.[59]

Nixon did complain, early and often, about the high cost and low quality of the intelligence he received. In July 1970, for example, he told his Foreign Intelligence Advisory Board "that the US is spending $6 billion per year on intelligence and deserves to receive a lot more for its money than it has been getting." He repeatedly threatened to slash the CIA's budget as a means of disciplining the agency. The CIA needed "a good thinning down," he said to Kissinger in November. The following July found him saying much the same thing to a roomful of federal officials: "The CIA tells me nothing I don't read three days earlier in the *New York Times.*" "The CIA isn't worth a damn," he added, before proposing a 25 percent across-the-board budget cut.[60]

Nixon's drumbeat of criticism produced some CIA cutbacks and management reshuffling. Unsatisfied with piecemeal measures, however, he initiated a major reform—or "shake-up," as he put it—of the U.S. intelligence community. Office of Management and Budget assistant director James R. Schlesinger led the review. Issued in March 1971, the Schlesinger Report, as the OMB study was known, found that the quality of finished intelligence remained static despite a doubling of the size and cost of intelligence production over the previous decade. The report attributed a significant portion of the cost growth to the acquisition of new, highly technical systems of intelligence collection. Satellites and other such systems revolutionized intelligence gathering, yielding unprecedented volumes of data. Yet they were also expensive. Their organization and management often crossed preexisting lines of authority, resulting in a patchwork of compromise solutions, or "treaties," among rival intelligence services, military as well as civilian, none of which exerted full and complete programmatic control. Their hoovering up of data encouraged members of the intelligence community to further prioritize collection so they could keep up. And the growing premium placed on information acquisition led to questionable acquisition decisions. "Because each organization sees the maintenance and expansion of its collection capabilities as the principal route to survival and strength within the community," the report explained, "there is a strong presumption in today's intelligence setup that additional data collection rather than improved analysis will provide the answer to particular intelligence problems. It has become commonplace to translate product criticism into demands for enlarged collection efforts."

As a reform, the Schlesinger Report recommended establishing a national intelligence director to hold responsible and accountable for the performance and cost of the entire intelligence community. Without a strong, impartial leader who could effectively manage the entire community, an under-regulated "collection competition" had broken out among intelligence agencies. Acquisition decisions were made, unsystematically and without adequate review, less by policy-level customers who were in positions to define national intelligence needs, the report found, than by producers and collectors of intelligence who, given the prevailing emphasis on collection within the community, had vested interests in developing ever more sophisticated and expensive means of gathering information. On paper, the director of central intelligence was responsible for coordinating the entire community. In reality, however, the DCI had too many conflicts of interest to act impartially. The DCI, the report explained, "is a competitor for resources within the community owing to his responsibilities as director of CIA, which has large collection programs of its own; thus he cannot be wholly objective in providing guidance for community-wide collection."

Established to advise the DCI, the United States Intelligence Board had evolved into the intelligence community's de facto governing body. Therefore, the board also had the capacity to provide effective supervision. However, the report found that the USIB had proven "generally ineffective as a management mechanism." Customers were not represented on the board. Instead, chaired by the DCI, the board was "dominated by collectors and producers who avoid raising critical questions about the collection programs operated by their colleagues." In other words, the USIB rubber-stamped proposals, including those brought by its chair, whose conflicted interest as DCI and CIA head made it difficult to act impartially.[61]

* * *

Schlesinger's report named neither Helms nor AZORIAN, which remained highly classified at the time. But the report was widely perceived as a rebuke of the sitting DCI and his leadership style. According to Helms's CIA biographers, the Schlesinger Report conveyed the "view that the several intelligence agencies constituted a group of contending baronies with which Helms was either unable or unwilling to cope."[62]

And AZORIAN exemplified many of the problems the president associated with the intelligence community. Proposed by Helms, a DCI he did not trust, endorsed by the USIB, and managed by a multiagency conglomerate, AZORIAN had ballooned into a far more expensive proposition than CIA accountants originally estimated. According to available data, costs skyrocketed—by more than 50 percent by 1971 and another 66 percent by 1972. Engineering modifications were chiefly responsible for the price hikes. Due to the prototypical nature of the project and the severe time constraints under which it operated, research and development of the lift system occurred simultaneously. Circumstances forced engineers to experiment and learn on the fly. Through trial and error, a participant recalled, they amassed "a considerable body of knowledge [that] enhanced the chances of success." And their determination to conquer the challenges of lifting a four-million-pound sub from three miles below is admirable. "We made mistakes," Global Marine executive Curtis Crooke allowed, but "we accomplished lots of things in a hurry."[63]

Yet those modifications were expensive, making the program more than twice as costly as Congress was led to believe in 1969–1970. And although Helms insisted that the CIA counted every penny, there is little indication that anyone was reviewing the agency's figures. On paper, OMB was supposed to scrub intelligence budgets with the same vigor it reviewed requests for any other purpose. In practice, though, no OMB representative sat on the USIB or any other high-level program review board. And the staff of the OMB unit dedicated to overseeing U.S. intelligence spending numbered no more than six, and sometimes fewer. "Incidentally," an investigator confided at one point, "if the press knew today that there is only one OMB employee at the CIA keeping tabs on its multibillion-dollar budget, there would be headline stories tomorrow blasting the president for totally inadequate fiscal oversight."[64]

The bottom line is this: lacking proper supervision, the CIA seriously underestimated the difficulty of raising the Golf. And the price of its miscalculation can be measured in AZORIAN's escalating cost, which combined with an economic downturn to jeopardize the program. "AZORIAN nearly foundered over cost increases," an internal history concedes. In August 1971, the month the president announced a series of austerity measures known as the Nixon Shock—including wage and price controls, an import surcharge, and the suspension of the dollar's convertibility into gold, all intended to combat rising inflation and unemployment, declining currency values, and other signs of a worsening economy—a high-level Executive Committee (EXCOM) met to review AZORIAN. Its chair, Deputy Secretary of Defense Packard, opened with a bombshell, announcing that, in his view, it was "necessary to terminate AZORIAN because of the risks involved, escalating costs, and the general budget situation." Extended discussion followed of AZORIAN's "cost growth problem," as the history called it, and whether the program could proceed under federal spending constraints.[65]

Ultimately, the EXCOM decided to proceed, after Helms reminded members of the high priority the USIB had placed on acquiring the AZORIAN target in 1970. But support was weak. And the president grew no less price-sensitive in the face of the U.S. economic slump. To promote the "more efficient use of resources by the community in the collection of intelligence information," he issued, in November 1971, a directive implementing a version of Schlesinger's recommended reforms.[66]

* * *

Remarkably, though, the White House had yet to fully vet AZORIAN by the start of 1972. Yes, Nixon probably learned about AZORIAN's existence during a September 16, 1969, meeting with his science advisor, who served as the president's representative on the three-person EXCOM with Packard and Helms. According to declassified files, Packard had proposed "that certain operations under the cognizance of the Navy" be assigned to the EXCOM, established to coordinate overhead reconnaissance. These operations included "a new activity in intelligence," and the science advisor wanted Nixon's authorization to proceed.[67]

No direct evidence of Nixon's reaction has emerged. According to a senior official, though, the "Executive Branch" approved, on October 20, "a classified United States Government program to accomplish certain secret tasks in furtherance of national security objectives of the United States."[68] This included approval of the "new organization" mentioned in chapter 1—which, readers will recall, some unofficial sources claim was the National Underwater Reconnaissance Office—to manage not only AZORIAN but the navy's suite of underwater reconnaissance programs.

But that was pre-Hughes. No known records indicate that the White House had weighed in since Raymond Holliday, the Hughes Tool executive, signed the November 1970 letter agreement. Maybe that was by design. Maybe CIA leaders elected not to inform the White House for security reasons, or to protect the president's plausible deniability of any knowledge of Hughes's involvement. But the earliest known post-Hughes reference dates from May 1972, when National Security Advisor Henry Kissinger called a contact in Hughes's orbit to say, "We need to have all of the information you may have on the Hughes-Nixon Loan."[69] Only then, and in that most unusual way, did representatives of the president of the United States, the nation's only elected official in full command of U.S. intelligence activity, begin to fully process an intelligence plan that collided not only with Nixon's political interests but also with his administration's foreign policy of détente with the Soviet Union.

3

THE RULES OF THE GAME

What if the Soviets discovered the truth behind the *Hughes Glomar Explorer*? How would they react to an American attempt to steal their nuclear submarine? Would "they say 'boys will be boys,' " shrug their shoulders, and raise their palms in defeat? That was Henry Kissinger's question the first (and only) time the high-level intelligence panel he chaired, the 40 Committee, met to review AZORIAN. Or "would they say 'You dirty SOBs'" and lash out?[1]

Kissinger's question resonated not because Cold War espionage was uncommon. Spying on the USSR always courted danger. And decision makers often considered the impact any failed intelligence operation might have on international relations.

It resonated because the emergence of Soviet-American détente—a development unforeseen by AZORIAN's originators—substantially raised the political stakes of getting caught. May 1972's historic Moscow Summit between American president Richard Nixon and Soviet general secretary Leonid Brezhnev "changed the rules of the East–West game," in the words of *Newsweek*. The two leaders signed agreements to limit strategic arms, reduce incidents at sea, and collaborate in space and other areas. They also signed a statement, "Basic Principles of Relations Between the United States and the USSR," outlining certain ground rules with the goal of promoting "businesslike cooperation" between the Cold War rivals. Actions, not words, would determine what course bilateral relations took, Nixon cautioned upon his return to Washington. Yet if each side lived up to its end of the bargain, then the deals reached at Moscow promised to provide a lasting "structure of peace." "The foundation has been laid for a new relationship between the two most powerful nations in the world," he declared.[2]

Widely hailed as a welcome reprieve from decades of East-West tension—and a possible beginning of the end of the Cold War—the Moscow Summit marked a high point for détente. But it also opened a new and uncertain period for the U.S. intelligence community, a creature of the Cold War designed to combat the communist menace. Together with Nixon's February 1972 trip the People's Republic of China, the opening to Moscow accelerated the breakdown of the Cold War consensus that had supported national security initiatives throughout much of the 1950s and 1960s. According to Anne Hessing Cahn, the CIA became a "vulnerable institution" without a clear mission and subject to attack on all sides.[3]

AZORIAN was in particular jeopardy. Initiated to give the United States an edge in its long twilight struggle against the Soviet Union, the project was by all accounts highly provocative. In many respects, it now seemed to be an anachronism ill-suited to the new state of Soviet-American affairs. Kissinger appeared poised to kill it before it could ruin détente—a centerpiece of the White House's foreign policy agenda, and an initiative in which both he and the president had personal stakes. Did the program's political dangers outweigh its anticipated intelligence gains? What impact would it have on bilateral relations? Would the president risk them, Kissinger asked in his memoirs, "for the sake of an intelligence coup?"[4]

* * *

No, answered many high U.S. officials. The May 1972 summit did not change the intelligence calculus behind AZORIAN. In August, the United States Intelligence Board recertified its 1970 requirement establishing the

G-722 as "the highest priority target." Although some officials voiced doubts, the Golf still held *"unique intelligence value"* in the eyes of the USIB. Recovery of its cryptographic materials still promised to represent *"a major milestone"* for U.S. cryptanalysts in their efforts to crack Soviet naval communications. Acquisition of its nuclear warhead and SS-N-5 missile system still promised to provide *"a much improved baseline for estimates of the current and future Soviet strategic threat."* In sum, the USIB continued *"to believe that recovery of the AZORIAN submarine would provide information . . . on subjects of great importance to the national defense."*[5]

Events in Moscow did alter the geopolitical equation, though. Nixon and his national security advisor, Kissinger, sought not to confront but, where possible, to negotiate with the USSR. The Kremlin would not be given carte blanche. Nor would superpower rivalry end overnight. But by identifying points of "linkage" among complementary interests, avoiding polemics, and engaging Moscow on a broad front, Nixon and Kissinger sought to enmesh the USSR in a thick, mutually beneficial framework—the "structure of peace" of which the president spoke—that would contain the Soviet Union, reduce global tensions, and enable the United States to safely withdraw from overextended defense commitments in Vietnam and elsewhere. The idea, Nixon recalled, was "to involve Soviet interests in ways that would increase [the Kremlin's] stake in international stability and the status quo." Deals alone could not prevent confrontations, Nixon realized, "but at least they would have to be counted in a balance sheet of gains and losses whenever the Soviets were tempted to indulge in international adventurism." "We seek," Kissinger told the Senate Foreign Relations Committee, "to moderate [Soviet] behavior" through a mix of pressure and conciliation.[6]

Moderate behavior. Balance sheets. Structured peace. Such talk spoke to détente's carefully calibrated code of conduct, which required participants to play by certain predetermined rules. Kissinger said as much, acknowledging that the administration's pursuit of world order placed "greater restraints on our behavior."[7]

That is not to say that détente prohibited competition. Quite the opposite, in fact: realists, Nixon and Kissinger predicated (to a fault, complained cold warriors and human rights activists alike) their approach on the assumption that each nation would continue to pursue its security interests. "We do not, of course, expect the Soviet Union to give up its pursuit of its own interests. We do not expect to give up pursuing our own," Nixon's 1972 foreign policy report explained.[8]

However, if superpower relations were to remain competitive, scholars Mike Bowker and Phil Williams write, then the "problem was to contain within bounds the tensions that were liable to be created by that competition. This required, on both sides, policies of restraint and mutual acceptance of the idea of legitimate or permissible behavior." "We do expect," Nixon's report continued, "self-restraint in the pursuit of those interests."[9]

At Moscow, Nixon and Brezhnev included restraint in the détente rule book, particularly by way of the twelve "Basic Principles" of Soviet-American relations. To promote "peaceful coexistence," the two leaders agreed, among other things, to limit armaments, avoid conflict, and refrain from violating one another's sovereignty. They also pledged, under the second principle, to prevent

> the development of situations capable of causing a dangerous exacerbation of their relations. Therefore, they will do their utmost to avoid military confrontations and to prevent the outbreak of nuclear war. They will always exercise restraint in their mutual relations . . . Both sides recognize that efforts to obtain unilateral advantage at the expense of the other, directly or indirectly, are inconsistent with these objectives.[10]

The Basic Principles consisted of little more than words, and the superpowers violated them at will. Yet the concept of mutual restraint was integral to Soviet-American cooperation. Without "self-containment," as political scientist Stanley Hoffmann termed it, détente ceased to exist.[11]

On their face, the Basic Principles outlawed certain kinds of espionage, raising questions about the relationship between intelligence gathering and Nixon's foreign policy. What role, if any, would espionage play in détente? Did greater Soviet-American cooperation raise the political threshold, reducing or even eliminating competitive Cold War spying? How far could spies go in acquiring intelligence without running afoul of détente's ground rules?

Not far, by one measure. Covert activity aimed at the Soviet Bloc—a common feature of the early and late Cold War—reportedly decreased in volume during the early 1970s. There were many reasons for the decline. But experts attributed some of it to détente, which was said to leave intelligence officers unsure as to whether policy makers would support assertive action. "This decline was a consequence of détente," wrote intelligence studies pioneer Harry Howe Ransom.[12]

The *Glomar Explorer* remained under construction at the time of the summit. The lift ship was not scheduled to sail to the target site for another two years. Nixon's return nevertheless prompted the Executive Committee, or EXCOM, the interagency panel that guided AZORIAN throughout its formative years, to seek "early evaluation of the political feasibility of conducting the mission in mid-1974, in the light of increasing concern that by that time the developing political climate might prohibit mission approval." In August 1972, Kenneth Rush, David Packard's successor as deputy secretary of defense and EXCOM chair, referred the matter to the 40 Committee, the National Security Council subcommittee charged with reviewing "all major and/or politically sensitive covert action programs."[13]

To be clear, AZORIAN was not a covert action—that is, an action conducted or sponsored by the U.S. government to further U.S. political objectives but planned and executed in such a way as to obscure official involvement from unauthorized persons. It was a major—and politically sensitive—clandestine collection operation, though. And Rush requested preliminary 40 Committee approval because, a Kissinger aide explained, he did "not wish to commit further resources to the program if there isn't a high probability that it will actually go ahead."[14]

AZORIAN's boldness—the audacity to think that Americans could reach down and steal a submarine out from under the Soviets' noses—placed the program in the crosshairs. And "steal" is not too strong a word, given AZORIAN's dubious legality. Although the Golf rested in international waters, the navy's Office of the Judge Advocate General argued, in 1970, that the United States could not lawfully retrieve the wreckage because commercial salvage laws did not apply to warships. "The tenets of international law, which are recognized by the United States, have maintained the position that the title to sunken warships remains with the flag government unless a specific notification of the intent to abandon has been made," the office explained. The Soviets had not officially abandoned their sub. Nor could abandonment be implied. As such, neither the wreckage nor its contents were legally salvageable under international law. Only the "flag nation has a right to determine what documents, classified material, etc., should be handed over in the event the vessel is salvaged or removed" by another nation.[15]

CIA lawyers defended AZORIAN. Decades earlier, in 1928, the USSR had salvaged a British submarine from the Baltic Sea and then incorporated the refurbished vessel into the Soviet fleet. Citing that precedent, the agency's Office of General Counsel insisted that salvaging the G-722 "would not be an illegal act in terms of international law." "We're always operating on the fringes," William Colby remarked at one point, "and international law is a fuzzy area."[16]

Kissinger ridiculed that argument. The 1928 precedent, he scoffed, "did not necessarily make it legal; it simply established that the Soviets got away with it." NSC staff agreed: "The Soviet submarine remains the property of the USSR, and our efforts to recover and exploit it are illegal."[17]

Salvaging the Golf amounted to piracy, grave robbery even, considering the fact that the G-722 was an underwater tomb. Ninety-eight Soviet submariners went down with their ship in 1968, and AZORIAN planners fully expected to recover the remains of some. In response to concerns raised by State Department diplomats, an interagency review group established procedures to handle human remains in accord with the Geneva Conventions. Each individual set of remains discovered aboard the sub would be treated with due respect and returned to sea, following Soviet naval customs, as Americans understood them. Any personal effects would be retained for possible future delivery to the USSR. Still, Moscow would undoubtedly voice grave concern if U.S. actions ever became known. "Morality,"

Kissinger acknowledged, was among the strongest arguments against AZORIAN.[18]

Officials realized that the Kremlin would occupy the high ground in the event of a disclosure. Colby said, "obviously we were secretly trying to steal this submarine. If [the Soviets] had known we were after that, it would have been legitimate for them to be able to try and stop us."[19]

What could the USSR do? One option would be to stage some sort of détente-killing diplomatic protest, repeating the playbook from 1960's U-2 incident, in which then Soviet premier Nikita Khrushchev made a public spectacle of the fact that Soviet air defenses had downed an American spy plane. Made on the eve of the first meeting between the Soviet and American heads of state in five years, Khrushchev's announcement helped torpedo the Paris Summit, ending hopes for a détente-like thaw in the Cold War. "If the Soviets were to discover our attempt, it could be exploited for propaganda and political purposes if the USSR desired," the NSC staff wrote of AZORIAN.[20]

U.S. officials foresaw another, possibly deadlier scenario. Because the *Explorer* would sail disguised as a commercial ship, AZORIAN managers considered the possibility of a military incident at sea to be remote. Soviet leaders were unlikely to order a replay of 1968's *Pueblo* incident, in which North Korean forces seized the USS *Pueblo*—an intelligence ship, like the *Explorer*—killing one American and holding dozens of crewmembers hostage for months. Still, U.S. officials never could rule out the possibility of a collision at sea occurring between the *HGE* [*Hughes Glomar Explorer*] and a Soviet craft dispatched to observe its activities. Nor could they eliminate the idea of boarding, ramming, or otherwise strong-arming the *Explorer* getting into the head of some overeager Soviet captain. Although contingency plans called for the U.S. Navy's Pacific Fleet to speed to the ship's defense in the event the Soviets took "severe hostile action," the *Explorer* would, for cover reasons, sail unescorted. Alone and unarmed, the *HGE* would be a sitting duck, "extremely vulnerable to physical harassment by another ship." Even a small noncombatant surface craft could effectively employ any number of harassment tactics against the *Explorer*, "ranging from close passes at the ship, to fouling of the ship's screw and/or positioning thrusters, to physically engaging and pushing the *HGE* sideways."[21] Any of which could, in a worst-case scenario, result in fatalities aboard the *HGE* as well as a superpower stand-off. Colby, who later acknowledged sending the *Explorer* into a potential *Pueblo*-like situation, imagined a sequence of events in which a Soviet attempt to thwart the operation caused an incident at sea that led to a "catastrophic climax."[22]

Finding AZORIAN's risk/reward ratio too low, many top Pentagon officials jumped ship. The assistant secretary of defense for intelligence, Dr. Albert Hall; the Defense Intelligence Agency director, Vice Admiral Vincent de Poix; and the chief of naval operations (CNO), Admiral Elmo Zumwalt Jr. all filed memoranda questioning the USIB's estimate of AZORIAN's intelligence potential and objecting to the program's "escalating costs and political risks." Hall and de Poix pushed for immediate cancellation of the project.

Zumwalt did not go quite that far. He did call for delay, though, a surefire way in Washington to kill almost any initiative. Registering "strong reservations about continuing AZORIAN," he recommended pausing to perform a cost-benefit analysis in "relation to the total DoD [Department of Defense] intelligence program."

Admiral Thomas Moorer joined the opposition. As CNO, Moorer once supported the CIA's plan. But in an August 28, 1972, memo to the 40 Committee, Moorer, now chairman of the Joint Chiefs of Staff (JCS), stated "that he could not support the proposed AZORIAN mission, primarily because of decreased intelligence value of the target with the passage of time since the G-722 sank in March 1968, the escalating costs which be believed would continue, and the possibility of strong reaction from the Soviets if they suspected the nature of the activity."

"Because of current and continuing political relationships and negotiations with the Soviet Union," EXCOM chair Rush agreed that it was "undesirable to execute AZORIAN as then planned." Like Moorer, Rush "predicted the Soviets would react strongly with physical force if they learned of the nature of the mission beforehand," a distinct possibility given the scale of the undertaking. Even if the Soviets were later to discover the true purpose of the *Explorer*, "U.S.–Soviet relationships and negotiations would be seriously damaged" once they did. All of which led Rush—a long-time Nixon confidant who, as ambassador to Germany in 1971, laid some of the groundwork for détente by brokering a four-power agreement on the status of Berlin—to recommend termination "in view of [the program's] high political and technical risks."[23]

* * *

AZORIAN was risky, Richard Helms conceded in a September 1972 memo to Kissinger. But research and development had already lowered the probability of mechanical failure from 90 percent, as originally estimated, to 70–80 percent—an acceptable level, in his view, given the possible intelligence gains. Prospects were likely to improve once the *Explorer* left the shipyard in November and underwent extensive testing prior to the actual lift mission, scheduled for the summer of 1974. Soviet-American relations might look different by that time. Only then could informed "political judgments" be made as to whether to proceed.

Besides, from a practical standpoint, AZORIAN was already well underway. Most of the costs were sunk. Canceling the program at this relatively late stage, with the *Explorer* nearing launch, would result in meager savings. Rather than transferring any unused funds from one intelligence account to another, Congress would probably delete program funding altogether, Helms predicted, resulting in a net loss for the intelligence community.

Then there was Howard Hughes to consider. Helms did not mention him by name. But he warned that terminating AZORIAN might seem capricious to Hughes Tool, Global Marine, and the other private firms that had signed on to develop the ship:

> On behalf of our cover story, our primary contractors have committed themselves publicly to a large ocean mining endeavor. Although there is sincere commercial interest along these lines, they would not have made a commitment to such a large expenditure at this time, and could not

follow through on it, without the Government's current involvement. I am concerned that we would have justifiable difficulties with these contractors over a termination.[24]

Maintaining good working relations was "a serious matter in intelligence programs where security and cover problems require a closer relationship between the Government and its contractors than is customary in other contractual areas," Helms continued. "Our reputation for stability within the contractor community is therefore an important matter, and I am concerned that in the wake of such a termination it would become more difficult to find corporations willing to participate with us in such a cooperative way."

Deciding whether to proceed with the multimillion-dollar project boiled down to a judgment call. In Helms's view, the positives outweighed the negatives. "On balance," he concluded, "I am in favor of continuing Project AZORIAN."[25]

* * *

Ordinarily, the intelligence chief's option carried significant weight in security matters. But Nixon was on the verge of firing Helms (for not doing more to shield him from the unfolding Watergate scandal, many believed, though the reason was never expressly stated). So it came as something of a surprise when Kissinger signaled, on December 11, that Nixon had approved AZORIAN. Kissinger did not explain why the president had given the green light to such a controversial program without benefit of a 40 Committee hearing. His memo said only that the president "was impressed by the project's creative and innovative approach."[26]

Nixon's critics, it must be said, would allege that his approval of the *Hughes Glomar Explorer* project was another product of a long-standing pay-to-play arrangement, in which Howard Hughes received government contracts and other favors in exchange for personal loans, political donations, and other gifts to Richard Nixon. The initial November 13, 1970, agreement remained secret, so critics did not know that it came as few as

FIGURE 3.1 Richard Nixon and Henry Kissinger meet in the Oval Office, February 28, 1972.

Source: Frame WHPO-8391-08, photographer Bryon Schumaker, White House Photo Office, Richard Nixon Presidential Library and Museum, Yorba Linda, California.

two weeks after a Hughes courier handed Nixon's associate, Bebe Rebozo, $50,000 in cash. Instead, they would point to a second black contract Hughes Tool received on December 5, 1972, just weeks after the president's aides solicited a $100,000 "emergency" contribution from the billionaire to cover last-minute expenses associated with Nixon's reelection campaign. One opponent claimed, "the CIA was looking for a project that would funnel hundreds of millions of dollars to Hughes to pay off Nixon's heavy political debts."[27]

The 1972 contribution was legal and aboveboard. Reporters could find only circumstantial evidence linking it to the no-bid contract. And officials denied any wrongdoing. They chose Hughes solely "because he is a dedicated patriot and superb at keeping secrets."[28]

But Nixon's decision predetermined AZORIAN's outcome. For when the 40 Committee eventually did convene in the White House Situation Room on June 5, 1974—some five years after the project's initiation—the *Hughes Glomar Explorer*, all $350 million of it, was already docked in Long Beach, California, undergoing final preparations for a mission scheduled to begin in just ten days. Launched from a Chester, Pennsylvania, shipyard in November 1972, the *Explorer*—a prototypical deep ocean mining ship operated by the offshore drilling firm Global Marine on behalf of Howard Hughes, according to press releases—underwent months of builder's trials in the Atlantic Ocean before sailing to California. Because its 115-foot beam was too wide to transit the Panama Canal, the ship had to sail all the way around South America. (Zelig-like, the *Explorer* journeyed to Valparaiso, Chile, where on September 12, 1973, it refueled, resupplied, and received seven "technicians" who had entered Santiago a few days earlier—"a bizarre coincidence quite unrelated," an official history insists, to rumors that the CIA assisted the military coup that resulted in the death, on September 11, of Chile's Marxist president, Salvador Allende. But that's another story.)[29]

On September 30, 1973, the *Explorer* arrived at its new home base, the Port of Long Beach, where the 618-foot-long vessel docked at Pier E—located within sight of a hangar that housed the Spruce Goose, Hughes's gigantic, World War II–era wooden seaplane that never delivered, despite the expenditure of millions of government dollars. After crewmembers

FIGURE 3.2 *Hughes Glomar Explorer* at sea.

Source: Wikipedia Commons, accessed May 23, 2022, https://commons.wikimedia.org
/wiki/File:USNS_Glomar_Explorer_(T-AG-193).jpg.

converted the ship from a white to black configuration, equipping it with
special classified gear to control the capture vehicle, exploit the submarine,
and secure ship-to-shore communications, sea trials began in January 1974
to verify the readiness of the ship's heavy-lift, pipe-handling, and other
systems. In February, the *Explorer* positioned over the submerged barge
to receive the claw-like capture vehicle. Integrated systems tests and training exercises followed off the California coast.[30]

Completed on May 12, the tests revealed significant problems with the
ship's well, the aircraft hangar-sized area that concealed the capture vehicle. During one test, thousands of tons of water generated violent wave
action that caused the well's nine-foot-thick steel gates to slam back and
forth, and up and down, uncontrollably. The force of impact made the whole
ship shudder, and badly damaged not only the gates but the gears that operated them.

The damage was reparable. But the episode sowed doubt. AZORIAN's mission director resigned. "He believed that the ship was unsafe and that continued efforts to recover the Soviet submarine would almost certainly lead to a disaster with potential loss of lives," Deputy Director David Sharp recalls.[31]

And repairs took time—time the mission did not have. Planners expected operations at the recovery site—located in the central North Pacific Ocean, some 1,560 nautical miles northwest of Pearl Harbor, Hawaii—to require at least three weeks, and as many as six, due to extreme weather, technical delays, or other contingencies. Operations could occur only during an annual weather window, a two-month period covering July and August, when sea conditions in the area afforded the highest probability of success. To take maximum advantage of that window, the *Explorer* needed to begin its two-week journey to the target site around June 15. If the ship was off schedule, the mission would have to be delayed for an entire year.[32]

* * *

CIA officers were growing concerned that AZORIAN's cover would not hold that long. After years of protection, the mask was slipping. Reporters, including *New York Times* investigative reporter Seymour Hersh, were known to be working the story. "Hersh has a story about the Soviet submarine," Colby, now DCI, had warned Nixon's foreign policy team in January.[33]

In May, former White House special counsel Charles Colson revealed details to a Washington private investigator. "The Hughes Tool Co., the Hughes interests, Summa Corp. [Hughes's main holding company following the 1972 sale of Toolco], is the biggest single contractor of the CIA. They do a lot of their contract-out work like this new Glomar Express [*sic*]," Colson said. "Maheu handles all CIA work for CIA."

Colson, facing trial for his role in the Watergate cover-up, spoke to the investigator in hopes of bolstering his claim that the CIA, not the White House, was the driving force behind the Watergate break-in. And the investigator's transcript of the tape-recorded conversation remained unpublished.

But word of its existence spread, prompting some to ask how Colson, a Nixon political aide whose portfolio encompassed only domestic matters, could know about a top-secret foreign intelligence operation.[34]

Hughes was in the news as well. Not Hughes himself, exactly—he was far away, living in seclusion atop a hotel he owned in the Bahamas—but his former aide Robert Maheu, the man Colson named. In May 1974, a federal court in Los Angeles heard testimony in the trial phase of Maheu's defamation suit against Hughes. Under oath, Maheu testified that Hughes encouraged him "to work out some kind of arrangement with the CIA whereby either he [Hughes] or the Hughes Tool Co. could become a front for this intelligence agency." According to Maheu, Hughes sought a working relationship with the CIA in order to shield his business activities in the cloak of national security. "He pointed out that if he ever became involved with the government—a regulatory body or an investigating agency—he thought it would be very beneficial to him."[35]

Maheu did not name *Glomar*. But his words made headlines and alarmed the CIA. Quietly, CIA staff explored the possibility that he might be in contact with some of the reporters who were working the story.[36] "I must remain concerned that some exposure might occur if the program were delayed for a year," one operative said. "Such exposure could eliminate the possibility of conducting the operation in 1975."[37]

With urgency, program managers canceled additional tests, including some critical ones scheduled to simulate the operation of the recovery system on the ocean bottom, at depths comparable to the 16,500-foot target site. Their cancellation, along with the poor results of the trials, led a ten-person technical review panel to give AZORIAN a vote of no confidence. According to Sharp, "they were unanimous in the opinion that we hadn't demonstrated readiness to attempt the mission."[38] Remarkably little of that concern appeared in the mission proposal submitted to the 40 Committee. AZORIAN's new mission director remained positively buoyant: *"All tests at 2,800 feet have been completed.* In spite of the fact that we have had to work through many problems, *all systems have worked satisfactorily. The crew has performed extremely well* . . . It is my recommendation that . . . we begin the mission (on or about 15 June)."[39] The probability of success stood at

40–50 percent—still low, officials conceded, but higher than the 20–30 percent estimated in 1972.[40] "*The AZORIAN system has the capability to recover the target section of the G-722,*" the mission proposal vouched.[41]

AZORIAN could be accomplished without incident. According to the proposal, the Soviets had no clue what the United States was up to. Though massive, involving dozens of ships and aircraft, the USSR's 1968 search had failed to locate the G-722, 40 Committee members were reminded. Because the search was so visible, Soviet officials probably assumed that American watchers guessed that a submarine had been lost. But if the Soviets knew that the United States knew the Golf's whereabouts, they had displayed no awareness of that fact for six years. To the contrary, all indications suggested that the Soviets themselves remained unaware of the Golf's location. At no point since 1968 had U.S. intelligence noticed any Soviet search or operational activities in the vicinity of the target site. This stood in contrast to the known location of a November-class submarine that sank in 1970 in the Atlantic Ocean, off the coast of Spain. Soviet vessels frequented that area.

U.S. intelligence detected "no undue Soviet apprehension" of two American research ships that had appeared in the vicinity of the target site since 1968. American authorities sent the ships not only to survey the site and collect data but to test Soviet sensitivity to the area and enhance AZORIAN's deep ocean mining cover. Conducted by Global Marine's *Glomar II* from September 1970 to January 1971, the first probe received close USSR surveillance. But American analysts attributed the reaction not to any Soviet sensitivity to the site per se, but rather to the fact that *Glomar II* inadvertently encroached upon the initial deployment of a Soviet Yankee-class submarine. In 1972, Soviet forces did not visibly react to the second ship, even though it closed to within forty-five miles of the target location.

"*A minimal amount of speculation departing from the cover facade is known to have occurred,*" the proposal continued. Generally, though, security held firm. Hughes's competitors accepted the legitimacy of his deep ocean mining enterprise. News outlets treated the *Hughes Glomar Explorer* as a commercial ship. And Soviet officials appeared unaware of the vessel's true purpose. Over the years, Soviet satellites had had ample opportunity to observe the *Explorer*'s development. Crews of Soviet commercial vessels presumably had surveilled the ship in both Chester and Long Beach. Yet American watchers saw no evidence that the opposition considered it to be anything other than a deep ocean mining ship.

Granted, the *Glomar Explorer* was likely to attract some attention once it set sail. After all, it was reputed to be among the world's most advanced commercial vessels, and Soviet intelligence would surveil it for scientific and economic reasons alone. Soviet naval intelligence was required to assess the activity of all ships approaching within fifteen hundred nautical miles of the Soviet land mass. And the *Explorer*'s destination, the recovery site, was located within a Soviet submarine transit lane five hundred nautical miles wide. But American experts figured that Soviet scientific and economic analysts would not see the *Explorer* for what it actually was—a platform to gather military-grade intelligence. Navy surveillance was expected to be relatively light because the unarmed "mining" ship posed no military threat. Besides, the site itself was located in international waters, far away (twelve hundred nautical miles) from the Soviet coast.

Even if someone did get curious, *Glomar*'s recovery system was designed to withstand close scrutiny. To be sure, the *Explorer* did have some vulnerabilities, the most serious of which was the possible leakage of residual plutonium from the Golf's warheads into the *Explorer*'s wake as the target neared the surface. At that critical stage, any surface ship hovering nearby could collect a water sample and return it to shore for analysis. According to the mission proposal, though, the risk of exposure was low. The recovery system's vulnerabilities existed "*in the very near field around the ship and can be exploited only by the Soviets using highly specialized collection equipment and techniques not considered to be deployed or available to the most probable group of potential surveillance platforms.*"[42]

* * *

Because Soviet intelligence archives remain closed, it is difficult even today to determine exactly what the Soviets knew. But they knew more than

Americans realized. According to a Russian account, the Soviet embassy in Washington received an anonymous tip in October 1970. Signed by a "Well-Wisher," the letter, reportedly addressed to the Soviet naval attaché, read as follows: "In March 1968 a Soviet submarine sank in the Pacific. The U.S. Central Intelligence Agency is using the minesweeping vessel 'Glomar' to hunt for the submarine; she departed Honolulu 17 October and will be at the point latitude 40 North, longitude 180 East in early November."

Certain aspects of the account, published years after the fact, do not ring true. The "Well-Wisher," for example, was probably a spy. And the naval attaché was almost certainly an intelligence officer working under official cover.

But the embassy's *rezident* (intelligence chief) knew that the loss of the *K-129*—or PL-574, as the Soviets also called the sub by its side number—remained a state secret in the USSR. No Soviet news outlet had ever reported the incident. No official announcement had been made, not even to the next of kin. Coldly, they were told nothing about how, when, or where their loved ones perished. Death certificates sent months after the *K-129* went missing stated only "declared dead."[43]

"To this day no one has informed us officially that they died in the ocean in the line of duty," a widow later complained. " 'Declared dead?' Where, in a fight? Or in a hospital bed?"[44]

Soviet authorities hushed up the affair. So how, the *rezident* must have asked, could this American "Well-Wisher" know so much? The embassy alerted Moscow, where the tip caused a commotion. Commander in chief of the Soviet Navy Sergey Gorshkov reportedly put dozens of staff members to work verifying the information. He briefed Minister of Defense Andrey Grechko, who ordered an immediate check of the area. Two ships arrived to find *Glomar II*, the ship that reported heavy Soviet surveillance when it surveyed the target site in late 1970. *Glomar II*, they found, "performed deep water work from 12 through 18 November at the point with coordinates latitude 40°04'05' North, longitude 179°57'03' East"—that is, almost the precise geographic location of the *K-129*, which until that time was unknown to Soviet authorities but was thereafter called "Point K." Observers watched the *Glomar II* join and lower pipes to an approximate depth of five thousand meters. They couldn't determine the nature of the ship's underwater work. But they noted some effort to camouflage its activity.

Glomar II left the area on November 19—without, it should be noted, collecting a core sample due to a mechanical malfunction. After tracking the ship until it entered Hawaiian waters, Soviet intelligence put two and two together and concluded: "A preliminary analysis of information about the vessel's activity for the period from 11 through 19 November provides grounds to assume that the vessel performed seabed exploration and collected samples of soil and water in search of an underwater object, presumably a submarine (side number 574)."[45]

An intelligence gold mine, the sub would be a boon to anyone who could acquire it, high-ranking Soviet officials agreed. But they took comfort in the knowledge that no one—not even the Americans, as clever as they were—could reach down more than five thousand meters to grab the treasure. Moscow's longtime ambassador to Washington, Anatoly Dobrynin, recalled, "our navy did not believe it possible to raise a submarine from such a depth." "Doubt about the technical feasibility prevailed" among navy brass, agreed Rear Admiral Victor Dygalo, the sub's division commander.[46] A third visit to the same site by another Global Marine–designed ship promised to excite additional interest, though.

* * *

Unaware of these deliberations, the White House announced that President Nixon would travel to Moscow beginning June 27 for another summit with General Secretary Brezhnev. Soviet-American relations had cooled noticeably since AZORIAN's preliminary approval. The 1973 October War had taken the superpowers to the brink of conflict in the Middle East. In the United States, détente's "structure of peace" was under attack from the left and the right, and sometimes both sides at once. Neoconservative senator Henry "Scoop" Jackson cosponsored an amendment to the Trade Reform Act of 1973 that denied most-favored-nation trading status to Moscow unless it allowed free emigration of Soviet Jews. Jackson, Secretary of Defense James Schlesinger, and other hawks opposed further SALT (or Strategic Arms Limitation Talks) concessions that, they claimed, squandered American nuclear superiority. Such developments left détente in deep trouble in both countries, a high State Department official told the *New York Times*, and Nixon was going to Moscow in an effort to reset relations.[47]

Of course, the official continued, Nixon had his own reasons for leaving Washington at the time. Watergate had metastasized into a vast scandal encompassing a wide range of abuses. The cancer on the presidency spread in January 1973 when former Nixon aides G. Gordon Liddy and James McCord were convicted for their roles in spearheading the Watergate break-in. It reached the White House that April when senior Nixon aides H. R. Haldeman and John Ehrlichman resigned, leading one Republican member of the Senate Watergate Committee to ask, "What did the president know, and when did he know it?" Public outrage grew following the so-called Saturday Night Massacre of October 20, 1973, in which a Justice Department official, acting on Nixon's orders, fired Archibald Cox, the special prosecutor appointed by the attorney general to independently investigate alleged White House misconduct. It grew further still in April 1974, when the president, claiming executive privilege, refused to surrender tapes of his calls and conversations that he had surreptitiously recorded, and that Cox's successor Leon Jaworski had subpoenaed, believing they might contain evidence of an attempted cover-up. No one yet knew how Watergate would end. But as the case worked its way toward the Supreme Court, the uncertainty cast a shadow over the presidency—and over superpower relations.

"Some concern is evident here about the effect of Watergate on détente," Walter Stoessel, the U.S. ambassador to Moscow, reported after meeting Brezhnev in March. Stoessel found the general secretary well entrenched. But hardliners like Minister of Defense Grechko and KGB chairman Yuri

Andropov were suspicious of American motives. And Brezhnev was under some pressure "to demonstrate that détente continues to have positive momentum." Brezhnev steadfastly supported Nixon, and he looked forward to his upcoming meeting with the president. According to Stoessel, though, he was concerned that Nixon's "political difficulties" would leave him unable to deliver something concrete.[48]

American officials tried to reassure their Soviet interlocutors that the United States, despite Watergate, and regardless of personalities, remained committed to improved relations between the two countries. Even so, Kremlin leaders were wary. With their imperfect understanding of American politics, many interpreted Watergate, in Ambassador Dobrynin's words, as some sort of "conspiracy by anti-Soviet . . . groups trying to scuttle Nixon's policy of good relations with Moscow."[49]

Andropov, for example, speculated that right-wing hawks were taking control of U.S. foreign policy. There was America's decision, during the October War, to put its military forces on DEFCON 3, the highest stage of readiness since the Cuban Missile Crisis; Secretary Schlesinger's vocal opposition to SALT II; Senator Jackson's denial of most-favored-nation status to the USSR—these and other developments led Andropov to warn Brezhnev that superpower relations might be entering a new, more confrontational phase. Nixon wanted to negotiate, Andropov assured Brezhnev. But the "Watergate affair" was flaring up. Impeachment was becoming more realistic. And Nixon, weakened by his "domestic problems," was less able to fend off "enemies of peace." Consequently, Andropov wrote, "a long and determined struggle with . . . the American 'hawks' lies ahead." Someone, probably Brezhnev, underlined large portions of Andropov's letter.[50]

Granted, Andropov, the KGB head, saw plots around every corner. And AZORIAN contingency plans gave the president *the option of initiating a bilateral dialogue with the Soviet Union via the 'hot line' or by other means in order to defuse the situation thus reducing the possibility of a military confrontation at sea.*[51] Still, in an environment of instability in which Kremlin leaders seriously considered the possibility that "enemies of peace" were driving events in the United States, sending a vessel to steal a warship containing the human remains of dozens of Soviet submariners courted danger—and to a greater extent than U.S. officials realized, given Moscow's foreknowledge of Washington's plans.

* * *

Against that background, members of the 40 Committee—Kissinger, Colby, JCS head Admiral Moorer, Deputy Secretary of Defense William Clements Jr., and Under Secretary of State for Political Affairs Joseph Sisco—convened in the Situation Room on June 5. According to the minutes, Kissinger began by asking, "what could go wrong with this operation?"

"Lots of things," Colby and Clements answered. Mechanical failure could doom the *Glomar Explorer*. So, too, could poor security.

Clements, a Republican who would go on to serve two terms as governor of Texas, "said that there were serious political problems that the Chairman and higher authority must consider."[52]

As Clements spoke, the Senate Watergate Committee was preparing to hold its twenty-fourth day of hearings into the Hughes-Rebozo matter, the cash gifts totaling $100,000 that Nixon's friend accepted from a Hughes emissary in 1969–1970. A highlight of the hearings occurred in March, when Nixon's personal attorney, Herbert Kalmbach, testified that Rebozo told him he had disbursed part of the funds to the president's brothers, his secretary Rose Mary Woods, and others. Kalmbach also testified that Rebozo later corrected himself to say that the disbursed funds came not from Hughes but from other, unidentified sources.

To investigators, Kalmbach's testimony indicated that Hughes's contributions went neither unspent nor solely toward campaign purposes, as Rebozo previously claimed. It indicated that Rebozo maintained a secret supply of cash—"Bebe's 'tin box,'" as Haldeman called it—contributed by persons in addition to Hughes. And it suggested that Rebozo may have drawn from that supply in returning the $100,000 to Hughes, given Federal Reserve analysis showing that some of the returned bills could not have been among the ones Rebozo originally received.

FIGURE 3.3 Longtime Nixon confidante Charles G. "Bebe" Rebozo flanked by members of the U.S. Capitol Police after questioning by the Senate Watergate Committee, March 21, 1974.

Source: Photo 740321012, Associated Press Images, www.apimages.com.

Based in part on Kalmbach's testimony, Watergate Special Prosecutor Leon Jaworski widened his probe in April, dedicating an entire task force to the Hughes-Rebozo matter. The task force investigated Rebozo for possible bribery, campaign reporting violations, income tax evasion, and perjury. It would be months before the task force completed its work, and weeks before the Senate committee issued its final report. (Published on June 27, the report devoted 198 pages to the Hughes-Rebozo affair.) But the hearings further damaged the president's standing by publicly documenting his ties to the shadowy billionaire.[53]

The hearings also named Robert Maheu, the former Hughes fixer who arranged payment to Rebozo. They combined with the publicity surrounding Maheu's May 1974 trial to generate concern among officials that disclosure of the Hughes connection to AZORIAN might rock the White

House. "On the domestic scene," an NSC paper warned, "note should be taken of the fact that Howard Hughes has played a prominent role in the cover for AZORIAN." While the cover was holding up, "recent publicity revealed that Hughes was anxious to become a 'front' for the CIA in an attempt to erect a shield to protect him from government regulatory and investigative agencies." "Given the current domestic political climate," the paper continued, passing over in silence what everybody in the room knew not to say—that Watergate was closing in on Nixon, and that exposure of yet another previously hidden Hughes connection would only throw gasoline on the fire—"potential severe embarrassment to the Administration could result from any public knowledge of Hughes' role in AZORIAN."[54]

"A 'flap' could be horrendous," remarked Clements. "In any event the operation cannot be kept secret."

Colby, whose enthusiasm for AZORIAN (and technical collection, generally) had grown since becoming CIA director the previous September, came to the program's defense. He "said he was not so sure it couldn't be kept quiet. He said we could tell 1700 of the 1800 [people] who know about the project that it failed and nothing was accomplished."[55]

Skeptical, Under Secretary of State Sisco "doubted that this would work." Too many people knew about the *Glomar Explorer*'s classified role. Somewhere, someone was bound to leak word. AZORIAN was too big to stay secret for long.

Shifting gears, Clements questioned AZORIAN's raison d'être: its intelligence value, the reward that justified the program's risks. Yes, the USIB, chaired now by Colby, had recently recertified its finding that acquisition of the items aboard the Golf—the cryptographic materials, the SS-N-5 missile, and its nuclear warhead—would yield uniquely valuable "information . . . on subjects of great importance to the national defense." But critics had questioned the board's conclusions in 1972. Now, two years later, Clements was even less "sure that we had anything to gain by recovering the six-year-old target."[56]

Dr. Albert Hall, the assistant secretary of defense for intelligence, was among several other officials in attendance. He conceded that "we do not know how the Soviet missile system works." The United States had never acquired a Soviet warhead, and "recovery might well lead to information which would provide a firm base from which to estimate for intelligence purposes."

Otherwise, Hall, a longtime AZORIAN opponent, echoed Clements's concerns. The SS-N-5 missile was now a decade old. He said, "the Soviets are now two generations beyond the target missile so recovery won't help us to know much about the current Soviet capabilities." And the sub's cryptographic equipment was of relatively limited utility. "The crypto is line of sight, ship to ship, not high level strategic so it is not going to be of much value."

CIA Deputy Director for Science and Technology Carl Duckett objected. The Golf's cryptographic capabilities were "not known for sure," he said. The "ship had been modernized and had been on station off our west coast just before it sank, so that it was reasonable to expect that it had higher quality communications and crypto equipment."

Admiral Moorer, the former CNO who initially backed AZORIAN only to jump ship in 1972, flip-flopped again. The codebooks, cipher machine, and other cryptographic gear aboard the Golf were far more significant than any nuclear material. Leaks did concern him somewhat. But AZORIAN had stayed secret for years, and he did not think that a disclosure would cause the Soviets to interfere with the *Explorer*'s operations.

It was at that point, on the subject of possible leaks, that Colby named Maheu, who in addition to having worked as a Hughes aide was also a former CIA contractor publicly associated with some of the agency's most notorious schemes. Years earlier, Colby explained, his predecessor, Richard Helms, had identified Maheu as a security risk. He had cut Maheu out of the loop before reaching out to Hughes. Helms deserved credit for taking preventative action, Colby continued. Otherwise, AZORIAN's Hughes connection would now be in the headlines.

Colby may have felt that the program had dodged a bullet. But talk of Maheu left Sisco, a respected diplomat known for mediating Middle East peace talks, even more opposed. Sisco "doubted that the project could move ahead without a leak; the chances were 100 to 1. Political repercussions would far outweigh any intelligence gain." He was not an intelligence officer, he acknowledged, "but he doubted the intelligence gain and he was certain it would leak. Relations with the Soviets would be affected, and there would be domestic repercussions as well and the President would have to take the heat."

Clements, waffling, "thought the domestic impact of a leak could go either way—pride that we had screwed the Soviets, or blasts of the President for allowing such a foolish thing to happen."[57]

The five-person committee was divided. (Hall, Duckett, and other lesser officials who attended were not committee members and did not have voting privileges.) Two members—Colby and Moorer—were in favor. But two others—Sisco and Clements, the latter despite his wavering—were opposed. Moorer vacillated.

Kissinger weighed in. His view was key not just because he was the president's national security advisor and de facto intelligence chief; as the 1973 Nobel Peace Prize winner (for negotiating the Paris Peace Accords that ended American involvement in Vietnam), he now stood at the very pinnacle of his career. In September 1973, he won Senate confirmation as secretary of state, becoming the first and still only person in American history to concurrently hold the nation's top two foreign policy posts. As Nixon grew ever more preoccupied with the scandal that would ultimately consume his presidency, Kissinger emerged as the unelected "president for foreign policy," historian Thomas Schwartz writes, exerting outsized control over national security decision making. Famously, it was Kissinger, not Nixon (too "loaded" to act due to heavy drinking, Kissinger told a deputy), who in October 1973 put U.S. military forces on DEFCON 3—one step shy of nuclear alert.[58]

To be sure, Kissinger was dogged by questions about his wiretapping of staff members, his secretive methods, his political acumen, and much else besides. But his reputation as the statesman chiefly responsible for the administration's crowning foreign policy achievements—the opening to China, détente with the Soviets, and the Paris Accords—allowed him to deflect much of this criticism. During a time of national crisis, Kissinger was widely perceived as the "indispensable man," Schwartz writes, the one person who was above it all, with the grand strategic vision to guide the ship of state to safe harbor. "God, I hope this doesn't bring Henry down," said a subordinate whose phone had been tapped. "He's the only guy keeping us afloat."[59]

Kissinger's renown grew on May 29, 1974, when news spread that he had done the impossible, having successfully brokered a disengagement agreement between the Israelis and Syrians along the border of the Golan Heights. This agreement, along with one Egypt and Israel had reached in January, ended the October War. Both deals were products of Kissinger's "shuttle diplomacy," his months of travel between Tel Aviv, Damascus, Cairo, and other capitals. "Henry Kissinger did it," *NBC Nightly News* anchor John Chancellor exclaimed. Kissinger managed to simultaneously launch a Middle East peace process, put the United States at its center, and push the Soviets to the periphery, all without triggering a superpower blowup. He was "the man of the hour."[60]

As the 40 Committee met, *Newsweek* was preparing a cover story on Kissinger's shuttle diplomacy. Published on June 10, the cover depicted him as a world-saving, gravity-defying superhero. "It's Super K!" the magazine announced.[61]

It was Kissinger, then, who was the decider with regard to AZORIAN. Whether the project could stay secret, and how its disclosure might affect superpower relations, were major sticking points. Everyone in the room agreed that the Soviets *could* react if they discovered the operation. But would they? That was another matter altogether.

Kissinger mused, "if the Soviets found out about the project wouldn't they say 'boys will be boys,' or would they say 'You dirty SOBs?'" The president would have to decide, of course. "On the plus side," Kissinger added, putting his thumb on the scale, "there is the value of intelligence to be gained, crypto, missile design, etc."[62]

★ ★ ★

The hawkish undertone of his remarks might have surprised those who presumed that Kissinger would axe AZORIAN because of détente. In fact, he proved to be among the program's staunchest backers. Why that was the case, and how the project moved forward, speaks to the history of détente—its rise and fall, its possibilities and limits, what it was supposed to achieve, and so on. It also speaks to the history of intelligence and diplomacy, generally, and to their uneasy coexistence.

Détente's spirit of bilateral cooperation did not foreclose superpower competition, identified by the president as a "hallmark of our relationship with the Soviet Union." ("The mix of cooperation and competition in American-Soviet relations makes it difficult to define the period of détente precisely," Raymond Garthoff observes.) The Cold War soldiered on. The United States and the USSR continued to jockey for position, arm themselves with deadly weapons, and spy on each other.[63]

Despite any appearances to the contrary, intelligence gathering proved integral to détente, playing a major role in shaping how superpower relations unfolded over the 1970s. Human agents continued operating on the ground. Satellites orbited overhead. And submarines roamed underwater. "Détente is not going to terminate mutual intelligence operations which the target country will consider obnoxious and the collecting country vital," observed Helmut Sonnenfeldt, the administration's Soviet expert. "Either country which wished to exploit a reconnaissance operation could cite airborne, underwater and overhead programs now being conducted."[64] In collecting the G-722, a target duly designated as a valuable source of foreign intelligence by the USIB, the CIA was merely following "the rules of the game," an official would tell *Newsweek*.[65]

Collection helped determine what course Soviet-American relations took, and foreign affairs influenced operations such as AZORIAN. Détente proceeded alongside a rapid Soviet military buildup that saw the USSR achieve rough strategic equivalency with the United States, one new feature of a rapidly changing geopolitical environment in which the relatively stable, bipolar order of the early Cold War gave way to a more complex, fluid world characterized by multipolarity, accelerating globalization, transnational issues, non-state actors, and much else besides. As U.S. decision makers struggled, amid those developments, to accurately gauge Moscow's military capabilities and political intentions, intelligence gathering assumed an added importance. How powerful was the USSR relative to the United

States? Were the Soviets adhering to SALT limits? What did the Kremlin intend? Significant throughout the Cold War, answers to such questions gained even greater currency because they went a long way toward determining the view of détente in Washington. Collection platforms such as the *Glomar Explorer* were well positioned to address them. "As we consider further reductions in the strength of our armed forces overseas, intelligence collection activities become increasingly important," Kissinger observed in a 1970 memo to Nixon. Espionage was a high-risk business, added Kissinger's then deputy, Alexander Haig. Yet "covert activity remains an essential arm of national security policies."[66]

To some degree, détente incentivized superpower competition. Nixon and Kissinger engaged the Soviets "across a broad front," as the president said upon his return from Moscow. Covering trade, arms control, science and technology, and more, bilateral accords encompassed so many areas as to create, on both sides, a "vested interest in peace" that the White House hoped would sustain momentum behind good Soviet-American relations, making their improvement difficult to reverse.[67] The diplomatic framework grew so thick, and both sides became so enmeshed in it, that neither Moscow nor Washington wanted to upset the status quo—so long, that is, as it continued to prove beneficial. Each participant was well aware of the extent of the other's investment in détente, of course, and with that knowledge came leverage. Détente itself, then, emerged as something of a bargaining chip, as linkage worked in reverse to encourage each superpower to take risks, push the limits, and test just how far it could go in pursuit of unilateral advantage without rupturing bilateral relations. Both the White House and the Kremlin, the scholars Bowker and Williams write, recognized that détente involved constraints but also opportunities "to exploit the problems of the adversary."[68]

A U.S. national intelligence analysis issued days before the 40 Committee meeting spoke to that point. Moscow, it said, conceived of détente as a vehicle for securing its geopolitical interests. To be sure, the Soviet balance sheet was growing more mixed. But the positives still outweighed the negatives. Détente remained "durable," because it allowed the USSR to access Western capital and technology, avoid conflict with the West, and limit the

U.S. military threat, all while consolidating its status as a superpower on par with the United States. "The USSR sees in détente the international atmosphere best suited to maximizing the power and security of the Soviet state and its influence abroad," analysts stated. "Moscow will not choose deliberately to abandon détente unless forced to do so by critical repercussions at home or in Eastern Europe."[69]

Soviet leaders, in other words, could make a fuss over their submarine if they wanted to do so. But Kissinger figured that they were too heavily invested in détente to throw it all away over an operation conducted far out at sea, miles from the Soviet coast. "On balance," Kissinger told *Washington Post* editors, referring to the general state of superpower relations, "I expect the Soviets to continue to opt for détente."[70]

Still, exploitation entailed brinkmanship, understood the *Post*'s editors, who defined détente as "an attitude, an understanding, a frame of mind in which the two great powers could pursue their various political interests, and conduct their rivalry with some sense of the need for pulling back on this side of the brink." The trick was to compete without crossing an invisible threshold that, John Lewis Gaddis writes, invited "escalation to the point that might threaten a direct Soviet-American competition."[71] The line was fine; the balancing act delicate.

Certain details led U.S. officials to believe that AZORIAN would fall safely on this side of the brink. Soviet authorities, American experts knew, had yet to acknowledge the loss of the G-722. It was just one of many subs the Soviets had lost in recent years, at a total cost of at least 177 lives. Whereas Soviet forces failed to find their own missing sub in 1968, U.S. intelligence had since managed not only to locate but to develop the ability to retrieve the Golf. These were all facts the Kremlin might not want to advertise. "If we were successful and the Soviets did not learn of it until after the fact, Soviet embarrassment and concern over what we may have gained from our acquisition might moderate their reaction," an NSC paper concluded.[72]

Soviet secretiveness, in sum, worked to maximize U.S. leverage and minimize American concerns about any ill effect disclosure might have on superpower relations. Kissinger well understood how secrecy worked behind the scenes to prevent instances of Soviet-American competition from breaking out into the open. He and Nixon had a penchant for conducting foreign relations in private. They evaded Congress, centralized foreign policy making in the White House, and established private back channels—that is, top-secret contacts between Kissinger and high-level foreign officials that paralleled public negotiations among subordinates on the same issue, often without the subordinates' knowledge.

They also favored clandestine activity. Nixon and Kissinger may have complained about the high cost and low quality of intelligence collection and analysis, but they didn't object to assertive CIA action. "An American President should never apologize for action taken to defend America's security," Nixon said in response to those who criticized Eisenhower's controversial 1960 decision to resume U-2 flights over Soviet airspace. If anything, Nixon and Kissinger found the CIA timid, too risk averse to take bold steps. "Far from being the hawkish band of international adventurers so facilely portrayed by its critics," Kissinger recalled, "the Agency usually erred on the side of the interpretation fashionable in the Washington Establishment. In my experience the CIA developed rationales for inaction much more frequently than for daring thrusts."[73]

At the end of the day, then, the Nixon White House took "an inconsistent and often opaque approach to intelligence," writes political scientist Brent Durbin, "one that coupled harsh criticism of the intelligence community with a heavy reliance on its products and assets." Nixon and Kissinger viewed the CIA, adds Christopher Andrew, "primarily as an instrument for the execution of White House wishes by secret methods," as demonstrated by events in Chile and elsewhere.[74]

Executive secrecy, critics complained, ran contrary to the nation's democratic principles. It also sidestepped congressional oversight to give the "imperial presidency" excessive control over American foreign policy. Nixon, though, insisted that it was key to his administration's diplomatic breakthroughs. "I can say unequivocally that without secrecy there would have been no opening to China, no SALT agreement with the Soviet Union, and no peace agreement ending the Vietnam War."[75]

Diplomatic historians know that confidentiality, despite its faults, was essential to détente. They point to Kissinger's back channel with Anatoly

Dobrynin, in which the two men privately discussed matters and exchanged information outside normal diplomatic and bureaucratic mechanisms. In their respective memoirs, Kissinger and Dobrynin hailed their "confidential channel" as a means of building rapport and exploring sensitive, controversial issues without involving the foreign policy bureaucracy or worrying that leaks would scuttle negotiations. They also hailed back-channel diplomacy for its ability to identify and contain potential problems before they could grow to jeopardize détente—as had been the case in October 1973, for example, when Kissinger called Dobrynin within minutes of learning that Egyptian and Syrian forces had moved against Israel in an effort, Craig Daigle writes, "to get matters under control before the shooting began." Despite some tense moments, the October War did not trigger a superpower confrontation. And the successful management of the "crisis demonstrated that tension could be localized and prevented from disrupting relations between Washington and Moscow," Dobrynin fondly remembered, as "the two countries found themselves deeply involved . . . as partners seeking the earliest possible end to [hostilities]."[76]

Less well-known is how Kissinger, with Nixon's approval, utilized his back channel with Dobrynin to mitigate Soviet-American "Intelligence Wars," as the ambassador called the relentless series of recruitment efforts, disinformation campaigns, and eavesdropping operations that the superpowers' intelligence services continued to wage. Kissinger and Dobrynin identified "mutual accusations of espionage" as potential sources of "irritation," Dobrynin recalled. To prevent an instance of spying from disrupting détente, as the U-2 incident had doomed 1960's Paris Summit, the two men sought to confine such accusations to their confidential channel:

> Kissinger and I discussed this delicate question privately, and he said he was authorized to propose that both sides agree not to disclose cases of spying. The United States, he said, was prepared to handle proven espionage as well as simple misunderstandings through private representations and, if necessary, by quietly recalling the suspects. To avoid leaks to the press, he would personally discuss the cases with the Soviet ambassador. I confirmed that the Soviet side fully agreed . . . Moscow took

similar measures which ensured that both sides adhered fairly strictly to this confidential and sound arrangement for a long time. . . . [77]

* * *

In the United States, détente's growing legion of right-wing critics would denounce just this sort of collusion, which suggested to them that the White House prioritized appeasing communists over battling Soviet advances. Yet Kissinger and Dobrynin's back channel served as a "safety valve that allowed détente to proceed," writes Richard Moss. Kissinger claimed that "inadvertent confrontations were prevented."[78]

Kissinger's conspiracy of silence with Dobrynin helps explain why he backed AZORIAN so forcefully. How would Moscow react in the event of a disclosure? Kissinger asked 40 Committee members. The chairman—who understood that secrecy was an unwritten rule of the game, and that this allowed AZORIAN to proceed despite the risks the mission posed to détente and everything else—answered his own question. The Soviets, he said, "would likely view it as an intelligence coup which we got away with."

Assistant Secretary of Defense Hall continued to question the Golf's intelligence value. Deputy Secretary of Defense Clements again "warned not to leave out the Howard Hughes involvement." But Kissinger's intervention changed the conversation. Nays turned to yeas. "We always knew we had a hot potato on our hands," Colby recalled. But Kissinger was always "fully supportive."[79]

Others quickly fell in line. Assistant Secretary of State for Intelligence and Research William Hyland, a Kissinger ally, "thought that the Soviet reaction would be nil."

Duckett, the CIA deputy director who quarterbacked AZORIAN from the beginning, dismissed the possibility of a disclosure. "We have been deep into this problem for four years without a serious leak," he proudly reminded committee principals.

Colby agreed. In response to Sisco's remark that the CIA stood little chance of accomplishing the mission without incident, Colby insisted that the odds of success were higher. Better than "1000 to 1," he said.

Kissinger, summarizing, said there were "two reactions to consider—public and Soviet."

Sisco wavered. He "thought that the public reaction could be positive—pride over the successful undertaking and accomplishment."

Clements caved. He "declared that if it were up to him, his judgment would be to go ahead."

Admiral Moorer, now almost fully back on board, "dismissed the argument that the Soviets would be a problem; the public problem would be domestic."

Kissinger, often criticized for coldly pursuing the national interest without sufficient regard for political, democratic, or other imperatives, kicked the Hughes issue upstairs—which in June 1974 effectively meant to himself. The "domestic problem was for the President to decide. The U.S. public will support it if it is in the national interest," he said.[80]

Hyland "said if the project were called off, we would be asked what was the justification for halting."

"Morality," Kissinger deadpanned.

The administration was damned it if did, damned it if didn't, said Assistant Secretary of the Navy for Research and Development David S. Potter, who stayed in the background but played a leading role on AZORIAN. "There was the same chance of a leak whether we went ahead with the project or not." So it might as well go ahead.

Kissinger, picking up on that theme, discussed the domestic implications. He said

> that if the project were stopped we would be asked why it was cancelled, why we went ahead with this when we knew four years ago that it was immoral. And if we go ahead now we will be asked why we did when we knew it was immoral. The President is faced with political considerations—public and Soviet; Howard Hughes's involvement; and a possible direct confrontation with the Soviets.[81]

Only the president could decide, repeated Kissinger, who said he would prepare a memorandum.

Committee principals were charged with making a recommendation, though. Kissinger asked where they stood. Colby said he "was prepared to take the domestic heat." Moorer voiced his support. Clements warned his colleagues "not to forget the spirit of détente," but he, too, voted in favor. That left only Sisco opposed. By a three-to-one vote—four, if one counts Kissinger—the committee approved.[82]

* * *

Kissinger's promised memo to the president, if it exists, has yet to materialize. The records of the 40 Committee remain unavailable to the general public. Despite my privileged access, I did not find it among the files while conducting research as a cleared State Department historian.

What little we do know comes from a memorandum for the record filed by a CIA officer detailed to the NSC. On June 7, the memo read, "higher authority" approved AZORIAN, albeit with one proviso. To prevent an incident that might embarrass the president while he was in the USSR summiting with Brezhnev, higher authority stipulated that actual recovery operations were not to begin until after Nixon left Soviet airspace on July 3.[83]

Clandestine operations could coexist with détente, it turns out, though, for reasons of diplomacy, perhaps not at the exact same moment. Delayed, the *Glomar Explorer* would begin its two-week voyage to the target site on June 20, five days later than planned, further compressing the mission's already tight schedule.

4

INSIDE JOB

July 2, 1974, found the *Hughes Glomar Explorer* in the middle of the Pacific Ocean, cruising at eight knots on a west–northwest course, near the end of its two-week, three-thousand-mile journey to the submarine site. Everything was going according to plan. President Nixon's trip to Moscow was wrapping up without incident. The *Explorer*'s true purpose remained secret. Final rehearsals were complete. In just two days—July 4, Independence Day, a good omen, crewmembers believed—the *Explorer* would arrive at its destination. After years of effort, success finally seemed within reach.

"We could do anything," it seemed to one CIA officer. Challenges surely lay ahead, but "with this crew and this beautiful ship, no task was too difficult. Mission impossible? Nonsense! 'Impossible' was not in our vocabulary."[1]

Back in Los Angeles, though, CIA staff received some news that forever altered AZORIAN's trajectory. Frank William "Bill" Gay, president and chief executive officer of Summa Corporation, the holding company formed in 1972 to control Howard Hughes's business interests following the public sale of Hughes Tool, called the program's local security chief. Gay was vague on the phone, saying only that he wanted to meet in person to discuss "something of critical interest to the agency." Things became clearer the next day, July 3, when the security head met with Gay and two Summa associates: Nadine Henley and Kay Glenn. The description of the sub-raising plan Hughes executive Raymond Holliday had written years earlier was missing, they said. Worse, thieves had stolen the memo during a recent burglary of Summa's Hollywood offices.[2]

The burglary had occurred weeks earlier, on June 5, 1974—the day the 40 Committee approved AZORIAN in Washington. Shortly after mid-night, Los Angeles time, four men reportedly overpowered a Hughes security guard while he was making his rounds outside the two-story, warehouse-like building, located at 7000 Romaine Street. The gang bound, gagged, and blindfolded the guard before forcing him inside. For hours, he later told a grand jury, he heard the men move from office to office, open-ing desk drawers, rifling through file cabinets, and blowtorching open safes. "Look at this. Take this," he heard them say as they searched the contents.[3]

The guard waited until he was sure the burglars were gone. He then freed himself and called the police at about 4:45 a.m. Officers arrived to find few clues other than the blowtorch apparatus, a screwdriver, and a pry bar. They also found open safes and the premises in disarray.[4]

According to published reports, stolen items included at least $60,000 in cash, jewelry, and other valuables, and papers—two trunks worth, some said. Holliday's memo was not among them, Summa officials assured the CIA on June 6, the day after the burglary. At that time, "they were fully confident that no [AZORIAN] related documents were among the 'take.'"[5]

On June 15, however, the building's switchboard received a phone call from a man who identified himself as Chester Brooks. He directed the operator to a park located across the street from another Hughes-owned office, in Encino. There, the caller said, Hughes officials would find a white envelope taped to a green trash can.

The operator alerted Nadine Henley, senior vice president and director of Summa. Through her office window, she could see a white object affixed to a trash can in the park across Ventura Boulevard. Inside the envelope, retrieved by an employee, she found two documents: a small white index card bearing the words "Air West," and a yellow legal paper including Hughes's handwritten instructions to "Bob," whom she identified in court as Robert Maheu, former head of Hughes's Nevada operations. Henley, a thirty-five-year Hughes employee, verified the handwriting's authenticity. The index card seemed genuine as well. At the time of the burglary, files pertaining to Hughes's 1970 acquisition of Air West Airlines had been stacked on a conference table in response to legal action.[6]

Having established his bona fides, Brooks phoned Romaine's switchboard on June 20, the day the *Glomar Explorer* left port. Los Angeles police taped the call. According to the transcription, he assured Henley "that this is not part of any conspiracy through the Maheu people or anything of that nature and we wish this man [Hughes] no personal harm of any, any kind." Brooks also demanded a million dollars for the return of the documents. Henley stalled for time, insisting that she couldn't pull that kind of money "out of my hat." But Brooks set a deadline. He would call back in about twenty-four hours. Communication would cease if he didn't receive a satisfactory answer at that time. "We have other channels," he warned.[7]

Brooks called back at the agreed-upon time the next day, June 21. Henley was away from her desk. (By prearrangement, she, Gay, and Hughes's attorney, Chester Davis, were aboard the *Explorer* participating in an event to bolster the fiction that it was a commercial vessel.) Kay Glenn answered instead. Brooks hung up, never to call again.[8]

What other papers might this Chester Brooks have, whoever he was? Glenn, Romaine's managing director, rechecked the files. The building enjoyed a storied history. Hughes had purchased it in the 1930s to serve as the headquarters of his moviemaking venture, Hughes Productions, where he edited the 1943 Western *The Outlaw*, starring Jane Russell. Romaine's climate-controlled vaults still held copies of his old films.

The facility took on a new purpose starting in the 1950s. As Hughes retreated from public life and moved from hideaway to hideaway—first Las Vegas, then the Bahamas, followed by Nicaragua, Canada (briefly), Nicaragua (again), Great Britain, and the Bahamas once more—Romaine became the nerve center of his extensive business empire, from aircraft manufacturing in Los Angeles and drilling in Houston, to real estate acquisition in Las Vegas and beyond. Managers at each locale enjoyed limited authority. But Hughes, compulsive about controlling his professional affairs no less than his personal surroundings, demanded to know everything. Despite what the media might say about his mental or physical health, Hughes, executives insisted, remained fully in charge. "We never made any major decisions without Mr. Hughes' approval," the Houston-based Holliday told a reporter.[9]

Equipped with a state-of-the-art operations center—including the switchboard, staffed 24/7, that Chester Brooks called—Romaine acted as the communications hub for Hughes's enterprises. That was particularly important in Hughes's case because he conducted so little business face-to-face. Reclusive, he communicated with top aides exclusively by phone or in writing. Many of those messages routed through Romaine, where a team of administrative assistants dutifully transcribed his calls, recorded his decisions, and maintained copies for the files—establishing a paper trail that enabled executives to stay on top of things, but which was vulnerable to outsiders too. Watergate investigators, for example, used the chain of custody of Hughes's records in their attempt to follow the money he gave to Nixon's camp.[10]

Holliday's 1970 memo outlining the agency's submarine pitch may have gone directly to Hughes at the Desert Inn. Some messages did, aides later testified. Or, it may have gone first to Romaine for relay to Las Vegas. Either way, Glenn explained when he met the CIA security man on July 3, 1974, the memo ended up at Romaine, because most of Hughes's penthouse papers were boxed up and moved to Los Angeles for safekeeping shortly after he left Las Vegas in November 1970. Romaine, in other words, was the primary archive for Hughes's personal effects—from the prints of his movies and the flight jacket he wore the day in 1947 he piloted the Spruce Goose for all of twenty-six seconds, to the memos and files that documented his business transactions.

Glenn, the custodian of the records, was slow to take stock, he admitted. He had been in and out of the country since the break-in and hadn't had an opportunity to perform an inventory. But he now recalled last seeing the Holliday memo about one month prior to the burglary—in early

May 1974 or so—while reviewing a tranche of Hughes's papers in response to court subpoenas. Pressed for time, he did not read the paper carefully. Realizing its significance, though, he reportedly removed the paper from the files with the intention of putting it somewhere else for safekeeping. He temporarily placed it, he believed, in the top drawer of a four-drawer file cabinet he kept in his office. Or maybe in his briefcase. He couldn't remember which.

Either way, the memo was missing; the burglars had taken Glenn's briefcase and cracked open the top drawer of his file cabinet. Many of the missing items—some of the cash, valuables, and records—came from that drawer, which locked and acted as a safe.

Glenn looked everywhere, he said. In other offices. On the backside of the filing cabinet. In its three bottom drawers (none of which the burglars disturbed, the CIA security chief noted). But he was unable to find it. Glenn concluded that the Holliday memo "is definitely among the take from the burglary and now in the hands of the extortionist."[11]

* * *

So much for planning. CIA officers had gone to great lengths to protect AZORIAN. They had cleverly disguised the *Glomar Explorer* as a commercial vessel. They had handpicked the supposedly secretive Hughes to front the scheme. They had designed the JENNIFER security system to enable thousands of people to handle officially classified information securely. And for years, those methods had successfully shielded AZORIAN. But the future of the agency's top-secret program now rested on a single scrap of loose paper—a potentially fatal flaw that no one foresaw from the very beginning due to the peculiarities of Hughes's organization; a paper written by a Hughes executive, no less, because there was no other way to communicate with the reclusive billionaire; a paper that existed entirely outside the JENNIFER system even though it contained highly sensitive data; a paper mishandled by inexpert Hughes officials (In a briefcase? Really? CIA security must have asked); a paper reportedly stolen from a Hughes-owned facility not authorized to store national security information.[12]

Stunned, CIA agents sprang into action. Their first task was to assess the risk posed by the Holliday memo. What did it say exactly? CIA officers didn't know because they had never seen it. Accounts differed. In her debriefing, Nadine Henley allowed that she hadn't actually seen the file in quite some time. But she remembered a one-page, handwritten document taken from a yellow legal pad, on which Holliday had described the AZORIAN program and "the agreed-upon structure of the Hughes/agency cover arrangement."[13]

Michael Davis, the Hughes security guard on duty the night of burglary, also remembered seeing a one-page document—but typewritten on "standard white paper." He later described its contents to representatives of the Los Angeles Police Department (LAPD) and the Los Angeles County District Attorney's Office. According to the transcript of the tape-recorded conversation, Davis, stammering, said, "Ah, it was a document, ah, it was to HRH [Howard Robard Hughes Jr.] from Raymond Holliday, and, ah, I'm a little vague as, ah, exactly what it said. It was in, ah, reference to the, ah, CIA contacting the, ah, Hughes people about, ah, financing the building of the Glomar. And in turn, that, ah, the IRS was going to turn their back on it."

Prompted by his attorney, Davis volunteered another detail. The document, he said, "also, ah, mentioned President Nixon's name—that he was aware of the transaction."[14]

CIA experts tried to reconcile these conflicting accounts. Was the paper hand- or typewritten? On yellow paper or white? Were there two versions—Holliday's handwritten original and a copy typewritten for the files by Hughes assistants?

Was the note really missing? In their debriefs, Gay and Henley were less certain of its whereabouts than Glenn. Maybe it was simply misplaced? After all, Chester Brooks, the attempted extortionist, said nothing about the CIA or a submarine on the phone. One would think he would have if he possessed a file documenting the agency's secret plans.[15]

Perhaps the thieves didn't realize the memo's full significance. It wasn't written on government letterhead. Nor did it bear a classification marking.

And it was fairly vague, even according to the guard's telling. Could AZO-RIAN go forward without securing the file?[16]

Maybe. Maybe not. Agents couldn't take the chance, especially not after they learned that the robbery fit into a larger pattern. Romaine was just one of several Hughes-owned buildings burgled in the Los Angeles and Las Vegas areas. In April, thieves had entered the Encino facility, taking, among other items, a telephone scrambler used to secure sensitive communications. According to a CIA analysis, someone skilled could use the device "to monitor Summa management conversations until the scrambler codes were changed." The intruders might have tapped phones or installed listening devices; the CIA didn't yet know. But a security breach extending well beyond the Holliday memo was certainly possible.[17]

On July 3, within hours of the meeting with Hughes officials, AZO-RIAN leaders convened in Washington to discuss the reports coming out of Los Angeles. Attendees included CIA Deputy Director for Science and Technology Carl Duckett, program manager John Parangosky, cover chief Walter Lloyd, and security head Paul Evans. The more they learned, the more concerned they grew. According to a declassified account, they learned, for example, that Romaine was no ordinary burglary. Other than Chester Brooks, the thieves had vanished without leaving a trace. LAPD detectives found no identifiable fingerprints at the crime scene. The acetylene tanks proved untraceable. These and other details led police to suspect a "professional torch job."[18]

"This particular burn on this safe was, in my opinion, done by someone that is very familiar with the use of a torch, and this is evidenced by the expertise and the way it was cut, and the amount of debris that was left from the burn," the LAPD officer in charge of the investigation, a twenty-three-year veteran of the force, would later explain to the grand jury, pointing to a photograph of an opened safe near Kay Glenn's office. "Normally," he continued, "if a person using a torch does not know how to correctly mix the two ingredients of acetylene and oxygen, you will get a very hot fire and it doesn't cut as quick. However, in this case it was very well done, in my opinion."[19]

Heavy security supposedly guarded Romaine. According to a biographer, Hughes's headquarters featured

> the finest and most sophisticated forms of electronic gadgetry usable in the counterespionage field. Various warning devices can be triggered by almost anything trespassing in the area under surveillance. There is a device which will sound an alarm if anyone tries to get information about documents inside the headquarters by use of x-ray outside the headquarters! There are lead-lined safes and burglar-proof vaults. There is electronic equipment to repel radio waves and to neutralize electronic snooping devices.[20]

Much of that was nonsense, of course. But those who knew Romaine best—current and former Hughes employees—vouched for the impenetrability of "the Bastille," as Nadine Henley called the hulking art deco fortress. "I always heard it was the most impregnable thing," Robert Maheu remarked. "It would have been easier to break into [former FBI director] J. Edgar [Hoover]'s office, that's the way it was described to me."[21]

Curiously, though, the burglars easily bypassed the building's security system. No alarms sounded. No security camera flashed. There was only the lone guard, and he saw little. "They knocked off Romaine like it was a corner delicatessen," an LAPD officer observed.[22]

Then there was the meticulous way in which the burglars worked. They went carefully, from office to office, as if they had a map of the place. They seemed to target Kay Glenn's office in particular. And their objective appeared to be documents—not cash or other valuables, many of which went undisturbed even though they were in plain sight. "The burglars seemed to know where they were going," Los Angeles County's deputy district attorney told the grand jury. "There were certain things that were not bothered with or tampered with. They seemed to know just what they wanted."[23]

To police, it all added up to an "inside job."[24] But who was "inside?" And why did they target Hughes's papers?

Maheu topped the CIA's list of suspects. To be sure, agents explored a number of avenues. And counterintelligence could never eliminate the possibility that a "foreign government—not necessarily USSR," was behind the burglary.[25] But Maheu ranked high for a number of reasons. His file showed that his security clearance had been revoked in January 1971 following several disturbing incidents. The last had occurred in December 1970, when an angry Maheu telephoned headquarters to complain "that the Agency had embarked on a new project with the Howard Hughes organization and had not gone through him."[26] No one thought Maheu burgled Romaine himself. But he had known ties to organized crime. Maybe, the thinking went, he hired someone to exact revenge against the agency, Hughes, or both.

Maheu's lengthy legal battle with Hughes was also reaching a climax at the time of the burglary. As police arrived on the scene the morning of June 5, 1974, a federal court in downtown Los Angeles was preparing to hear testimony in the trial phase of Maheu's $17.5 million defamation suit against his former employer. This was the same case in which Maheu had testified, in May, that Hughes once expressed interest in becoming a front for the CIA in order to win government favor.

That wasn't the only explosive claim Maheu made. During the trial, he also testified that Hughes, boasting he could "buy any man in the world," directed him to give large sums of money to leading politicians, including $100,000 to Richard Nixon, through his friend Bebe Rebozo. To support such claims, Maheu's attorneys produced examples of Hughes's handwritten instructions drawn from Maheu's private collection. Hughes's papers contained additional documentation, they claimed, because Hughes, ever meticulous, insisted on tracking every little detail, down to individual deliveries of cash. They subpoenaed these materials, which were said to physically reside in the Romaine Street warehouse, where, a Hughes aide told the court, most of the billionaire's penthouse papers went shortly after he left Las Vegas in 1970.[27]

On June 14, 1974, days after the burglary, Hughes's lawyers produced a written statement signed by Kay Glenn, Romaine's custodian of records. Glenn couldn't personally appear in court to answer questions, they explained, because he was out of the country, in the Bahamas, giving Hughes a post-incident report. In the statement, Glenn denied having "any

Company files which contain any memorandum between Mr. Maheu and Mr. Hughes or between Mr. Hughes and Mr. Maheu." Glenn had custody of some of Hughes's personal files, he acknowledged. To his recollection, though, they contained no records fitting the description of those subpoenaed by Maheu's team.[28]

Glenn's carefully worded statement raised as many questions as it answered. Perhaps, a CIA official speculated, citing a working LAPD theory, "the burglary was staged to obtain a Secret memorandum involving Hughes and Robert A. Maheu."[29] The Holliday memo might have been specifically targeted to create leverage or obscure the burglary's true purpose. Or it might have been swept up in a wider search for something else. In any event, authorities were virtually certain that the removal of documents was the primary motivation for the burglary, and that the cash and other valuables were taken only in an attempt to obscure that fact. "It would appear that the purpose of the burglaries was to locate and steal these documents for whatever use they are intended," a CIA memo concluded.[30]

Summa executives blamed Maheu. Nadine Henley and Kay Glenn reported to Bill Gay, Summa chief executive and the head of the triumvirate that had pushed out Maheu years earlier. The ensuing legal feud was long, bitter, and very public. In interviews with authorities, Gay's team repeatedly accused Maheu of masterminding the burglary. His motive, they suggested, was to obtain information to bolster his lawsuit—or publicly embarrass Hughes. He had known ties to organized crime, they reminded the CIA. He and his associates were certainly capable of committing the crime. They had stolen from Hughes in the past, Summa executives claimed—that's why he had been removed as head of Las Vegas operations.[31]

Authorities wondered if Summa officials themselves weren't somehow involved in the burglary, so eager were they to name names. LAPD detectives found them uncooperative. They appeared reluctant, for example, to specify what papers were missing or how many. And they seemed strangely disinterested in recovering the stolen goods. Executives may have been evasive for national security or internal reasons. (Hughes, upon learning of the burglary, issued instructions demanding a detailed report "before anything is touched."[32]) But their behavior fed an impression that something fishy was going on. "The Corporation has been less than cooperative with the LAPD during the conduct of its investigation into this matter," CIA officials noted.[33]

Two Summa employees failed to pass polygraph examinations administered by police. One was the security guard, Michael Davis, who Summa promptly fired after he refused to take the test. The other was Ralph Winte, the corporate security chief who in 1972 helped Nixon's White House Plumbers plan to burglarize the offices of *Las Vegas Sun* publisher Hank Greenspun. Winte kept his job despite the fact that he seemed to possess illicit knowledge, in the unanimous opinion of the examiners who reviewed his polygraph results.[34]

"A current theory existing within the LAPD is that the burglars may well have been hired by the Corporation itself," reads a CIA memo.[35] Summa was under legal assault on several fronts, this theory began. The Securities and Exchange Commission (SEC) was actively investigating Hughes's 1970 acquisition of Air West airlines. Days prior to the burglary, SEC attorneys subpoenaed Summa for documents relating to the case, in which Hughes faced indictment for possible illegal manipulation of the airline's stock, costing shareholders some $60 million. At the same time, the judge in the Maheu trial ordered Summa to furnish documents pertinent to those proceedings. Attorneys in both cases had reason to believe the requested records were housed in the Romaine Street facility. Yet in each instance Summa lawyers said they could not produce any files—despite the fact that one of the documents Chester Brooks, the attempted extortionist, used to establish his bona fides pertained to Air West. The timing seemed too convenient, leading some, including the attorney who defended the man police identified as Brooks, to argue that "there was no victim of this alleged burglary; there was no burglary; and in fact the entire burglary scenario was invented to absolve the Hughes corporation from the production of documents required by court order."[36]

"Hughes and his agents [may have] been motivated to make it appear that there was a theft in order to avoid complying with our SEC subpoena, other civil subpoenas growing out of the Maheu libel trial, and [the judge in the Maheu case's] demand that any original documents of Hughes be produced," added the attorney leading the SEC's Air West inquiry.[37]

An LAPD officer reached a similar conclusion. "It is the investigating officer's opinion," a July police report declared, "that someone within the corporation set up or supplied information for this burglary. It is not known at this time if the purpose of the burglary was for money or for certain documents that were removed. It should be noted that a subpoena duces tecum had been served on the Hughes Corporation . . . three days prior to the burglary."[38]

* * *

The Romaine case entered a thicket of bureaucratic red tape, questionable statutory responsibilities, and conflicting jurisdictions. Legal restraints prevented the CIA from exerting police powers. Any direct contact with the LAPD risked drawing unwanted attention to the investigation.

On July 3, though, CIA officers, acting under the director's statutory responsibility to protect classified data, reached out to the Federal Bureau of Investigation for help cracking the case. The FBI lacked jurisdiction to formally intervene. No clear evidence of interstate crime yet existed. Authorities could not even verify that national security information had been stolen.

In Washington, though, agents could check headquarters files for field reports from Los Angeles. From the files, FBI Director of Foreign Intelligence and Counter Espionage William O. Cregar couldn't determine whodunnit. But the evidence, the twenty-year FBI veteran agreed, pointed to Hughes, Maheu, or some combination thereof. Cregar advised his CIA contacts "that Hughes may attempt to place the blame for the burglary on Maheu [while] simultaneously attempting to ascertain how strongly the Agency feels about the loss of the sensitive document and hope that the Agency may offer to intercede in the Maheu trial to the benefit of the Hughes Corporation."[39]

Importantly, the FBI contacted the LAPD on the CIA's behalf. According to a court filing, two FBI agents personally briefed LAPD officers working the case. The agents did not name *Glomar* or say anything about a submarine, nor did they fully describe the contents of the document in question. They only "told the LAPD there was a national security document involved, that if they found the document, they would recognize it, and they were to forget they had ever seen it."[40]

According to CIA cables, police received instructions to hand over any files they recovered prior to entering them into evidence. Sensitive materials were supposed to "be immediately returned to [federal authorities] without being reviewed, indexed or otherwise molested by LAPD." Under no circumstances were police to speak (to the press, especially) about the papers—or the fact that government agents were looking for them. Otherwise, national security would be seriously compromised.[41]

Look, but not too closely—that was the message LAPD officers took away from the briefing. "We were supposed to close our eyes, seal the documents in a pouch, and deliver them unread to the FBI," scoffed one detective. "That's actually what they told us. I don't know how we were expected to find the stuff with our eyes closed."[42]

* * *

Meanwhile, the *Glomar Explorer* sailed—its crew only dimly aware, due to security restrictions governing ship-to-shore communications, of the paper chase unfolding in Los Angeles. As scheduled, the ship arrived at the recovery site on July 4. Crewmembers began preparing for the recovery operation. They deployed transponders and buoys and calibrated the automatic station-keeping system that enabled the ship to maintain a fixed position on the water's surface, directly above the submarine 16,500 feet below. They opened the well gates, allowing water to rush into the belly of the ship and around the capture vehicle.[43]

Docking legs had lowered the capture vehicle roughly a hundred feet below ship before foul weather struck on July 11. A typhoon "created havoc in the well of the ship," according to an eyewitness. Huge, twenty-foot waves sloshed back and forth, "putting extremely high stress" on the legs holding the two-thousand-ton capture vehicle. "Malestrom [*sic*] in the docking well," reads the ship's log.

Operations paused for one week. "No mining activity," the log reads. Crew used the time to make repairs. But the delay accelerated the mission's already tight deadline.[44]

Work was set to resume on July 18, when the *Chazhma*, a Soviet tracking ship equipped with a helicopter, appeared through the fog. According to a Soviet analyst, the Pacific Fleet commander directed the *Chazhma* to rush to Point K to determine if the *Explorer* "was performing some kind of special assignment." Upon arrival, the *Chazhma* closed within sight of the *Explorer* so that personnel on deck could take photographs with binocular cameras. Its helicopter circled above, snapping pictures from every angle.[45]

The *Chazhma* also signaled the *Explorer*. The Soviet ship indicated that it was sailing home, to Petropavlovsk, when it happened upon the *Explorer*. "What are you doing here?" it asked innocently.

Crew aboard the *Explorer* did not realize that a "Well-Wisher" had tipped the Soviets to their true purpose. Nor did they know the full extent of the security breach that had occurred on Romaine Street. At sea, they remained unaware that the CIA was investigating whether the USSR was behind the burglary. But they knew enough to know they were being watched.

"We are conducting ocean mining tests—deep-ocean mining tests," the *Explorer* answered, keeping up the facade.

"What kind of vessel are you?" probed the *Chazhma*.

"A deep-ocean mining vessel," the *Explorer* repeated.

What type of equipment was aboard the *Explorer*? the Soviets wanted to know.

"We have experimental deep-ocean mining equipment onboard," the Americans answered.

"How much time will you be here?"

"We expect to finish testing in two to three weeks."

AZORIAN's director, anticipating a Soviet attempt to board the ship, issued emergency instructions. Some crewmembers occupied the bow to prevent the helicopter from lowering personnel there. Others prepared to defend the control room long enough to destroy sensitive materials.[46]

Without inspecting belowdecks, the *Chazhma*'s commander could not verify that the *Explorer* was attempting to raise the *K-129*. From his vantage point, he saw only an oversized "vessel of completely incomprehensible design," featuring a tall, oil derrick–like structure in the middle, racks of pipes, and "mechanical robots" poised to automatically lift sections of pipe from the racks, screw them together, and send them downward. His interpretation of the Americans' objective was the simplest. "All signs are that they're seeking oil," he reported to his superiors.[47]

Boarding the *Explorer* risked provoking a Cold War incident at sea. Instead, the *Chazhma*'s commander ended the stand-off. "I wish you all the best," the Soviet ship signaled before leaving Point K, bound for Petropavlovsk.[48]

* * *

Relieved, the *Explorer*'s engineers pressed ahead. They transferred the capture vehicle's full weight—all four million pounds of it—onto the pipe string that would slowly lower the mechanism down to the submarine. "Running pipe," reads the log entry for July 21, the day the first sixty-foot section entered the derrick housing the ship's automatic pipe-handling system.[49]

Mechanical malfunctions, stoppages for maintenance and repairs, and other delays slowed progress. Even so, the claw was three thousand feet below on July 22, when the *Explorer*'s radar spotted another ship off in the distance. Visibility was poor, and spotters couldn't positively identify the vessel until it sailed up next to the starboard side of the *Explorer* and began circling at a distance of just two to three hundred feet—close enough that they could read the hull number, *SB-10*, and count forty-three faces on deck. According to a CIA history, the crew was mostly a mishmash informally "dressed in fatigue-type outfits, swim trunks, shorts, and other such apparel." One person stood out, though: a woman wearing a printed dress.[50]

Officially, the *SB-10* was an oceangoing salvage tug. But CIA officers knew that the Soviets often used such ships for intelligence purposes. NATO, the

FIGURE 4.1 The *SB-10*. Note the woman in the printed dress.

Source: Courtesy of Ray Feldman.

North Atlantic Treaty Organization, categorized them as AGI: auxiliary, general intelligence. "Clearly," AZORIAN deputy director David Sharp writes, "the mission of the *SB-10* was purely intelligence collection."[51]

As it circled, some aboard the *SB-10* inspected the *Explorer* with binoculars. Others snapped photographs. One person used a sextant and an alidade to measure the *Explorer*'s substructure.[52]

Then, as suddenly as it appeared, the *SB-10* sailed off again to hover at a distance—mostly unseen by the naked eye, but ever present, radar showed. Its vigil continued for two weeks, each day following a similar routine: Sudden appearance. Close inspection. Hasty retreat. Repeat. Which proved both annoying—the tug developed a habit of materializing at the most inopportune moments—and dangerous: The *SB-10* sometimes closed within fifty yards, forcing the *Glomar Explorer* to sound its foghorns or flash its searchlights in warning.[53]

The *SB-10* carried divers trained to perform hull inspections, minor repairs, and other shallow-water operations. Its appearance heightened concern about a possible security breach. But experts figured that the tug's "presence near the recovery site was related to Soviet Pacific Fleet submarine operations and transit." And AZORIAN's mission director guessed that the Soviets would not send divers down to inspect the underside of a foreign ship—a hazardous task under any circumstances, much less in the middle of the open ocean. Without proof—the underwater equivalent of Gary Powers's U-2 spy camera, say—they could not confirm any suspicions they might have about what was actually happening below deck.[54]

Meanwhile, "mining" operations aboard the *Explorer* proceeded—in part to keep up appearances for the benefit of the *SB-10*'s watchers, but mainly to complete the job before the annual weather window closed. August 10 was the deadline set by the mission plan. Only eighteen days remained, and the claw still had miles to go to reach the submarine.

Silently, the claw plunged downward. It reached 5,600 feet by the end of July 23; some 13,800 by July 26; and more than 16,000 on July 29, when the vehicle's lights and closed-circuit television cameras clicked on to give controllers a glimpse of the treasure they'd been hunting for years.[55]

"Everyone on board was caught up in the anticipation of seeing the target for the first time," one participant recalled.[56] Cleared personnel rushed to the ship's control center, where screens displayed images beamed from the TV cameras below. They were amazed at the high quality of the black-and-white images. "The water was incredibly clear," one remembers. "We could see the whole length of the target object with the pan/tilt cameras. And, reassuringly, the target looked almost exactly as we expected." That is, a submarine listing to starboard and heavily damaged both fore and aft. But a sub whose sail area housing the ship's central nervous system—its control and radio rooms—remained remarkably intact, still almost perfectly preserved all these years later.

Just one thing looked out of place: viewers noticed something—a hammer, maybe—lying on the hull. Funny, no one recalled ever seeing it in any of the hundreds of photos of the target they'd studied prior to the mission. What was it, and how did it get there? They were stumped, until a pipe handler solved the mystery. He recognized the object as a tool commonly used on the *Explorer* and remembered dropping one overboard at some point. Amazingly, the hardware had fallen more than three miles down to land on top of the Golf—a measure of just how precisely the *HGE* was positioned over the target.[57]

* * *

In Los Angeles, meanwhile, an investigator in the district attorney's office received a tip from an informant. Leo Gordon, a burly 6-foot, 2-inch, 210-pound character actor typecast as a heavy in prison movies, legal dramas, and police procedurals like *Perry Mason* and *Adam-12*, said that Donald Woolbright, a salesman from whom he had once purchased a used car, had recently approached him with an interesting proposition.

"I don't know whether I should tell you this," Woolbright began, according to Gordon's subsequent testimony before the grand jury. "But I have something that's very big and I don't know quite how to handle it."

What did he mean? Gordon asked.

"What would you say if I told you I had two boxes of Howard Hughes's personal documents?" Woolbright replied.

"Well," Gordon thought, "where did they come from?"

From the burglary of Hughes's Romaine Street offices, the one that made the newspapers back in June, Woolbright affirmed. Woolbright hadn't personally taken part in the burglary, he assured Gordon. Rather, he said, "there were four men brought out from St. Louis specifically to do the job." An "inside job," he clarified, led by "heavy people" to steal Hughes's secrets. Sure, the take included some valuables and cash well in excess of the amount reported stolen. But that was only a smoke screen to obscure the real objective. According to Woolbright, "somebody was in the know and it [the burglary] was set up to" take Hughes's papers, now stashed somewhere in

Las Vegas until a buyer could be found. "The whole object of the burglary was to get the papers and the money was ancillary," Gordon later testified, summarizing Woolbright's remarks for the benefit of the grand jury.

Woolbright claimed to know all this because sometime after the burglary he had received a phone call from "a man from St. Louis, named Bennie." Neither the caller's name nor his voice rang a bell. Woolbright was wary, he said, until Bennie explained, by way of introduction, that they once met "at Tex and Joe's funeral in St. Louis."

Bennie called because he needed a "bag man," someone who, in return for a portion of the proceeds, would negotiate ransom for the return of the papers and do any necessary legwork. At first, Woolbright explained, Bennie's associates tried to blackmail Hughes. But negotiations broke off because they "smelled something funny." Now they were giving Woolbright, a Missouri native with a lengthy criminal record, "a whack at it." He approached Gordon because the actor was also a writer—he had a number of screenplay credits, for TV shows like *Bonanza* and *Maverick*, and *Tobruk*, a 1967 war movie starring Rock Hudson—and Woolbright thought that Gordon might have contacts in entertainment or publishing, where, he believed, "someone would pay handsomely for these documents because they are all handwritten by Mr. Hughes."

Gordon was skeptical. But he and Woolbright spoke with several possible buyers, including an attorney who asked to see samples of the papers. No problem, Woolbright responded. Days later, he phoned to report that "he had just come back from Las Vegas in his Corvette with Bennie, and the papers were in the trunk." He and Gordon returned to the attorney's private office, where Woolbright produced two files, both of which were later introduced into court as evidence. The first was a three-page letter handwritten by Hughes on yellow legal paper. Dated 1968, the letter, addressed to the Atomic Energy Commission, complained about nuclear tests taking place in Nevada. Affixed to the letter was a white, three-by-five-inch index card with a typewritten notation indicating that the matter had been taken care of and bearing a signature: "Mahue [*sic*]," Gordon testified.[58]

"If I were you, I would drop it," the attorney advised after taking one look at the documents. "You are playing with dynamite."

Over coffee, Gordon and Woolbright agreed they'd reached a dead end. "Well," Woolbright said, "we tried our best shot and I guess we are too lightweight to handle it. It is too big for us. I'll just have to give this stuff back to the people [Bennie's associates] and forget it."[59]

A convoluted tale, not all of which was true. Gordon, who had a criminal record of his own (he had served time in San Quentin State Prison for armed robbery and assault with intent to commit murder), nevertheless relayed the story to the investigator in the district attorney's office. Soon thereafter, the investigator played Gordon a tape recording of a phone call that the Hughes switchboard had received from a man who identified as himself as Chester Brooks. Did he recognize the voice? the investigator asked.

It was Donald Woolbright, Gordon answered.

Donald Woolbright's voice matched that of Chester Brooks, the attempted extortionist? Was Gordon certain?

"Yes. There's no question, that's his voice."

Gordon's tip lengthened the list of suspects. News that organized crime—"a gang from St. Louis," as AZORIAN's West Coast Program Office cabled—may have carried out the burglary did not necessarily disqualify Maheu, Hughes, or their allies.[60] "Heavy people" reportedly operated behind the scenes. But it introduced a new and potentially dangerous element, forcing CIA officers to seriously consider the possibility that the Mafia had burglarized Summa's offices "to gain leverage on Hughes's Las Vegas operations." Or to extort the billionaire. Or to sell the documents to the highest bidder. A Hughes business rival, maybe. Tabloids, perhaps. Even a foreign entity.[61]

The CIA's search intensified. On August 5, the agency's acting security chief notified FBI director Clarence M. Kelley that new information had come to light from a "fairly reliable" source (Gordon). According to this source, the Summa burglary "was committed by five individuals from the Midwest and was mob-sponsored." Moreover, the contents of Hughes's stolen papers were "said to be highly explosive from a political view and, thus, considered both important and valuable to Hughes and others as well." Stakeholders included the CIA, a claim based on reports that a national security document was among the items taken. "Efforts are now being made to sell the material," reportedly to a foreign buyer.

These details demanded a larger federal role in the investigation. For national security reasons, though, the FBI would have to move quietly, should Kelley choose to act. "If, as a result of your possible investigation, information is developed concerning the highly sensitive intelligence . . . project involved, it is requested that prior to taking any action your Bureau coordinate with this office."[62]

The FBI deepened its involvement. But Los Angeles officials remained in charge, and federal intervention proved to be counterproductive in some respects, further complicating an already complex case. A deputy district attorney grew to distrust the federal agents, feeling as though they "were obstructing his investigation."[63] The FBI, "or some [other] agency"—he couldn't yet say for sure which one—appeared to be working at cross-purposes behind the scenes, putting "pressure on the DA . . . not to investigate the matter," he told a fellow prosecutor.[64]

Distrust wasn't just due to the turf battles that commonly divide local and federal law enforcement officials, though they certainly occurred. It also stemmed from the cryptic ways in which FBI agents operated: telling police to look for the missing document, but not too closely; encouraging them to act, but not before checking with headquarters; insisting that national interests were involved, but not specifying what those interests were. And lurking behind it all appeared to be some unseen forces orchestrating events.

Who were they? Were they there to serve or protect? What, exactly, were they looking for? Outsiders didn't know for sure. But rumor was never in short supply where Howard Hughes was concerned. In the fevered summer of 1974, it ran wild in the hallways and bars where officers of the court congregated. Working from the premise that national security really was at stake, some joined the deputy district attorney in guessing—correctly, as it turned out—that the CIA was the hidden hand. One local official involved in the burglary investigation told reporters that Hughes's Romaine Street archive housed correspondence documenting his working relationship with the agency, a relationship, the official said, that extended well beyond a single operation. According to the Associated Press, stolen records included files showing that "the Hughes organization was used as a 'pay-master type front' for undercover CIA agents around the world."[65]

Then there were Hughes's aides. They were so unhelpful, so reticent, as if they were hiding something. Perhaps they staged the "inside job" in cahoots with the CIA, with the intent of removing compromising evidence before it fell into the wrong hands. The "break-in was done by the CIA," one source claimed.[66]

Others sensed that the national security claim was bogus, invented by federal agents to hide other secrets—bad secrets—the government wanted to keep hidden. They could open their daily newspapers to find that security claims weren't always sacrosanct. On August 5, days after the U.S. Supreme Court ordered President Nixon to deliver tape recordings and other material subpoenaed by Watergate investigators, the White House released a transcript of a tape-recorded conversation Nixon had had with aides in the Oval Office on June 23, 1972. Dubbed the "Smoking Gun," the tape proved that the president had engaged in an attempted cover-up. Listeners heard Nixon and his then chief of staff, H. R. Haldeman, discussing a plan to obstruct the FBI's investigation into the Watergate break-in by directing the CIA to falsely claim that national security was at stake. The tape's release weakened support for the president within his own party. In Congress, key Republican holdouts announced that they would not stand in the way of impeachment proceedings, making Nixon's removal from office a foregone conclusion.[67]

Many were struck by the similarities between the events at Romaine Street and the Watergate break-in—a sign, some said, of the White House's desire to discover what Robert Maheu's friend, Democratic National Committee chair Larry O'Brien, knew about the Hughes-Rebozo funds. "It's the best theory we have on the Watergate break-in," a Senate Watergate Committee staffer told a reporter.[68] The committee couldn't reach a definitive conclusion, in part because key persons refused to cooperate. Rebozo exercised his Fifth Amendment right not to provide incriminating evidence. Hughes himself proved unreachable. Prosecutors found it impossible to personally serve him with a subpoena to appear in court, secluded as he was behind heavy security, atop a hotel he owned in the Bahamas. "We were advised that Hughes had made a determined effort to avoid service of any kind of process, particularly since leaving Las Vegas in 1970," reported Watergate assistant special prosecutor Paul Michel, head of the office's Hughes-Rebozo task force. Efforts to get Hughes's chief counsel to cooperate voluntarily went nowhere.[69]

Were documents detailing the Rebozo payments hidden inside Romaine? Yes, Maheu testified—prior to the burglary, anyway. "Received call from [an unidentified official from the] FBI [who] states home office in Washington interested. They feel Watergate is involved," an LAPD report read. The CIA, too, considered the possibility that the Romaine break-in was, "politically motivated to aid or deter Watergate investigation/inquiry."[70]

"I think the Romaine Street Break-In is no ordinary burglary-robbery," William Turner, the enforcement officer in charge of the SEC's Air West investigation, wrote Michel. "My guess is that it is a continuation of Watergate—the unique contents of those files and the unique relation between Hughes, Maheu, and the CIA as well as the sophisticated manner in which they were removed lead me . . . to this conclusion." The fact that the documents had yet to surface fed Turner's impression that those who removed them "were not extortionists but people who have had and do now have an interest in their not reappearing."[71]

Michel could never establish that Watergate-related files were among the stolen materials. The task force closed without indictments, concluding "that the interest of the burglars and their confederates was purely a monetary one; it was simply a case of blackmail." But it did find "substantial evidence" of misconduct. And federal intervention caused suspicion to fall over the case, hindering the search for the missing AZORIAN file. The investigation "was a disaster," one prosecutor said. "Nobody knew what was up. The Hughes people were so goddamn mysterious, we couldn't get a thing out of them, then the FBI steps in and starts playing cat-and-mouse—saying it's your case, but don't ask what's going on—and lurking behind everything there's the CIA."[72]

* * *

In the *Explorer*'s control room, operators began the final descent. By remotely controlling hydraulic thrusters, they positioned the capture vehicle directly over the illuminated submarine. They then fully extended the claw's fingers and carefully lowered the enormous, warehouse-sized contraption down the final few feet, leaving just enough room for four breakout legs positioned at each corner to clear the Golf. Hours of simulator training paid off, for soon the capture vehicle rested firmly on the bottom, within one foot of its intended location. Not bad, considering that the controllers were working on the water's surface, more than three miles above. "It was almost a perfect touchdown," writes Sharp, the deputy mission director. "Mining machine on bottom," reads the ship's log for July 31.

The next step—driving the claw's tines into the seabed so that they could close under the submarine prior to liftoff—didn't go as smoothly. Because the *Glomar II* survey ship had failed to collect a core sample, AZORIAN planners had to guesstimate the density of the soil surrounding the target. They erred on the conservative side. But the soil proved to be even harder than expected. Three times controllers tried to force the tines into the earth. Each time they failed, despite offloading a million more pounds of tension onto the capture vehicle with every attempt. Its "operators were getting nervous," Sharp recalls. The vehicle itself weighed four million pounds, meaning they only had another million or so to work with. And the claw's davits were not designed to withstand that kind of force. They "were intended for pulling up, not pushing down," said Ray Feldman, an engineer with Lockheed, the capture vehicle's developer.

Operators had no choice. A fourth attempt succeeded in driving each of the claw's eight grabbers several feet into the seabed, enough to secure the target. Seawater flowed down through the pipe string to hydraulically power the four legs that pushed up to help the load break free of the muck.

Breakout went according to plan. Yet another problem appeared just before liftoff, though. The heave compensator system, designed to dampen the transmission of movement between the *Glomar Explorer* and its heavy-lift equipment, failed. Engineers shut off the seawater hydraulics to make repairs. Without power, the legs settled back to the ocean bottom. Operators maintained tension on the pipe string. Still, the claw's fingers were left to support much of the combined weight of the capture vehicle and the submarine. "It couldn't have come at a worse time," Sharp remembers. "We could only cross our fingers and hope for the best."

As they waited, the *SB-10* buzzed nearby, circling the *Explorer*, darting in and out, this way and that. "SB-10 dangerously close amidships to port—our windward side. Estimated less than 50 yds dist[ant]," reads the overnight log. Worried about a possible collision at sea, the *Explorer*'s captain signaled the *SB-10* to keep clear, but he received no response. Moments later, the *SB-10* moved out to sea, only to suddenly rematerialize out of the dark, cross in front of the *Explorer*, and stop off the starboard side.[73]

Finally, after nearly twenty hours, engineers completed repairs. Seawater again flowed into the legs, lifting the capture vehicle a second time. "Commence pulling pipe," announced the August 1 log.[74]

Groaning under the load, the *Explorer*'s system slowly lifted the submarine. It reached almost three thousand feet by the end of August 2; roughly eight thousand feet—nearly halfway up!—as August 4 dawned. Each length of pipe reduced tons of stress on the lift system. Success appeared at hand. "No one was relaxing," a participant recalled, "but there was a sense arising that we were, indeed, going to make it." Crew reveled at the thought of stealing the Golf out from under the *SB-10*. What a lashing the tug's crew would get someday when the Kremlin realized what had actually happened below water![75]

Then crewmembers felt a jolt. Feldman, the Lockheed engineer, rushed to the control center, where the TV monitors were located. Everything looked okay. The screens showed the target nestled safely in the claw's grasp, in the same condition as it had been since liftoff.

Relief spread through the control room, until someone remembered to hit the refresh button. New, more recent images appeared on screen. They confirmed engineers' worst fears: much of the payload was gone. As part of the nuclear-armed submarine plummeted back to the seabed, crewmembers braced themselves for a possible explosion.[76]

5

FISH OR CUT BAIT?

What is the latest on our ship project in the Pacific?" Gerald Ford asked the National Security Council on August 10, 1974. The former vice president had assumed the presidency just twenty-four hours earlier, following Richard Nixon's resignation. Ford convened the meeting—the first such NSC gathering of his administration—to affirm the transition of power, and also to get a situation report on the *Glomar Explorer*, which was still at sea. What happened? he wanted to know.

"Well sir," CIA director William Colby began, "the tines were damaged when we picked up the sub and we lost [part of the target]." Thankfully, the submarine's nuclear warheads hadn't detonated on impact, as some aboard the *Explorer* had feared. But the claw had come up shorthanded. As he spoke, the ship was sailing toward the Hawaiian Islands, where trained personnel stood ready to inspect the haul.

"It is very hard to tell what they have," Colby cautioned. It would take time—a month or more—to identify every item inside the *Explorer*'s well. But he was hopeful that specialists would find valuable material.[1]

Colby broached the possibility of a second mission, though, in case they failed to find the uniquely valuable hardware whose retrieval had driven AZORIAN from the outset: the sub's ballistic missiles, nuclear warheads,

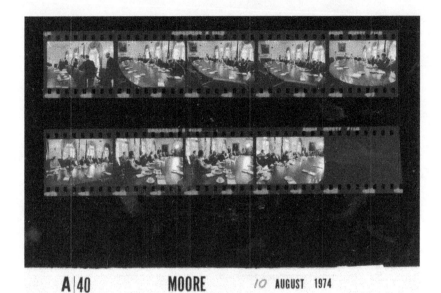

A|40   MOORE   *IO* AUGUST 1974

FIGURE 5.1 William Colby, Henry Kissinger, James Schlesinger, and other officials arrive in the White House Cabinet Room for the August 10, 1974, National Security Council meeting, the first such NSC gathering of the Ford administration.

Source: Contact sheet A0040, White House Photographic Office Photographs, Gerald R. Ford Presidential Library, Ann Arbor, Michigan.

and code gear. NSC members discussed sending an intelligence-gathering submarine to photograph the target so that experts could determine if the wreckage remained sufficiently intact, after again falling thousands of feet to the seabed, to justify another try. Surveying the site did not commit the president to a follow-on mission, Ford's aides assured him. "This is just to take pictures and see the situation," said the deputy national security advisor, Lieutenant General Brent Scowcroft.[2]

* * *

What, exactly, the claw captured remains a state secret to this day. For years, exaggerated claims appeared in print, based in part on misinformation deliberately spread by American officials attempting to confuse the Soviets into taking unnecessary (and expensive) countermeasures. *Glomar* fully accomplished its mission, *Time* magazine reported in 1976. The ship purportedly raised the entire 324-foot-long submarine—a physical impossibility, given that the *Explorer's* interior docking well measured only 199 feet in length. "It was all one hell of a success," a senior navy officer bragged.[3]

CIA officers aboard the *Glomar Explorer* knew the truth before the ship reached port. Once seawater was pumped from the well, they could look down and see the top of the capture vehicle—and a dark, twisted mass beneath. "It wasn't a pretty sight," recalled deputy mission director David Sharp. "It was so mangled that it was difficult to identify the features. To me it was just a gray mass of metal that bore very little resemblance to a submarine. It was impossible for me to say, 'Oh, there's a torpedo tube,' or 'Over there's the mount for the deck guns.' It was massive, and gray, and looked very formidable."[4]

A partially declassified Pentagon report characterized the AZORIAN mission as "partially successful, resulting in retrieval of a [text redacted] section of the original target." Colby provided additional details in the French edition of his memoirs, published beyond the reach of CIA censors. The *Explorer*, he wrote, brought "to the surface only the forepart, about one-third [of the target], while the aft fell to the bottom of the sea with its nuclear missiles, its guidance apparatus, its transmission equipment, its codes, in other words with all the things the CIA had hoped to gain through this unprecedented operation."[5]

Collecting even that much represented a significant achievement. So far as is known, the United States had never before acquired such a large portion of a Soviet submarine. By subjecting the steel to metallurgical analysis, U.S. experts could gauge the hull's strength and determine how deep Soviet subs could dive—knowledge that could be put to great use in undersea warfare.[6]

As cutting torch handlers carefully peeled back the outer and inner hulls, they reportedly found uneven and pitted welding, as well as hatch covers and valves that were crude by U.S. standards. Wooden two-by-fours had even been used to support some compartments. Though surprising, these findings were important as well, for they enabled American analysts to downgrade their estimates of Soviet capabilities.[7]

Exploitation teams also discovered nuclear-tipped torpedoes. Electricity powered some; steam others, sources later told the *New York Times*, "indicating that the submarine's firing tubes were not interchangeable." Though that finding worsened American impressions of Soviet forces, recovering the torpedoes was an important achievement, the late intelligence historian Jeffrey T. Richelson observed, because they gave "U.S. analysts their first look at the Soviet devices. Data concerning the homing devices incorporated into the torpedo design would be of aid in developing countermeasures."[8]

Personnel found documents too. According to a CIA congressional briefing, recovered papers included "Notebooks on Sonar Systems."[9] They also included a journal kept by an officer who served aboard the Golf, the *Times* reported. Arguably the most valuable item collected, the journal, readable after chemical treatment, reportedly provided "a partial description of the Soviet cryptographic codes and nuclear system in effect in 1968."[10]

Americans also found human remains entombed inside the G-722. Crewmembers smelled the stench of decaying corpses long before exploitation teams saw them. As the *Explorer* sailed south and summer temperatures warmed the well, the distinctive odor permeated the entire ship, resisting even the ten-knot breeze the *Explorer* generated as it steamed toward Hawaii.

Eventually, the teams located the remains of six Soviet crewmen. Surprisingly, Sharp recalls, "the bodies were mostly intact, with their features very well preserved." When the hull imploded, he explained, "the wall of water coming forward into the bow forced everything—equipment, mattresses and sailors—into the forward section containing most of the sleeping quarters. The mattresses compressed around the sailors, protecting them from the fish and crabs that were all over the ocean bottom and which would have otherwise stripped their bones bare."[11]

According to a CIA account, three submariners were found without personal identification, and could not be identified. Three others carried ID:

Victor Lokhov, Vladimir Kostyushko, and Valentin Nosachev, each of whom was just twenty years of age when their ship went down. The *Explorer*'s surgeon listed the cause of death as "explosion and crushing injuries incurred while working on duty vessel."

Anticipating that they would find human remains, AZORIAN leaders were prepared to bury the dead at sea. And they kept meticulous records in case Soviet authorities ever asked. "From the time of their recovery from the submarine's hull until the burial ceremony, the remains were handled with the utmost care and respect," reads the CIA account. No autopsies were performed. Two burial rehearsals occurred "to ensure that the actual ceremony would proceed smoothly and with the appropriate dignity."

On September 4, 1974, the *Explorer* paused for the burial at sea. Immediately prior to the ceremony, a six-person honor guard, clad in white, transported each set of remains to a burial vault, a heavy steel container measuring eight by eight by four feet in dimension, and outfitted with six shelves to support each individual body. During transportation, a Soviet naval ensign, carried aboard the *Glomar Explorer* specifically for this purpose, was draped over the deceased. After each of the six were placed in the burial vault, together with a representative portion of the *K-129*, the vessel on which they had served and perished, personnel mounted the ensign behind the vault, alongside the American flag. The ceremony, attended by some seventy-five crewmembers and videotaped for posterity, began with the national anthems of the United States and the Soviet Union. It continued with a service approximating an actual Soviet Navy burial at sea ceremony, followed by the American equivalent. An interpreter translated both services into Russian.

Crew then slowly closed and hoisted the vault over the side of the *Explorer*, while an officiant read words of committal and benediction. A hymn played. "At 1921 local time, during the final light of evening twilight," the account ended, "the vault, now completely flooded, was released into a calm sea and fell free to the ocean floor." Casualties of the Cold War, Victor Lokhov, Vladimir Kostyushko, and Valentin Nosachev reached their final resting places in the waters of the Pacific, some ninety miles south-west of Hawaii.[12]

* * *

AZORIAN's ledger was grim: a few documents, some hardware, and a bunch of dead bodies. From an intelligence standpoint, the documents and hardware were certainly useful. However, experts later told the *New York Times*, they were "insignificant" compared to the enormous resources poured into AZORIAN—resources that, in retrospect, could have been invested more productively, some U.S. officials claimed.[13] For years, the *Glomar* "mess" drained funding from other, worthier collection programs, complained Major General George Keegan Jr., chief of intelligence for the U.S. Air Force. Underdeveloped, these programs left the U.S. intelligence community at a disadvantage vis-à-vis the Soviet Union. "In the field of assessing the evolving naval threat, we are now in the Stone Age," Keegan wrote.[14]

High officials could've cut bait at that point. Everyone involved knew from the outset that the sub-raising mission was nearly impossible—a "10 percent activity," one participant later described it.[15] They could've stopped secure in the knowledge they had done everything in their power to catch a prize that remained just out of reach. It was late 1974, after all, and times had changed since the program got underway back in 1968. Almost every top figure present at the creation—including Richards Nixon, Helms, and Russell—was out of office, or, in Russell's case, dead. In many respects, AZORIAN was a legacy of a bygone age in which American confidence soared high, the U.S. economy boomed, the government enjoyed budget surpluses, and national secrets remained safely locked away. Sitting leaders had an opportunity to move on, especially since the case for collecting a now twice-damaged, two-by-four-supported, 1950s-vintage vessel was weaker than ever.

The lure of treasure proved irresistible, though. "Our intelligence exploitation of the part that was recovered was of such significance, and the prospects of what we might obtain if we were to recover more of the submarine were so promising, that plans were made for a second mission," reflected Henry Kissinger, still wearing two hats as secretary of state and national security advisor.[16] Besides, *Glomar* had come so far, had gotten so close. Officials had already sunk so much into the program—$250 million and counting. Why not tens of millions more, given that such a relatively small investment might yield a large intelligence payoff?

First, they had to determine whether a second attempt, code-named MATADOR, was even possible. What condition was the target object in? Was it still in one piece after again plummeting to the ocean bottom, or had it shattered on impact? Did the remains of the G-722 rest on flat or rocky terrain? On level ground or a slope? On soil soft or hard? In other words, was the target object recoverable?

The photographs taken by the surveillance submarine Ford's aides discussed addressed those questions. The photos and the name of the sub that took them remain classified. Published sources identify a nuclear attack submarine subsequently converted into a navy special project (i.e., intelligence-gathering) submarine. Outfitted, like the *Halibut*—the spy sub that had photographed the G-722 back in 1968—with remote-controlled cameras capable of operating at extreme depths, the special sub reconnoitered the Golf in late 1974. According to navy officials, the pictures showed that it was unrecoverable. "It dissolved just like that," snapped a former high-ranking naval officer, "like an Alka-Seltzer in water. It spread all over acres on the ocean floor." "It shattered," said another. "The judgment was made that there was no possibility to recover anything more."

Navy officers were not uniformly against MATADOR. Dr. David S. Potter, under secretary of the navy, actively supported the program. Many objected, though, including Captain James F. Bradley, the deepwater surveillance pioneer who opposed the CIA effort from the outset. Though retired, Bradley remained influential—and certain that the heavy lift technique was impractical, a view AZORIAN's outcome did little to disprove. Another opponent, Admiral James L. Holloway III, chief of naval operations, worried that MATADOR would force the Pacific Fleet to come to the rescue of the *Glomar Explorer*, and into an unnecessary confrontation at sea with the Soviet military.[17]

Had AZORIAN acquired a Soviet code machine, along with information specifying how it operated, the mission would have ranked among the greatest exploits in intelligence history, alongside Allied code-breaking efforts in World War II, reasoned Rear Admiral Bobby Ray Inman, the director of naval intelligence. But the possibility of obtaining the Golf's cryptographic gear was too "remote" to justify another attempt. The photos showed that the target had suffered additional damage. "The target is now broken," an ad hoc committee of the United States Intelligence Board confirmed. "Some equipment and documents, apparently spilled from the target vehicle during the recovery attempt, are dispersed throughout [a] debris field," along with segments of the G-722's hull. No items other than the hull segments were identifiable. There was no guarantee that the claw could grab the most desirable objects. A return trip simply wasn't worth the additional expense, in the view of Inman, the future National Security Agency director, not when there were cable tapping and other higher-performing underwater reconnaissance programs to fund.[18]

The USIB saw things differently. The board's position was crucial. Its 1970 prioritization of the AZORIAN target effectively foreclosed debate on that program, shutting down critics again and again. Now, the USIB reviewed the case for MATADOR.

Chaired by a respected member of the Defense Intelligence Agency (DIA), the USIB committee found "that there have been no significant intelligence developments since the last Board assessment [of the Golf's value prior to the AZORIAN attempt] in May 1974 which would detract from the unique intelligence potential of equipment believed to be aboard the original MATADOR target." Although the intelligence value of these items would have "decreased slightly" by mid-1975, when the *Glomar Explorer* was set to sail again, "our basic priorities and estimate of overall gain from acquisition of equipment and documents have not changed measurably."

Cryptographic machines and related documents; nuclear warheads; SS-N-5 missiles; navigation and fire-control systems—all would have remained uniquely valuable in the eyes of the committee, which considered one of the target object's two sections to be most "likely to contain items of highest intelligence value." The section lay on the ocean bottom in a "potentially recoverable" position. The committee recommended "that this section be accorded priority if recovery of either hull section is attempted."[19]

No significant intelligence developments? The USIB's AZORIAN judgment had faced some resistance over the years. But the committee's MATADOR assessment struck the State Department's intelligence chief, Assistant Secretary of State for Intelligence and Research William Hyland, a USIB member, as "too optimistic and positive. It is misleading to estimate that our 'basic priorities and estimate of overall gain from the acquisition of equipment and documents have not changed *measurably*.'" The target had broken into pieces. Debris littered the ocean floor. Items aboard the Golf were dated to begin with. They would be even older by the time the *Glomar Explorer* sailed again. "Thus," Hyland concluded, "the overall gain from a second mission is almost certainly to be of much less value than the original [1970] estimate."[20]

A second USIB member rejected the committee's report. DIA's director, Vice Admiral Vincent de Poix, wrote that "the possible gain from acquisition [of the target] is not commensurate with the sharply increased risks of Soviet discovery." Nor was it worth the expenditure of additional resources, added de Poix, a thirty-year navy veteran, whose agency was then suffering post-Vietnam budget cutbacks that would reduce its workforce by one-third.[21]

Three USIB members, including the CIA's representative, concurred with the committee report. Two others abstained. "I find that there are mixed opinions in the [U.S. intelligence] community as to whether or not we should proceed with the second mission," Deputy Secretary of Defense William Clements Jr. advised Kissinger in November 1974.

Clements recommended moving forward nonetheless. Admittedly, keeping the mission secret for another year would be challenging. He wrote, "security is problematical—particularly, in the present Washington environment." But the yearslong project had an exemplary record (aside from the June 1974 burglary of Howard Hughes's Hollywood office, which Clements neglected to mention). And he assured Kissinger that every effort would be made to maintain that same high standard moving forward.[22]

Despite all the craziness, *Glomar*'s deep ocean mining cover remained watertight. To be sure, Hughes's business rivals continued to question the *Glomar Explorer*'s unorthodox design. Why, they wondered, did the ship have tall towers at each end? They seemed unnecessary to mine the seabed. And what about that pipe string? It looked too heavy and thick to suck up manganese nodules. Yet experts took the enterprise seriously, because they knew Hughes to be a shrewd businessman, unconventional though he might be. As French undersea explorer Jacques Cousteau later explained, "we all knew that Howard Hughes does not involve himself in uneconomic undertakings."[23]

The Soviets were fooled too, it seemed. American intelligence officials reviewed the actions of the *SB-10*, the Soviet ship that had closely monitored the *Explorer* at the recovery site. They concluded "that the Soviets did not suspect its true purpose although there was considerable Soviet interest." Colby, for one, expressed confidence that the *SB-10* paid such close attention only because the *Explorer* was positioned near an active Soviet submarine transit lane. A return appearance by the American ship would excite additional Soviet surveillance. But CIA cover staff planned a fresh blizzard of publicity, and Clements felt certain that it would succeed in obscuring the ship's "mining" activities.[24]

MATADOR required an extra $56.3 million—maybe more, depending on contingencies. That amount was significant, certainly. But it might yield Soviet codes, and they were priceless, suggested Clements, rebutting the price-sensitive de Poix.

MATADOR's calendar didn't call for the actual mission to begin until July 15, 1975, a date determined by the annual weather window. Even so, the schedule was "very tight," Clements wrote. At that moment, the *Glomar Explorer* harbored in Long Beach, within sight of the Spruce Goose, where technicians were busily overhauling the ship's heave compensator, heavy-lift, and pipe-handling systems. Hundreds of miles away, engineers at Lockheed's Redwood City facility worked inside the *Hughes Mining Barge-1* modifying the capture vehicle to match the dimensions of the new target, and using HY-100, a stronger, less brittle steel. These improvements were essential. But they would take time to complete. And the recoupled components would have to undergo extensive testing—"critical" in this case, Clements insisted, because inadequate testing may have contributed to AZORIAN's failure.

Clements thus called for quick and favorable action by the 40 Committee. Members were divided. But most supported MATADOR, he assured Kissinger.[25]

FIGURE 5.2 The *Hughes Glomar Explorer* docked at Pier E, Port of Long Beach, in the fall of 1974 undergoing preparations for the MATADOR mission. Note the hangar housing the Spruce Goose in the upper left-hand corner.

Source: Courtesy of Ray Feldman.

Crucially, supporters included the nation's intelligence chief. On November 23, Colby wrote the following: "After careful review it is my opinion that the costs, cover/security and technical considerations are acceptable when considered on balance with the significant value of the potential intelligence material expected to be in the section which would be recovered." In particular, the cryptographic gear held the "highest value" in Colby's view.[26]

* * *

Clements was right to flag security as a concern. Keeping intelligence secrets was more difficult in post-Watergate Washington. After decades of near invisibility, some of the deepest, darkest recesses of the U.S. government were coming out of the shadows, illuminated by sunshine-era journalism that increasingly brought the nation's security establishment into public view.[27]

New York Times investigative reporter Seymour Hersh was already working the story that would definitively blow *Glomar*'s cover, based on leaks from well-placed sources in the U.S. intelligence community who were opposed to the program's high risk and, in their view, low reward. He put the story aside for a moment to focus on another scoop that changed intelligence history. "Huge CIA Operation Reported in US Against Antiwar Forces, Other Dissidents in Nixon Years," the *Times*'s page-one headline blared on December 22, 1974. Hersh's bombshell claim that the CIA aimed "a massive, illegal domestic intelligence operation" at thousands of American citizens dominated the news. It drew upon a leaked CIA report, known as the "Family Jewels," listing activities that exceeded the agency's legislative charter. Compiled in the wake of Watergate, the 702-page collection documented not just covert mail openings, warrantless wiretappings, illegal break-ins, and physical surveillance of journalists, but also human experiments and plots to assassinate foreign leaders.[28]

Coming on the heels of news that the CIA had covertly attempted to undermine Salvador Allende's democratically elected government in Chile, the story cast a sinister light on the agency, which now stood accused of repressing civil liberties both at home and abroad. Together, Kissinger recalled, the Hersh story and the Family Jewels "had the effect of a burning match in a gasoline depot." Colby agreed. "All the tensions and suspicions and hostilities that had been building about the CIA since the Bay of Pigs and had risen to a combustible level during the Vietnam and Watergate years, now exploded," he wrote.[29]

President Ford tried to limit the damage by appointing, on January 4, 1975, a blue-ribbon commission chaired by Vice President Nelson Rockefeller to investigate CIA activities within the United States. The activist 94th Congress was not easily deterred, however. Held less than ninety days after Nixon's resignation, the elections of November 1974 produced a Democratic landslide and an influx of new, and more liberal, legislators. These "Watergate babies," as senior members derided them, arrived determined to clean up Washington, in part by launching a legislative "revolution" against the outsized power of the "imperial presidency."[30] Committees in both chambers quickly launched intelligence investigations, the most notable of which were led by Senator Frank Church (D-Idaho) and Representative Otis Pike (D-New York). These probes drove the "Year of Intelligence," as *New York Times* editors called 1975, already well underway by the time the 40 Committee convened in the White House Situation Room on January 22.[31]

But Clements was wrong about the locus of the immediate threat. MATADOR had unraveled not in Washington, but in Los Angeles, where authorities were still searching for the memo reported stolen from Hughes's Romaine Street offices in June 1974, the one that spelled out some of the sub-raising mission's secret details. The hunt for the missing file took another turn in September. That month, LAPD detectives hatched a sting operation. Using Leo Gordon, the actor who tipped off the district attorney's office, as an intermediary, they planned to lure their prime suspect, Donald Woolbright, into a trap. Police believed that Woolbright, a.k.a. "Chester Brooks," allegedly the caller who attempted to extort Hughes officials, could lead them to the "gang from St. Louis," the underworld figures said to be behind the break-in. And they planned a sting operation in which an undercover officer would pose as a private buyer interested in purchasing the stolen goods.[32]

Originally, the scenario called for an LAPD officer to work undercover. Concerned about a possible leak, though, police asked the FBI to provide an undercover agent instead. FBI officials hesitated to intervene. Such action might inadvertently alert the culprits to the fact that federal authorities were involved, hindering the LAPD's efforts to retrieve the missing document.[33] After consulting the CIA—science and technology director Carl Duckett personally authorized the bureau to offer up to a million dollars for any paper "identical to the Project document in question"[34]—the FBI assigned a special agent to assume the identity of a California representative of a New York law firm interested in acquiring Hughes's personal property.[35]

Everything was arranged. The trap was set. At police direction, Gordon, the actor-informant, phoned Woolbright to say that he had found "somebody who seemed to be quite interested and had the wherewithal to make a deal."

As Gordon later told a grand jury, the two men agreed to meet at a Denny's restaurant on Ventura Boulevard, not far from the park where Summa officials discovered the envelope containing bona fide samples of Hughes documents. Woolbright was "edgy," though, worried they were being watched. So they went to a coffee shop instead, where Woolbright peppered Gordon with questions. Who was this buyer? Why was he interested? Where did Gordon find him?

Gordon tried "winging" a story, he said. But Woolbright didn't buy it. They hadn't spoken in weeks, not since they had given up trying to fence the papers in August. Why had Gordon called him out of the blue? It didn't add up.

Days later, on October 1, at a third locale, Woolbright demanded answers. "I want to know exactly what you are doing, exactly who you are dealing with, who you are talking to, and what the whole setup is?"

"All right, I'll level with you," Gordon caved. "The police are onto it. The Feds are onto it. They know you and they know me and all they are interested in right now is recovering those documents because national security is involved." The "buyer" was actually an FBI undercover agent, he revealed.

Though federal agents were involved, Gordon thought he and Woolbright could swing a deal to avoid prosecution—if Woolbright delivered the papers, that is. Were they still obtainable? Gordon asked. Maybe, answered an evasive Woolbright, but they were somewhere else now—in Florida, possibly—and he would need some earnest money to get a sample folder from the people who held them. These were "heavy" people, Woolbright reminded Gordon. "They are not about to hand over a folder just on [my] say so." Five thousand dollars should do it, he suggested. Gordon gave him thirty-five hundred—"to make up, you know," for narcing to the police.

With that, Woolbright vanished. He told Gordon he was headed for the airport to catch a connecting flight to Miami. "My God, don't tell the police or the Feds I'm on my way to Denver," he said. "I don't want any tails on me because if I show up with a tail, I'm a dead man."[36]

That was baloney, of course. Woolbright didn't go to Denver or Miami. Police weren't yet sure where he went. All they knew was that he was on the lam. Without him, they were back to square one, because he was the only real lead they ever had in the case. Asked later how they let him slip away, LAPD chief Ed Davis answered, lamely, "We have a lot of crime here, and we are understaffed."[37]

The following day, October 2, law enforcement officials compared notes behind closed doors. Sadly, no known transcript provides a verbatim record of what must have been a spirited exchange. The best account available is an official summary, which notes, diplomatically, that FBI agents "expressed surprise and consternation at the turn of events." The LAPD were the only ones who were supposed to know the undercover FBI agent's true identity. Somehow, though, their informant, Gordon, had learned not only that the "buyer" was actually a federal agent, but also that national security was involved. Someone had blown the FBI agent's cover and allowed Gordon to go rogue, spilling the beans over coffee while he met Woolbright alone, with only his handler from the district attorney's office nearby. Now Gordon was claiming entrapment and demanding immunity for both himself and Woolbright. This was not how the plan was supposed to go.[38]

From the CIA's perspective, the outcome was a "fiasco."[39] Officials discussed various options, including granting immunity in exchange for the documents, buying them up front, or launching a full FBI investigation.[40] None brought them any closer to securing the piece of paper on which the CIA's top-secret mission hinged. A burst of FBI activity—interviewing subjects, retracing the LAPD's leads, and so on—would only serve to call additional attention to the thing the CIA was trying to protect, everyone agreed. Whoever possessed the file would probably photocopy it, assuming they hadn't already done so.[41] Until Woolbright surfaced, all they could really do was wait—and hope that the other shoe never dropped.

* * *

White House review of MATADOR was exemplary, according to the final 1976 report of the Senate Select Committee to Study Governmental Operations with Respect to Intelligence Activities. Chaired by Senator Church, the committee

> found that in general the President has had, through the National Security Council, effective means for exerting broad policy control over at least two major clandestine activities—covert action and sensitive technical collection. The covert American involvement in Angola and the operations of the *Glomar Explorer* are examples of that control in quite different circumstances, whatever conclusions one draws about the merits of the activities.

These cases demonstrated that the CIA, generally, was "not 'out of control,'" despite Church's previous claim that the agency was a "rogue elephant on a rampage."[42]

NSC review procedures were more formalized than they had been when AZORIAN entered the pipeline. Church Committee investigators (and later historians) could assess the NSC's performance because the White

House began keeping more comprehensive 40 Committee records in 1974, the year Congress passed the Hughes-Ryan Amendment to the Foreign Assistance Act, requiring the president to issue findings certifying that covert activities served the national interest before expending congressionally appropriated funds. Gone were the freewheeling days in which 40 Committee chairman Henry Kissinger conducted business mostly by telephone, or in private with the president, sometimes bypassing the committee entirely. Now, the committee regularly met in person to review intelligence proposals. Aides transcribed the proceedings. Kissinger forwarded recommended actions to the president for approval. And assistants kept the records—from the presidential finding and the meeting minutes to the mission proposal—on file.[43]

By design, these and other reforms sought to instill confidence in the U.S. intelligence establishment, on the defensive in 1975 due to disclosures of wrongdoing and, more broadly, the post-Vietnam collapse of the Cold War consensus. It was hoped that the improved procedures would ensure that serious-minded leaders made intelligence decisions in an orderly fashion, after careful deliberation and due consideration of the facts.[44]

President Ford and his advisors approved clandestine activities that they believed were in the national interest, following a routine that was dutifully minuted, collated, and filed. As systematically as they worked, though, Henry Kissinger and the other serious-minded men seated around the Situation Room's conference table on January 22 struggled to process the events in Los Angeles—events that were anything but orderly or routine. Not that high officials hadn't considered extraordinary plots like domestic spying or assassination before, as various disclosures throughout the Year of Intelligence would reveal. These events, though, pertained to the CIA's essential mission: foreign intelligence collection. Neither Kissinger nor the four other members present—Deputy Secretary of Defense Clements, Under Secretary of State for Political Affairs Joseph Sisco, Joint Chiefs of Staff chair General George Brown, and Colby—reconciled the two.

Significantly, no one said anything about the paper chase ongoing in Los Angeles, even though at least three of the five were aware of the "Hughes Affair," as insiders called it. Colby knew all about the whole sordid episode from the very beginning, of course. According to an NSC report, Clements and Sisco each received post-burglary briefings. Two of three lesser officials present—Deputy National Security Advisor Brent Scowcroft and Assistant Secretary of State William Hyland—were briefed, as well.[45]

That's five people confirmed, of the eight in the room. Yet the "fiasco" in Los Angeles went unmentioned, at least according to the memorandum of conversation, which isn't a verbatim transcript. Maybe the aide (a CIA officer on detail) who took minutes didn't hear the discussion, or chose not to include it, for reasons of plausible deniability should the record become public.

Or maybe knowledgeable participants did not think that the affair warranted high-level attention. After all, the search for the missing file occurred mostly at the working level, some three thousand miles away in Los Angeles. Newspapers hadn't reported on the burglary investigation in months. The trail was cold, and the principals in Washington had reason to believe it wouldn't reach across the country to impact their deliberations. Weeks earlier, in late November 1974, the CIA learned that the LAPD investigation was inactive. An agency memo reads, "in effect they are doing nothing at this time." As a result, federal authorities were "content to wait and see."[46]

Yet the CIA general counsel was well aware of the fact that the Los Angeles County District Attorney's Office sought to indict Woolbright on felony counts of receiving stolen property and attempted extortion. Grand jury proceedings were supposed to remain secret. Under discovery rules, though, Woolbright's defense team was entitled to information available to the prosecution, which in this case included FBI and CIA reports. Defense attorneys would surely request those materials. And once they did, the circle of knowledge would widen considerably, making it that much harder to prevent word from spreading—especially in early 1975, when public suspicion of the CIA was high.[47]

Not a word of these developments escaped the lips of 40 Committee members, even though they spoke directly to the matter of mission security. Instead, Colby began the meeting in the customary way, with a briefing covering conventional matters, like mechanical malfunctions and cost overruns. Some $275 million already had been, or soon would be, spent on the sub-raising project, he calculated. (Tens of millions had gone toward construction costs since Clements's November 1974 estimate.) So, he said, "we are talking about an expenditure of only about $25 million more to complete the job."

Another, relatively minor issue involved whether to conduct a deepwater test prior to the actual lift operation. Clements "favored the test because it was designed to prove the system which failed." "If the test revealed things that need correction," he added, "the corrections could be made and then we could go on with a better chance of success."

Colby opposed the test because performing it would give the *Glomar Explorer* only two weeks in which to work at the recovery site before the annual weather window closed. For safety reasons, the ship had to depart the area before the Pacific hurricane season peaked in August. Deepwater tests might increase confidence in the system, but they would leave the ship with a razor-thin margin for error, and postponing the mission for another twelve months was out of the question. Nobody thought the project would remain secret that long. Even Clements realized "that we can't go another year; security risks will be too great"—the closest anyone came to acknowledging MATADOR's precarious security situation. Nineteen seventy-five represented *Glomar*'s last shot at the G-722. If the ship failed, Colby reasoned, it might as well fail at the recovery site.

The committee thus had two decisions to make, Kissinger announced. "One, whether to do a second operation or not, and two, whether to risk failure or schedule deep water tests. What we find in the tests won't help [in 1975]," he added, effectively settling the matter. If approved, MATADOR would go ahead that summer as planned, without a deepwater test.[48]

* * *

Colby did depart from the script in one respect. He announced his intention to report MATADOR to the President's Commission on CIA Activities

Within the United States, the blue-ribbon panel Ford established in response to Seymour Hersh's December 1974 exposé. Colby felt obligated to tell the Rockefeller Commission "because of the Howard Hughes connection."

Colby's declaration prompted a remarkable exchange concerning the new Year of Intelligence sunshine, what light it might shed on not only MATADOR but clandestine activity generally, and whether and how to limit it:

> KISSINGER protested that there was no connection with domestic spying—that this was clearly a foreign intelligence operation. He said he would clear this with the vice president. The commission's charter is to determine whether the CIA spied on Americans.
>
> COLBY said the commission's charter covered CIA activities in the US.
>
> KISSINGER said Mr. Colby could not go before the commission.
>
> COLBY said he would go to the vice president and ask for an exemption. He is familiar with this pattern. He [Rockefeller] asked for a list of addresses of our domestic installations and I asked permission to leave a couple out.
>
> KISSINGER asked Mr. Colby to make sure that General Scowcroft knew of his discussions with the vice president. He foresaw no problems there. Some of the commission's staff members insist that they want to write books; they'll have to fire them, of course. But you can't put stuff like MATADOR before them.
>
> BROWN said that Mr. Colby was expendable, but the system was not.
>
> COLBY said he recognized that, and he thought that he would have to resign sometime—simply declare that he could not continue to perform as DCI and maintain his obligations to preserve security if he had to reveal everything.[49]

The matter decided, Kissinger returned to MATADOR. Leadingly, he asked, "am I correct that everyone here is in favor of a second attempt except State?" Not exactly, answered the assistant secretary of defense for intelligence, Dr. Albert C. Hall. DIA opposed MATADOR, he announced, "because the intelligence gain was minimal and going back again to the same area would trigger Soviet interest."

Under Secretary of State Sisco joined Hall in opposition. Sisco, arguably the mission's most persistent critic, objected to MATADOR for many of the same reasons he opposed AZORIAN, only more so. According to the minutes, Sisco dissented because the "risks were greater, the costs do not justify the marginal return, and he is more against going ahead now than he was before."

General Brown, as chair of the JCS, voiced similar concerns. MATADOR was riskier than AZORIAN, and AZORIAN cut things close. He said, "if we go to the area for a second time and have a failure we will attract more Soviet attention."

Kissinger displayed little patience for this line of inquiry. The 40 Committee had already litigated the Soviet case in 1974. He saw no reason to relitigate it now. He said he "could understand the risks if the target were in the middle of Murmansk Harbor, but it is in the middle of the Pacific, the open sea." It was true, in other words, that the salvage operation was probably illegal under international law. No government agency other than the CIA ever argued otherwise. But it was less provocative than, say, tapping underwater Soviet cables in the Sea of Okhotsk, and the United States was already doing that under the IVY BELLS operation. So there was really no reason not to proceed. Espionage was a commonly accepted practice in international relations. America was simply following the rules of the game.

Hyland, the State Department's intelligence chief, fully understood the rules. Soviet-American relations had cooled since the November 1974 Vladivostok Summit, where negotiators reached general agreement on a SALT II deal that set ceilings on each side's strategic arms. American hawks opposed the deal's limits on American weaponry. Soviet leaders decried Congress's December passage of the Trade Act of 1974, including the Jackson-Vanik Amendment linking the emigration of Soviet Jews to the USSR's receipt of most-favored-nation status. In that more uncertain environment, "the Soviets would seize upon any incident," said Hyland, a former CIA officer and respected Kremlinologist who had carefully studied the diplomatic history of the 1960 U-2 incident. He worried that someone in the Kremlin—perhaps not Leonid Brezhnev, who was personally invested in détente, but a hardliner like KGB head Yuri Andropov—would make a political spectacle out of an American attempt to steal a submarine, much as Nikita Khrushchev had in 1960, when Gary Powers's U-2 overflew Soviet airspace. The possible presence of human remains aboard the target increased the likelihood of a backlash.[50]

Kissinger was having none of it. Super K's star no longer shined quite as brightly as it had when the 40 Committee approved AZORIAN in June 1974. He faced growing political opposition from members of Congress as well as human rights activists, and strong rivals for influence inside the Ford administration, led by Donald Rumsfeld, the White House chief of staff. But he remained the central figure in American foreign policy, the essential bridge between presidential administrations who continued to dominate the NSC process as both secretary of state and national security advisor.[51] Détente was his policy, his handiwork. He alone among the principals had been present since AZORIAN's creation—since 1969, when President Nixon signed off on a new intelligence organization to manage the interagency project. And he was as certain as ever that, even in the event of an unmasking, the mission would have a negligible effect on superpower relations.

According to the minutes, he said, "if the Soviets wanted an incident they would react, but would they want an incident?" The implication was that they would not. The Kremlin had too much at stake to scuttle détente over an intelligence incident occurring miles out at sea.

Sisco restated his objections. He "thought the risks were greater and very exploitable—that the Soviets would really explode. Also, the expense is simply not defensible."

Clements admitted that MATADOR's anticipated intelligence gain wasn't defensible if the 40 Committee "were being asked to approve $250 million now." But those costs were sunk. So "we are talking about $25 or $30 million to complete the job and therefore we ought to go ahead."

In reality, the gross cost had climbed northward of $300 million. But the principals should think in terms of net, suggested Scowcroft, the deputy national security advisor. The government might realize a future return on its investment. Couldn't the CIA find another, post-MATADOR use for the *Glomar Explorer*? he asked.

Probably not, Colby answered. But all the talk about Howard Hughes's interest in manganese nodules had spurred commercial interest in deep ocean mining. CIA officials hoped to sell the ship for $40 to $50 million once the mission was complete.

With a final flurry, the meeting wrapped up:

KISSINGER said he foresaw no problem in justifying to the American public this attempt to obtain Soviet [text redacted from the original, but presumably a reference to "cryptographic machines and related documents," the mission's motivating force, according to the USIB] and that warranted taking some Soviet risks.

HYLAND said we wouldn't spend $60 million for Soviet [text redacted].

COLBY said we were only talking about $30 million and that he would gladly give that [text redacted].

KISSINGER asked what the alternative was.

HALL said that he had originally opposed the operation but so much had been done that he was in favor of finishing the job.

Hall's last-minute reversal left only the two State Department representatives—Sisco and Hyland—in opposition. (Brown, though critical, appears to have gotten on board.) Kissinger invited Sisco to put his objections in writing so that they could be put before the president. He assumed Ford would approve, though.[52]

* * *

The next morning, Kissinger huddled with President Ford in the Oval Office to review the performance of the 40 Committee, particularly that of one member. William Colby's tenure as director of central intelligence was in question from the moment Hersh's bombshell hit newsstands. Behind closed doors, Ford spoke of firing him, not because he was responsible for the domestic spying abuses Hersch uncovered—each had occurred in the past, with the approval of his predecessors—but because he appeared too open, too eager to cooperate with investigators, sometimes without consulting the White House. "Colby's not only telling all, he's telling more than all," former DCI Richard Helms cried after Colby turned over to the Justice Department evidence that Helms had misled Congress about CIA activity in Chile.[53]

Colby's biographers tend to disagree with this assessment. "Colby was for more transparency and accountability, but he did insist that the CIA had an unconditional right to keep secret its 'sources and methods,'" writes one. Colby's reputation for openness "obscures the degree to which Colby actually worked to protect CIA secrets," writes another.[54]

That said, Colby's methods were unorthodox. No CIA director had ever been so candid—least of all Helms, revered in some circles as the "man who kept the secrets." Colby's rationale was simple. "The CIA," he recalled, "was in very real danger of ultimately being crippled as an effective weapon in the defense of the nation's security if not in fact threatened with being destroyed outright." The remedy, he believed, "was to lift as much as possible that thick cloak of secrecy that had traditionally veiled the agency and its operations from the scrutiny—and, more important, the understanding—of the public at large."[55] Or, as he responded in 1974 to a critic who insisted that airing the CIA's dirty laundry would irreparably harm the agency, "There are some 'bad secrets' which are properly revealed by an aggressive press [and] there are some older 'non-secrets' which no longer need to be kept secret and which we should gradually surface, but there are some 'good secrets' which deserve greater protection than we have been able to give them, in part by reason of their association with 'secrets' of lesser importance."[56]

Reasonable though it may have been, Colby's candor was anathema to Henry Kissinger. On January 23, he reported the following to the president:

> *Kissinger:* We had a 40 Committee meeting. We can't conduct covert
> operations. Colby is a disaster and really should be replaced. Colby

is shellshocked—he wanted to testify on AZORIAN because it was a domestic operation. He said he would work it out with the VP—I said it was none of the VP's business.

Ford: That's stupid.

Kissinger: There are so many people who have to be briefed on covert operations, it is bound to leak. There is no one with guts left. All of yesterday they were making a record to protect themselves about AZORIAN. It was a discouraging meeting. I wonder if we shouldn't get the [congressional] leadership in and discuss it. Maybe there should be a Joint Committee [to investigate intelligence activities, a move some supported in the wake of reported abuses].

Ford: I have always fought that, but maybe we have to. It would have to be a tight group, not a big broad one.

Kissinger: I am really worried. We are paralyzed.[57]

In the days ahead, Kissinger and other national security conservatives often claimed that the Year of Intelligence immobilized the U.S. intelligence community with excessive red tape, preventing the type of bold action the CIA once took to protect national security. Little of that concern was evident in his briefing memo to Ford, though. "With justifiable pride the intelligence community climaxed a six-year effort" by lifting a Soviet submarine from the ocean floor in 1974, the memo began, exuberantly. A portion of the sub fell back to the seabed, marring this "unique accomplishment." But the United States had another opportunity to claim the prize—and on Ford's watch, no less.

The USIB had given its imprimatur. The board, Kissinger wrote, "reaffirmed its view that the equipment aboard the target is of 'unique intelligence potential' and its estimate of the overall gain from a successful recovery has not 'measurably' changed." To be sure, extending the operation invited some additional risk. Operational security remained firm, though. MATADOR's deep ocean mining cover story was widely accepted. The Soviets showed only routine interest in the first recovery attempt and gave no indication they suspected *Glomar*'s true purpose. Therefore, "it is reasonable to expect that they will accept a return to the site as what it will appear to be—a second deep ocean mining trial."

Obtaining the target required an additional $36 million (though estimates varied). Importantly, however, Kissinger emphasized that these "funds are available via reprogramming [of the black budget]; no new funds are necessary." Besides, $275 million had already been spent or committed. For a fraction of that original cost, the United States could acquire an intelligence gold mine.

The 40 Committee had reviewed the plan. Sisco raised some objections, Kissinger duly reported. Sisco "questions whether recovery of [the target] offers sufficient return to warrant the expenditure; he believes risks are greater and that a return to the exact spot of ocean will feed Soviet suspicion; and that new uncertainties in U.S.–Soviet relations add to the substantial political risks should there be a Soviet reaction."

All other 40 Committee members—plus, Kissinger noted, former CIA director and now secretary of defense, James Schlesinger—favored MATADOR. "The consensus is that the potential intelligence return from a successful second mission would be significant enough to accept the cost, cover/security and other risks." Kissinger advised Ford to approve the mission.[58]

* * *

President Ford initialed his approval on February 6, 1975. For twenty-four hours or so, that must have seemed like a wise move. On February 7, however, the *Los Angeles Times* published a page-one story that changed everything.

6

COLBY'S DIKE

President Ford was holding an afternoon meeting with his national security team on February 7, 1975, when Director of Central Intelligence William Colby interrupted. "I hate to raise this but the *Los Angeles Times* just asked whether we had raised a piece of a Soviet submarine," he said. Moments earlier, a reporter had phoned CIA Deputy Director for Science and Technology Carl Duckett asking for confirmation.[1]

The call came too late to prevent the story from appearing in that morning's paper. Headlined "U.S. Reported After Russ Sub," the front-page account revealed that the *Hughes Glomar Explorer* was not a deep-sea mining vessel, as claimed, but the centerpiece of a "supersecret" mission undertaken by the CIA and Howard Hughes.[2] The story also had a punch line. Citing "reports circulating among local law enforcement officers," it suggested that the operation came to light because of the CIA's efforts to hide it. CIA personnel had enlisted the FBI in the search for the memo describing the submarine mission that, Hughes aides said, *might* have been among the documents stolen during the June burglary of Hughes's

Romaine Street warehouse. Without specifying the identity or location of AZORIAN's target, security officers briefed select FBI agents, urging them to be on the lookout for a "sensitive paper." FBI agents repeated the briefing to LAPD detectives investigating the burglary. And as a Los Angeles County grand jury prepared to charge the police's chief suspect, Donald Woolbright, with possession of stolen property and attempted extortion, someone leaked the news to William Farr and Jerry Cohen, *Los Angeles Times* reporters covering the local beat.[3]

Federal officials believed the leak came from the LAPD, though suspicion also fell on the district attorney's office, its informant, Leo Gordon, and Woolbright's defense team. "From what we know now," a CIA detailee explained to Deputy National Security Advisor Brent Scowcroft, "it appears that the *Los Angeles Times* story does indeed stem from 'local law enforcement officers' and can be traced to the CIA-to-FBI-to-Los Angeles police-to-the-intermediary revelations that CIA was interested in a memorandum which the extortioner *might* have which revealed CIA-Hughes discussions about recovery of a Soviet submarine."[4]

Meanwhile, Woolbright remained at large. And the whereabouts of the document—Hughes Tool executive Raymond Holliday's 1970 memo to Hughes outlining the CIA's proposal—were unknown. After months of investigation, the detailee could report only that "there is *no* confirmation that the memorandum . . . still exists or that it was among those papers taken during the burglary."[5]

In hindsight, some accused CIA personnel of mishandling the situation. Officials should have waited to see how the investigation unfolded before rushing to contact police, critics complained. After all, the extortionist mentioned neither the CIA nor a submarine in his calls to Hughes's offices. Such talk began only months later, after FBI agents, officials from the LAPD and the LA County DA's office, Gordon, and even Woolbright became aware of the government's interest in the case. A former CIA officer with direct knowledge of the case claimed that security operatives "overreacted" to the Romaine theft. Acting on incomplete, even misleading information as to the whereabouts of Holliday's memo, they briefed criminal investigators, unnecessarily expanding the circle of knowledge and inadvertently disclosing AZORIAN.[6]

* * *

The sequence of events that led to the *Los Angeles Times* disclosure made CIA officers look like Keystone Cops foolishly chasing after a scrap of paper that might not have been missing in the first place. The disclosure itself blew the *Glomar Explorer*'s cover, presumably dooming the operation. Surely, the Soviets could now connect the dots—the observed movements of the *Explorer*, the ship's proximity to a submarine transit lane the previous summer, the reports that had come across the transom over the years indicating that the craft was not what it appeared to be, and so on—and conclude that the *Explorer* was designed to salvage the *K-129*.

Or, Colby thought, perhaps the operation could still go forth despite the leak. He recalled an episode from World War II when another American newspaper, the *Chicago Tribune*, had published a front-page story revealing that the United States had broken Japan's top-secret naval code. "Nevertheless," he remembered, "the Japanese continued using that code—and the Americans kept intercepting and deciphering it; apparently the Japanese High Command had not gotten word of or hadn't believed the *Chicago Tribune* story."[7]

Colby believed the Soviets might discount the American news just like the Japanese had. After all, the *Los Angeles Times*'s claim—that the CIA had allied with a shadowy billionaire on a "supersecret" project to raise a sunken Soviet submarine from the ocean bottom—was on its face hardly more plausible than the operation's cover story holding that the *Explorer* was a deep ocean mining vessel. Perhaps incredulous Soviet intelligence officers would dismiss the truth once again.[8]

Moreover, the scoop, which had been rushed to press, was "garbled and error-ridden enough to throw anyone off the scent," according to Colby. The story had mistakenly placed the *Explorer*'s salvage effort in the Atlantic Ocean. It misidentified the ship's possible target as one of two Soviet submarines that sank off Spain in 1970 and Newfoundland in 1972. And it provided only the sketchiest details about the lift operation "reportedly" carried out by the CIA, failing to specify when that attempt occurred, whether it was successful, and, if not, whether the agency planned a second one. Together, such imprecision added up to a "real chance" that the Soviets would regard the story "as just another of the hysterical tales about the CIA then crowding the press."[9]

Some reasoned that, even if Soviet officials did accept the substance of the press report as fact, they might prefer to ignore reality. According to deputy mission director David Sharp, acknowledging that the CIA had caught them unawares "would suggest serious failures of the KGB's intelligence apparatus," jeopardizing the careers of intelligence and naval officers alike. More importantly, the news could prove personally and politically humiliating to Chairman Leonid Brezhnev, invested as he was in détente with the United States. Colby believed "that there might be some—albeit small—chance that the Soviets would prefer to ignore the allegations in the *Times* and hope that the story about the recovery of one of their submarines would simply 'go away.'"[10]

If the observable actions of the *Glomar Explorer* and its crew hewed closely to the cover scenario, Colby reasoned, then perhaps the ship's second voyage could proceed that summer as planned. But that all depended on his ability to buy time by killing the story.

And so began one of the more notable examples of prior restraint in CIA history. According to scholar Loch Johnson, prior restraint is perhaps the most contentious of the ways in which the CIA has historically attempted to manipulate the press because of its potential to pit security concerns against democratic practices. To what extent should the free press cooperate with the CIA in suppressing sensitive information that, in the agency's opinion, might injure national security but that the public, at least from a democratic perspective, ought to know?[11]

In principle, the answer comes to us from the U.S. Supreme Court. In 1971 the court ruled against the Nixon administration's efforts to suppress publication of the Pentagon Papers. Censorship, the court declared, was reasonable only if disclosure caused "direct, immediate, and irreparable damage to our Nation or its people." That ruling, though generally seen as a victory for the First Amendment, left significant room for interpretation as to what met the test of immediate damage. It often fell to editors to make case-by-case determinations about whether publication would disclose more "necessary" secrets—for instance, the details of ongoing intelligence operations, the exposure of which would demonstrably harm U.S. security—than "unnecessary" secrets, like efforts to conceal wrongful decision making or government waste.[12]

When does the public's right to know trump the government's duty to withhold national security information? To many—including *Washington Post* executive editor Ben Bradlee, who oversaw coverage of Watergate and found covering national security stories to be particularly "dicey"—the line seemed unclear. Editors, he said, strove for balance. But intelligence officials monopolized classified information. And so editors often made decisions without all the facts. Under duress, Bradlee found it difficult to reconcile competing claims. "On the one side there's a claim by a government official of some standing that what you're about to print will harm the country's security. But on the other side you have the conviction that you're being conned, that what is at stake is not any national security, but just plain embarrassment."[13]

The line was clearer to Colby. Soon after hearing from Duckett, Colby—acting under the authority of the National Security Act of 1947, which empowered DCIs to protect intelligence sources and methods from unauthorized disclosure—sent two members of the West Coast Program Office to speak with William Thomas, editor and executive vice president of the *Los Angeles Times*. Nothing could be done about the initial report; a copy of the final edition was already splayed on Thomas's desk when they arrived. But further disclosure, the officers said, would cause "grave harm to national security." Without going into unnecessary detail, they explained that *Glomar* was still an important and ongoing intelligence operation. They admitted that the *Explorer* had indeed attempted to salvage a sunken Soviet submarine. The CIA had not recovered everything it wanted to obtain, though, and the agency planned to complete the mission in the future. Program officials could not be certain how much the Soviets knew about the plans. But more publicity was guaranteed to alert them, perhaps ending the ability of the United States to acquire the rest of the sub or to conduct other, as yet unspecified undersea intelligence work. Calling attention to U.S. efforts to capture Soviet assets might also antagonize Moscow, possibly disrupting détente and provoking an international incident.[14]

Thomas expressed regret for releasing the initial story. He said he would have killed it had he realized the security implications sooner. Farr and Cohen, the reporters, were still conducting interviews. Moving forward, though, he pledged to "exercise the full authority of his position to keep the results from ending up in the *L.A. Times*."[15]

Thomas buried a follow-up report on page eighteen of the next day's edition, where, one journalist later remarked, it became "almost invisible, hidden in the interior forest of the *Los Angeles Times*'s advertising pages." And with that, coverage stopped. Days passed without another word of the affair appearing in print. Encouraged, the West Coast Program Office of the CIA (WCPO) expressed hope that the agency's suppression effort just might succeed: without corroboration of the *Los Angeles Times*'s claims by another media outlet, there was a good chance that "the story may not be believable and could fade away with time."[16]

Washington Post reporters picked up wire reports of the *Los Angeles Times* stories. Colby turned off the *Post*'s coverage just as easily as he had the *Los Angeles Times*'s by phoning publisher Katharine Graham to alert her that the story involved a matter of national security. Graham checked with managing editor Howard Simons (Bradlee was out of the country at the time) before calling Colby back.

"It is all agreed with us that it is not anything we would like to get into," she said. "We have no problem not doing it."

Reporters continued to follow leads, but with Graham's decision, the *Washington Post*—the newspaper that had published the Pentagon Papers and uncovered Watergate—joined the *Los Angeles Times* on the sidelines. "You are very kind," said Colby to Graham. He praised her rectitude as "a great tribute to our journalists."[17]

The *New York Times* was poking around too. American officials were "horrified" to learn that Seymour Hersh knew much of the truth behind

Glomar. To many of his peers, Hersh—winner of a Pulitzer Prize in 1970 for his exclusive disclosure of the My Lai Massacre in Vietnam by American soldiers—was among the best investigative journalists in the business. To many high government officials, however, the hard-charging reporter was a gadfly. The thirty-six-year-old's reputation was already well established by the fall of 1973, when he picked up a tip about a "crazy scheme" by the CIA to recover something valuable from the ocean bottom. Details remained elusive, and Hersh didn't yet have all the facts. But his sources consistently expressed concern as to whether the lift technology would work and what effect discovery of the operation might have on superpower relations. They also questioned the program's price tag, which seemed exorbitant in the wake of the October 1973 oil embargo staged by OPEC, the Organization of the Petroleum Exporting Countries. The embargo helped plunge the once indestructible U.S. economy into a deep recession—the deepest since the Great Depression. The country was suffering its first case of stagflation, an unprecedented mix of stagnant economic growth and high inflation that flummoxed economists. And spending hundreds of millions on an elaborate scheme to raise a vintage Soviet submarine no longer seemed like such a bright idea during an era of austerity. The "people who talked to me were worried about money," Hersh recalled, "all the money being poured into the project" at a time when American workers were suffering, the U.S. government was awash in red ink, and officials slashed federal outlays for everything from defense and intelligence to milk subsidies for public school lunches.[18]

Hersh never named his sources, and their identity became a source of speculation. CIA operatives presumed the compromise came from a high-level navy officer who, in Sharp's words, "saw the CIA program as a threat to the growth of the Navy's own undersea warfare operations." Leading suspects were Captain James F. Bradley and Dr. John Piña Craven, the architects of the navy's competing plan and known critics of the CIA-led effort. Leaking damaging information about *Glomar* to the media struck Washington insiders as "a surefire way to kill the program."[19]

Hersh's sources did include navy officers. But they also included CIA personnel. A senior agency official—"somebody who sat in the catbird's seat for a long time," he said, and "knew everything"—provided the crucial first tip. Another high-level person was "blabbing," Hersh told Colby, who took the hint seriously enough to order all knowledgeable personnel "to keep their mouths shut."[20]

Quietly, Hersh began asking questions. Not quietly enough, it seems, for in January 1974 he received a call from Colby, who asked the reporter not to say—much less write—anything else. He couldn't be more specific on the phone. But if the two could meet, he would explain why.[21]

Hersh agreed to meet Colby at the *New York Times*'s Washington bureau. Colby planned "to level with [Hersh] and appeal to his patriotism." That is, rather than offering denials or making demands, Colby planned to "soft-shoe it," to "argue him around" by confirming *Glomar*'s basics but explaining how disclosure would harm U.S. interests. Colby took a relatively straightforward approach because the times demanded as much. To threaten the reporter with legal action or invoke national security without explanation would have been counterproductive in the post-Vietnam era, when journalists were suspicious of government officials. "So," he recalled, "in order to convince them of the legitimacy of what I was asking in this case, I took the gamble of responding to their questions to the minimum degree necessary to show my good faith, and only then, when I was sure they comprehended the seriousness of it, did I request that they hold back stories on the *Glomar*."[22]

National Security Advisor Henry Kissinger thought Colby was "crazy" for trying to reason with a muckraker like Hersh. "Appealing to that guy's sense of discretion will do you no good," one U.S. official said. Colby would have more success encouraging *New York Times* executives to "come down on [Hersh]."[23]

Colby did reach out to Hersh's superiors, including publisher Arthur Ochs "Punch" Sulzberger, who notified managing editor A. M. "Abe" Rosenthal that Hersh was inquiring into a matter that involved national security. Otherwise, Colby ignored official advice when he met Hersh on the first of February.

Watergate was the lead story at the time, and the *Times* was running well behind the *Washington Post* in covering it. So Hersh proposed a deal:

he would lay off the submarine story if Colby told him something useful about Watergate in return. "We were dishing," said Hersh. Hersh wouldn't specify what transpired other than to say he came away with a good lead and no regrets for making the trade. "It more than made sense to me. I would do it again."[24]

Colby, too, was satisfied. He received "a firm commitment" from Hersh not to report on the matter as long as it remained secret. And Hersh, despite his reputation as an adversarial journalist, kept his end of the bargain. He sat on the story for more than a year, giving the *Glomar Explorer* ample opportunity to complete its first mission in 1974, as planned.[25]

With the *New York Times*, the *Washington Post*, and the *Los Angeles Times* all "sewed up," Colby grew confident in his ability to hold the story—not forever, but long enough to complete MATADOR. Indeed, U.S. intelligence detected no response whatsoever from the Soviets to the February 7, 1975, *Los Angeles Times* disclosure. Remarkably, the *Glomar Explorer*'s cover remained intact. Crewmembers continued to ready the ship for a second voyage. And Colby praised the responsibility displayed by members of the press. "They really have been very good," he told Scowcroft.[26]

* * *

Then Colby learned that Hersh—"energized" by the *Los Angeles Times* report, the publication of which effectively ended his year-old nondisclosure agreement—was again working the story. As before, Colby reached out to Punch Sulzberger, who "very gently passed on the word" of caution to editors and met personally with Hersh in an effort to keep the lid on. His message was much the same as well: *Glomar* was an important and ongoing intelligence operation the United States hoped to complete; further disclosure would end it, harm national security, and perhaps motivate an international incident. The *Los Angeles Times* had patriotically agreed to withhold additional coverage so that the *Explorer* could try again, and Colby asked the *New York Times* to match that patriotism.[27]

Circumstances had changed, however, and Colby met stiffer resistance this time around. Hersh now knew a great deal more about *Glomar*. To him, the facts showed that the program was a "waste of money and a silly idea." The lift technology had failed in 1974, as his sources had predicted it would. Those same sources indicated that what little material had been obtained was not all that valuable. And having failed to retrieve the main target despite the expenditure of hundreds of millions of taxpayer dollars, CIA officials were now attempting to "cover up"—trigger words in Watergate's aftermath—an intelligence "fiasco." In sum, *Glomar* was an example of CIA mismanagement. Shedding light on the agency's dark recesses, where special-access programs like *Glomar* were immune from appropriately rigorous review, would avoid such missteps moving forward, Hersh suggested. *Glomar* served, he believed, as "the perfect allegory, the perfect way to question what was wrong with U.S. intelligence."[28]

Neither did Hersh buy Colby's "security 'mumble jumble,'" as the reporter called it. Despite Colby's claim to the contrary, the *Los Angeles Times* disclosure had blown *Glomar*'s cover wide open. Soviet agents could read the newspaper too, and they would not stand idly by while American intelligence recovered one of their submarines. *Glomar* was over and done with, whether the CIA wanted to admit it or not. "We can't use it again," one source averred.[29] So why, Hersh wondered, was Colby so intent on keeping the story from the public? To hide an intelligence failure? To protect Howard Hughes?

Journalists, Colby realized, "were mighty skeptical" of the CIA in 1975.[30] Vietnam and Watergate had shaken public faith in the intelligence community no less than the U.S. government as a whole. To his credit, former CIA director Richard Helms refused to fully participate in Nixon's efforts to cover up White House ties to the Watergate break-in, which is probably what led to Helms's 1972 dismissal. But the agency's hands weren't entirely clean. Five former CIA employees were among those directly tied to the break-in, including E. Howard Hunt Jr., who received aid from the agency on other black-bag jobs. Such facts became known despite efforts by Helms and others to keep them out of the public eye, leading some to claim that the deep state, rather than Nixon, had masterminded the Watergate burglary.

In response, Helms's successor, James Schlesinger, issued a directive in May 1973 ordering CIA employees to report "any activities now going on, or that have gone on in the past, which might be construed to be outside the legislative charter of his Agency." Totaling some seven hundred pages, the resulting "Family Jewels" compilation documented extra-charter activities that extended well beyond Watergate. It also served as the basis of Hersh's December 1974 domestic spying exposé that triggered the "Year of Intelligence."[31]

Investigations were just beginning when Colby first attempted to impose prior restraint on the press. But new and startling revelations occurred even as those efforts continued. During a January 16 luncheon with *New York Times* leaders, President Ford explained why the purview of the Rockefeller Commission, the blue-ribbon panel the White House had established to forestall congressional action, was limited to CIA domestic activities. To go further risked uncovering things that would "blacken the name of every president back to Harry Truman," Ford said.

"Like what?" asked Rosenthal.

"Like assassinations!" Ford reportedly blurted out, perhaps forgetting that he was speaking before a room full of newspeople.[32]

After extensive debate, *New York Times* editors decided what they'd heard wasn't fit to print. The story was too explosive. Besides, Ford's remarks were off the record, they determined. But word of the president's remarks spread nonetheless. On February 28, journalist Daniel Schorr reported on *CBS Evening News* that "President Ford has reportedly warned associates that if current investigations go too far, they could uncover several assassinations of foreign officials in which the CIA was involved." Although details remained closely held, Schorr speculated that the agency might have some literal skeletons in its closet.[33]

Schorr's disclosure widened the scope of the intelligence investigations. Both the Rockefeller Commission and the Senate's Church Committee expanded their probes to include assassinations. News of the CIA's possible involvement in plots to kill foreign leaders further discredited the agency in the eyes of many Americans, journalists included. The news media began to take a harder look at the CIA.

Like Congress, the press can provide important oversight by holding intelligence agencies accountable; it can regulate by revealing, experts say.

And during the "era of trust" the press did sometimes expose abuses, as happened in 1967 when the alternative magazine *Ramparts* revealed the CIA's covert ties to student and voluntary groups. Generally, though, the mainstream media took a deferential position to the U.S. national security establishment, the intelligence community especially. The tenets of objective journalism, the professional standard that prevailed at the time, encouraged reporters to relay "just the facts" authorities provided. Questioning the official view in print, holding power accountable—such practices were considered unorthodox, disreputable even. Meanwhile, many news executives actively assisted the CIA. Punch Sulzberger's father, the late publisher Arthur Hays Sulzberger, for example, signed a secrecy agreement that allowed the agency to disguise approximately ten of its officers as *New York Times* journalists between 1950 and 1966. Dozens, perhaps hundreds, of American reporters secretly carried out paid assignments for the agency, from collecting intelligence and distributing news plants, to serving as back channels with foreign contacts. That is, until these controversial practices were exposed and officially discontinued in the mid-1970s.[34]

Most journalists weren't CIA assets, of course. They simply shared the same Cold War mind-set that guided the agency's congressional partners: To defend the nation against communism, the spy agency had to operate in secret. Deep probing could only hinder its work. Intelligence leaders deserved trust. These views still prevailed when AZORIAN got underway. "The nation must to a degree take it on faith that we too are honorable men, devoted to her service," Helms declared in an April 1971 address before the American Society of Newspaper Editors, his first public speech in five years as intelligence director. Helms's audience applauded. "They were newspapermen," writes intelligence historian John Ranelagh, "and they accepted Helms's word; few felt there was sufficient evidence to challenge it."[35]

But Vietnam—and the official deception behind the failed war, as the 1971 publication of the Pentagon Papers made plain—broke that trust, Steven Usdin writes, turning "journalists from willing allies of the CIA into wary adversaries." Watergate, including not only Nixon's lies but his attempts to hide his crimes behind the pretense of national security, widened the credibility gap. And the scandal, unearthed by journalists, elevated the stature of the Fourth Estate, widely seen as a defender of the public interest against official corruption.[36]

In short, a normative change occurred in the course of *Glomar*'s life span. News coverage "opened up," according to journalism professors Katherine Fink and Michael Schudson. Reporters did not abandon the tenets of objectivity. But a new generation of journalists emerged who were less deferential to and more critical of established power than had been the case among their immediate forbears. Influenced by the reform-minded muckraking journalists of the Progressive Era, they asked hard questions, contextualized the facts, dug for additional ones, and exposed lies in an attempt to hold authorities to account.[37]

The rise of investigative journalism is among the reasons why some have characterized the early to mid-1970s as the dawn of the "sunshine era," when watchdog reporting and openness legislation raised American expectations of government transparency. ("In the sunshine era, we do not expect so many closed-door meetings to take place," *Washington Post* and *Newsweek* editorialist Meg Greenfield wrote of the change.[38]) Sunshine advocates took a dim view of secrecy—which, having long served to protect CIA activities like *Glomar*, now suddenly became a liability, attracting unwanted attention. "Years of total secrecy had made the CIA extremely vulnerable to suspicion and sensation," Colby recalled.[39]

Secrecy claims stopped shielding the agency from scrutiny just as AZORIAN/MATADOR reached maturity. "Everything was fair game," Hersh recalled of the post-Watergate era. Government officials used to wave "the Cold War flag all the time," claiming that "the Soviets would invade California" if the *New York Times* printed this story or disclosed that information. But that argument "wasn't working anymore. It was a free time."[40]

Such freedom endangered national security initiatives like *Glomar*, officials countered. "Security is problematical—particularly, in the present Washington environment," Deputy Secretary of Defense William P. Clements Jr. wrote in his MATADOR report to Kissinger. Heightened security concerns factored into the 40 Committee's deliberations pertaining to the 1975 mission.[41]

MATADOR brought the debate to a head, in part because Colby's preventative efforts forced journalists to weigh secrecy in national security and foreign policy against the competing, and growing, demand for transparency. Was *Glomar*, as Colby insisted, a necessary secret? Or was it, as Hersh believed, an unnecessary one? What did the public need to know? What did the public *not* need to know? Many reporters who heard Colby's case came away convinced that his "efforts to quash the story marked one of those moments when the phrase 'national security' was used not to save national secrets, but national embarrassment," according to *New York Times* reporters Sherry Sontag and Christopher Drew. "If anything, Colby's gambit left most journalists increasingly skeptical about acquiescing to requests by intelligence officials to hold back on such stories."[42]

MATADOR, unlike other activities disclosed during the early months of the Year of Intelligence—domestic spying, foreign assassinations, and so forth, all of which had been discontinued by the time they came to light—was still an ongoing intelligence operation. And the CIA was operating in its legitimate sphere, collecting foreign intelligence, as opposed to monitoring Americans or plotting to kill foreign leaders. Officials planned to send the *Explorer* on another voyage in the foreseeable future, declared Colby, an assertion that put additional weight behind his argument that news organizations must prioritize national security. Journalists could face accusations of damaging American interests if they chose to publish the story over official objections. That responsibility weighed heavily on *New York Times* managing editor Abe Rosenthal. Rosenthal had played a decisive role in the newspaper's decision to publish the Pentagon Papers, which put his credentials as an advocate of openness beyond reproach. At the same time, however, he—a self-described anticommunist whose "feeling for American values and institutions bordered on the reverential," according to onetime *New York Times* journalist David Halberstam—had a gut feeling that it would be a mistake to publish the *Glomar* story. Ordinarily, Rosenthal did not believe in delaying publication. Here, though, he "felt that the goals were so important that a reasonable case had been made for delay." "The advantage of publishing it immediately did not outweigh the disadvantage of writing about a military operation of some importance."[43]

Hersh pressed his case. "Lest I seem cavalier about secrets, the fact is that I know almost every major ongoing reconnaissance operation . . . and have for years. I'm not going around shooting off my mouth about it," he wrote in an outraged memo to Rosenthal and *Times* Washington bureau chief Clifton Daniel. However, "when one of the programs seems risky and overpriced and there's a legitimate news peg, it doesn't make sense not to tell the American people about it." Besides, Hersh asked Rosenthal, in what way did *Glomar* differ from Vietnam, which remained an ongoing military operation in 1971 when the *Times* published the Pentagon Papers?[44]

Rosenthal stood his ground. On March 3, 1975, *New York Times* leaders decided to postpone coverage of the *Glomar* story "until the CIA either completed a second attempt to salvage the submarine or abandoned the project altogether—or until someone else published the story." Rosenthal's stand extended *Glomar*'s life span. And his reticence—along with that of Bill Thomas, Katharine Graham, and other news executives—demonstrated the extent to which security claims retained power. Members of the press, especially senior ones, remained mindful of their responsibility to protect national interests, even as the rules governing the release of classified data loosened in 1975. Despite recent history—including Nixon's false claims of national security in Watergate—"editors and publishers up and down the line, including those of the *New York Times*, accepted Colby's argument," remarked former associate editor Harrison Salisbury. The case, Kathryn Olmsted agrees, shows that the post-Watergate press remained deferential to executive authority.[45]

* * *

Yet the mere fact that editors of a leading newspaper seriously considered publishing the details of an ongoing collection effort that the director of central intelligence himself had certified as essential to the nation's security was one measure of the press's new stance toward the CIA. During the era of trust, journalists had routinely self-censored stories about ongoing U.S. intelligence operations, in part because they saw it as their duty to keep certain information from the public in the interest of national security. "Then, it had not occurred to me that we should print such things," the *New York Times*'s Tom Wicker wrote later. He recalled an instance from 1964 in which a high government official had candidly told him and two other writers about some of the CIA's black activities, including, the official said, complicity in the murders of two foreign leaders. Wicker, then a mid-career correspondent, remembered being shocked but not outraged by the disclosures, since, like most Americans, he was deeply impressed by the "national-security mystique." To reporters of his generation, "national security seemed to have [a] literal meaning. What was done under its arc was not something to be interfered with or too deeply questioned." National security claims were so strong that he and his colleagues made only cryptic records of the official's remarks, lest their notes fall into irresponsible hands.[46]

Eleven years and one cultural revolution later, the definition of the public's right to know had grown substantially. *New York Times* executives left a meeting with Colby and Duckett on February 27, 1975, unsure how to proceed. Things rested on the "knife's edge," said Colby. Duckett guessed the CIA stood no better than a fifty-fifty chance of keeping *Glomar* out of the headlines.[47]

Executives wavered enough for Colby to call in reinforcements. Perhaps a call from Super K would restore confidence. Kissinger duly phoned Washington bureau chief Clifton Daniel. According to the transcript of their telephone conversation, he began by reiterating Colby's anti-disclosure argument:

> *Kissinger:* Bill Colby told me about his conversation with you, and I don't want to tell you what to do. I just wanted you to know that a decision, whether to go ahead, whether to cancel, has not been made and that we would very much like to have the option to continue, in light of the fact that there is some information there that would be uniquely valuable to have.
>
> *Daniel:* I'm making a note on that.
>
> *Kissinger:* What we have to do is to keep watching this over the next months, and then see what the recommendation will be.

Daniel said he would relay Kissinger's message to his colleagues in New York, where publication of the story was under active and "very serious" consideration.[48]

Evidently, editors there still doubted whether the administration was protecting *Glomar* for national security or other reasons, because Daniels called back hours later to seek clarification:

Daniel: You said we would very much have the option of continuing it. They ask if that's just an expression of desire or whether you consider it a matter of great importance.

Kissinger: We consider it a matter of importance. I don't know how much Colby told you. It might give us [text omitted from the original transcript].

Daniel: He said the same, more or less. You are endorsing what he said[?]

Kissinger: . . . I endorse it, that's why we've gone after it.

Daniel: The second question is, as the Russians [must] know about this operation and they are worried they lost a submarine, what is the reason for continued secrecy[?]

Kissinger: They never raised it with us. I think [they will] once it's on the front page of the *New York Times.* I think it was only in a San Diego newspaper.

Daniel: It was on the front page of the *Los Angeles Times* . . . The *Washington Post* did not use the story.

Kissinger: Well, it's never been raised with us.

Daniel: My final question is, the submarine, as I understand it, is a 1958 model but it went down . . . [in] 1968. Has everything changed since then?

Kissinger: Our technical people think that by knowing the design, it would give us a pretty good clue to where we're going from there.

Daniel: Alright, I think that's all.[49]

Rosenthal opted to delay publication. But New York's indecision did not go unnoticed. *Los Angeles Times* editor William Thomas picked up "vibrations" indicating the *New York Times* was wavering. Thomas, under increasing pressure from the newsroom to print the story, was "getting edgy." He allowed reporters—not just Farr and Cohen but others working in Los Angeles, Honolulu, Houston, and Washington—to continue their investigations. Soon, he had a fuller, more accurate account of the *Glomar* program ready to go to press. The *Los Angeles Times* would not be the first outlet to disclose additional details, he assured a WCPO security officer. But if he got the sense that a competitor was about to scoop him, he would have no choice but to publish.[50]

Another measure of the erosion of the press's traditional deference to the state was the number of news organizations now pursuing the story. Colby may have buttoned up the nation's top three newspapers, but rumor had spread "like a goddamn ripple all over the place." And the *Glomar* operation, after years of watertightness, started to leak uncontrollably. ABC, CBS, NBC, and PBS television networks; National Public Radio; *Time*, *Newsweek*, and *Parade* magazines; the *Philadelphia Inquirer* and the *Boston Globe*; and the Associated Press and United Press International were all following *Glomar* leads, sometimes with multiple reporters. And that list didn't include local outlets—in Tulsa, Oklahoma, for instance, which Colby identified as a security risk because it was home to some roughnecks who staffed the *Explorer*'s crew—that might have been doing so without the CIA's foreknowledge. Nor did it include freelance investigative reporters such as James Phelan, the Howard Hughes specialist who Colby learned was interviewing sources as well. "The freelancers will get us," Colby worried.[51]

With *Glomar* springing so many leaks, the DCI said, "I feel like the boy in front of the dike, and I am running out of fingers and toes." The situation seemed hopeless; too many people knew too much for the dam to hold for long. "If you can contain this, there will be a medal for you in Garfinckel's window," one newsman told Colby, referencing a DC-based department store chain. Colby plunged ahead nonetheless, in part because *Glomar* was too important, too innovative not to. "It has to be fought for. It is damn good," he insisted.[52]

But Colby was mindful, too, of the way in which the *Glomar* "story could hurt us now," a reference not only to the operation itself but to the heavy beating the CIA was taking at the time.

"The dimensions of the problems have changed substantially now," Scowcroft agreed.

"They are all just waiting to write that great, sanctimonious, sickening prose," said Colby.[53]

So he spent weeks racing from newsrooms and editorial offices to televisions stations "trying desperately to plug any leaks." Any indication that a reporter was asking questions would send him to that reporter's employer with a plea to withhold publication. Sometimes he arrived before the employer knew what questions were being asked. That was the case when the DCI spoke with one confused NBC executive:

Colby: I would like to say if you hear anything about CIA and the ocean, you sit on it until you have had a chance to talk to me. You will recognize it when it comes.

NBC executive: Oceans, as in water?

Colby: Yes. I cannot be more specific over the phone for good reasons, but I would be very happy to explain it to you or anyone else in the next day or so.[54]

As Colby went from newsroom to newsroom, he explained that outlets like the *New York Times* had agreed to withhold publication. Although the DCI conveniently overlooked the fact that Hersh, like his rivals at the *Los Angeles Times* and the *Washington Post*, continued to follow leads, he was careful to point out that Hersh was among those cooperating. And if even the "ferocious Seymour Hersh had backed off the story," to quote Wicker, then the consequences of publishing must be pretty severe, or at least that's what Colby implied.[55]

Hersh's reputation was such that the mere mention of his name bolstered Colby's case. So, too, did Colby's promise to notify all organizations involved if he could not persuade any one outlet to join the embargo. The list of his interlocutors grew so long that he began to carry in his wallet the telephone numbers of those he was obliged to alert.[56]

The dam held, but only just barely. Almost every major outlet had some part of the story, and everyone knew that everyone else had it too. Afraid of being scooped, journalists worried that their competitors would be the first to break the news. Bill Thomas believed the *New York Times* would publish; Abe Rosenthal thought the *Los Angeles Times* would; and both worried that another organization would beat them to the punch. As Donald Barlett and James Steele, the Pulitzer Prize–winning journalists who led the *Philadelphia Inquirer*'s investigation, observed, the "natural mistrust that exists among competing news media, the fear that a rival was about to break an exclusive story, began to take hold," counterbalancing whatever qualms they had about revealing national security data.[57]

"There were too many reporters working the story," Hersh later said of Colby's prevention effort. "It was very competitive. Everyone was doing the story. He couldn't hold it."[58]

And sure enough, the dike cracked on March 14. Based on grand jury testimony in the Woolbright case, the freelance reporter James Phelan wrote in the *New York Times* that the Romaine Street burglars boasted of having stolen documents discussing "an arrangement" between the CIA and Howard Hughes's Summa Corporation, including at least one memorandum "explaining to Mr. Hughes in detail the relationship that would exist between his corporation and the CIA." Phelan offered no other details, and his report did not add much to what was already in the public domain. Nevertheless, his story concerned Colby, mainly because its appearance reflected growing restiveness among journalists. "The *Times* got in a back hand at you," remarked Thomas, the *Los Angeles Times* editor, who phoned Colby to ask if the *Times*'s disclosure had broken the news embargo. "That nearly jumped my skin out," answered Colby, insisting that the restriction remained in effect.[59]

The fissure cracked wider on March 18 when Colby learned that the story had fallen into the hands of Jack Northman Anderson, the columnist who years earlier had exposed Hughes's $100,000 cash gift to Richard Nixon's crony Bebe Rebozo. Anderson, described in a CIA report as "opinionated, self-righteous, ambitious and highly envious (therefore belligerent) toward anyone in a position of power, especially 'Establishment' types," was regarded as an agency nemesis on par with Hersh. His track record of ferreting out and publishing information, some of it classified, that officials wanted to keep hidden earned him a spot on the CIA's watch list. In 1972, the CIA began surveilling him at work and at home. The snooping lasted only a short time, and it had since stopped, but nevertheless, by 1975 Anderson knew the agency had spied on journalists in violation of its charter, and this soured him on requests from Colby or the CIA.[60]

Anderson's instinct told him to publish the *Glomar* scoop, and quickly. Every reporter in Washington already had the story, it seemed. The news was bound to break before papers could publish his syndicated column, which had a four-day distribution time between the final edit and publication. Besides, the Soviets surely knew what the Americans were up to. And *Glomar* "smacked of boondoggle and cover-up" to Anderson, a self-identified muckraker who "covered the shady side of government" and penetrated "the fraud behind official pretenses" in order "to expose the corruption beneath the surface."[61]

Anderson resolved to broadcast the news on his nightly radio broadcast. Yet even he, the teller of so many other government secrets, was nervous about the national security implications of spilling the details of an ongoing intelligence operation. Hours before going on air, he had two of his assistants phone Colby first. As Anderson typed his radio copy, Colby tried to persuade them to join the crowd of journalists who had agreed to withhold publication; they would be in good company if they did so, he explained.

"Everyone else is sitting on it," said Colby.

One assistant, Les Whitten, was not impressed. Perhaps cooperating journalists were responsible. Or perhaps they were "doing a half-assed job," he remarked.[62]

Still, Anderson remained undecided. Colby called back an hour later to make his case once again, this time directly to Anderson. Anderson received Colby's claims with considerable skepticism, however.

"We have talked to Navy people, and I mean these are really high Navy people who know their business on the technical side, and they say there are no (secrets) in this," said Anderson of the 1950s-vintage Golf, which in his sources' estimation didn't hold data valuable enough to justify the expenditure of hundreds of millions of taxpayer dollars on a high-risk venture to steal it. Some experts had "been opposed to the operation from the very start."

"There have been differences of opinion in this whole thing," acknowledged Colby. But the program had undergone internal review, and each time referees came away convinced that its potential rewards exceeded its risks. "The review has been careful all the way up, and it came to a review a long time ago, and it was reviewed two or three times in building up to the activity in which the negatives were given full consideration and thought about, and it was decided it was worth a try."

Anderson questioned Howard Hughes's involvement. Hadn't Hughes received a sweetheart deal to front *Glomar*? Didn't the operation amount to a payoff for the billionaire's previous support of President Nixon? Wasn't the CIA now trying to keep the story out of the papers to protect Hughes, with whom the agency had an extensive relationship? Colby denied the accusations, insisting that the CIA had initiated *Glomar* for purely "technical" reasons.

"I am concerned," said Anderson, "that some of your own people may be overly influenced because they want to keep Howard Hughes—"

"That has nothing—this is a compartmented relationship with that outfit," Colby interrupted. "It has nothing to do with the [indistinct text omitted from the original transcript]. When we went to Hughes, the [decision?] was that [Maheu] would have nothing to do with it. There are people here who are enthusiastic about it—for the goal and the scope of the undertaking."

"We are going to have to do more talking," said Anderson. "I am impressed with what we have heard from Navy sources."

"I would be glad to sit one of our technical experts down with you."

Glomar was a legitimate security secret, Colby insisted, and he was determined to keep it. He compared *Glomar* to the Manhattan Project, the secret World War II–era undertaking to build the atomic bomb, a sizeable effort that suffered occasional security lapses but remained classified due to the patriotism shown by "good Americans." "It is like the Manhattan Project that leaked all over, but people held it. If we get through this . . . ," Colby trailed off before again listing the news organizations that were holding the story: the *New York Times*, the *Washington Post*, the *Los Angeles Times*, and so on. A "hell of a lot of good people" were cooperating, including some of "my severest critics," Colby said, without naming Hersh.

Anderson doubted the story could hold much longer. "It is bound to break loose," he said. "This is something we have to take into consideration."

Besides, disclosing *Glomar* was in the public interest, Anderson said. The columnist's declaration prompted a pointed exchange with the DCI as to what was in the public interest: Exposing *Glomar* to the light of day? Or keeping the ongoing intelligence operation secret?

> *Anderson:* We want to cooperate with you at all times, and we will do the best we can, but we have to be guided by what we think is in the public interest.
>
> *Colby:* That public interest part, I agree with you on that, and that is my pitch. If there were anything bad about this, I could not argue with you.
>
> *Anderson:* There was a lot of money spent and a contract with Howard Hughes . . .
>
> *Colby:* For which he did not make much money. He did a good job for us, and it has been audited . . . You are in the far-out edge of [indistinct text not transcribed in the original]. People said this could not even be . . . done. There were people absolutely convinced you could not do a thing this big—the [indistinct text] could not stand it. The fact is—

Glomar pushed the outer limits of what was technically possible, and perhaps beyond, Anderson interjected.

"That is my point," replied Colby.

"We will make a decision," Anderson said before hanging up.[63]

Moments later Colby spoke to Scowcroft. "I think our story is about to break, more or less. Jack Anderson has some sources that are putting his kind of [spin] on it. Howard Hughes and that sort of thing."

Colby had given Anderson "a very hard pitch," he explained. He swayed the columnist somewhat, he thought, but probably not enough to prevent him from revealing the operation. Although Anderson hadn't given him a definitive answer, Colby guessed the news would soon spill.[64]

Colby pulled out his wallet and began dialing journalists. His message: Jack Anderson had the story. And Colby was calling, as promised, to say the news was about to break.

Remarkably, Colby still held out hope of limiting the damage. Anderson was a credible journalist, to be sure. But the columnist also had a reputation as a lone wolf who howled endlessly about alleged government malfeasance, and his word was often not the last on any subject. (Asked years earlier why the CIA sought to prevent a major newspaper from printing certain information that had already appeared in the public domain, one of Colby's predecessors, John McCone, explained that the data in question "was published by Jack Anderson in his column . . . and we didn't worry about that. But now when it comes out in the *New York Times* it is like the State Department issuing a White Paper.")[65]

If the disclosure could be limited to Anderson, then perhaps the mission could still go forward without incident. "I still want to try to keep it down if I can," Colby explained to a *Washington Post* representative. "It is really not a matter of keeping it from Americans—it is a matter of [not] making it a big issue" and of keeping it from "foreigners," that is, the Soviets. The news was so full of stories about the CIA—domestic spying, assassinations, covert action, and so forth—that *Glomar* might fall unnoticed through the cracks, or so Colby hoped.[66]

* * *

As expected, Anderson broadcast the story that evening over the Mutual Radio Network. Using the *Hughes Glomar Explorer*, the CIA had successfully raised approximately one-third of a Soviet submarine from the bottom of the Pacific during a covert operation the previous summer. But, he continued, the agency failed to recover the other two-thirds, including the sub's missiles, warheads, and communications gear—everything the spy agency wanted—which broke free and plunged back to the seafloor. Anderson identified the wreckage as a diesel-powered model from 1958, an "older class of submarine made obsolete," he said, by the introduction of the Yankee class of nuclear-powered, ballistic missile–carrying submarines starting in the late 1960s. To salvage the aged sub outfitted with technology that was "outmoded" by 1975, the CIA had spent an estimated $350 million.

Anderson told listeners that Colby tried to suppress the story. Other reporters complied. And Anderson, lest anyone accuse him of being loose with state secrets, said that he, too, had helped the CIA keep other matters quiet in the past. This time, however, Anderson opted to broadcast the *Glomar* story because, he explained, "Navy experts have told us that the sunken sub contains no real secrets and that the project, therefore, is a waste of the taxpayers' money." Colby sought to withhold publication "not because the operation was a secret, but because it was a $350 million failure."[67]

The DCI's imposition of prior restraint grew out of a desire "to cover up a $350 million blunder," Anderson added, sharpening his allegation, powerful in the wake of Watergate. "I don't think the government has a right to cover up a boondoggle," he added. "I have withheld other stories at the behest of the CIA, but this was simply a cover-up of a $350 million failure—$350 million literally went down into the ocean." The CIA was merely trying to hide its embarrassment at giving a billionaire, Hughes, millions more "for a one-shot attempt . . . to get an obsolete submarine."[68]

Before going on the air, Anderson phoned Seymour Hersh to ask if what he'd heard was true. Had *New York Times* editors censored a more comprehensive account Hersh had written? Yes, confirmed Hersh, who phoned Clifton Daniel, his bureau chief, to say that Anderson had scooped the *Times*.

Soon thereafter, Hersh learned that his account would at long last appear in print the following day. He called Rosenthal to chide him. "Wouldn't Bill Colby's argument about national security still be valid? The august *New*

York Times was taken far more seriously by Russia than Jack Anderson, was it not? Why run the story?" Hersh asked irritably.

Rosenthal, according to Hersh, "ignored my whining and said, simply, 'Shut the fuck up and get the story ready.'"[69]

Appearing under a triple-deck headline across five columns at the top of the *Times*'s front page, Hersh's March 19 account compounded the CIA's woes. Deeply researched, the lengthy piece detailed the spy agency's recovery operation, describing everything from how U.S. intelligence located the downed sub in 1968 to what went wrong in 1974 and why program managers wanted to try again in 1975. Although it got some details wrong—misidentifying the name of the security system, JENNIFER, as the program code name, for example, and mistakenly placing the recovery site some 750 nautical miles northwest of Oahu—the article provided the closest look the public would have at AZORIAN/MATADOR for quite some time.

Like Anderson's broadcast, Hersh's article characterized the agency's lift effort as "unsuccessful." Despite years of preparations and hundreds of millions of taxpayer dollars, the mission secured none of its primary objectives: neither the sub's missiles and warheads, nor its codebooks and cryptographic gear. Instead, the *Glomar Explorer* hauled up only part of an old sub, described as a 1958-model craft, containing little other than the remains of Soviet submariners who went down with the ship. "It was a failure," one source, identified as a U.S. intelligence official, said of the operation.

Other officials took exception to that description. One source, a high-level member of the Ford administration, characterized the effort as "50 percent successful" since some useful data had been recovered. Preliminary review of the salvaged materials indicated that the Soviets "had significantly altered the structure and design" of the Golf since its 1958 construction, information that could prove "invaluable" in the estimation process and arms control talks. Even if it was only "partly successful" in execution, a high-ranking official said, the project was "fantastic" in conception. CIA experts had kept hidden for years a massive, inventive project designed to gather intelligence that was deemed crucial to U.S. security. Had the salvage effort been fully successful, it "would have been the biggest single intelligence coup in history," insisted Colby.

But of course *Glomar* hadn't fully succeeded, and Hersh quoted other sources who said the program had provoked a "bitter dispute" within the U.S. intelligence community from the outset. Critics doubted the value of the targeted missiles and code materials, which they depicted as "outmoded." One opponent, identified as a retired navy admiral with knowledge of the program from his time on active duty, complained that the only "real" intelligence gained was "the metallurgical stuff" resulting from analysis of the submarine's hull and interior. "The codes wouldn't mean that much today," the retired officer continued, "even if you recovered their code machine. They have a tremendous number of discs and circuits and you wouldn't know what combination was used." Even if the codes could be broken, they would be intelligible only for a limited period because of what the admiral depicted as "a random restructuring of the various circuits and codes that was completed by the Soviet submarine communicators every twenty-four hours."

Another source said the program ran into "deep trouble because there were all kinds of technical problems" with the CIA's complicated recovery plan, whose expense proved troublesome as well. Because of the need for secrecy, none of the contracts awarded to Hughes's company, Global Marine, or the other subcontractors involved competitive bidding. According to insiders, serious cost overruns caused the price tag to soar above $350 million.

The high risk of the operation had sparked internal debate as well. Some critics expressed concern about the program's potential impact on superpower détente. Others raised the alarm about the possibility of "violent" interference from the USSR, maybe even military action. For cover reasons, the *Explorer* sailed without naval escort, said sources, who suggested the ship's crewmembers were left undefended against possible hostile action. The risk of a clash was especially high because the U.S. effort to recover the sub—containing as it did the remains of Soviet seamen—was probably illegal, not to mention immoral, insiders noted.

Together, such concerns raised two big questions in the minds of Hersh's sources. "Was it worth the hundreds of millions of dollars involved to learn what kind of equipment was being utilized by the Russians? Was there any information available that would have justified the operation?"[70]

To judge from the tone of Hersh's piece, the answer to both questions appeared to be no. And now that the *New York Times* had published its account, other news outlets felt free to follow with theirs. Despite Colby's attempts to plug it, the dam broke open wide. CIA officers braced themselves for the flood of criticism—the "great, sanctimonious, sickening prose"—that was sure to come. It seemed the Year of Intelligence was about to get worse.

7

NEITHER CONFIRM NOR DENY

Every major newscast and daily led with the *Glomar Explorer* story on March 19, 1975. All across the country, NBC anchor John Chancellor said, Americans were talking about the futuristic ship that was supposedly built by Howard Hughes but was actually at the center of a CIA operation.[1] Questions abounded. Could the White House confirm the reports? Did the president approve the CIA plan? Had he heard from the Kremlin?

Crickets. Despite repeated requests for comment—thirteen by one news outlet alone—queries went officially unanswered by U.S. government spokespeople.[2]

Meanwhile, President Ford huddled with his national security team to coordinate a response. Defense Secretary (and former CIA chief) James Schlesinger advised the president to officially acknowledge the submarine operation. The administration could not plausibly deny the story because William Colby had already confirmed much of it in his conversations with journalists. Nor could the administration offer the standard "no comment," a line that would be taken by the press as tacit confirmation of the project's existence. Besides, Schlesinger added, the mission was "a marvel—technically, and with maintaining secrecy."[3]

Confirming the press reports could help the administration from a public relations standpoint. Schlesinger argued that getting out in front of the story—providing as full and complete an account as possible without compromising intelligence sources and methods—was the way forward. Continued silence would only deepen skepticism of the CIA, which was already under a cloud of suspicion. "If we move now we can take the high ground—if not we will be pilloried."[4]

Had Henry Kissinger been in attendance he surely would have disagreed. But the notoriously secretive secretary of state was shuttling among Middle Eastern capitals trying to negotiate another peace deal. That left Colby, whose performance during the Year of Intelligence would receive mostly negative reviews. Colby's critics charged that he was too open, that he shared more information with journalists and members of Congress than a director of central intelligence should have. Kissinger, for example, characterized him as a "runaway CIA director" whose oversharing did irreparable damage to America's security service.[5]

Given Colby's historical reputation, one might suspect that he took a tell-all approach. He did not. Colby's reading of history told him that the advantages of keeping mum were simply too great. "I go back to the U-2," he said. Ford, Schlesinger, and the others present could no doubt recite the basics of the U-2 affair, and how the downing of a spy plane piloted by Francis Gary Powers on the eve of the 1960 Paris Summit led to the meeting's cancellation. But Colby, who arrived at the White House carrying a copy of Nikita Khrushchev's newly published memoirs, pointed out a detail they might have missed. The former Soviet leader, Colby noted, recalled being well aware of the dozens of times U-2 reconnaissance aircraft had overflown Soviet airspace since 1956, which was infuriating enough. "But what had really upset him," Colby continued, was Dwight Eisenhower's admission that he had approved Powers's ill-fated mission. Eisenhower's public acknowledgement stripped away any remaining pretense that Powers's plane had accidentally veered off course while performing weather research, as the U.S. cover story claimed, or that anti-Soviet "militarists" within the

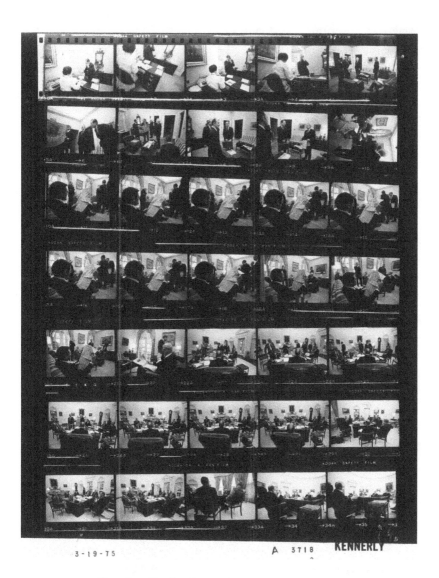

3-19-75   A 3718   KENNERLY

FIGURE 7.1 President Ford and his aides meeting on March 19, 1975. Note the newspaper Donald Rumsfeld, William Colby, and others are reading, the *Washington Star*, featuring a page-one story on the *Glomar Explorer*.

Source: Contact sheet A3718, photographer David Hume Kennerly, White House Photographic Office Photographs, Gerald R. Ford Presidential Library, Ann Arbor, Michigan.

American government had launched the provocative flight without the president's permission, as Khrushchev tactfully suggested might have been the case. Khrushchev, for political reasons, couldn't allow Eisenhower's admission to go unchallenged in Paris. To save face, he demanded an apology from the president for violating Soviet sovereignty. Eisenhower refused, rose from his seat, and led the U.S. delegation out of the summit. The meeting—the first between Soviet and American heads of state in five years—ended before it began, increasing Cold War tensions after a brief thaw. "If I had to do it all over again," Eisenhower conceded years later, "we would have kept our mouths shut."[6]

Colby advised Ford to follow a strict "no comment" policy with regard to *Glomar*. Were the president to repeat Eisenhower's mistake of confirming a clandestine activity targeting the Soviet Union, the intelligence director foresaw a possible scenario in which Leonid Brezhnev followed Khrushchev's example and took some sort of face-saving retaliatory action that would similarly jeopardize bilateral relations—and perhaps trigger an international incident. "I think we should not put the Soviet Union under such pressure to respond."[7]

Colby drew an imperfect historical analogy. True, the U-2 and the *Hughes Glomar Explorer* were both technologically advanced collection platforms aimed at the USSR, the compromise of which, coming at pivotal moments in the Cold War, underscored the importance of maintaining plausible deniability. And the two systems shared a common ancestry: many people who pioneered U.S. overhead reconnaissance had also developed AZORIAN under CIA special project manager John Parangosky, himself a U-2 veteran. But the similarities largely ended there. Whereas the U-2 overflew Soviet airspace, the *Explorer* sailed in international waters. The ship's most sensitive work occurred below deck, making it difficult for the Soviets to catch the Americans red-handed.

"In 1960 the Soviets had all the bragging rights," explained David Sharp, the deputy mission director whose résumé also listed the U-2. They had the wreckage of the aircraft and also its pilot, Powers, alive and well. In 1975, however, the situation was different. "Sure, the Soviets held the legal high ground, but the United States had part of their submarine—recovered within plain view of Soviet surveillance ships. The bragging rights belonged to the United States."[8]

Remarkably, those bragging rights gave U.S. intelligence officers hope that the *Glomar Explorer* could make its voyage that summer as planned despite the media disclosure—another reason to remain silent. CIA analysts knew full well that news of the *Explorer*'s exploits had penetrated the Iron Curtain: both the Voice of America and the British Broadcasting Corporation carried accounts, in Russian, to listeners in the USSR. But published reports told a tale of repeated Soviet failure. They confirmed that the *K-129* had been lost in 1968—a sensitive fact that Moscow had yet to officially admit. They revealed that the United States could attempt to recover the downed sub only because of the Soviet Union's inability to locate it. And they implied that Soviet intelligence failed to discover the true purpose of the American "deep ocean mining program" even though it had operated mostly in plain sight for years. From experience, CIA analysts knew that the Kremlin typically remained stonily silent when faced with public humiliation. If Moscow followed the script, then maybe—just maybe—MATADOR could proceed.[9]

But that all depended on American officials holding their tongues as well. Plans were underway for Ford and Brezhnev to meet at that summer's Conference on Security and Cooperation in Europe in Helsinki. But superpower relations remained uncertain. Given that fact, it was all the more important not to do or say anything that would unnecessarily antagonize Brezhnev, that would put the Soviet leader in a box and force him to lash out—with words or force—to restore credibility.

Colby's advice prevailed. ("Boy, was Schlesinger wrong on that," Ford remarked.)[10] After talking virtually nonstop for weeks in an effort to suppress the *Glomar* story, Colby suddenly cancelled interviews, causing the *Los Angeles Times* to cry, "Administration Won't Talk About Sub Raised by CIA." "The backgrounding has been done," he explained, "and at this point I have to stop talking. Honestly, we can have international problems and I have to be careful."[11]

* * *

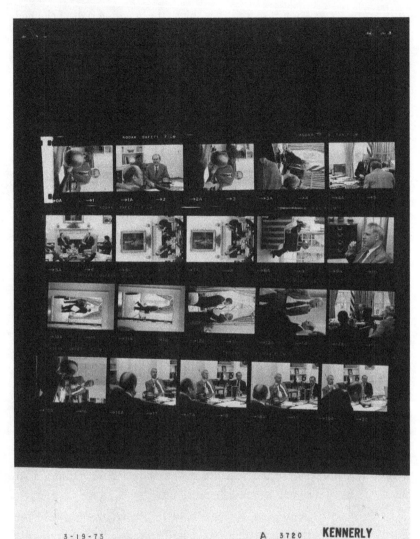

3-19-75　　　　　　　　A 3720 **KENNERLY**

FIGURE 7.2 James Schlesinger and William Colby speaking with President Ford in the Oval Office, March 19, 1975.

Source: Contact sheet A3720, photographer David Hume Kennerly, White House Photographic Office Photographs, Gerald R. Ford Presidential Library, Ann Arbor, Michigan.

"Well now, Comrade Maslov," began commander in chief of the Soviet Navy Sergey Gorshkov. "(Expletive). A submarine?" Ordinarily, the sixty-five-year-old Gorshkov, a Hero of the Soviet Union widely credited with overseeing the navy's growth into a global force, was not a voluble man. Quiet, he avoided official functions, preferring to spend weekends with his wife at their dacha outside of Moscow. But reports of an American attempt to steal the *K-129* prompted an angry call to Admiral Vladimir Maslov, the newly appointed commander of the Pacific Fleet.

"Not at all, comrade commander in chief," replied Maslov, who had taken command only a few months earlier, in late 1974, perhaps unaware that his predecessor had once sent ships to Point K to investigate reports that the *Glomar Explorer* was performing some sort of clandestine activity.

"What does 'not at all' mean?" shouted Gorshkov, so worked up, one of Maslov's staffers recalled, that his asthmatic breathing could be heard on the other end of the line in Vladivostok. "Do you think I am a (expletive)? A submarine?"

Gorshkov demanded an immediate report on "Project JENNIFER," as the *New York Times* called it. What were the Americans doing? Who had failed to stop them? How could they be stopped?[12]

Meanwhile, the Soviets maintained a posture of official silence. American observers expected them to eventually act based on larger policy goals. "If they decide a hardening of relations is called for, the reaction could be nasty," diplomats told *Los Angeles Times* Washington bureau chief Jack Nelson. "But if they want to keep détente as the norm for U.S.–Soviet relations, the reaction could be cautious."[13]

The U.S. intelligence community did detect some operational moves. A President's Daily Brief (PDB) reported that most Soviet intelligence collectors and oceanographic ships operating in the Pacific continued to follow routine procedure. But some had taken unusual action. On March 21, two TU-95 reconnaissance aircraft flew in the vicinity of the recovery site, loitering there for several hours. That same day, ATA *MB-11*, a seagoing tug reconfigured for intelligence collection, proceeded to an area about 750 nautical miles northwest of Oahu, the location the press had misidentified as the recovery site. Finding nothing, the tug then proceeded to the actual recovery site, arriving there on March 28.

Watchers noticed some political moves as well. On March 20, Oleg Yermishkin, second secretary of the USSR's Washington embassy, told *Time* magazine's Strobe Talbott that he personally viewed the *Glomar* episode as a "setback to détente." Yermishkin also said that chargé d'affaires Yuli Vorontsov—acting instead of Ambassador Anatoly Dobrynin, who, like Kissinger, was negotiating in the Middle East—had sent a strongly worded cable to Moscow urging the Kremlin to lodge a protest. Four days later, during a conversation with a United Press International (UPI) correspondent, Valentin Kamenev, the embassy's chief press officer, expressed "distress" in response to media accounts claiming that the CIA had recovered the remains of some of the *K-129*'s submariners. Referring to "certain decencies in international law and behavior," Kamenev implied that the Foreign Ministry was weighing its options. Another contact told the same UPI reporter that Soviet officials were "very sensitive" to the fact that the United States had yet to repatriate the remains. "If we had recovered your submarine off Murmansk," one said, "we would have given back the bodies."

Other moves appeared conciliatory. The embassy's naval attaché buttonholed a U.S. Navy officer at a social function and asked—"in a plaintive, almost beseeching tone," according to the PDB—if the United States planned to deny the published stories. Prior to a March 29 meeting of the Law of the Sea Conference in Geneva, Soviet representative Valentin Romanov took Leigh Ratiner, his American counterpart, aside to ask what the American delegation planned to say if the subject of *Glomar* arose in the public forum. U.S. officials would have no comment, Ratiner answered. "Good," Romanov replied, "we do not want to say anything either."[14]

Notably, Moscow had yet to lodge any public complaint. TASS, the Soviet news agency, issued no statement. No word of the *Glomar Explorer* appeared in the state-controlled media. Soviet diplomats filed no formal protest.[15]

CIA officers could not know for certain what lay behind the silence. According to one theory, the Soviets discounted the published reports of the *Explorer*'s actions, still incredulous that anyone could raise the *K-129*, which at 324 feet long was more than half the known length of the *Hughes Glomar Explorer*. That thinking, though wishful, was not entirely unreasonable: after all, the Soviets had no way of knowing that the sub had broken into smaller pieces more susceptible to recovery.[16]

Another, more widely held theory postulated that the Soviets fully accepted the reports as fact but were unwilling to acknowledge the cold, hard truth. Silence served several purposes. It enabled the Kremlin to avoid the embarrassment of having to admit, to domestic and international audiences alike, the loss of the Golf for the first time. It allowed Soviet leaders to sidestep "the obviously superior technical capabilities" demonstrated by the United States in not only locating but recovering a portion of the sub. It permitted Moscow to downplay the equally obvious weaknesses of the Soviet intelligence apparatus. And it maximized Soviet intelligence's ability to deceive the United States, to limit whatever gains the Americans may have made by denying them any additional information as to what valuable material was or was not aboard the *K-129*.[17]

A third theory held that the Soviets were still gathering facts and taking a wait-and-see approach before making a move. *"We assume the Soviets were taken by surprise when the story of the submarine recovery effort broke,"* the March 27 PDB reported. All accounts published in the American press had misplaced the recovery site. Some had misidentified the targeted submarine. What the United States had done and, more important, whether its intent ran contrary to détente remained unknown. "The Soviet leadership will have many questions for the navy and the intelligence services about the validity of the press stories." It would take time to sort out the answers, and the CIA doubted the Soviets "will ever be fully satisfied that they know the whole truth."[18]

Soviet motives may have been opaque. One thing seemed clear, though: the episode passed so quietly as to have little evident effect on superpower relations. CIA Kremlinologists could find *"no evidence of any unusual activity or new line from the Soviet leadership."* General Secretary Brezhnev's public schedule continued unchanged. Premier Alexei Kosygin's public remarks included "positive reference" to Soviet-American cooperation. And

Foreign Ministry officials continued to plan joint activities in Moscow marking Victory in Europe Day. Always a barometer of the state of Soviet-American relations, the tone of these commemorations took on added significance in 1975 not only because they marked the thirtieth anniversary of Nazi Germany's surrender to the Allies at the end of World War II. They were also notable, wrote leading Sovietologist Helmut Sonnenfeldt, now State Department counselor, because "there may be developments which may make our participation in this highly symbolic celebration incongruous."[19]

The CIA took these signals to mean that the *Glomar* disclosure might pass without causing lasting damage. "Whatever their visceral feelings, the Soviet leaders have felt no compulsion to rush before the world with protests or denials," reported the March 27 PDB. "So far Soviet officials are conducting themselves as though they either have no instructions, or the instructions are to pursue 'business as usual.' The 'no-comment' policy of the US has undoubtedly helped Moscow avoid public commentary."[20]

* * *

Bilateral relations appeared so unaffected that U.S. officials moved to complete MATADOR. On March 28, the 40 Committee reconvened to discuss the program's future. Numerous factors weighed against a second mission, including the diminution of secrecy. "Secrecy has been viewed in the past as essential to the operation," Colby noted. His predecessors could depend on reporters to look the other way. But the veil had been lifted, and the press was certain to "monitor and flag" the scheduled movements of the *Hughes Glomar Explorer*, eliminating the element of surprise. April's sea trials to test the post-AZORIAN modifications, May's mating of the capture vehicle with the ship, and June's integrated systems tests—each step taken to prepare the *Explorer* for its July departure would receive heavy news coverage, he predicted, putting pressure on Moscow to respond. Backed into a corner publicly, the Kremlin might be forced to take action, such as formally lodging a diplomatic protest or forcibly thwarting the operation. Lodging a protest could lead to an "international furor—as in [the 1960] U-2 incident"—that ended with the United States blamed for scuttling world peace. Using force could cause an incident at sea, perhaps leading to a "catastrophic climax." Approving MATADOR was tantamount to sending the *Glomar Explorer*'s crew on a potential suicide mission.[21]

Given the prevailing political climate, Colby foresaw the administration becoming an inviting "target for claims of money waste, brinkmanship, and strong arming." The CIA would be subjected to intensified investigation by the media and Congress, an unwelcome development that might very well expose the "substrata" of intelligence sources and methods used by the agency in carrying out not only AZORIAN/MATADOR but other clandestine activities. "This will become a political football, with renewed cries to curb the intelligence establishment and possibly generate an avalanche of leaks," Colby predicted. (In a separate meeting, members of the President's Foreign Intelligence Advisory Board also voiced concern about "the potential political hazard of failure at this time with intelligence under investigation.") Those reasons and more led Colby to advise against MATADOR. "The conclusion of my own weighing of the above arguments is, I regret to say, that it is inadvisable to undertake a second mission," he informed Kissinger, who still chaired the 40 Committee in his capacity as national security advisor.[22]

Public disclosure had almost certainly led the Soviets to take countermeasures that diminished the intelligence value of MATADOR's target. Even so, the leaks did nothing to change the United States Intelligence Board's latest assessment of the target's value. The target still held "unique intelligence potential," according to the board. And in the estimation of other 40 Committee members that assessment was enough to go ahead with MATADOR, despite the mission's heightened risk. Erroneous and conflicting media reports regarding the identity of the targeted submarine, the location of the recovery site, and the extent of AZORIAN's success might have confused the Soviets enough to allow the United States to complete the mission before they could get organized. Plus, the lack of a formal protest on the part of the Kremlin encouraged some U.S. officials to believe that their Soviet counterparts might not interfere with a second recovery mission, even if they had put two and two together.[23]

James Schlesinger, for one, held out hope of completing MATADOR. Only days earlier, he had advised Ford to come clean, to lay it all on the table. Now, the secretary of defense, a hawk increasingly critical of the White House's pursuit of détente with the USSR, thought it best to wait and see how things played out before voluntarily canceling a potentially valuable Cold War intelligence operation. A majority of 40 Committee members found his views persuasive. The committee decided to continue preparations for MATADOR but to withhold judgment on the actual mission until just before the *Explorer*'s scheduled departure. Officials reserved the option of canceling the operation at any time if the Soviets exhibited a strong reaction.[24]

* * *

Less than twenty-four hours later, Soviet ambassador Anatoly Dobrynin strode into Kissinger's State Department office. The Soviet Navy had completed its review of JENNIFER. Many questions remained unanswered. But its findings prompted Minister of Defense Andrey Grechko to address a memorandum to the Central Committee of the Communist Party of the Soviet Union, the collective policy-making body for party and state activities. Grechko recommended that Ambassador Dobrynin lodge a formal protest demanding that the United States cease efforts to salvage the *K-129*. The Central Committee approved Grechko's recommendations, and so Dobrynin arrived in Kissinger's suite carrying a note. "Moscow paid attention to the [press] reports," it began, "regarding the fact that certain U.S. services have conducted for some time the work of raising the Soviet submarine that sunk in 1968 in the open sea in the area northwest of Hawaii." The *Glomar Explorer* reportedly carried out the operation, which succeeded in raising part of the submarine, the note continued.

As critics had predicted would be the case from the very beginning, the Soviet Union challenged the legality of the U.S. salvage effort. Under maritime law, Dobrynin recalled, a sunken "man-of-war cannot be raised without the permission or knowledge of its government, which is its owner."

His note objected to the "raising [of] any parts and property of the submarine belonging to the USSR."[25]

Dobrynin also raised "special concern" about the fact that the remains of Soviet sailors had been unceremoniously "thrown out into the sea." Dobrynin's account of the burial at sea ceremony performed aboard the *Glomar Explorer* differed substantially from a written description that Robert Gates, then director of central intelligence, would present Russian president Boris Yeltsin after the end of the Cold War in 1992 describing the "care and respect" with which the *Explorer*'s crew had treated the remains of the six seamen identified aboard the *K-129*. Still, Dobrynin's note insisted, "matters related to the submarine and the dead seamen are the prerogatives of the Soviet Union alone."

Dobrynin closed by demanding explanations with regard to the published reports. Specifically, the ambassador demanded complete information as to the identity and status of the human remains. He also insisted upon the discontinuance of any ongoing U.S. operations pertaining to the submarine.[26]

Dobrynin's démarche raised the possibility of a U-2-like crisis. U.S. officials took care not to be seen dancing on the graves of Soviet submariners. But many American news outlets were not so diplomatic. The *Atlanta Constitution*, for example, declared that the United States had scored a "major intelligence victory" over the Soviet Union. To be sure, the CIA had not gotten everything it wanted. But in going to the bottom of the sea to steal part of a submarine out from under the Soviets' noses, the agency demonstrated America's Cold War superiority. "We are technologically able to discover and reach a foreign submarine at a depth of 17,000 feet, whereas the Soviets apparently were unequipped to pinpoint the craft at all," the *Chicago Tribune* bellowed.

Moreover, the *Tribune* expressed little concern about the disclosure's possible political repercussions. The Soviets were not "cloistered innocents." They knew that intelligence gathering was routine, part of the game. And the paper predicted that news of America's underwater exploit would have no bearing on détente so long as that policy continued to play out to the Soviets' benefit, as defined by the Kremlin. Détente "will exist as long as the Soviets consider it in their interest for it to exist—not a day more, not a day less."[27]

Such triumphalism put additional pressure on Moscow to respond in some way. Dobrynin's protest appeared to confirm that the Soviets viewed *Glomar* as a "setback to détente." News of the U.S. salvage attempt was one of several "accumulated irritants" that created greater "uncertainty" in Moscow as to Washington's intentions, according to a brief Kissinger received from Sonnenfeldt and Assistant Secretary of State for Intelligence and Research William Hyland. The "submarine salvage operation will certainly not have helped those in the Politburo who are arguing in favor of good relations with the US." The memo pointed out that Soviet leaders had sent Dobrynin hurrying back to Washington with instructions to sound out Kissinger on a range of issues, none more important than the White House's attitude toward détente. And Dobrynin, an architect of détente probably "under somewhat of a cloud" back home due to fraying superpower ties, arrived at the State Department for his meeting with Kissinger determined to get answers, to appear forceful in the face of America's perceived provocation.[28]

Thanks to declassifications, we now know that the *Glomar Explorer*'s revelation intensified otherwise routine "Intelligence Wars," as Dobrynin called a series of tit-for-tat actions taken by the Soviet and American intelligence services. Growing to encompass disinformation, eavesdropping, and, eventually, the arrest and expulsion of suspected spies, these "wars" began in the spring of 1975, when Soviet intelligence bombarded the U.S. embassy in Moscow with microwave radiation. The purpose of irradiation (to jam or intercept embassy communications) was clear. Its outcome was predictable: the United States strongly objected, in part because of irradiation's possible ill effects on the health of embassy staff, including Ambassador Walter Stoessel Jr., who later developed leukemia. And Dobrynin and Kissinger tried to keep the fallout under wraps before it could escape into the open and cause what the Soviet ambassador called the "erosion of détente." "We are trying to keep things quiet," Kissinger said at one point.[29]

But why, U.S. analysts asked, did Moscow choose that particular moment in time to take a step certain to antagonize Washington? Their answer: to respond to news of the *Glomar Explorer*. Wide publicity given to U.S intelligence "successes" such as the *Glomar Explorer* and U.S. submarine penetrations of Soviet waters, an interagency intelligence memo concluded, caused Soviet "embarrassment and dismay," reduced Soviet expectations for détente, and encouraged Soviet intelligence to take retribution against American targets to show resolve and to restore lost credibility.[30]

In some respects, then, *Glomar* tested the limits of détente. Yet, as Kissinger explained to President Ford, a close reading of Dobrynin's note revealed certain encouraging signs. The note referred only to "reports" of the submarine mission, a subtle but significant diplomatic signal that gave both sides room for maneuver in how they managed the situation. Plus, the ambassador's actions—delivering a message in private rather than manufacturing a public spectacle—suggested that Moscow wanted to resolve the matter quietly without endangering détente, which remained Soviet policy.[31]

That was certainly the impression Dobrynin conveyed in an exploratory, pre-meeting telephone conversation with Kissinger on March 27.

"How is détente getting along?" probed Kissinger, still uncertain as to the effect of the news.

"Well, I think," answered Dobrynin. "What is your opinion?"

"Well, my opinion is, why not?" a relieved Kissinger joked. "On our side," he added, "we are determined to continue our course and in fact to extend it."

"Yes," Dobrynin responded, "this is the same as our course, our policy. I tell you authoritatively."[32]

And this was the message Kissinger reinforced after their March 29 meeting. "I thought our talk was very good," he said, "and really from our side there is no intention of doing anything except to proceed in a positive direction."

"This was what you mentioned to me," Dobrynin replied. "It makes it very clear to me."[33]

The CIA reached the same verdict as Kissinger. First and foremost, Soviet leaders wanted the United States to cease its underwater activity. At the same time, they hoped to maintain a "general détente posture toward the US. This total reaction," the agency continued, was "calculated to hold the best chance of preserving a relationship in which the Soviets have considerable [interests] at stake, while communicating to the US that it must act within certain restraints"—mutual restraint, as codified in the Basic Principles signed at the 1972 Moscow Summit—"or bear the onus of destroying détente."

That is to say, Soviet leaders wanted détente to continue, if possible. They wanted *Glomar* to pass in silence. And they wanted Washington's help in making the whole humiliating affair go quietly away. "The Soviets appear to convey the desire that the United States cooperate in holding down publicity and, equally important, that there be no official U.S. government acknowledgement of MATADOR."[34]

A Soviet diplomat confirmed as much in a conversation with a UPI correspondent. Foreign policy drove the Soviet blackout. Publicizing *Glomar* "might cause anti-American feeling and harm the process of détente," the diplomat said.[35]

Official silence served the interests of intelligence as well. Published reports offered conflicting versions of the *Explorer*'s intelligence haul. Most accounts stated—accurately, time would tell—that the ship's capture vehicle recovered only the forward third of the Golf. But some claimed, inaccurately, that it held onto more. Citing intelligence sources on the "fringe of the CIA," the *Washington Post*, for example, reported that the *Explorer* retrieved the entire submarine—missiles, warheads, and code machine included.[36]

Knowledgeable officials did nothing to clear up the confusion because it left their Soviet adversaries confused as well. And in the intelligence business, Thomas Powers explains, it is axiomatic "that information is most useful when your opponent doesn't know you have it. A corollary would be that second best is to confuse your opponent about what you've learned when you can't deny him knowledge of the operation altogether."[37]

From published reports, the Soviets knew, as Dobrynin's note indicated, that the Americans had raised part of the *K-129*. However, they had no ability to verify exactly how much or what portion of the Golf had been compromised. To maximize Soviet uncertainty about what it had or had not learned, the CIA gave the highest possible degree of security protection to the details of the intelligence gained from the operation. "Significantly," Sharp writes, "the intelligence *not* gained from the analysis was given equivalent security protection."[38]

Such deliberate ambiguity sought to put the Soviets on the defensive, to force them to assume that everything aboard the *K-129*—the missiles, the codebooks, the cipher gear, all of it—had been compromised. The goal was to push Soviet submarine forces into making substantive, not to mention expensive, operational changes, up to and including issuing fresh codes and developing new cryptographic hardware. To U.S. intelligence officials, the situation amounted to an unexpected windfall. But that windfall depended on the maintenance of utmost secrecy.[39] In that regard, *Glomar* grew oddly more secret even as it became better known.

Henry Kissinger may not have been an intelligence officer, but he knew a thing or two about the geostrategic value of deception. "Uncertainty," he wrote in *The Necessity for Choice*, his 1961 treatise on foreign policy, "has a certain utility. It makes the calculations of [one's opponent] more difficult."[40]

Which helps explain his recommendation to President Ford for how the United States should respond to Dobrynin's note. A full and complete confirmation of the espionage operation was out of the question for the aforementioned reasons. Another option was to offer a "quasi-confirmation" by providing the names of the Soviet submariners whose recovered remains CIA experts had been able to identify. Even such a limited admission "would be extremely risky," though, for any official, written confirmation would effectively "challenge the Soviets. Even if they did not react at present, they would have it in reserve and could spring it at any time. Moreover, there is no explanation that would assuage them. In particular, we cannot argue the legality or legitimacy of the operation without starting a polemic, and the Soviets cannot possibly concede its legality as their note indicates."

Instead, Kissinger proposed an oral reply. It would say "that we do not confirm, deny or otherwise comment on alleged intelligence activities and that there will be no official U.S. position on this matter." The proposed language conformed to Ford's March 19 decision not to comment, Kissinger added.[41]

Ford approved. Kissinger then gave the following verbal reply to Dobrynin: "The United States has issued no official comment on the matters related to the vessel *Glomar Explorer*. It is the policy of this government not to confirm, deny or otherwise comment on alleged intelligence activities. Regardless of press speculation," he concluded, "there will be no official position on this matter."[42]

* * *

In his reply, Kissinger gave the first known instance of what later became known as the "Glomar response": "We can neither confirm nor deny the

FIGURE 7.3 Anatoly Dobrynin and Henry Kissinger aboard a helicopter, January 25, 1974.

Source: U.S. Department of State photo, accessed May 23, 2022, https://flickr.com /photos/9364837@N06/2380409304.

existence of . . ." Commonplace today, that doublespeak originated in 1975 to provide the official answer to all public requests for data about what was then still an officially classified mission, including those filed under the Freedom of Information Act, the landmark openness law that Congress strengthened in 1974. Arguably *Glomar's* most durable legacy, the response serves today as the standard non-denial denial, an innovation that emerged in the mid-1970s—the sunshine era—to hide dark practices from the light of day.[43]

Notorious among scholars, watchdogs, and journalists for frustrating transparency efforts, the Glomar response performed a historically significant role from the standpoint of foreign relations. Diplomatic historians do not refer to a *Glomar* analogy. Perhaps they should, because unlike the better-known U-2 analogy, drawn by William Colby and others to illustrate the costs of poor decision making, *Glomar* provides a lesson in how effective information management can work to resolve international crises.[44]

Kissinger's evasive answer to Dobrynin's note was an end product of their nondisclosure agreement, in which the two diplomats arranged to confine "mutual accusations of espionage," potentially troublesome for détente, within their confidential channel. Such collusion risked glossing over provocations. But leaving reports of the *Glomar* operation both unconfirmed and undenied also provided a fig leaf that allowed the USSR to save face, the superpowers to sidestep a showdown, and their posture of détente to continue. In word if not in deed, the Glomar response reaffirmed that restraint, sorely tested in the coming weeks as the United States evacuated Saigon ahead of communist forces who overran the South Vietnamese capital, still governed superpower competition at a crucial juncture in the Cold War. And *Glomar's* diplomatic history—from Colby's reticence in the face of the media disclosure to Dobrynin's low-key protest—provides a case study showing how intelligence and diplomacy can coexist (albeit uncomfortably) under the cloak of secrecy, how nations can and do routinely gather intelligence, generally without sparking international crises.

To be sure, words—or the lack thereof—weren't enough to stop MATADOR; a show of force was required as well. Kissinger's Glomar response left Dobrynin's final demand—that the United States end its submarine foray—conspicuously unaddressed.

The ambassador's protest did raise the stakes, though, clearly signaling that Moscow would strenuously object to any attempt by the United States to complete the operation. And the CIA's forecast grew more bearish as a result. Were the *Explorer* to sail in the face of their objections, the Soviets would naturally conclude that the United States "was not only determined to compromise their security, but that it was willing, if not anxious, to humiliate them." Because of the public way in which that humiliation was likely to play out, the agency predicted they would go to great lengths to frustrate the ship's mission, perhaps with disastrous consequences.[45]

But how far would the Soviets go? Dobrynin's quiet approach had already revealed Soviet leaders to be invested enough in détente to sweep *Glomar* under the rug. Would they look the other way again if the *Explorer* went back to finish the job? Could the United States leverage détente to forge ahead?

Or what if the CIA waited until things cooled down? Soviet authorities had done their due diligence by dispatching the ATA *MB-11* to the location where the *Glomar Explorer* had operated the previous summer. But the tug couldn't stay there forever. And of course it wouldn't find anything because the *Explorer* was long gone, and the Soviets lacked the technological ability to surveil the ocean bottom. Perhaps, finding nothing, they would lose interest and leave the recovery site unattended. Besides, the news cycle was short; the media would eventually move on to the next big story and forget all about the CIA spy ship. Could the *Explorer* then safely return to the recovery site in July as planned?

U.S. officials didn't yet know for sure. Until they did, preparations continued to ready the *Hughes Glomar Explorer* for its scheduled departure. Despite Dobrynin's protest, officials still held out hope of completing the mission, of recovering the uniquely valuable intelligence inside the Golf.[46] Granted, the likelihood of that happening was remote. But the lure of pulling off a major intelligence coup remained strong. MATADOR had come too far, too much had been invested in the *Explorer*'s development to give up now that the end was within reach.

Clarity arrived in the form of a submarine that a U.S. frigate spotted some 100 nautical miles off the California coast in April 1975. The frigate didn't get a good fix on the sub. American naval analysts could not positively identify the advancing vessel, which they classified only as "non-US, non-friendly." Neither could they definitively tie its activity to MATA-DOR. But they supposed it was Soviet because the sub appeared to work in conjunction with two Soviet fishing trawlers located south of San Francisco. And the CIA figured that the sudden appearance of a Soviet submarine in the vicinity of American waters could only mean one thing: the sub was positioned to track the *Explorer*—all the way to the recovery site, if need be.[47]

Greater certainty came that same month, when a tug, identified as the fleet ocean ATF *MB-26*, relieved the ATA *MB-11* at the recovery site. CIA officials did not know that Soviet leaders had assigned ships to constantly maintain station at Point K to deter Americans from working there. But they observed that the tug held its position after relieving its predecessor on station, as opposed to passing it in transit some distance away. To the trained eye, these facts indicated that the Soviets intended to maintain constant surveillance. Were the *Glomar Explorer* to return, it would likely find the ATF *MB-26* or a similar vessel already situated there.[48]

What would happen in that event? Perhaps nothing. Maybe the Soviet ship, an unarmed auxiliary noncombatant, would back off and allow the *Explorer* to complete its work undisturbed. But the CIA knew from experience that the Soviets typically employed auxiliary units under naval command and control to discourage, by harassment, activity they suspected of having a covert aspect. The agency expected the ATF *MB-26* to physically interfere with the *Explorer*, which was especially worrisome because the ship was "extremely vulnerable" to interference. "Designed and configured wholly as a commercial vessel, having no arms or armor, with many of its vital operating systems exposed above the main deck and shielded only from the weather by paint, rubber and plastic," the ship contained several highly specialized systems for maintaining accurate positioning and stability during heavy-lift operations, each of which was highly susceptible to physical harassment.

Though unarmed and small relative to the *Explorer*, noncombatants like the ATF *MB-26* could inflict serious damage. Maneuverable, they could come within yards of the American vessel to employ any number of harassment tactics, ranging from closely passing the ship to fouling its screw, damaging its positioning thrusters, and physically pushing it sideways. The *Explorer* was most vulnerable during recovery operations. With its heavy-lift system under tremendous stress, even the slightest physical displacement—a twisting motion here, a lateral movement there—could cause the pipe string to snap and recoil upwards, potentially doing catastrophic damage to the ship and its crew. "If pushing tactics were employed," the CIA concluded, the *Explorer* "would have to cease operations, and were the recovery system to become damaged, the ship would be rendered virtually immobile."[49] The *Glomar Explorer* was a sitting duck.

If those actions proved insufficient, the Soviets could resort to a final option to thwart U.S. efforts. They could dispatch a combatant vessel to "threaten or intimidate" the *Explorer*. Deploying a man-of-war against what was ostensibly a civilian vessel would be a provocative move, one that the CIA considered unlikely. But the possibility could not be ruled out in a case where diplomatic overtures had failed and the Soviets felt they had no other recourse to indicate their "high level" of concern. And stationing a combatant at the recovery site, though risky, did offer an advantage: it would put Moscow in the driver's seat, putting the Soviets in control of events. "They might calculate," the CIA reasoned, "that the US would be forced to give way or escalate the matter in some fashion which would make Washington bear the responsibility for what evolves thereafter."[50]

It was a grim assessment. Remarkably, though, some U.S. officials urged the 40 Committee to approve MATADOR when the committee reconvened on June 5 to decide whether or not to proceed. The committee had delayed making a final determination to see how the situation developed. As they spoke, the *Explorer* stood harbored in Long Beach undergoing final preparations for a scheduled July 4 departure on a two-week journey to the recovery site, where it would spend an estimated thirty days, ostensibly testing ocean mining equipment but actually attempting to recover the remains of the Golf target.

"There were no Soviet reactions to the sea trials," said CIA deputy director for science and technology Carl Duckett, "and there was a surprising lack of publicity." Better yet, what testing had been completed revealed no problems, showing all systems to be in "first-rate condition." "From the technical standpoint," said Duckett, always a strong booster, "there is a very high probability of our success if a second mission is authorized."

Bill Clements agreed. The deputy secretary of defense noted that the first mission had only a fifty-fifty probability of success. But AZORIAN had amounted, in retrospect, to "an expensive R&D activity." Engineers had learned a great deal. So "technically the chances of success are much improved this time."[51]

* * *

Glomar had reached its most dangerous point. Had the 40 Committee recommended MATADOR's approval, President Ford might well have sent the *Explorer* on a high-risk journey to the recovery site. There, the superpowers would have stood toe-to-toe on the brink of an armed conflict, all so the CIA could salvage the damaged remains of a 1950s-vintage submarine, a target that many top officials believed held limited value.

Thankfully, cooler heads prevailed. The main question was no longer whether the lift hardware would work, but rather "what the Soviets would do," interjected Kissinger, who expressed serious reservations about the submarine operation for the first time. Dobrynin had lodged a back-channel protest, he told the 40 Committee. And a Soviet tug remained at the recovery site. Officials had delayed the meeting in hopes that the Soviets, observing no activity there, would eventually leave. But they hadn't left. The ATF *MB-26* remained on guard more than two months later, a fact that weighed heavily on the panel's deliberations. "The Soviets intend to maintain their surveillance at the target site," Kissinger observed.

A "second mission would be too risky," remarked State Department intelligence director Bill Hyland.

Undeterred, Duckett mentioned that some members of Congress who had been briefed "wanted to go ahead." The CIA would owe its congressional overseers an explanation if it didn't follow through.

Kissinger responded that he "saw no way we could go back when there is a Soviet ship right at the site and what we propose to do is clearly illegal."

Colby refused to concede the illegality of the operation, but he agreed that "the risk of Soviet reaction was too great" to go ahead.

To Kissinger, it appeared "that the Soviets will block a second attempt and that it would really take very little to disrupt our efforts." True, contingency plans called for the U.S. Navy's Pacific Fleet to render assistance in the event the Soviets took "severe hostile action." But it would take time for the navy to sail to the recovery site, and its arrival could escalate matters if Soviet forces were present as well. Nobody wanted a repeat of the *Mayaguez* incident, in which Cambodian forces seized, on May 12, 1975, a U.S. merchant ship, the USS *Mayaguez*, in international waters. Determined to avoid another *Pueblo*-like hostage crisis, Ford took decisive action, ordering a military mission to rescue the boat's crew. The president managed to secure the captives' release, and his strong response won plaudits for demonstrating American resolve after Saigon's fall. But more than forty U.S. servicepeople died in the fighting. And, though the Soviets were unlikely to replay the Cambodian action, the *Mayaguez* incident served as a reminder both of the vulnerability of unarmed American vessels to foreign attack and of the grave risk to U.S. soldiers ordered to rescue their crews.[52]

"Why get into an argument with them [the Soviets] on this?" asked Kissinger. Nobody answered, and the 40 Committee voted to recommend Project MATADOR's termination. "There was not a chance that we could send the *Glomar* out again on an intelligence project without risking the lives of our crew and inciting a major international incident," Colby recalled.[53]

*　*　*

"It is now clear that the Soviets have no intention of allowing us to conduct a second mission without interference," Kissinger informed the president, citing the oceangoing tug that remained on station. "Our recovery system is vulnerable to damage and incapacitation by the most innocent and frequent occurrences at sea—another boat coming too close or 'inadvertently' bumping our ship." "Aggressive and hostile" action was also possible, including a direct confrontation with Soviet naval vessels. The 40 Committee had concluded that the risk of a Soviet reaction was too great to warrant a second recovery attempt, and Kissinger advised Ford to terminate MATADOR. The president initialed his approval on June 16, 1975, quietly bringing the program to a close some seven years and one month after U.S. intelligence first located the wreckage of the G-722.[54]

Soviet leaders took de-escalatory steps too. In April, at a diplomatic reception in Moscow, Alexei Kosygin greeted Stoessel with what struck the U.S. ambassador as "ostentatious cordiality." "Within earshot of many Soviet and East European bigwigs," the premier assured Stoessel of the Soviet Union's "desire to continue on the path of détente despite 'those' who try to drive a wedge between the two countries." Kosygin went on to express pleasure that W. Averell Harriman—an "old friend" who had overseen the World War II–era Soviet-American alliance as U.S. ambassador to Moscow from 1943 to 1946—was scheduled to return to Moscow to lead the U.S. delegation observing Victory in Europe Day. And Kosygin asked Stoessel to pass along his and Brezhnev's "warmest wishes" to Kissinger and Ford.[55]

On April 10, Brezhnev sent a message to Kissinger for delivery to Ford. The general secretary, the translated message began, had "attentively considered" what Kissinger said during his March 29 conversation with Dobrynin "regarding the firm intention of the United States government and of the president personally to continue the policy of relaxation of tensions and also regarding the fact that the president did not intend to undertake any actions either of an internal or international nature which might bring into conflict the United States and the Soviet Union or harm their relationship." Soviet leaders, the message continued, "take note of the president's assurances in this respect and on their part would like to reemphasize that their own intentions are also the same. Of this, the president can rest firmly assured. We . . . stand for the deepening and widening of mutual understanding and cooperation between our countries."[56]

Dobrynin called Kissinger to reinforce Brezhnev's message moments before the embassy dictated it to the White House. "It is something that Brezhnev wanted you to tell the president," Dobrynin said of the note, which was supposed to convey two impressions—one, that Soviet leaders had noted the president's assurances; and two, that Brezhnev's intentions were the same as Ford's—namely, "the firm assurance and mutual understanding and cooperation between our countries." Dobrynin went on to sketch out more detailed plans for a Brezhnev-Ford summit meeting to coincide with the upcoming Conference on Security and Cooperation in Europe, scheduled to begin in Helsinki in late July. He invited Kissinger to Moscow for preparatory talks in May.[57]

Soviet officials continued to include *Glomar* among their list of grievances against the United States. When Kissinger met Andrei Gromyko for those preparatory talks in May, the longtime Soviet foreign minister covered a number of issues, including "the matter of our sunken submarine." "This was a fact that wounded us," Gromyko said, "though we did not give vent to our feelings, for reasons that should be obvious." When Ford met Brezhnev in Helsinki in July, the president expected the general secretary to complain about détente-harming developments such as "the intelligence activities of the US that have received a great deal of publicity."[58] And the tit-for-tat "Intelligence Wars" that *Glomar*'s disclosure sparked still raged just below the surface of détente.

Yet Moscow's restraint—the refusal of Soviet officials to "give vent to our feelings" of "wounded" pride, as Gromyko put it—matched Washington's. And it indicated "a willingness to maintain the posture of détente." Or at least it appeared that way to CIA analysts. "The U.S. government's 'no comment' posture has achieved the objective of not forcing an official Soviet comment on this subject," the agency concluded in May. Kissinger and Dobrynin's conspiracy of silence operated behind the scenes as a face-saving device that enabled the superpowers to avoid becoming embroiled in the sort of public posturing that doomed previous fence-mending efforts. As Colby later boasted, *Glomar*, unlike the U-2, never became the center of an international incident.[59]

In that sense, then, the Glomar response served as a diplomatic master-stroke in miniature, one that gave legs to détente, enabling the appearance of good Soviet-American relations to continue a while longer. Henry Kissinger certainly thought that was the case. Secrecy, he told President Ford months later, was the major "difference between the U-2 and the *Glomar*," the key variable that explained why "the one was a blow up and the other wasn't."[60]

8

SHIVERING FROM OVEREXPOSURE

The White House's refusal to address the March 1975 press reports may have avoided a Cold War showdown. But it left the CIA to face the tough questions alone. "What would be on a submarine that sank in 1968 that we didn't know about in 1974 or 1975?" asked Senator Stuart Symington (D-Missouri), a onetime CIA loyalist who had since broken with the agency over its secret paramilitary war in Laos. "If they were looking for codes, well, anybody would know that the Russians wouldn't be using the same codes." Symington said he would have expressed concern had he been consulted in advance. But he insisted he hadn't been briefed by the CIA, even though he had been a senior member of the Senate Armed Services intelligence subcommittee ever since the program's inception.[1]

Symington couldn't verify reports of the operation's $350 million cost because the spending was buried in other items spread across the federal budget over a number of years. Only select legislators—just seven on all of Capitol Hill, CBS's Daniel Schorr estimated—knew where. Most elected representatives remained in the dark, including some who, like Symington, sat in Congress's innermost sanctums. And no public document specified the program's cost, Schorr commented, even "though the Constitution says there must be a public accounting for public money."[2]

Symington announced that he would summon CIA director William Colby to appear before Congress. "I want to know what they did and how much it cost and who they told about it," Symington said. He promised to hold CIA leaders to account.

Representative Lucien Nedzi acknowledged that he had been briefed as chair of the House Armed Services intelligence subcommittee. But he wanted another look now that he chaired the House Select Committee on Intelligence, the panel formed in February 1975 to spearhead the lower chamber's review. "This is obviously a big project," said the Michigan Democrat. "For us to ignore it would not be proper under the circumstances."

"If the CIA can spend $350 million to pay Howard Hughes to raise an obsolete eighteen-year-old Russian submarine, then I think the agency needs a cost-to-benefit ratio," remarked Senate intelligence committee chair Frank Church (D-Idaho). "Now wonder we're going broke," added Church, who pledged to look into the matter as part of his committee's probe. "You know," he explained, "there are limits to how much we can spend for this or any other activity."[3]

To Senator Jacob Javits, the disclosure showed that the CIA had been "practically autonomous" for too long. "We have got to fashion means to supervise and monitor everything it does and see that it is authorized by Congress," said the New York Republican. Congressional supervision should cover intelligence gathering, Senator Alan Cranston (D-California) specified.[4]

Inability—Congress's to limit the scale of the program, and the CIA's to pull it off—raised eyebrows. The spy agency's failure to complete the mission, find the missing paper, or keep it all under wraps made it seem incompetent. Even supporters had to admit that security officers' clumsy attempts to secure the sensitive file made them look less like James Bond spymasters than "boys playing at cops and robbers."[5]

The Hughes connection may have been the most damaging disclosure, though. Hughes may have once been highly regarded, but by 1975, the sixty-nine-year-old had fallen into disrepute. Since leaving Las Vegas, he had crisscrossed the globe in an effort, critics speculated, to avoid the long arm of American law. News of his pact with the CIA found him under prosecution by the Justice Department on federal charges of stock manipulation and conspiracy growing out of his 1968 purchase of Air West airlines. And the Watergate Special Prosecution Force continued to scrutinize his $100,000 gift to then president Richard Nixon's friend, Bebe Rebozo. Reporters could find only circumstantial links between Hughes's giving and the taxpayer-funded contracts he received to front the *Glomar* operation. But the *Los Angeles Times* did obtain the transcript of the conversation in which Charles Colson cast doubt on the deal. The ex-Nixon aide told a private investigator that former Hughes fixer Robert Maheu "handles all CIA work for CIA," implying that he may have effectively purchased the naming rights to the *Glomar Explorer* in giving the Hughes cash to Rebozo.[6]

Colson served a prison sentence for obstructing justice in the Watergate probe, and the investigator suspected he made his statement to deflect blame from the White House. His claim, though, led reporters to review the sworn testimony Maheu had given in 1974 in his defamation suit against Hughes. Maheu told a Los Angeles jury that Hughes wanted to serve as a front for the CIA to protect his businesses from federal regulation.[7]

Maheu's claim seemed baseless at first. It rang truer now that the secret behind the *Hughes Glomar Explorer* was out. "He wanted it so that Uncle Sam could never take after him," Maheu explained. "If he got in a jam with the Internal Revenue Service or the Securities and Exchange Commission, they couldn't afford to touch him because of what he was doing with the CIA."[8]

* * *

Assassination, covert action, domestic spying—*Glomar* paled in comparison to the various shocks that had rippled outward during the Year of Intelligence, each of which discredited and weakened the CIA. But news of the agency's alliance with one of the world's most furtive men on an ill-fated mission did nothing to raise its stature. Initially, the headlines only made things worse.

Watergate was in the rearview mirror by March 1975, with former CIA director Richard Helms having kept the agency out of the spotlight. But disclosure of the *Hughes Glomar Explorer*'s true purpose moved the Church Committee to reopen the case. The committee would find, Watergate investigators told reporters, that E. Howard Hunt, the Nixon White House Plumber who co-organized the June 1972 break-in at Democratic National Committee headquarters, was employed at the time by the Robert R. Mullen Company, a DC-based public relations firm that acted as a CIA front and listed Hughes's corporation as a client; that Hunt and his fellow Plumber, G. Gordon Liddy, worked with Hughes representatives on another plan to break into a Las Vegas safe said to contain Maheu's files documenting his former boss's political contributions, including to Rebozo; and that, although that black bag job was aborted, investigators strongly suspected that the Watergate burglars targeted the files of Maheu's friend, Hughes's onetime Washington lobbyist, DNC chair Lawrence O'Brien.[9]

What motivated the break-in? Was there really a Hughes connection to Watergate? A CIA link? Investigators couldn't say for sure. But the appearance of impropriety made the CIA look guilty by virtue of its association with the shadowy tycoon at a time when revelation after revelation of previously unimaginable deeds—of high government officials plotting and covering up crimes—made anything seem possible. Conspiracy appeared to lurk around every corner. And *Glomar* dredged up a past the CIA wanted to forget, recalling Senator Howard Baker's claim that Americans had seen only some of the animals crashing around in the forest.[10]

Watergate wasn't the only skeleton *Glomar* unearthed. To be clear, Robert Maheu wasn't supposed to be part of the CIA's submarine plan. Helms considered him a security risk. And Colby praised his predecessor for having the foresight to exclude Maheu from the outset.

But once Maheu's name resurfaced in conjunction with *Glomar*, reports linked him to one of the most notorious schemes in CIA history: the Kennedy-era plot to assassinate Cuban leader Fidel Castro in league with organized criminals. Church Committee investigators subpoenaed Maheu. After receiving immunity from prosecution, he appeared before the committee in May 1975, testifying that he had indeed served as the CIA's go-between with known Mafia figures on plans to kill Castro.[11]

CIA defenders were quick to point out that those plans never came to fruition. Castro continued to harangue the United States from Havana. To Senator Church, however, Maheu's confirmation of the murder plot offered further proof that the CIA behaved, as he famously said, "like a rogue elephant on a rampage." Word of the plot increased his committee's determination to take a deeper look at the spy agency—and its ties to the Hughes organization.[12]

The full extent of that relationship remains undisclosed to this day. But more became known as a result of *Glomar*'s end, which inadvertently put the "Invisible Billionaire" on display. "For a man who has made an obsession of his personal privacy," Hughes was in the news more "than the most avid publicity seeking movie star," the *Las Vegas Sun* observed following the mission's unveiling.[13]

Journalists reported that the Hughes Aircraft Company built intelligence satellites and employed former high-ranking CIA officials.[14] They reported that Hughes entities served to disguise CIA clandestine activity across the world. And they reported that Summa was one of at least twenty American companies that provided commercial cover for CIA operatives. The list, an intelligence source told the *New York Times*, read like a "who's who" of businesses in fields such as heavy industry, petroleum, banking, travel, public relations, and journalism.

Though nonofficial cover is a long-standing intelligence practice, its existence was generally unknown at the time, even within participating corporations. To protect the safety of undercover agents working overseas, the CIA's clandestine service tried to limit knowledge to the smallest possible number of executives. Which explained why the service preferred to work with corporations, like Hughes's, that were "wholly owned by a single individual, closely held, or headed by a dominant and aggressive chief executive officer," said the source, who went on to describe operational methods—namely, how cover arrangements worked, who the CIA recruited to serve as clandestine agents, and what techniques agents used to cultivate their fictional identities.

Commercial cooperation came at a price. How much and what kind of compensation individual businesses received in exchange for lending their names and reputations to shield covert CIA activities varied from case to case. Officials maintained that Hughes Tool, for example, earned only a modest profit for producing the pipe string the *Glomar Explorer* used to lower the capture vehicle. But other firms forced the CIA to "pay through the teeth," the *Times*'s source said. And some "attempted to take advantage of their special relationships by approaching the agency to seek some official favor from the government."[15]

Congressman Michael Harrington called for an investigation. Months earlier, in late 1974, Harrington, a vocal CIA critic, had helped expose the covert effort to destabilize Salvador Allende's democratically elected Marxist government in Chile. The role that an American firm, International Telephone and Telegraph, played in that effort alerted the Massachusetts Democrat to the obscure links that existed among certain domestic corporations and U.S. intelligence agencies, and to the possible dangers those links posed to open society.

News reports of the *Glomar Explorer*'s stopover in Chile during the height of the 1973 military coup that toppled Allende heightened Harrington's concern.[16] But what really troubled him were other reports indicating that U.S. contractors such as Hughes Tool knowingly filed false tax, disclosure, or other statements that misrepresented the character and purpose of the *Glomar Explorer*, and also that self-identified CIA agents pressured local and federal authorities to look the other way. Harrington cited these accounts as evidence of wrongdoing: the CIA and its contractors, he alleged, had attempted to thwart federal regulations or evade U.S. law in order to shield the sub-raising mission. And he wondered whether the CIA had been fatally compromised by its association with Hughes—an individual, Harrington noted, whose past corporate practices had put him in an adversarial relationship with the Department of Justice, the Internal Revenue Service, and other arms of the federal government.[17]

Like others, Harrington believed that Hughes received a sweetheart deal. He suspected that the lack of competitive bidding for black contracts inflated *Glomar's* multimillion-dollar price tag. And he wanted to know whether Hughes received other considerations in exchange for his participation, and if they included protection from federal authorities, as Maheu alleged. "Should domestic corporations be allowed to violate U.S. regulatory laws in order to carry out covert programs for the CIA? Should the CIA, in turn, be allowed to pressure our independent regulatory commissions to violate their own statutes to further the covert operation?" Harrington asked in a May 1975 letter calling upon the chair of the House Government Operations Subcommittee on Legislation and National Security to approve an investigation.

The Hughes-CIA nexus suggested that the "corporate-intelligence complex," as Harrington called it, was large and growing. How far it extended was anyone's guess. And the House, he argued, should determine what functions businesses performed for the intelligence community, how those functions were performed within the constraints of the U.S. legal system, and whether legislative controls were needed.[18]

* * *

Colby, consumed with trying to keep the submarine program out of the headlines, had played mostly defense to that point. But the attacks on the CIA had grown too strong. The year's revelations left the CIA "extremely vulnerable," he recalled. Opponents demanded the regulation, the dismemberment, even the abolition of the agency. "Abolish the CIA!" the ordinarily moderate *Newsweek* shouted in April.[19]

Glomar's unmasking, in particular, threatened to strip the CIA of its cloak of secrecy. According to the executive editor of the *U.S. News and World Report*, the public's insistence on the right to know had grown to rival the ability of authorities to protect national security data. The result—exposure of an active intelligence operation—was predictable, he wrote. Should this trend continue, it could force America's spies to come in from the cold. And if that happened, the beneficiaries would be not the American people, but those who wished them harm.[20]

Time agreed. *Glomar*'s outing was the clearest indication yet that the intelligence investigations had left the CIA "Shivering from Overexposure."[21] The agency, the magazine suggested, faced the deepest existential crisis in its twenty-eight-year history.

Importantly, however, *Glomar* also offered the CIA's defenders a place to take a stand. Things may not have gone exactly as planned. Technically, though, the underwater mission was a marvel. The degree of skill and ingenuity displayed by the CIA in plumbing the depths was impressive. And AZORIAN's underlying premise was unassailable: acquiring military-grade foreign intelligence was what the CIA was supposed to do. Plus, MATADOR was ongoing at the time of its disclosure. In those respects, the program stood apart from prior Year of Intelligence disclosures. By revealing it, the news media was susceptible to charges of harming national security.

"Your triumphs are unheralded, your failures are trumpeted." Colby cited those words—spoken by President John Kennedy during a 1961 visit to CIA headquarters—to argue that the agency needed to go on the offensive and tell its side of the story. Normally an asset, secrecy had become a liability in the sunshine era, Colby realized. Excessive secrecy magnified the CIA's vices, concealed the spy agency's virtues, and contributed to the cloud of scandal that darkened even legitimate collection activities like *Glomar*.[22]

Colby vowed to break the silence, to speak out on behalf of the besieged agency to which he had devoted his life's work. "This meant," he recalled, "that I had to cooperate with the investigations and try to educate the Congress, press, and public, as well as I could, about American intelligence, its importance, its successes and its failings. The agency's survival, I believed, could only come from understanding, not hostility, built on knowledge, not faith."

Traditionally, intelligence chiefs avoided the public eye. Colby's departure from this norm met with strong opposition from current and former officials who insisted that openness could only damage intelligence institutions. But he felt that the situation demanded some degree of public accountability, and that he could be relatively transparent without exposing essential secrets such as the names of clandestine agents, the details of collection methods, and the identities of ongoing activities.[23]

So William Egan Colby took center stage. To be sure, directors of central intelligence had given speeches before. Richard Helms, for instance, once urged newspaper editors to take it on faith that intelligence officers were honorable men devoted to the nation's service. But in 1975, the agency reached out to the public as never before, with the goal of bolstering its standing by projecting an image of competence and openness and, counterintuitively, by putting a positive spin on secrecy. In the process, the CIA established one of the bases of its modern public affairs strategy, a strategy, scholars say, that dramatically reshaped how Americans perceived the spy agency.

Colby served as the campaign's chief proselytizer. "A public informed of the CIA's accomplishments and capabilities will support it. A public aware of its true mission and the limits of its authority will accept it," he wrote. "A public convinced of the CIA's value will help protect its true secrets."[24]

Glomar qualified as a true secret in Colby's book. President Ford's gag order prohibited him and other U.S. officials from directly addressing the operation in public. It didn't prevent them from speaking indirectly or on background, though. And what they said was influential because, as the *Washington Post* noted, outsiders weren't fully equipped to judge the top-secret program. Only insiders could claim to know all the facts, including what the *Explorer* did or did not haul up.[25]

National security provisions effectively gave intelligence experts the last word. Current and former officials used it to defend the program, starting with the CIA's decision to join forces with Hughes. Whatever arrangement the agency may have once had with Robert Maheu was strictly "compartmented" and had no bearing on *Glomar* or any other working relationship with the vast Hughes empire, they assured reporters. The CIA chose Hughes to front the sub-raising mission not because Richard Nixon said so, but because of Hughes's reputation as a dedicated patriot and trusted keeper of secrets.[26]

As for the mission itself, one unnamed source, identified only as a top CIA official, told *Time* that the sunken Soviet sub, though admittedly older, contained a treasure trove of otherwise unattainable information. Never before had American experts acquired a Soviet nuclear warhead, cipher machine, or codebook, much less a submarine. And the CIA targeted those items in hopes of gaining fresh insight into the state of Soviet nuclear technology, encrypted communication, and naval capability—that is, in hopes of gaining an edge in the underwater Cold War that raged, readers learned, mostly sight unseen beneath the surface. Raising the Golf offered "an absolutely unique, unprecedented opportunity to capture an entire Soviet code room," said a ranking U.S. intelligence official.[27]

A former official denied published reports claiming that "JENNIFER," as reporters mistakenly called the mission, had faced significant opposition within the national security community. "I don't recall any raging debates about cost or about the importance of [the operation]," the official told *Newsweek*, ignoring the actual disagreements that did occur about those very issues. The salvage mission was legal and unprovocative. Nations spied on one another as a matter of course. "If [Soviet nuclear missiles and codes are] not important to our nation's security, then I don't know what the hell is," the official continued. "I would say that if there was a chance to do it and we did not do it, we have got to be the stupidest people in the world."[28]

Most news accounts reported that the *Explorer* recovered only about one-third of the sub. But, again, assessments of the ship's haul remained officially classified. And as time went on, accounts began to circulate claiming that the ship had actually retrieved the entire submarine—missiles, warheads, code gear, and all. Attributed to intelligence sources, these accounts proved to be inaccurate, and many journalists believed that officials deliberately leaked them to confuse the Soviets. What effect, if any, these reports had on foreign agents remains unknown. But they certainly muddied the waters at home, fostering an impression that the mission was an almost total success.[29]

"It was a fantastic operation," said a high-ranking American, who singled out the ingenious cover the CIA developed to hide the true intent of the enormous undertaking. Other officials praised the sophisticated technology the agency deployed to reach the ocean bottom. The *Glomar Explorer* marked a revolutionary advance in intelligence tradecraft, one source told

U.S. News and World Report. "Think of what the U-2 launched in terms of intelligence coverage. The submarine-salvage ship now also opens a whole new field of technology."[30]

As for Colby, he spoke on the record but in conditional terms. Had a salvage operation like the one described in the news succeeded, he said, without confirming or denying anything, it "would have been the biggest single intelligence coup in history."[31]

Colby also turned the tables on the press, using the disclosure as a pretext to lecture the public about secrecy's role in protecting America. Some intelligence secrets were essential to national defense, he told *Time* correspondent Strobe Talbott; keeping them required restraint on the part of the media and Congress.[32]

Intelligence officials amplified that message. They told the *New York Times* that the unmasking of an active collection operation like JENNIFER was the clearest indication yet that the inquiries being performed by the media and Congress were doing irreparable harm to the CIA. "We're just so battered at this point," one agency officer said. No secret was safe anymore, said another. "I fear for the country, I really do. I just don't believe that we can compete with the Russians anymore."[33]

Officials enumerated their concerns. Employee morale plummeted in the face of negative reporting that caused a presumption of irregularity to fall over all CIA activities, collection included. Disillusionment spread among junior officers. And an exodus occurred among senior staff, including CIA western hemisphere operations chief David Atlee Phillips, who resigned to organize the Association of Retired Intelligence Officers to defend the agency.[34] (Before exiting, Phillips urged Colby to go public too. "I submitted for his consideration the thought that any organization with a public relations problem of the magnitude of the one tarnishing CIA's image needed some kind of public relations effort to keep matters in perspective."[35])

Soaring ambition had once infused the CIA. And that confidence, that can-do spirit had pushed the agency to do the impossible, to go where no other spy service could, be it to the heavens to collect data with high-altitude aircraft or to the bottom of the sea to salvage a downed Soviet submarine.

But sources told *Time* that intelligence officers—from field agents to headquarters staff—were growing overly cautious, too fearful of being second-guessed in the newspapers or hauled before some congressional committee to mount risky, out-of-the-ordinary operations. *Glomar* might be the last program of its kind, the newsweekly warned. And if excessive supervision prevented such risk taking in the future, national defense would be in jeopardy.[36]

Without secrecy, insiders said that foreign intelligence services and sources, doubtful of the CIA's continued ability to keep their assistance private, were growing less cooperative. And foreigners weren't the only ones pulling back. Leaders of American companies that provided cover or did contractual work for the CIA were also expressing concern that their reputations and businesses would be harmed should their aid become public knowledge.[37]

Businesspeople could point to the unmasking of Hughes's intelligence work, to Representative Harrington's proposed probe of the "corporate-intelligence complex," or to a formal inquiry the Securities and Exchange Commission opened in response to published reports identifying Global Marine Inc. as the firm that designed and operated the *Glomar Explorer* on the CIA's behalf. SEC investigators probed whether the California company misled investors by filing reports in the early 1970s that, in support of the cover story, erroneously identified the ship as the centerpiece of a commercial ocean-mining enterprise. Global Marine faced possible federal penalties, and the company's misfortune served as a cautionary tale, an example of the financial and legal costs that could come from cooperating with the CIA in the new age of transparency.[38]

JENNIFER's unauthorized disclosure cost the United States another shot at recovering the submarine, officials explained, leaving some of the materials U.S. intelligence chiefs had certified as invaluable to national defense unexploited on the seafloor. Never again could the *Explorer* be used in a classified role—its cover had been blown, wasted along with the millions of dollars poured into its development.

Those were significant losses. But some of the program's cutting-edge tradecraft—the intelligence sources and methods CIA's Directorate of

Science and Technology employed to lift the sub from three miles down and hide the massive recovery effort in plain sight for years—was compromised as well, splayed on the front page for anyone (foreign agents included) to see. And the exposure of operational methodology—the "substrata" of intelligence work, as Colby called it—was what most concerned some intelligence officers.[39]

"'We don't care about the newspapers or the news coverage,' one said. 'What we care about is the *other* stuff'—how the cover was organized, how the agency set up missions, and how [it] went about keeping [its] work secret. If such methodology were public knowledge, then daily activities of future covert missions . . . would be very difficult to keep undercover."[40]

Colby, in an April 7 address to the American Newspaper Publishers Association, blamed the "climate of sensationalism" for putting national security at risk. Colby voiced no objection to openness per se. An adversarial relationship between the press and the government was healthy. "Bad secrets"—which he defined narrowly as domestic surveillance and other missteps of the past—needed to be exposed. But "good secrets" also existed, and Colby insisted that they were necessary if the U.S. intelligence community were to fully contribute to America's defense.

Necessary secrets included the characteristics of highly sensitive, highly technical collection systems. Without naming the *Glomar Explorer*, Colby said that the U-2 and "certain other activities" of which his listeners might have recently become aware had revolutionized intelligence gathering, enabling the United States to hoover up vast amounts of previously inaccessible data that provided analysts with greater clarity as to what Soviet military planners were doing behind the Iron Curtain. However, he added, such systems—and the bureaucracies that managed them—tended to be large, expensive, and susceptible to exposure. The slightest breech could render them useless, enabling America's foreign adversaries to take evasive action.

To protect state secrets, Colby urged news executives to exercise greater responsibility in handling sensitive information that came to their attention. The press, he suggested, had behaved irresponsibly of late. But he had reason to believe that a sense of duty was returning. Again, without naming *Glomar*—a story then in the news after editors withheld it from publication for thirty-nine days following the initial *Los Angeles Times* leak—he said he found journalists more receptive to arguments that certain information ought not to appear in print for security reasons. And he expressed hope that the trend would continue, for the indiscriminate release of legitimate secrets put intelligence collection as well as national safety at risk. "Intelligence by its very nature needs some secrets if its agents are to survive, if its officers are to do their work, and if its technology is not to be turned off by a flick of a switch."[41]

* * *

Colby did not get the same applause editors had given Helms. Too much change had occurred in the media's—and the nation's—relationship with the CIA. His message resonated nonetheless—"particularly," an internal study found, with "the media outside the Eastern liberal press."[42]

Nationwide, more than two-thirds of newspaper editorials declared "The Great Submarine Snatch" a major victory for U.S. intelligence as well as American know-how. "An astonishing feat," crowed the *Cincinnati Post*. "Remarkable," exclaimed the *Long Island Press*. "A triumph of American technology, an example of intelligence-gathering at its best," announced the *Arizona Republic*.[43]

Such support was unexpected given the prevailing anti-CIA climate. And not everyone got on board. The *Nashville Tennessean*, for example, found it hard to believe that a businessman like Hughes "with his reputation for turning a profit did not have some incentive in addition to his patriotism" for cooperating with the CIA. The Hughes connection disturbed the *Dayton Daily News* in light of the large and well-documented contributions the billionaire had given over the years to Nixon, whose administration approved the multimillion-dollar submarine program. Tellingly, Black newspapers like the *Atlanta Daily World*, the *Baltimore Afro-American*, and the *Pittsburgh Courier* paid no attention to the story, passing over in silence reports that the government had gone to such great expense at a time when so many Americans were in need.[44]

But most outlets were too captivated by JENNIFER's novelistic quali-
ties to voice doubts. Underwater espionage, impossible technology, a reclusive billionaire—the story of the *Hughes Glomar Explorer* read as if it had
been ripped from the pages of "Jules Verne, with an update from Ian Fleming," remarked *Los Angeles Times* editors. Enthralled, the paper ranked the
CIA operation among "the greatest exploits in the history of espionage."[45]

Glomar's space-age technology amazed the news-consuming public.
Outlets published photographs showing the *Glomar Explorer*, artwork
illustrating (often inaccurately) what techniques the ship used to raise the
submarine, and stories examining how those sophisticated methods might
conquer the oceans. Enthusiasts likened the lift operation to the most
advanced U.S. collection efforts known at the time, including the Berlin
Tunnel, the U-2 spy plane, and GAMMA GUPPY, a signals intelligence
program that intercepted conversations Soviet leaders had on their limou-
sine telephones. *Time* said that the mission amounted to an underwater
moonshot insofar as it "pushed the limits of engineering and technology
almost as far as Project Apollo," the space program that took American
astronauts to the moon in 1969. Never before had an intelligence service
gone so far to recover something as large as a submarine from such a great
depth, the newsweekly notified readers.[46]

"Following all the painful headlines of recent months," *Newsweek*
remarked, the CIA showed "it could take on a real-life Mission Impossible, and make it nearly possible after all." What enabled the CIA to do the
impossible? Imagination, said news outlets. Only an inventive intelligence
service could develop a plan to do what others couldn't—and keep the ambitious undertaking secret for years. The mission, said the *New York Daily
News*, displayed the CIA at its best, "alert, imaginative, energetic and ingenious." "Audacious and imaginative," JENNIFER exemplified top-quality
spy work in the eyes of the *Chicago Tribune*.[47]

Even the editorial board of the *New York Times*—publisher of so many
Year of Intelligence scoops—commended the CIA's underwater foray. "Certainly imaginative," the effort opened new frontiers, the *Times* said. Like
Apollo, it brought a hitherto inaccessible environment within the ambit of
the United States. What exactly the country could accomplish there

remained uncertain. But it obviously opened a new playing field for intelligence collection, and possibly also a new platform for the projection of U.S. power. Some claimed, unironically, that the project had already pioneered a new industry—deep-sea mining—and put American firms squarely in the lead![48]

To supporters, the story of how America's spies went to the ends of the earth rebutted talk of U.S. decline, offering reassuring evidence that the United States, despite all the trials and tribulations of the sixties and seventies, remained ahead in its Cold War competition against the Soviet Union. *Chicago Tribune* editors, for example, encouraged readers to take "pride and comfort" in the knowledge that Americans were technologically able to locate and reach a foreign submarine at a depth of more than three miles, whereas the Soviets were apparently unable to pinpoint the craft at all. True, JENNIFER failed to achieve complete success. All in all, however, the *Tribune* found that the project merited "a 'well done' rather than a congressional investigation."[49]

"Something's Right with America," the *Philadelphia Inquirer* affirmed in a headline. Self-doubt wracked the country, but the exploits of the *Glomar Explorer*—a product of American initiative built in nearby Chester, Pennsylvania, the *Inquirer* boasted—provided 50,500 long tons of proof that the United States still had the right stuff to lead. In that sense, the ship, arguably the world's most technically advanced, acted as both "a marvelous accomplishment and a proud promise."[50]

To *New York Times* columnist James Reston, JENNIFER demonstrated that the United States retained a commanding lead in the "Battle for the Oceans," as he called the Cold War's inner-space race. "Washington is in trouble these days on the ground that it can't run an economy, that it has no imagination, no leaders and no vision of the future. Maybe it's not as unimaginative or crippled as it looks," remarked Reston, for Washington—unlike Moscow, apparently—possessed the ability to "hear a bump on the bottom of the ocean thousands of miles away, and find a submarine on the vast floor of the Pacific."[51]

A rare bit of good news in an otherwise dismal period for the CIA, *Glomar* changed the conversation, refocusing attention on what the besieged agency was doing right, as opposed to what it had done wrong. "The CIA Was Doing Its Job," declared a *Washington Star* editorial, which observed that, in attempting to recover the Soviet sub, the agency had done precisely what it was supposed to do: discover as much as possible about the military capabilities and intentions of America's most powerful adversary. "It wasn't shadowing U.S. dissidents around Washington or New York." Nor was it plotting to assassinate foreign leaders. Rather, "it was out on the high seas performing a function that was legitimate and potentially of high intelligence value."[52]

Gathering intelligence was a core mission of the CIA, and news organizations across the country applauded the agency for going to extreme lengths to fulfill it. "Hooray for the CIA!" cheered the *Atlanta Constitution*. "Let's hear one for the good, old CIA," the *Anchorage Daily Times* implored.[53]

* * *

Stranger than fiction, the *Glomar* story fascinated readers. But should it have been told? No, foreign policy conservatives answered. Concerned that transparency was moving too far, too fast, resulting in the indiscriminate release of sensitive information, hawks rallied around *Glomar*. They pointed to the program's revelation as a prime example of the cost of openness, and the media became the villain in their version of events.

"One of the most damaging and irresponsible leaks in United States intelligence history," veteran *New York Times* military correspondent Hanson Baldwin wrote of the disclosure. Journalists, he conceded, struggled to balance the public's right to know with the imperative of protecting national security. But he believed news organizations—including, pointedly, his employer, the *Times*, which had put its imprimatur on Jack Anderson's account—behaved recklessly in this case. Acting in the name of press freedom, the news media damaged America's defense of freedom from communist dictatorship by exposing an ongoing intelligence operation aimed at the USSR—and a highly technical one at that. Blowing *Glomar*'s cover, he said, deprived the United States of a valuable collection asset that had taken many years and extensive resources to develop. Henry Kissinger, for his part, ranked *Glomar* among the "most pointless—and damaging—disclosures" of his eight-year tenure in office.[54]

Ronald Reagan led the counterattack. The former California governor seldom attended Rockefeller Commission meetings, critics clucked. Yet his membership on the commission made him a national authority on intelligence matters. From that perch, he defended the sub-raising mission as a justifiable attempt to measure Soviet military capabilities. Testing a line that would become a standard feature of conservative messaging, he also accused the liberal media of being insufficiently concerned about national security. "I just think it was irresponsible to publish it," he told a news conference. "Freedom of speech and freedom of the press are wonderful, but sometimes I think we shouldn't say something just because we have found it out."[55]

Asked about the public's right to know what the CIA was doing, Reagan responded, "I don't think the public has a right to know if the government legitimately knows it cannot inform the public without at the same time informing the Soviet Union and thus rendering this (information) useless from the standpoint of national security." "I think the people understand that," he added.[56]

Reagan also devoted radio commentaries to the *Glomar Explorer* and its role in the unfolding intelligence investigations. Reagan began recording nationally syndicated broadcasts in 1975 to raise his profile in anticipation of a possible presidential run. Reaching twenty to thirty million listeners each week, they dealt with domestic and foreign policy, including national defense and intelligence. *Glomar*, he said in one broadcast, represented an achievement of historic proportions. But it had fallen victim to a "witch-hunting mood" that bedeviled the media and Congress into doing "inestimable harm . . . to this Nation's entire intelligence gathering ability." As evidence, Reagan cited intelligence personnel who, unlike in the forward-leaning days of yore, were "retreating into a 'don't stick your neck out' posture," that is, who were growing too cautious to again mount an ambitious undertaking like JENNIFER. The CIA's ability to protect Americans by monitoring America's foremost adversary, the Soviet Union, would surely suffer if the media and Congress continued to air the agency's dirty laundry.[57]

Shooting the messenger was an attempt by CIA defenders to shift blame onto the news media for exposing the agency's controversial activity and away from the activity itself. It prompted a wide-ranging debate about the media, the government, and their competing duties with respect to national security data in an age that demanded greater transparency. What secrets needed keeping and why? How far did the new openness extend? Had the public's right to know grown to eclipse the executive branch's ability to protect national security? Should journalists prioritize informing the people or guarding public safety? And on which side of the divide did the *Glomar* story fall? The collective response, observers realized, would go some way toward determining the post-Vietnam, post-Watergate ground rules governing the publication of sensitive data.[58]

Jack Anderson pugnaciously defended his actions. Legitimate secrets existed, he conceded. The imperative of public safety sometimes overrode the right of the people to know. And in those instances, he said he cooperated when U.S. officials urged him to exercise restraint.

In *Glomar*'s case, however, Anderson found Colby's arguments for silence unpersuasive. Officially, the operation was secret. Practically, however, word was already out by the time Colby asked him to withhold publication. The *Los Angeles Times* had published its initial, February 8 report. Dozens of news organizations were following leads. And some of the thousands of federal employees or private contractors who knew about some aspect of the massive undertaking were leaking.

It strained credulity to believe that Soviet intelligence remained unaware of U.S. activities, as Colby insisted was the case. "So the Russians knew. We knew they knew. They knew we knew they knew," Anderson wrote in his March 25 Washington Merry-Go-Round column. Only the American people did not know. But Colby insisted they couldn't be told without "rubbing [the Soviets'] noses in it."

"What was at stake in publishing, then, was not national security but international etiquette, not American secrets but Soviet face, not the sabotage of a second *Glomar* mission but the ruffling of Russian tail feathers,"

Anderson declared. Diplomatic considerations were important. But he regarded them as insufficient reason for "cutting off the news—the windpipe of the American system."

According to Anderson, American taxpayers deserved to know that millions were spent outside of the regular appropriations process on a CIA "gamble to recover an archaic diesel sub, obsolete missiles and outdated codes." Granted, U.S. analysts could have gleaned valuable intelligence from the submarine had it not fallen apart. But was such data worth a sum that could have financed other national priorities, such as homes for the needy, alternative energy research, or other, more efficient means of spying on the USSR. Was *Glomar* truly a military necessity, he asked, or merely an "admiral's toy?"

Such questions could not be answered definitively. But they wouldn't have surfaced at all without the press. As such, *Glomar* served as a powerful reminder that the chief duty of the free and independent press in the American republic was to expose the dark practices of government. Or, as Anderson put it, that reporters "exist not to lie down with the lions but to fend them off, to cause the turmoil by which the free system cleanses and energizes itself."

Journalists needed reminding, Anderson said, because executives' handling of the *Glomar* story showed that the news business had grown overcautious again since Richard Nixon's resignation. Shaken by the fact that they helped oust a president, some top editors and reporters had begun to wear a "hair shirt" in an effort, he claimed, to prove "how patriotic and responsible [journalists] are, [to] prove that we're not against the establishment, the government, that we're not all gadflies." "Older blather" about the press's responsibility to protect state secrets reentered newsroom discussions, drowning out talk about the news media's duty to uncover abuse. "The old pre-Watergate, pre-Vietnam ideals of partnership with government, of cozy intimacy with the high and mighty, of a camaraderie of secrets shared by this peerage but kept from the public, begins to appeal once more to a press concerned that its abrasive successes have earned it a bad name and a hostile reception," Anderson wrote. This retreat was unfortunate, he believed, because the country was ill served by an unwatch-ful press.[59]

The media and its handling of the submarine story *became* the story. News organizations reviewed the press's performance. All agreed that, in *Glomar's* case, national security considerations complicated a problem newsrooms routinely faced: determining when to print a story or when not to. Weigh-ing the public's right to know against the imperative of protecting public safety was not easy. What posed clear and present danger to the nation—the legal threshold for determining what information could or could not be published—often remained unclear. And security restrictions forced edi-tors to make tough decisions without all of the facts, without full access to the classified data officials possessed. Judging the veracity of security claims made by trained intelligence professionals amounted to educated guesswork. "The only place where you could get [complete] information is the CIA itself," said *Washington Post* executive editor Ben Bradlee, "and I'm not sure I'd believe them anyway."[60]

Many sided with Jack Anderson. *Washington Post* ombudsman Charles Seib found that editors surrendered too easily to Colby's national security argument. Editors generally agreed that Colby's job description gave him a license to deceive. Yet they didn't do enough to verify his claims, Seib said. Instead, they accepted them "with a readiness they would have found naïve in one of their reporters." *Glomar* was an illegitimate secret in Seib's view. And media brass, despite their self-congratulatory talk about the press's ability to hold power accountable, were "prime patsies" for protecting it.[61]

New York Times columnist Tom Wicker was similarly struck by the fact that executives of virtually every major news outlet in the country took Colby at his word, despite all of the evidence that had accumulated in recent years showing how government officials routinely invoked national secu-rity to shield themselves from political embarrassment. To Wicker, the widespread cooperation with the spy chief's restraint efforts disproved claims that the media was "anti-government, anti-security, anti-conservative, or pro-leftist." But it also suggested that the press, fearful of being branded as unpatriotic, had little appetite for taking on the intelligence community following Watergate. The "national security mystique," as Wicker called it, remained strong—so strong as to override competing arguments on behalf of publishing a juicy story like *Glomar*.[62]

The *Columbia Journalism Review* reached a clear verdict: Anderson's disclosure endangered no one. Colby's case for censorship rested more on embarrassment than security. By those tests, the *Review* concluded, "the submarine story should have been reported."[63]

News executives stood behind their decisions. *Los Angeles Times* editor William Thomas insisted he had done his homework, questioning CIA officials on at least seven different occasions. However, he said, "I never found anything that could trip them up." "Also the immense amount of technical detail, the graphic detail, the descriptive detail led you to believe [their version of] the story was true."[64]

"We were told that this was an important, ongoing military operation," *New York Times* managing editor Abe Rosenthal explained. "We believed in this case that the advantages of immediate publication did not outweigh the considerations of disclosing an important, ongoing military operation."[65]

Colby made a "rational argument and he laid out the facts as he saw them," added *Washington Post* publisher Katharine Graham. The paper's editors found his security claim persuasive, and they decided not to run the story. Graham was a little uneasy about the decision. But, she said, "if [officials] can prove to you that you are going to hurt your country [by publishing a story] I see nothing wrong with cooperating. And, of course, that is what, in effect, they said."[66]

"Obviously," *Post* editors declared, "this newspaper feels there was valid reason to hold the story while it did. We do not believe that our devotion to the principles and practices of a free press is undercut by the exception made in this case. On the contrary, a willingness to make such exceptions when confronted with compelling arguments from a government in exclusive possession of all the facts of the matter is a mark of a responsible free press."[67]

Such nuanced, inside-baseball arguments about who did what and why made little impression outside the Beltway, where the news media was held collectively responsible all right—but for harming, not protecting,

America's interests. First Amendment protections empowered the press to check government, and journalists performed a public service in uncovering CIA abuses of the past. But newspapers across the country agreed that freedom of the press did not give the media license to damage U.S. security, especially in real time.

Never mind that Seymour Hersh had sat on the *Glomar* story for more than a year, or that Rosenthal had resisted that story's publication in the *New York Times*. The *Detroit News* said the nation paid "a heavy price" for the *Times's* account. Published over Colby's objections, it corroborated Jack Anderson's radio broadcast, encouraging other organizations to publish their versions. Plus, Hersh's piece disclosed a wealth of intelligence details, ranging from how the United States located the Soviet sub to what salvagers recovered. Publishing such data was irresponsible, the *Detroit News* maintained. Should it continue, such conduct threatened to destroy the CIA, reducing America's chance of winning the Cold War.[68]

"We treasure our free press, realizing that freedom of expression and our constitutional system are inseparable," *San Diego Union* editors announced. But any member of the media who knowingly published details of an active intelligence operation over the objections of the nation's spy chief abused their First Amendment privileges. Only the Soviets stood to profit from the disclosure of a state secret like JENNIFER. The paper urged journalists to be more responsible moving forward.[69]

Openness was detrimental to U.S. interests—that was the main lesson cold warriors took from the *Glomar* affair. The superpower competition persisted in spite of détente. Transparency placed the United States at a disadvantage vis-à-vis the USSR, and each new disclosure gave Soviet agents additional insight into CIA activity. U.S. leaders required more, not less, secrecy to defend the nation effectively.

"This is not a marshmallow world. Anyone who thinks the United States can lower its guard and dismantle its intelligence-gathering apparatus is living in a dreamland. Soviet leaders and the KGB no doubt are rubbing their hands in glee over the public fix the CIA has gotten into," observed the *Washington Star*, which joined other publications in calling on Congress to pass tougher security laws that punished not only U.S. officials who leaked classified data without authorization but the journalists who published it.[70]

"Secrecy is vital," declared the editor of the *Tucson Daily Citizen*. In its zeal to peel it back, the press restricted the CIA. And that was dangerous, *Time* explained, because the Soviet Union maintained an extensive espionage network. To compete, the United States had to have "an agency more or less like the CIA, and such an agency must, up to a considerable point, function in secret."[71]

The implications were clear: No longer could the CIA suffer from overexposure. Legitimate secrets needed protection. Put on the defensive, *Los Angeles Times* editors apologized for having disclosed *Glomar* in the first place. The agency's pathbreaking attempt to surveil the deep was worthwhile and provided, they said, "a sobering and salutary reminder of the importance of the intelligence operation. It is a timely reminder, too, because some people, shocked by the abuse of trust and by the violation of law that has characterized some of the things the CIA has done, would do away with spies altogether." Yet it would be a grave mistake, editors continued, to let the national outrage "divert resources from the vital task of maintaining an excellent intelligence apparatus"—especially the part of the apparatus that was technologically adept enough to collect data by launching satellites, unscrambling foreign communications, or embarking on "one of the most astonishing salvage operations in marine history." *New York Times* editors also issued a mea culpa. The CIA's extraordinary submarine mission served, they said, as "a useful reminder of how essential good intelligence is for the national security" in the nuclear age.[72]

* * *

Glomar contributed to the establishment of a post-Vietnam, post-Watergate equilibrium between openness and secrecy, a rebalancing of the public's right to know against the state's ability to withhold information in the name of national security. That was the conclusion reached by Washington columnist Joseph Kraft, who wrote that the submarine incident served to "right the balance." Recent headlines had made the CIA seem like "a kind of post-graduate Ivy League playground where rich boys and girls spied on their countrymen between clumsy efforts to make and unmake foreign governments—preferably by assassination." But *Glomar*'s disclosure showed that intelligence activities "can have a serious purpose which fully justifies secrecy." Undertaken with "high organizational skill and considerable technical ingenuity," the CIA's semi-successful sub-raising mission—an appropriate attempt to collect military data, Kraft noted—gave the country "solid evidence of the high quality and great importance of the work being done by the intelligence community." Colby's national security claims were genuine, Kraft wrote, not a smoke screen to cover up failure or impropriety. And news executives' careful handling of the story demonstrated that the press had not embarked on a "relentlessly hostile, undiscriminating effort to get security agencies," but was instead prepared to treat classified matters responsibly.

According to Kraft, the affair reestablished some degree of trust. It imparted "a modicum of balance and sanity to the raging debate about this country's black operations." Looking ahead, he anticipated that the media and Congress would take greater pains to protect state secrets.[73]

Others sensed the change as well. Watergate heightened public awareness of and sensitivity to government secrecy, giving birth to the "son of Watergate," as CBS's Daniel Schorr dubbed the Year of Intelligence. Like Jack Anderson, however, many journalists saw the powers that be close ranks over *Glomar*. News executives cooperated with Colby's censorship effort "in large measure to prove in the wake of Watergate that they were not irresponsible, that they did have a real sense of the national interest," claimed Roger Wilkins, who earned a Pulitzer at the *Post* before moving to the *New York Times*. Media leaders, Wilkins continued, wanted to demonstrate to government officials that, despite their aggressive coverage of intelligence stories in early 1975, they remained "members in good standing of the club."[74]

Glomar had a chilling effect, then, demonstrating the challenges of covering the intelligence beat and the susceptibility of the press to charges of sacrificing national security for the abstract principle of openness. Fearful of being labeled unpatriotic, concerned about losing access to policy makers and other insiders, the Washington press corps showed signs in March 1975 of becoming "judicious again," according to *New York Times* national security correspondent Leslie Gelb. "Judicious" was one word; William Greider preferred "submissive." To Greider, then a *Washington Post* reporter, the extent to which news executives cooperated with Colby showed that the press, despite all the talk of its being a fearsome watchdog, was content to play the "cozy lapdog" where national security was involved. At the beginning of the Year of Intelligence, the press "snarled at the CIA with its new ferocity," Greider wrote, "but when Director Colby came up with a small bone (the Howard Hughes submarine caper), it rolled over on its back to have its tummy rubbed."[75]

All told, the *Glomar* story acted as "something of a political boon for the CIA," *Washington Post* editors remarked. Following months of painful headlines, news of the far-reaching operation allowed the agency to bask in unexpected praise, cleansing its stained reputation somewhat. The disclosure reinforced the agency's status as an essential collector of intelligence. And the blowback restrained the press, limiting the journalistic revolution before it could expose more secrets U.S. officials classified as crucial to national defense.[76]

In fact, the CIA fared so well that some wondered whether Colby had wanted the story to leak all along. Schorr found Colby's behavior puzzling, especially for someone who supposedly wanted to keep *Glomar* out of the papers. As Colby went from newsroom to newsroom to quash publication, for example, he not only confirmed the sub-raising mission's existence but answered questions, offered clarifications, and volunteered previously unknown details, all in an apparent effort to ensure that news executives understood why the story ought to be withheld. Along the way, Colby or his aides also told journalists who else was covering the story, how their rivals planned to proceed, and, in some cases, what leads they were following—spurring an already competitive situation. "In a way, Colby stimulated pressure to get the story out," remarked Schorr, who suspected that Colby wanted *Glomar* to become public to counteract the bad press the agency was receiving, that he sought "to divert attention to one great thing the CIA did that wasn't illegal, immoral or lethal."[77]

Others suspected that Colby performed a limited hangout, that he volunteered some information in order to withhold other, still-unknown facts from the public. According to this theory, the submarine tale acted as a fallback cover story that distracted reporters from pursuing other, perhaps more sensitive lines of inquiry, like the extent of the agency's relationship with Hughes or the scope of U.S. underwater activity. Perhaps the *Glomar Explorer* was only the tip of the iceberg. Perhaps, *Time* suggested, it served as "the supreme cover for a secret mission as yet safely secure."[78]

Colby dismissed such talk as nonsense. As DCI, he took seriously his legal responsibility to protect any and all intelligence sources and methods from unauthorized disclose. He supported the submarine mission. And he went to great lengths to keep it under wraps, even beyond the point where others thought it was a lost cause. "It has to be fought for. It is damn good," he once told reporters.[79]

But evidence shows that officials did consider capitalizing on *Glomar*'s publication. According to a February 1975 CIA memorandum, drafted while Colby was still struggling to hold the news, the program's disclosure, while harmful in some respects, would provide a case in point demonstrating the need for tougher secrecy laws to protect future intelligence operations from unauthorized disclosure. "The nation would therefore be cutting its losses on this one program, with an aim of overall future benefits." After all, the memo noted, the agency was not obligated to tell the press the whole truth."[80]

Colby reportedly disapproved of this approach. But if it appeared the news was going to break anyway, his duties called for him to shape the narrative to the CIA's advantage. Seasoned journalists familiar with how Washington worked presumed that he used his wide-ranging backgrounders to tell the official side of the *Glomar* story. He briefed reporters, Seib, the *Washington Post* ombudsman, wrote, "to keep some control over the form [the story] would take."[81]

Post managing editor Howard Simons believed that Colby wanted a major newspaper like the *Post* or the *New York Times* to give *Glomar* a "huge splash" in order to show "the agency masterfully pulling off a highly technical spying mission in the hope that news of such a feat would give the beleaguered CIA a public relations lift." "I never heard of an intelligence chief telling an editor more about a matter than the editor knew," Simons said. Colby "was determined to use *Glomar* to repair the CIA's reputation," recalled former *New York Times* associate editor Harrison Salisbury.[82]

"My opinion," *Parade* editor Lloyd Shearer wrote days after the news broke, "is that the CIA wants the story out. At a time when it's been accused of meddling in domestic affairs, when it's being investigated by several congressional committees, it can point to Project JENNIFER as a superb covert operation. Just imagine putting together a project involving more than 4,000 men and keeping it secret for seven years," added Shearer, who was struck, like others, by *Glomar's* scope.[83]

Whatever his motives, Colby seemed pleased with the results. *Glomar*, he later recalled, taught intelligence outsiders "to distinguish between the sensational and the real, the legitimate secrets and the boondoggles."[84] Journalists would publish other intelligence stories. But they had learned the lesson. Would lawmakers?

9

HOLD THE LINE

C IA legislative counsel George L. Cary was leaving a White House meeting on March 7, 1975, when presidential counselor John O. Marsh Jr. pulled him aside for a private chat. Although not widely known outside of Washington, the forty-eight-year-old Marsh was familiar to Cary as a savvy Beltway insider who served four terms in the House and a stint in the Pentagon as assistant secretary of defense for legislative affairs before moving to the White House, where in 1974 he smoothed Gerald Ford's transition to the Oval Office as the then vice president's national security advisor. Cary and Marsh knew each other well enough to speak "bluntly and directly," Cary recalled. So Marsh got right to the point: Frank Church, the Democratic chair of the Senate's select committee, seemed intent on conducting a wide-ranging review of intelligence activities. Intelligence director William Colby was being too cooperative. And the White House was growing concerned about the volume of privileged material that was being disclosed and "the crippling effect it might have on national security mechanisms and presidential authority."

Remarkably, Marsh raised particular concern not about disclosures having to do with domestic spying, or even the assassination plots that Ford had let slip in his February meeting with *New York Times* editors. He mentioned neither the CIA's efforts at mind control via Project MKULTRA, nor the National Security Agency's practice of domestic espionage through Project SHAMROCK, nor any number of potential trouble spots the Church Committee could get into. Rather, he singled out *Glomar*. And his stated reason for doing so had less to do with national security than domestic politics. The goal was withholding from the Democrat-controlled 94th Congress information that could twist individual threads of inquiry into a tangle of apparent wrongdoing, a knot of scandal that could, in the anti-establishment climate of 1975, have far-reaching implications for both the CIA and the White House. According to Cary's account, "Marsh expressed concern that the current investigations would result in the disclosure of links between the *Glomar Explorer* operation and the Hughes Corporation, and between covert U.S. activities in Cuba and Robert Mahue [*sic*] of the Hughes Corporation, as well as Mahue's involvement in Watergate and several other developments." The White House was taking "a more active role" in shielding such matters from congressional review, Marsh said, and he asked Cary to help "hold the line."[1]

Hold the line. Marsh didn't elaborate. But Cary could guess why Ford aides might want to obstruct Congress. Because if investigators were allowed to rummage through the files, they might discover that ex-Hughes executive Robert Maheu was the CIA's chief contact with organized crime on plans to assassinate Cuban dictator Fidel Castro in the 1960s; that Maheu had facilitated Hughes's under-the-table payments to Nixon's friend, Bebe Rebozo, in 1969–1970; and that the Watergate break-in may have been motivated by a desire to learn what Maheu's associate, Democratic National Committee chair Lawrence O'Brien, knew about Nixon's secretive dealings with Hughes.

To be clear, Gerald Ford had nothing to do with Richard Nixon's green-lighting of AZORIAN. Unlike past CIA activities investigated by Congress, though, *Glomar* was directly attributable to him. Plausible deniability would vanish if investigators gained access to White House sources. The files of the 40 Committee documented the fact that Ford himself had authorized MATADOR in February 1975. National Security Council records showed that he had been briefed about the failed recovery attempt in August 1974. And interviews with staff might reveal that his involvement dated from his days as House minority leader. "Ford had known about the operation from the beginning," James Cannon, his assistant for domestic affairs, recalled. "While he was still in the House, Ford had helped the CIA get the $300-million House appropriation to build . . . the *Glomar Explorer*."[2]

Ford, then, was partly responsible for funneling hundreds of millions of taxpayer dollars into a boondoggle to recover an obsolete submarine, as Senator Church saw it—and a fat payday for Hughes, the billionaire scofflaw. That look was bad enough in the austerity economy of 1975. But the Hughes connection to Watergate made things worse. Ford's September 1974 pardon of Nixon for any crimes the former president might have committed while in office haunted Ford's presidency. It fueled speculation that he had secretly agreed to pardon Nixon in exchange for Nixon's resignation, which elevated Ford to the presidency. Those allegations may have been baseless: Ford acted in the national interest, he said, to help the country move on from the Watergate scandal. But they hounded Ford. Rumor circulated that he, too, had accepted contributions from Hughes. And he and his advisors sought to avoid anything connected to Watergate—or Nixon, who cast a long shadow. Dredging up a matter like *Glomar* could possibly derail Ford's 1976 election bid and metastasize the intelligence crisis, resulting in unwanted limitations on presidential authority.[3]

Cary took Marsh's words seriously enough to take an unusual step for an experienced CIA officer trained not to write things down on paper unless absolutely necessary—especially details relating to an active intelligence operation, as MATADOR still was at the time. He drove back to CIA headquarters in Virginia and made a detailed record for the files. Not the next morning, or the one after that—but immediately following his White House meeting with Marsh. And it was a record that documented exactly what was said, by whom and under what circumstances, and on paper whose provenance placed it not in DS&T operational files, where it would be safely off-limits under sources and methods protections, but in legislative (i.e., nonoperational) files more subject to outside review, should anyone care to look. By CIA standards, Cary's action constituted a security breach. Yet he evidently felt the need to document what was said.

* * *

Senator Church's select committee, along with the one led in the House by Representative Otis G. Pike, were serious endeavors. They aimed to expose intelligence missteps in order to improve community performance. And they spoke to the extent to which Congress and its relationship with the CIA had changed since lawmakers first sanctioned the sub-raising mission in 1969. Then, Richard Russell and his ilk defended the CIA from attack. Now, with him gone, the surviving "old lines," as Cary's predecessor called the agency's protectors, were under heavy siege.[4] Elected in Watergate's aftermath, the activist 94th Congress convened in January 1975 determined to clean up Washington, in part by leading what the *Washington Post* termed a "revolution" against the outsized power of the imperial presidency.[5]

No presidential arm seemed more imperious than the intelligence community. Published days before Congress was seated, Seymour Hersh's December 1974 report discredited not only the community but its congressional overseers. To critics, the fact that spy agencies had been able to collect data on thousands of American citizens for years without watchdogs making so much as a noise showed that those "watchdogs" had been asleep all along. House insurgents pushed to remove several committee chairs, including the two who chaired the chamber's standing committees with intelligence oversight responsibilities: seventy-three-year-old F. Edward Hébert (D-Louisiana) of Armed Services and seventy-four-year-old George Mahon (D-Texas) of Appropriations. Hébert lost his post.[6]

Amid calls to curb, reorganize, or even abolish the CIA, Congress also empowered the select committees to perform sweeping reviews. They proceeded to subject the intelligence community to unprecedented scrutiny. Empaneled in January 1975, the Church Committee alone held 126 hearings, interviewed over 800 persons, and reviewed innumerable files documenting subjects ranging from assassination plots and covert actions to illegal mail openings and warrantless searches. Issued in April 1976, its final report found that "mechanisms for, and the practice of, congressional oversight have not been adequate."[7] As a remedy, the chamber established the Senate Select Committee on Intelligence (SSCI), Congress's first standing committee devoted exclusively to intelligence matters.

For these and other reasons, 1975–1976 won acclaim as a watershed moment in the history of intelligence oversight—and of government transparency more broadly. According to former Church Committee staffer Loch Johnson, the SSCI "ushered in a new and promising era of intelligence oversight."[8] To reformers, Congress's improved ability to illuminate the darkest recesses of government secrecy promised to impose greater discipline on America's spy agencies. Closer supervision would prevent spy agencies from committing abuses—or rushing, historian Arthur Schlesinger Jr. wrote in the *Wall Street Journal*, "into bizarre and profligate projects, like Howard Hughes and the *Glomar*." Henceforth, CIA officers figured, it would be more difficult to launch a similarly ambitious scheme to collect foreign intelligence.[9]

Difficult maybe, but not impossible, for many of the promises to investigate turned out to be hot air. Studies have shown how Ford administration officials worked with allies on Capitol Hill to prevent the congressional revolt from entering particularly sensitive areas or placing undue (in their view) restrictions on clandestine activity. Generally speaking, heads didn't roll. The CIA emerged intact. And the "substrata" of intelligence secrets that Colby feared would rise to the surface stayed on the downlow. According to Kathryn Olmsted, the CIA and its sister intelligence agencies "clearly emerged the winners of their long battle with the investigators."[10]

Glomar worked to hold the line against disclosure. The story broke too early to have the decisive effect other events (the tragic assassination of CIA station chief Richard Welch in December 1975, say, or the unauthorized publication of a version of the Pike Committee's report in February 1976) had on the investigations' outcome. But it played a more pivotal role than historians realize, starting with the way in which the program's unmasking served as a rallying point for foreign policy conservatives, against not just the media but the liberal 94th Congress and the self-inflicted damage it was supposedly doing to national defense. True, the sub-raising mission didn't go exactly as planned. And one could question it on cost and other grounds. But its underlying premise was unassailable: Collecting *foreign* intelligence was the CIA's raison d'être. "The CIA Was Doing Its Job," opined the right-leaning *Washington Star*. If the agency couldn't gather military-grade information on the Soviet Union, America's chief rival, supporters argued, then it really couldn't do anything at all—and America, they added, needed a fully functional spy apparatus to win the Cold War.[11]

In that sense, *Glomar* served as a point of departure from *domestic* intelligence collection, the revelation that put hawks on the defensive throughout the first months of the Year of Intelligence. The unauthorized disclosure of the still-active program allowed agency loyalists to take the offensive. "There is no reason to question the propriety of this action," declared South Carolina's Strom Thurmond, the ranking Republican on the Senate Armed Services intelligence subcommittee. In attempting to obtain the useful material thought to be aboard the submarine, "the CIA was only performing the intelligence-gathering functions for which it was created." Instead of condemning JENNIFER, as the project was publicly known, Americans should be offering praise, for the effort, he said, represented "not only an impressive technological achievement, but a timely reassurance of the vigilance and initiative of the American intelligence community."[12]

Similar statements of support came from Senate majority whip Robert Byrd (D-West Virginia), Senate Appropriations chair John McClellan (D-Arkansas), and Richard Russell's protégé, Senate Armed Services chair John Stennis (D-Mississippi). "I knew about, gave surveillance [of], and fully supported this project from its beginning," Stennis's statement began. "It was a highly valuable undertaking, and of the highest interest. It invaded no one's rights." Rather than criticism, the CIA deserved commendation for launching such an ambitious collection effort—the type of job, he noted, for which the agency was created.[13]

History, one could argue, was not on these lawmakers' side. Reforms enacted by the 94th Congress prevented chairs like Stennis from acting as autocratically as they once had. He would lose much of his influence in 1976 when the SSCI took intelligence oversight responsibilities away from his Armed Services Committee.

But statements of support also came from legislators positioned to shield the CIA over the long haul. They included House Appropriations chair George Mahon, who stubbornly remained at the controls despite efforts by House rebels to unseat him. JENNIFFER was a "gamble," he acknowledged, but a worthwhile one. The mission "would have been a good idea if it [had] worked."[14]

They came, too, from the Church Committee's vice chair, Senator John Tower. To him, the operation appeared "extremely valuable." "If the roles were reversed," the Texas Republican remarked, "I'm sure the Soviets would not have any inhibitions about [stealing a downed American submarine]."[15] And from Senator Barry Goldwater, the committee's senior Republican. "I'd have been madder than hell if they hadn't done it," the Arizonan said of the CIA's sub-raising effort. "That's their business, to collect information and intelligence." It was high time that Americans realized that they needed spy agencies to watch the USSR, just as the USSR watched them, Goldwater argued.[16]

His words resonated. Mail poured into his office from constituents endorsing his unapologetic defense of CIA activity. "Bully for you," a Tucson resident wrote.[17] Another forwarded a *Tucson Daily Citizen* editorial, "There Has to Be Secrecy," in which the paper's editor, Paul A. McKalip, bemoaned the bad publicity CIA activities were receiving of late. *Glomar*'s unmasking demonstrated, McKalip wrote, that America's spy service couldn't successfully operate in a fishbowl. Congress and the news media both needed to back off and let the CIA do its job—in secret, without much in the way of oversight. "What I am saying," he concluded, "is that there can be circumstances in which secrecy is vital."[18]

Prescott's deputy sheriff enclosed an *Arizona Republic* editorial that praised the CIA's sub-raising mission in the face of attacks on the agency.

Despite First Amendment concerns, he called for federal prosecution of reporters who published national secrets—as Jack Anderson allegedly had by disclosing *Glomar* on air. "I personally cannot understand why we allow ourselves to be continually weakened from within as a nation by allowing these types of things to go on," the deputy closed.[19]

Because Goldwater, a former Republican presidential nominee, was a nationally known conservative, letters also arrived from like-minded citizens across the country. A New Jerseyan commended him for standing up for the good men and women of the CIA. "These patriotic [Americans] do not deserve the ridicule they have been recently subjected to by some of our liberal politicians and newspaper people. The average citizen is 100% behind the CIA." "Keep up the good work," he encouraged Goldwater, "it is appreciated by those who still love this country."[20]

Goldwater's correspondents were self-selective. Many Americans criticized the multimillion-dollar sub-raising plan.[21] But the grassroots reaction indicated that support for the intelligence inquiries was soft—and that the CIA could be successfully defended on national security grounds. "This is not the Watergate investigation," a Democratic member of Congress acknowledged. "Nobody ever talks to me about it on home trips, and I hear very little about it here [in Washington]."[22]

The show of public support strengthened Goldwater's resolve to protect the CIA. To be sure, Goldwater needed little encouragement to obstruct the Church Committee's inquiry. He was opposed from the start. But as more and more mail arrived—from San Antonio, Texas, and Columbus, Ohio, to Nashville, Tennessee, and back again to Mesa, Arizona—his outgoing letters grew bolder, from April 4, when he assured the New Jerseyan that he would do his utmost to preserve the CIA; to April 13, when he promised the Tucsonan who sent the McKalip editorial that he would work to prevent the agency's "destruction"; to April 16, when he took a partisan step in his response to the deputy sheriff who wanted to jail leakers:

> We are in close agreement on the subject of national intelligence and you
> can be sure that I will continue to make my strong views known. I can
> only suggest that perhaps it is the Democrats, who control the House,

Senate and all Committees, who should be hearing from citizens who believe as you do that secrets are vital to the security of our nation, and were meant to remain secrets.[23]

* * *

At the other end of Pennsylvania Avenue, *Glomar*'s disclosure prompted the White House to take a "more active role," as Jack Marsh said, in order to prevent not only good secrets but bad ones from spilling out, the type that could have a "crippling effect" on presidential authority and national security institutions. William Colby would continue to feature prominently in the saga that played out during the Year of Intelligence. But his mercurial behavior throughout February and March—racing from newsroom to newsroom to plug *Glomar*-related leaks, even as he spoke openly to journalists about the still-classified operation—did little to inspire confidence in him in the White House, where he was already under fire for cooperating with the news media.

In fact, Colby wasn't so loose-lipped. Time and again, we have seen how he told not the whole truth but versions of the truth, curated to protect national security, the reputation of the CIA, or both. We've also seen how he worked to shield the *Glomar* secret, and how he counseled silence even after the operation's cover was blown.

Yet his inability to keep MATADOR secret further discredited him in official eyes. Within hours of Jack Anderson's broadcast, reports circulated in Washington that the president would ask Colby to resign. To *Newsweek*, the intelligence chief's hold on office "looked newly precarious" following disclosure of the less than fully successful operation.[24]

The White House press secretary denied the rumors, and Ford would wait until November to replace Colby. Significantly, however, knowledgeable sources confirmed that the White House was now prepared to take over the job of coordinating the administration's response to Congress's intelligence inquiries. To that point, the White House had tried to distance the president from the controversy, allowing the nation's intelligence chief to serve as gatekeeper. Colby, though, had proven "too damned coopera-tive with the Congress" to perform that role any longer. Acting unilater-ally, the "runaway CIA director," as Henry Kissinger called him, reputedly handed over postmortems and inspector general reports and internal memos and more, sometimes without White House preapproval. He allowed investigators virtually unfettered access to agency records. And these fish-ing expeditions threatened the security of clandestine activity like MAT-ADOR. Only quick action by Chief of Staff Donald Rumsfeld, Kissinger claimed, managed to prevent official disclosure of the CIA's sub-raising mission.[25]

They also affected the balance of power in Washington. "What Colby has done is a disgrace," Kissinger declared. Notoriously secretive, Kissinger stood at the forefront of those who, in Colby's words, "argued that intelli-gence was inherently a presidential function and that the Congress should be kept out of it." Lawmakers, they warned, could not be trusted with intel-ligence secrets. Sharing sensitive data with the antiestablishment 94th Con-gress was tantamount to releasing it to the world, and Ford's advisors vowed to surrender executive material only after a tenacious fight and when there was no alternative.[26]

To Kissinger, Colby's candidness served no purpose other than to pro-long the intelligence crisis. The longer the investigations went on, the more damage they could do: Damage to the CIA's cover arrangements, certainly. Damage to the agency's relationships with foreign partners. And damage to its image, its morale.

But damage, too, to the creativity, the inventiveness that made cutting-edge operations like *Glomar* possible. "The fact of these investigations could be as damaging to the intelligence community as McCarthy was to the For-eign Service," Kissinger warned, smearing the 94th Congress's probes by association with those led by red-baiting Senator Joseph McCarthy in the 1950s. "The result could be the drying up of the imaginations of the people on which we depend."[27]

Near complete secrecy used to shroud intelligence officers from accountability—and that was a good thing, Kissinger explained, because second-guessing could cause them to become too cautious, too risk averse to propose the kind of bold action needed to acquire intelligence, exfiltrate agents, or influence events. ("Cramped caution" became the refuge of once freewheeling CIA personnel as a result of congressional overregulation, Kissinger later wrote. "It became far easier and safer to bury oneself in bureaucratic paperwork than to stick one's neck out in a profession in which the risks at home sometimes exceeded those in the field.") National security would suffer. "That," Kissinger asserted, "is my overwhelming concern."[28]

The White House takeover began in March, and by all accounts it marked a key turning point in the Year of Intelligence. Entrusting an NSC official, a White House counsel, or both to litigate each and every congressional request for executive information signaled a get-tough attitude on the part of the administration. It reflected, the *New York Times* reported, a change in "the whole atmosphere" of interbranch relations.[29]

* * *

It's not clear what, if any, next steps followed Jack Marsh's conversation with George Cary, in which the White House aide urged the CIA legislative counsel to "hold the line." Available records are silent. But we do know that the White House, operating in concert with allies on the Church Committee—Goldwater, Tower, and Howard Baker (R-Tennessee)— worked to limit the committee's findings. Issued in April 1976, the committee's final report cited *Glomar* to arrive at a milder-than-expected conclusion. In contrast to Church's claim that the CIA had behaved like a "rogue elephant," the committee

> found that in general the president has had, through the National Security Council, effective means for exerting broad policy control over at least two major clandestine activities—covert action and sensitive technical collection. The covert American involvement in Angola and the operations of the *Glomar Explorer* are examples of that control in quite different circumstances, whatever conclusions one draws about the merits of the activities. The Central Intelligence Agency, in broad terms, is not "out of control."[30]

That conclusion was accurate, as far as it went. The 40 Committee did exert broad policy control. However, it left some areas unexplored. The Senate committee, notes former CIA inspector general L. Britt Snider, "did not conduct in-depth investigations of the agency's principal mission areas: clandestine collection abroad and analysis."[31]

Representative Otis G. Pike sought answers. In July 1975, the New York Democrat took over the chairmanship of the House Select Committee on Intelligence (HSCI) from Lucien Nedzi, who had been forced to resign after it was discovered that he had received a private briefing about some of the Family Jewels abuses in 1973—and yet had taken no action. Mired in controversy, the committee had little to show for its first five months of work. Pike, a fiscal conservative who represented a heavily Republican district on Long Island, was determined to move forward—and quickly—with a probe that subjected the intelligence establishment to a cost-benefit analysis.

How much did intelligence cost American taxpayers? What bang did they get for their buck? How well did America's intelligence services perform? Were they accountable?

Glomar offered an obvious starting point. A longtime member of the Armed Services Committee, Pike had chaired the House investigation into the 1968 seizure of the USS *Pueblo*. His subcommittee concluded that official negligence had placed the intelligence ship in harm's way. He saw possible parallels between the *Pueblo* and the *Glomar Explorer*. According to *New York Times* reporters Sherry Sontag and Christopher Drew, *Glomar* struck Pike "as a massive failure at best, or an all-out boondoggle, a blank check written to the Howard Hughes corporations, perhaps even a political payoff."[32]

Administration officials worried that close inspection of *Glomar* would uncover other, bigger secrets. "Intensified investigation," Colby warned at one point, could very well expose a "substrata of sources and methods." In *Glomar*'s case, this included the precise nature of the CIA's relationship with Hughes and other private contractors; how the spy agency financed, secured, and managed the sub-raising effort; and the identity of the "new organization" instituted in 1969 to coordinate the CIA-navy hunt for the Golf. The fact of the office's existence remained unacknowledged by the U.S. government six years later—a notable exception to the many other secrets that had been revealed over AZORIAN/MATADOR's life span. Yet its portfolio had grown to include a suite of highly classified underwater intelligence programs, and some of them were staring to leak.[33]

In May 1975, *New York Times* reporter Seymour Hersh revealed that specially equipped American submarines routinely penetrated deep inside Soviet territorial waters under a top-secret program code-named HOLYSTONE. These missions were valuable. Submarines went where satellites couldn't, reportedly maneuvering in close enough to tap underwater cables, observe missile launchings, and trail opposing submarines. They gave U.S. experts unprecedented visibility of Soviet underwater activity. Navy technicians, for instance, acquired acoustic signatures that allowed them to identify and track specific Soviet vessels, even at long distance. "We can follow boats through their life cycle," one expert said of the United States' ability to monitor Soviet submarines from launch to decommissioning.

HOLYSTONE incursions were also dangerous. By 1975, U.S. submarine reconnaissance efforts had resulted in at least nine collisions with Soviet vessels, an untold number of near misses, and over 110 possible detections. These incidents risked a superpower clash—not to mention the lives of American and Soviet sailors. The risks were not limited to HOLYSTONE. According to a former CIA official, they were "symptomatic of many of the current Pentagon collection and reconnaissance programs." Hersh's sources spoke out, they said, to alert Congress that these programs operated in almost total secrecy, and without adequate supervision.[34]

Hersh stopped short of identifying the National Underwater Reconnaissance Office (NURO), the organization's name, according to published reports. But his account prompted lawmakers to widen their probes. In July, the Church Committee tentatively scheduled hearings on "High Risk Collection Programs—NURO."[35]

For whatever reason, those Senate hearings never actually occurred. The House select committee pressed ahead, though, causing officials to try to check its investigation before it unmasked highly classified programs they considered essential to national security. During an April meeting of the

President's Foreign Intelligence Advisory Board, a member reported that Congressman Ronald Dellums (D-California), the HSCI's only African American member, was already "on to the underwater programs." No one knew for "certain whether the underwater activities Dellums had run across were related to MATADOR or other Navy programs." But a board member could verify that another legislator "had been asked to turn him [Dellums] off."[36]

Dellums refused to be sidetracked. Under Pike's leadership, the HSCI held hearings. It called the director of naval intelligence, Admiral Bobby Ray Inman, to testify. Inman had known about AZORIAN since 1973, when he served in Hawaii as assistant chief of staff for intelligence of the Pacific Fleet. Like many naval officers, he harbored serious reservations. The CIA-led program seemed unlikely to succeed. It was also expensive, subtracting resources from navy-led programs that, in his estimation, had "higher payoff." But the program was already well underway, and as a mid-career officer he was in no position to reverse course.[37]

Now that he directed naval intelligence, Inman shrugged off advice from those who urged him to stonewall, who said Pike couldn't be trusted with defense secrets. Testifying in closed session, he reportedly leveled with the select committee in an attempt to swing members around to the navy's view that its underwater programs—and its programs alone—were worth protecting. Mistakes had been made, he admitted. Submarine mishaps had occurred, and there had been too little coordination between U.S. foreign policy and intelligence agencies. He promised to investigate. But throughout it all, he steadfastly defended submarine reconnaissance. Laying out the facts as he saw them, Inman explained that underwater programs provided unique intelligence—that is, information unobtainable by other means—that actually saved money by helping the navy tailor its plans to a well-defined Soviet threat.

By all accounts, Inman's performance disarmed the Pike Committee. He appeared eager to cooperate. He came armed with facts, not excuses. In so doing, Inman—who went on to direct the National Security Agency—distinguished himself from other U.S. officials in the eyes of Pike's staff.[38]

William Colby couldn't be as candid. Underwater intelligence put him in a jam. As intelligence chief, he was obligated to protect any community program deemed vital to national security. Plus, he backed *Glomar*. ("It has to be fought for. It is damn good," he told reporters.[39]) And as CIA director, he had no desire to impugn the agency's work.

So the spy chief threaded the needle, using misdirection to steer the Pike Committee away from underwater collection. During his appearance, Colby put on a cloak-and-dagger show. According to chief counsel Aaron Donner, the committee was already meeting in executive session when a phalanx of serious-looking CIA security specialists made a dramatic entrance. Wearing dark suits and earphones, they swept the hearing room with electronic gear, searching for listening devices in corners and under tables and chairs. Colby followed, briskly trailed by a second contingent of CIA officers carrying black valises. The cases snapped open, revealing large plastic bags, which the officers carefully placed on a long table set before the congressmen.

Everyone fell silent. From the dais, all eyes looked down at the bags, struggling to peer through the plastic. They could see that they contained pieces of rusted iron of various shapes and sizes. And it was clear that the items were important from the reverential way in which they were handled. "They were treated like pieces of the True Cross," Donner recalled, by CIA officers who appeared to be "trying to give us a certain aura of great import and secrecy."

Try as they might, though, committee members couldn't positively identify the items—that is, until Colby spoke up, ending the suspense. Lawmakers were looking, he solemnly declared, at pieces of a Soviet submarine hefted from a depth of 16,500 feet by the wizards of Langley.[40]

Glorifying clandestine activity to win over Congress enjoys a storied tradition. "I'll just tell them a few war stories," Allen Dulles once said of his approach to congressional testimony. Drawn from his days in the Office of Strategic Services, the wartime precursor to the CIA, Dulles's tales of derring-do usually involved human agents bravely operating behind enemy lines. As espionage evolved over the years, though, technology figured more prominently in CIA presentations—presentations often designed, disaffected former officers Victor Marchetti and John Marks wrote, to mythologize intelligence "as some sort of mysterious, often magical, profession capable of accomplishing terribly difficult, if not miraculous, deeds."[41]

In 1966, Richard Helms, anticipating some uncharacteristically hard questions from senators about rising intelligence costs, brought along his deputy director for science and technology and a bag full of spy gadgets to an appropriations subcommittee hearing. As the DS&T head discussed the benefits of satellites and other technical collection systems the CIA was putting into operation, the senators inspected the hardware—including a camera concealed in a tobacco pouch, a radio transmitter hidden in a set of false teeth, and a tape recorder disguised as a cigarette case. One persistent senator kept trying to ask about the high cost of DS&T's systems. Predictably, however, the James Bond–like devices attracted most of the attention, even though they came from another directorate. And Helms walked out of the hearing room with a fully funded DS&T budget. "Senators became so enthralled with the equipment," Marchetti and Marks reported, "that no more questions were asked."[42]

Colby expanded this practice in 1975. "One day we held an executive session for the House committee and brought in a whole bunch of toys," Colby's special counsel, Mitchell Rogovin, recalled. "The phone-in-a-shoe-type thing. Most of the members were interested in all that James Bond stuff."[43]

The intent was clear to Donner. "They wanted to put on shows for us," the HSCI special counsel said of the CIA effort. "This was to sidetrack us."[44]

Show-and-tell sessions did not always divert Congress. Colby's September 1975 display of a dart gun capable of silently firing poison pellets—a "nondiscernable microbioinoculator," he called it—had the opposite effect, reinforcing the Church Committee's impression that the CIA was out of control, that it had not only plotted assassination but maintained stores of deadly toxins in contravention of a presidential order to destroy them. But they certainly made an impression—particularly, some felt, on "Pike's marauders," the junior members of his committee whom intelligence professionals feared most because they had the least experience with national security matters. "You've got the children all excited," the chairman grumbled during one CIA briefing.[45]

Few briefings left a more lasting impression than Colby's on *Glomar*. Donner vividly remembered it years later. "People were shaking their heads with absolute awe," Donner told an interviewer in 1983.[46]

"Colby's performance was masterful," Sontag and Drew concluded. Awestruck, Pike Committee members were too busy inspecting the rusted chunks of the Golf to scrutinize other materials Colby and his deputies had brought along to contextualize MATADOR. He evaded their questions about costs with vague explanations that exact totals were unavailable because they were hidden in several budgets. "By the time the show was over, not a single member of the committee had remembered to raise the question of Howard Hughes."[47]

Pike's marauders moved on, becoming embroiled in a losing battle with the White House over Congress's right to access and publish classified data. In January 1976, the House voted not to release the committee's report until the president certified that it did not contain national security information. Famously, however, the *Village Voice* obtained a leaked copy. Published on February 16, the report provided unprecedented visibility of the secretive world of submarine intelligence. And it was critical in many respects. "The Navy's own justification of the program as a 'low risk' venture is inaccurate," the committee found. In reality, risks were "unacceptably great." Past risk assessments tended to be "ritualistic and pro forma," and review procedures "inadequate." Consequently, the committee recommended stronger management "to avert another *Pueblo*, or worse."

Otherwise, the Pike Committee—by all accounts, the most assertive of the boards that conducted intelligence investigations in 1975—offered a remarkably positive assessment. Supervision of the submarine program had improved of late, the committee was happy to report. "At present it appears to be extremely well managed." As for performance, the committee had nothing but praise. "The program clearly produces useful information on our adversaries' training exercises, weapons testing and general naval capabilities," its report said of U.S. submarine reconnaissance.

This report stood in stark contrast to the committee's other, damning evaluations of the intelligence community's recent performance, and it said less about U.S. submarine operations than it might have. Discussion of the subject amounted to just eight paragraphs. Not a word was said about *Glomar* or cost. And the office that administered the nation's underwater reconnaissance effort went unnamed.[48]

Thus ended the public's first real opportunity to assess the underwater Cold War. To be sure, stronger review mechanisms were put in place. And the CIA took a back seat to the navy after *Glomar* funding dried up. Otherwise, underwater operations continued much as before. If anything, they received additional funding—and support from Congress. "Within the submarine ranks it was business, and silence, as usual," according to Sontag and Drew. "NURO," they concluded, "had survived the *Glomar* fiasco."[49]

* * *

To that point, the Year of Intelligence had been mostly retrospective in its probes, focusing on past U.S. intelligence actions. Reflection would certainly continue until the Church and Pike Committees issued their findings in early 1976. But debate about the future of American intelligence began in earnest in September 1975, when the House Appropriations Committee considered the fiscal year 1976 defense budget—the first major intelligence spending measure to come before the chamber since the CIA's time of troubles began.

Glomar surfaced a final time to shape that debate, managed by George Mahon, the Appropriations chairman the Watergate babies failed to unseat. "Mr. Anonymous," as a journalist dubbed the Texas Democrat, kept his cards close to his vest—so close as to go unnoticed in comparison to his more voluble peers. Mahon's reticence, though, masked the extent of his influence. First elected to Congress in 1934, he rose in 1949 to head the Defense Appropriations Subcommittee, vested (on paper, at least) with the power of the purse over intelligence spending. For the next thirty years, Mahon served as the House's chief intelligence overseer—the chamber's closest living equivalent to Richard Russell.[50]

Intelligence professionals appreciated the quiet but effective way in which Mahon, who took the Appropriations gavel in 1964, maneuvered to safeguard their interests. William Colby considered him "a longtime friend and protector of the CIA." Mahon, a biographer observes, was a frugal man of modest means who habitually resoled his own shoes, and a fiscal conservative who generally resisted federal spending. His parsimony, though, didn't extend to security measures, which he liberally funded. A dedicated cold warrior, Mahon oversaw a vast expansion of military-related appropriations. When he became subcommittee chairman, the defense appropriation totaled $13 billion. By the time he retired three decades later, he had authorized defense appropriations in excess of $1.5 trillion—including the multimillion-dollar effort to retrieve the Soviet submarine from the bottom of the Pacific.[51]

Defending the CIA became more difficult in 1975. Mistakes had been made, Mahon conceded. He didn't agree with everything the CIA had done. But he continued to parrot the same line he had always uttered in the face of calls for transparency: Airing the agency's dirty laundry was wrong—"dead wrong," he told a constituent. Strong intelligence was vital to national security and divulging privileged information could only aid America's enemies.[52] Silence was golden, anonymity a virtue.

Unlike Hébert, Mahon kept his chairmanship because he was adept enough to make concessions, where necessary. Henceforth, he announced in 1975, intelligence chiefs would have to defend budget requests before the full, thirteen-member Defense Appropriations Subcommittee. Long sought by reformers, this procedural change significantly expanded House oversight. Previously, only a small, informal group of senior subcommittee members—meaning Mahon and, perhaps, the ranking Democrat and Republican—had reviewed intelligence budgets. Now, for the first time, a larger number of appropriators who may or may not have been trusted supporters of the CIA gained access to, and regulatory authority over, agency finances. And by all accounts, CIA's FY 1976 funding request received the closest review in memory. After what one participant described as "a frank and full" discussion of the agency and its activities, the subcommittee recommended, on September 25, 1975, a $263 million cut.[53]

No longer, it seemed, could appropriators be accused of handing the CIA a blank check. Still, the review was not close enough for Representative Robert Giaimo (D-Connecticut). A longtime subcommittee member, Giaimo was among those who first gained access to CIA financials in 1975, his sixteenth year in Congress. It must have been an eye-opening experience, for he offered an amendment to publish, as a line item in the FY 1976 defense budget, the total amount appropriated to the CIA.

Despite months of disclosures and reviews and promises to bring the CIA to heel, this most rudimentary bit of spending data remained hardly more known than it had been during Richard Russell's day. True, the circle of knowledge had widened somewhat to include the thirteen defense subcommittee members. And there had been unofficial disclosures: Marchetti and Marks pegged the agency's annual budget at $750 million in their 1974 tell-all, *The CIA and the Cult of Intelligence.*[54]

Officially, however, such estimates went unconfirmed. The actual figure remained a closely guarded CIA secret. House rules prevented the few lawmakers who were in the know from sharing it with those who weren't— even with the other 42 members of the 55-person Appropriations Committee who did not sit on the defense subcommittee. The overwhelming majority of the 435-member House did not authoritatively know how much intelligence spending was tucked into the FY 1976 defense appropriation bill—not to mention what the money was for, or whether it was justified. Yet they were supposed to appropriate public funds for intelligence purposes, sight unseen.

Without access to this basic information, Giaimo argued, representatives couldn't cast an informed vote. They couldn't, therefore, satisfactorily discharge their constitutional duties as prescribed by the Appropriations Clause. ("No money shall be drawn from the Treasury, but in Consequence of Appropriations made by Law; and a regular Statement and Account of the Receipts and Expenditures of all public Money shall be published from time to time.") And they couldn't begin to exert real accountability over the CIA. Even the Rockefeller Commission, the most cautious of all the investigative boards, recommended some degree of transparency, he pointed out. "Congress should give careful consideration to the question whether the budget of the CIA should not, at least to some extent, be made public, particularly in view of the provisions of Article I, Section 9, Clause 7 of the Constitution," the commission reported in June.[55]

Publication, Giaimo said upon introducing his amendment, would end the "old practice . . . of voting in the dark" and begin a new era of intelligence accountability. Using the CIA's annual budget as a benchmark, regulators could get a better handle on what portion of defense spending went toward intelligence, and how the agency's price tag compared with the costs of other federal priorities. Looking ahead, they could combine the FY 1976 figure with future budget numbers to chart the rise or fall of CIA spending over time, and that insight, too, could inform congressional decisions.[56]

Exerting the power of the purse, Giaimo and his supporters said, was Congress's surest means of restraining the spy agency. They cited *Glomar* as a prime example. Had Congress properly scrutinized CIA spending in the past, some of the abuses and excesses that were now being investigated might never have gotten off the drawing board. Take MHCHAOS. Or Chile. Or *Glomar*. "We must ensure that extravagant programs like the *Glomar Explorer* are made to compete effectively against other claimants on the public purse," one House member said. "I think it is time that the sunshine were allowed to come in a little bit."[57]

Giaimo's side was careful not to name names. But George Mahon must have taken their comments personally. After all, it was he, papers in his own files show, who had known about the *Explorer*'s classified role long before it became public; he who, as a House Appropriations leader, had signed off on intelligence budget requests for decades; and he who now stood accused of failing to restrain CIA activity—publicly accused, as the *Washington Post* would say, of doing "a lackadaisical and inept job of oversight in the past," of being among the prime "handmaidens of executive abuse and patsies for executive power."[58]

Mahon led the fight against Giaimo's amendment. He began with another concession: Henceforth, he announced, all House members could review intelligence budget numbers before voting to appropriate defense funds. Certain restrictions applied: congresspeople, for example, had to sign a registry to review classified materials in a secure area. But his move—made in coordination with the White House, internal records show—effectively undercut opponents, removing a key basis of support for publicizing CIA data.[59]

He also sharpened his attack on Giaimo's proposal. Publication would indeed provide a benchmark, as Giaimo claimed, but one that would also be visible to foreign adversaries, who, Mahon argued, could use the figure to measure America's clandestine effort. "I doubt that making the budget public is in the public interest because you tell the world—Russia, Castro, China—the level of our intelligence efforts," he told a newspaper.[60]

Mahon dusted off Richard Russell's favored response to accountability calls. Revelation of the tinniest bit of budget data, Russell cautioned until his death in 1971, would give foreign adversaries a "blueprint" of America's clandestine capabilities. The risk of unintentionally telegraphing clandestine U.S. activity to foreign powers was particularly acute, Mahon and his allies now said, in cases where highly technical—and therefore often highly expensive—collection programs were involved. Were foreign intelligence services to observe a sudden rise—or "conspicuous bump"—in CIA expenditures, without a commensurate change in personnel, they could conceivably conclude that the United States had developed a costly intelligence collection system that was technology- rather than labor-intensive. And if they gained additional insight through open sources, industrial espionage, or other avenues, they might succeed in identifying—and counteracting—the system.

In Russell's day, the U-2 served as the proving example of the "conspicuous bump" theory. Had the foreign intelligence budget been public when the expensive aircraft was under development in the 1950s, the theory went, the Soviets could have countered the U-2 sooner—perhaps with fatal results for American pilots.[61]

Now the *Glomar Explorer* took its place alongside the U-2. "It is not just the publishing of a raw figure that is at stake," explained Congressman Jack Kemp (R-New York). "It is whether that figure waxes or wanes over a period of time due to extenuating circumstances that would be telegraphing to an adversary that there was something going on that was extremely vital to the security of the United States in terms of intelligence gathering." Witness, he said, the case of the Russian submarine. Had Soviet experts had advance notice of CIA expenditures, they might have disrupted the *Glomar Explorer*'s mission to raise the watercraft.[62]

If America's opponents couldn't put two and two together, then members of Congress might inadvertently do the math for them. "If one year a promising technical means of collection were developed against hostile powers at a given budget figure and the next year that figure had swollen tremendously," said Representative Robert Daniel (R-Virginia), lawmakers were certain to ask questions. Their inquiries might very well attract unwanted attention. "Would we not then be clueing the target country so they could then defend themselves against this means of collection?" asked Daniel, a former CIA officer, one of several exes who served in Congress over the years. "A vote for this amendment will be a vote to enhance the knowledge of opposing intelligence services about our own intelligence community."[63]

Publishing the annual CIA budget was a step toward ruin, doomsayers alleged. If Congress kept pressing for transparency, enough information—totals and subtotals and more—would enter the public domain for foreign targets to identify even the most well-concealed program. "This would be particularly true of our highly sophisticated—and, I might add, highly expensive—technical collection systems," Mahon would say. "Investments of hundreds of millions of dollars could be jeopardized."[64]

Common sense argued against releasing CIA budget data. Besides, reforms had been made. Intelligence appropriation procedures were more transparent than ever before. After years of voting in the dark, House members could view the figures for themselves.

"So, I do think we have gone far enough," Mahon concluded. "If we know ourselves what the situation is, why do we insist on telling the Soviet Union and Red China and everyone else?" To satisfy public opinion? Not according to his soundings: Middle Americans weren't clamoring for national security data to be released. "I do not think many of the people feel it would be wise for us to spill our innermost secrets of the government to the whole wide world."

A vote for Giaimo's amendment would not sit well with constituents—Mahon's least of all: "When I go home to Texas I do not want somebody to meet me on the street and say, 'Congressman, why did you vote to give away our secrets to the USSR and the Communist conspiracy? The information was available to you. We trust you. We thought you would protect our interests. We did not need to know the information.'"[65]

* * *

Mahon could speak with confidence because he did his homework—or, rather, someone did it for him. In early 1976, residents of Mahon's Nineteenth Congressional District received an "opinion ballot" from the National Write Your Congressman Club asking, "Should Congress control the CIA?" Like other surveys distributed by the avowedly nonpartisan Dallas-based club, this poll was designed to encourage its members to pressure their elected representatives about important issues of the day. It began with excerpts from statements by prominent figures who took opposing sides on the intelligence question—followed by space in which recipients were encouraged to indicate their position, and instructions explaining how to mail the completed ballot to their congressperson.

On the left: An excerpt from Arthur Schlesinger Jr.'s *Wall Street Journal* piece, in which the Harvard-trained historian, New York college professor, and Democratic activist used the *Glomar Explorer* to illustrate the need for closer congressional supervision. Careful accounting of the intelligence budget represented the surest means, he argued, of reining in the CIA, an agency that had "far too much money. One consequence of having too much money is the temptation to rush into bizarre and profligate projects, like Howard Hughes and the *Glomar*. Another consequence is a lot of people sitting at a lot of desks and trying to justify their existence by thinking up things to do"—including allying with a mysterious billionaire on a half-baked scheme to raise an obsolete submarine with a giant claw. Halving the CIA's budget, Schlesinger wrote, "would eliminate most of this nonsense, release mindless covert operators for jobs as Hollywood script writers and compel the CIA to concentrate" on more serious methods of intelligence collection.[66]

On the right: Arizona senator Barry Goldwater, who read into the *Congressional Record* a statement claiming that Congress's yearlong investigations had done nothing but harm national defense. Congress leaked (more than "the men's room at Anheuser-Busch," he once quipped.) Unauthorized disclosures of "the systems, innerworkings, and budgets" of U.S. intelligence agencies had already aided America's enemies. Additional revelations would further damage the community's ability to serve the national interest.[67]

Arthur Schlesinger was a dedicated cold warrior, and his fiscally conservative message bridged some of the distance that separated him from most residents of Texas's Nineteenth District, a dusty patch of cotton farms and oil fields stretching from the state's western border to Lubbock in the east, and from the plains of the Panhandle south to the petroleum-rich Permian Basin. Yes, agreed a minority of respondents—17.2 percent, to be exact—Congress should impose limits. They included Midland dentist K. J. Kimbrough. "Although the operation of a good, efficient intelligence agency without the necessity of policing would be nice," Dr. Kimbrough wrote in the space provided, "it is in fact not possible. For Congress not to control these agencies is an expensive situation and is a problem just waiting to happen." And they included my late grandfather, Lubbock realtor Basil L. Webb Sr., a sixty-three-year-old Dust Bowl veteran whose wife, my grandmother Robbie Marion Webb, a fellow Depression survivor, habitually saved every little thing that might conceivably prove useful because—she would explain, when pressed—"you just never know."[68]

Typically, my grandfather, tight-lipped like Mahon, didn't elaborate. But to frugal West Texans, *Glomar* seemed like an extravagance, particularly with austerity's return in the mid-seventies. "I feel some budget cut may be needed to cut expensive and unneeded projects," opined an Idalou grocer. "The CIA could do some improving as far as spending money," added a farmer from Amherst.[69]

Savings were important, but security was paramount in most of their neighbors' eyes. Despite détente, a concept so reviled in these parts that President Ford stopped using the word during the 1976 Republican primaries, the Cold War remained ongoing. To win it, the CIA needed the freedom to act, the creativity to dream up bold schemes like stealing a foreign submarine out from under the Soviets' noses. "The CIA is our best protection against foreign agents and spies. Leave them like they are. Let them . . . do their duty," a Hale Center junkyard owner advised.[70]

Congressional regulators, some feared, would tie up America's foreign intelligence services with red tape, just as they had private enterprise. "I, for one, think it is high time that the Congress cease from attempting to regulate and control everything in this country," H. L. Hagler wrote in the space provided and, when it proved inadequate, on the back page of the legal-sized survey. Lawmakers had already "strangled the oil & gas industry" with excessive regulation, claimed Hagler, a self-identified oil worker from Midland, a capital of the Permian Basin. Now they were meddling with intelligence, and he had no doubt they would hog-tie it as well. His recommendation: "Put capable, qualified people in charge [at the CIA], and give them a free hand" to do whatever they deemed necessary to defend America's interests.[71]

No, more than 81 percent answered, Congress had no business restricting the CIA. "Hell no," emphasized a Littlefield dry cleaner, voicing a common refrain. The agency should answer only to the president, in part to minimize leaks from Congress, where members and staff gave reporters inside information to expose wrongdoing or kill mistaken initiatives—but also, for more selfish reasons, to smear political opponents or advance personal agendas. Unauthorized leaks did irreparable damage to American security. Those "caught leaking info. should be lined up & shot," he asserted.[72]

Granted, Texas's Nineteenth District was fiercely conservative—among the reddest in a red state, a place where military measures always polled well. Respondents were self-selecting. And despite the National Write Your Congressman Club's avowed nonpartisanship, its actual intent appears to have been to drum up support for the CIA. Distributed shortly after CIA station chief Richard Welch's December 1975 assassination turned opinion firmly against the investigations, the club's survey insinuated that oversight proposals were controversial not because of past intelligence abuses but because "of the danger of security leaks to the enemies of this country."

By any measure, though, 81 percent was a remarkable figure—all the more so because it followed months of shocking disclosures of instances in which the CIA had exceeded its charter or pursued (in Arthur Schlesinger's words) "bizarre and profligate" schemes. And it was entirely consistent with what many people had been saying all along. A Lubbock salesman, for example, had written Mahon in mid-1975 to report that he regularly spoke with clients across Mahon's district. These conversations indicated "that the law-abiding average citizen wants to leave the CIA and the FBI free to do the job they are supposed to do"—protect America from enemies foreign and domestic. "The majority of U.S. citizens," wrote another constituent, "do not insist on the 'people's right to know.'"[73]

The silent majority spoke, and with a force that struck Mahon. He defended the CIA throughout its time of troubles. But after sampling the feedback that poured into his office, he directed staff to strengthen his letters to state his position "in a more dogmatic way."[74]

"Our intelligence agencies are indispensable to the welfare and security of the United States," came the reply to my grandfather, Basil Webb, the Lubbock realtor who registered concern about *Glomar*'s high cost. Sure, those agencies had erred in the past. But any attempt by Congress to second-guess them could endanger Webb's safety, as well as that of his four children and his grandchildren, who numbered ten at the time. Détente notwithstanding, communism remained, in Mahon's view, the world's greatest threat to freedom. America's spies couldn't provide maximum protection if they were handcuffed with restrictive laws, reporting requirements, or other red tape. Besides, he predicted, congressional micromanagement would inevitably cause sensitive intelligence data to appear in the public domain, and recent experience had shown that the release of such details could harm national security. He closed by pledging to redouble his efforts to maintain "a strong CIA."[75]

* * *

Not only Texans but Californians and New Yorkers and many in between felt much the same, to judge by the vote on Giaimo's amendment. After days of intense debate—a debate, the *Wall Street Journal* reported, that concerned the proper balance between the public's right to know and the need for national security secrecy—267 legislators representing forty-seven states voted in October 1975 against the measure. Just 147 voted in support.[76]

Foreign policy hawks reveled in the victory. Throughout 1975, Congress styled itself as the defender of the people's right to know. Frank Church and Otis Pike and others made headlines calling for openness and accountability. But the fact that so few House members voted to publish the CIA budget showed that, when push came to shove, most stood solidly behind the security state. "The sunshine fad for openness," a columnist in Mahon's district bragged, had been dimmed before it could do additional harm to America's interests.[77]

Reformers agonized at the defeat. "These guys in the House just don't want to know," sighed Giaimo, disappointed that only a minority of his colleagues bothered to review CIA financials when given the chance.[78] Politically, it was safer not to know what the agency was doing, for to know was to bear some responsibility for those actions should they go awry.

To syndicated columnist Mary McGrory, the Year of Intelligence appeared to have turned a corner. "Things went better for the CIA this week than at any time since last December, when Seymour Hersh of the *New York Times* revealed that the agency had engaged in massive illegal domestic surveillance," she observed. In addition to Giaimo's defeat, Pike lost a key confrontation with President Ford that week over Congress's right to unilaterally declassify documents. Public television also stopped airing Church Committee hearings, a sign that audiences were losing interest. Langley, she speculated, probably saw the light at the end of tunnel.[79]

According to McGrory, the "old intelligence hands" had regained control, Mr. Anonymous chief among them. "Mahon remains as powerful as ever," remarked a *Washington Post* congressional correspondent. After the vote, the congressman proceeded to do what he had done every year for decades: put the annual intelligence outlay where no one (other than select insiders like himself) could see it. That is, inside the Pentagon's enormous budget, under an innocuous-looking line item like "Research, Development, Test and Evaluation, Navy," where *Glomar* funds were stashed. The aggregate amount annually appropriated by Congress to the national foreign intelligence program remained unpublished, arguably in violation of the Constitution's Appropriations Clause. Remarkably, it would stay that way for another thirty-two years—until 2007, when Congress finally voted to release the number.[80]

It is difficult to square that outcome with the view that 1975 marked the dawn of a new era of intelligence accountability. Deprived of a basic data point, American taxpayers remained in the dark, unable to determine how many of their annual tax dollars went to fund intelligence activity—much less, Giaimo remarked, "to question [that amount] and . . . analyze its growth from year to year." In that sense, he said, they remained no more informed—and were perhaps even less so—of American clandestine activity than the average Soviet spy.[81]

Taylor Branch put it best, as Pulitzer Prize winners often do. Branch hadn't yet won the prize for *Parting the Waters*, the first volume of his trilogy chronicling the life of slain civil rights leader Dr. Martin Luther King Jr., when he reviewed the intelligence investigations for the *New York Times Magazine* in 1976. He marveled at the results. Probes by two congressional committees and one presidential commission "stretched the imagination with showbiz material" about plots to assassinate foreign leaders with Mafia hitmen. They proved beyond a shadow of a doubt that the U.S. government had spied, Big Brother–like, on King and other American citizens. And they established, in contrast to Watergate, that abuses of power were not limited to one presidential administration or political party.

Those revelations forever changed how many Americans perceived the United States and its role in the world, Branch acknowledged. Yet a surprising number of subjects escaped discussion. The Church Committee's report remained silent, for example, about the network of American contractors and subcontractors who secretly assisted the CIA. It said little about the agency's rumored use of members of the press to gather and spread information. And it failed to break new ground on the agency's commercial cover arrangements, despite unconfirmed reports that several top firms acted in this capacity. "There was no exploration," Branch wrote, "of the agency's work with the corporate interests of the late Howard Hughes—in spite of confirmed reports of the $300 million *Glomar Explorer* project for raising a sunken Soviet submarine."

Omissions occurred where investigations cut too close "to the bone" of the CIA's essential mission. High officials, Branch claimed, gave ground on "marginal" issues like assassination in order "to protect the means and practice of covert action," which he defined, broadly, as action taken both to shape foreign politics and collect foreign intelligence. As a result, the CIA emerged with its powers still largely hidden and essentially unchallenged. Contrary to expectations, "the vaunted trial of the CIA has already become a memory. And the agency itself has survived the scandals with its covert operations intact, if not strengthened."[82]

For better or worse, continued secrecy allowed American spy agencies to retain a degree of flexibility when it came to imagining bold schemes like the *Glomar Explorer*. Not as much as before, certainly—nor as much as someone like Robert Gates would have preferred. "At the end of the investigations," recalled the future CIA director, who served on the NSC from 1974 to 1976, "CIA had few secrets left other than the names of sources and some of its technical collection capabilities." But it was more than seemed likely at the beginning of the year, when the CIA appeared to be on the ropes, all the momentum was behind disclosure, and no national secret seemed safe. After Watergate, *New York Times* columnist Anthony Lewis observed, it was generally expected that executive agencies like the CIA would have to be more forthcoming moving forward. Somewhere along the way, though, that expectation changed. "Secrecy and national security are winning political slogans these days," he wrote in February 1976 after President Ford issued a reform plan that, critics said, did more to protect than punish the U.S. intelligence community. "The issue," a frustrated Church agreed, "has become how to keep secrets rather than how to preserve freedom."[83]

The line, in other words, had held. And it held with support from the *Glomar Explorer*. Built to salvage a Soviet submarine, the ship ended up shielding the CIA from transparency.

CONCLUSION

On June 25, 1981, Harriet Ann "Hank" Phillippi finally received the answer to the Freedom of Information Act (FOIA) request she filed more than six years earlier, in March 1975, after news outlets divulged the *Glomar Explorer*'s true purpose and then CIA director William Colby's attempts to kill the story. Phillippi, a Washington correspondent for *Rolling Stone* magazine at the time, requested "all records relating to the Director's or any other agency personnel's attempts to persuade any media personnel not to broadcast, write, publish, or in any other way make public the events relating to the activities of the *Glomar Explorer*, including, but not limited to, files, documents, letters, memoranda, travel logs, telephone logs or records of calls made, records of personal visits, or any other records of any kind of communications."[1]

Phillippi was under no illusions. Signed into law in 1966, FOIA exempted nine categories of federal records from disclosure. Exemption 1, for example, covered information classified to protect national security; exemption 3, information prohibited from disclosure by another federal statute, including the National Security Act of 1947, which charged the CIA director with protecting intelligence sources and methods from unauthorized disclosure.

But Phillippi didn't request operational records, the kind likely to identify sources, methods, or other sensitive aspects of intelligence tradecraft. She requested nonoperational files documenting Colby's contacts with the news media. Surely, they were subject to release under FOIA, a landmark open access law that set a high standard for similar measures worldwide. Strengthened by Congress in 1974, the act required agencies to search for and review records requested by "any person" to determine if they were disclosable. It empowered federal courts to fully review agency decisions, to include *in camera* examinations of classified records to ascertain whether such records were properly withheld under the law's exemptions. And it placed the burden on agencies to prove their denial claims. Concerned that judicial review, in particular, could disclose data classified by executive branch officials, President Gerald Ford vetoed the bill in October, months after giving lip service to open government in his inaugural remarks. In November, however, the House and Senate overrode his veto by a combined vote of 436–58, earning praise for advancing the people's right to know.[2]

The amended law went into effect in early 1975. By all accounts, it worked to increase government transparency. "As a result [of the measure]," *Time* reported, "officials are speedily granting many of the requests for information, a mass of formerly withheld material is being turned over to academic researchers, reporters, and other citizens." Peak FOIA had arrived.[3]

Phillippi had not reckoned with Walter Lloyd, however. After *Glomar*'s unmasking, Lloyd, the program's cover director, and a lawyer by training, was transferred to the CIA's Office of General Counsel. As associate general counsel, he handled requests for information about CIA activity. Phillippi's FOIA request landed on his desk—the desk of a man trained in the art of deception who had managed to hide a 618-foot-long ship in plain sight for years.

In response, Lloyd did not want to claim that the CIA possessed no records responsive to Phillippi's request. False statements were challengeable in court as a possible violation of FOIA law, which required federal agencies to conduct searches in good faith. But *Glomar*'s true purpose remained officially classified, despite what Colby may have told reporters on background.

MATADOR was still active, and U.S. officials refused to acknowledge the submarine mission in order to keep their options open, save Soviet face, and protect whatever intelligence may or may not have been gleaned.

Federal statute required directors of central intelligence and their subordinates, Lloyd included, to protect intelligence sources and methods. Besides, any pertinent records the agency possessed were classified for national security reasons. Therefore, he reasoned, they were exempt pursuant to FOIA provisions 1 and 3.

For some time, Lloyd struggled to reconcile these conflicting legal responsibilities. Then, in a moment of inspiration, he hit upon the answer, or nonanswer, really. "We can neither confirm nor deny the existence of the information requested, but hypothetically, if such data were to exist, the subject would be classified and could not be disclosed." Previously used by Henry Kissinger in a private, diplomatic exchange, the so-called Glomar response entered the legal lexicon for the first time as a rationale to deny information to members of the public.[4]

In an April 4, 1975, letter addressed to "Mr. Hank Phillippi," the CIA denied her FOIA request.[5] Phillippi filed an administrative appeal. The CIA quickly rejected it too. In a response, dated May 21, Deputy Director for Science and Technology Carl Duckett, the official whom Richard Helms once nearly defenestrated for proposing such a "crazy" submarine scheme,

determined that, in the interest of national security, involvement by the U.S. Government in the activities which are the subject matter of your request can neither be confirmed nor denied. Therefore, he has determined that the fact of the existence or non-existence of any material or documents that may exist which would reveal any CIA connection or interest in the activities of the *Glomar Explorer* is duly classified Secret in accordance with criteria established by [executive order]. Acknowledgement of the existence or non-existence of the information you request could reasonably be expected to result in the compromise of important intelligence operations and significant scientific and technological developments relating to the national security, and might also result in a disruption in foreign relations significantly affecting the national security.[6]

* * *

Non-denial denials have a storied history in America. In 1916, Ford Motor Company representatives "would neither confirm nor deny" rumors they were planning to reprice the popular Model T automobile. In 1958, Eisenhower administration officials declared that it was U.S. government policy "neither to confirm nor deny the presence of . . . nuclear capable weapons in any other country."[7]

But the introduction of the Glomar response forever altered the balance between government transparency and national security in America. Under FOIA, as amended by Congress in 1974, an individual who submitted a records request to an executive agency could expect to receive one of three responses. The agency could (1) identify and release responsive records; (2) determine that it possessed no responsive records and inform the requestor of that fact; or (3) identify responsive records but determine that they were exempt from disclosure under one of the act's nine exemptions. The Glomar response introduced a fourth possibility: an agency could refuse to confirm or deny whether responsive records existed, on the grounds that acknowledging their existence (or nonexistence) could reveal sensitive information and therefore harm the public interest.[8]

That response, critics say, enabled agencies like the CIA to sidestep the law's search and review requirements. It permitted the agency to withhold materials indefinitely, without fully justifying its actions. And it left requestors in the dark as to whether responsive files existed, or how to take legal recourse. As Lloyd explained, "We'd tell the [FOIA] requestor that we could neither confirm nor deny the existence of any records responsive to the request, but if we *did* have any such records, they would be classified. So, either way, they're screwed!"[9]

Represented by the American Civil Liberties Union and Ralph Nader's Public Citizen Litigation Group, Phillippi filed a complaint in the

U.S. District Court for the District of Columbia. She moved to force the agency to provide detailed statements justifying why each individual document should be exempt from disclosure. In response, Justice Department lawyers submitted affidavits from national security officials affirming that any and all *Glomar*-related files the CIA might have in its possession should remain undisclosed. After *in camera* examination of two classified CIA affidavits, the district court sided with the government, ruling that the information Phillippi requested was protected from disclosure by exemption 3 of the FOIA, exempting information prohibited from disclosure by another federal statute, in this case the National Security Act of 1947.[10]

Undaunted, Phillippi appealed to the DC circuit court, which reached a judgment in November 1976. By that time, the Year of Intelligence was a distant memory. ("The topic faded away so quickly as to make the whole episode look like a fad," Taylor Branch remarked.) The *Glomar Explorer* was in mothballs, unused despite CIA assurances that it would fetch millions on the open market. And former Georgia governor Jimmy Carter, a Washington outsider who promised post-Watergate reform, government transparency included, was president-elect. Weeks after Carter's victory, the three-person court handed down a split decision. Reversing the district court's decision on procedural grounds, it ruled, narrowly, that the lower court erred by immediately resorting to *in camera* proceedings, rather than first requiring the CIA to publicly justify its decision to the maximum extent possible. The circuit panel remanded the case to the district court for further proceedings.[11]

The Carter administration reviewed the government's position. CIA director Stansfield Turner concluded that disclosure of CIA involvement would not damage national security. The national security advisor, Dr. Zbigniew Brzezinski, concurred. And in May 1977, the government acknowledged that CIA officials had attempted to dissuade members of the press from publishing stories concerning the *Glomar Explorer*'s activities. Months later, the CIA released 16 documents in full and another 134 in part. Those files provided the source material for a second round of published accounts

that gave the public a fresh look at the *Glomar* mission and Colby's quix-
otic efforts to keep it secret.[12]

* * *

At the same time, the CIA denied 4 documents in full and deleted
portions of the others. It also acknowledged possessing another 128,000
documents logged into the program's control system. Comprising a vast
archive, those files remained beyond public view.[13]

Phillippi pressed ahead with litigation seeking release of the deletions,
described as involving "sensitive" operational details properly falling under
FOIA exemptions 1 and 3. They no longer qualified for national security
exemption, she argued, because so much about the *Glomar Explorer* was
already in the public domain. In 1978, for example, the French version of
Colby's memoirs appeared in bookstores, complete with its unexpurgated
account of the *Explorer*'s recovery of "the forepart, about one-third [of the
target], while the aft fell to the bottom of the sea with its nuclear missiles,
its guidance apparatus, its transmission equipment, its codes, in other words
with all the things the CIA had hoped to gain through this unprecedented
operation." This was in addition to the briefings he had given, as director
of central intelligence in 1975, to some forty journalists, none of whom possessed security clearances or signed nondisclosure agreements as precondi-
tions for receiving agency data. Many of those reporters went on to publish
accounts based, in part, on what Colby and other CIA officials had told
them. In light of these disclosures, the agency could safely release the disputed data without harming national security.[14]

Phillippi cited press reports claiming that the *Hughes Glomar Explorer*
raised part of the submarine, all of it, or performed "some still-secret third
function." According to a court filing, these reports suggested that government officials had told different members of the news media conflicting
versions of the story, perhaps in an attempt to purposefully mislead them as
to the mission's payoff. Therefore, she insisted, there was a substantial and
overriding public interest in knowing the actual purpose and accomplishments of the *Glomar* program. "This is a particularly significant question in

view of the great cost of the *HGE* and the fact that the program was conducted under contract with Howard Hughes organizations."[15]

Hughes had been dead for years. He died in April 1976, aboard a plane bound for Houston from his final Acapulco hideaway. (According to the autopsy report, Hughes's "remarkably emaciated" six-foot, two-inch body weighed just ninety-three pounds. Pathologists noted needle punctures and other possible signs of a "propensity to self-medicate."[16]) Whatever else he knew about Watergate and the CIA went with him to the grave. The Watergate Special Prosecution Force never managed to subpoena, much less interview, him, protected as he was behind private security, in a penthouse atop a hotel he owned. Above the law to the end, he was the only major Watergate figure who eluded prosecutors, columnist Jack Anderson noted bitterly.[17]

Hughes's CIA connection generally escaped verification as well. Asked by a reporter to describe the relationship, President Ford demurred: "The only link that I think I can comment on is the one that involved the *Glomar*, where one of his companies was involved in the construction of that ship and its operation. Other than that, I don't think it is appropriate for me to discuss a relationship that may or may not have existed."[18] The Romaine Street burglary went unsolved.

In any event, the district court ruled for the CIA. Exemption 3 only required the CIA to demonstrate that release of the deleted material could "reasonably be expected to lead to unauthorized disclosure of intelligence sources and methods." In concluding that the agency had made the requisite showing, the court noted that disclosure of the data sought by Phillippi might reveal the true purpose of the *Glomar Explorer* project and the extent to which its goals had or had not been achieved. Such disclosure, the court added, could impair relations between the United States and the unnamed country targeted by the operation.[19]

Phillippi appealed to the DC circuit court, the court that had ruled in her favor, on a technicality, in 1976. There, *Phillippi* collided with a similar case, *Military Audit Project v. William Casey, Director of Central Intelligence, et al.* Like *Phillippi*, *Military Audit* began soon after the press disclosures of 1975, when a representative of the Military Audit Project, a nonprofit

ent letters to the CIA and Defense Department requesting
the FOIA to "the contract and all other documents pertain-
to the planning, design, construction, leasing, use and disposition of
the *Glomar Explorer*."[20] Citing exemptions 1 and 3, the agencies Glomared
the requests. The DC district court dismissed the plaintiff's challenge.
And after years of legal maneuvering, the case ended up before the circuit
court, where it dovetailed with *Phillippi*.

Argument opened in February 1981, weeks after the presidential inau-
guration of former California governor Ronald Reagan, winner of a landslide victory over Carter in the 1980 election, partly on the strength of his
pledge to bolster national defense. Military Audit counsel, too, argued that
the government had nothing left to hide. In the years since *Glomar*'s
unmasking, not only had a former CIA director described the ship's mission in his memoirs, but the U.S. Senate, the National Science Foundation,
and the General Services Administration had each reported additional
details. None of these partial disclosures—official in some cases, Military
Audit lawyers noted—had caused demonstrable harm to national security,
despite previous claims by U.S. officials to the contrary. This rendered
implausible any claim that withheld material was still entitled to national
security protection. Therefore, the CIA and Pentagon should fully release
all *Glomar*-related records in their possession.[21]

Though there may have been some publicity, Justice Department lawyers responded, the government had not officially confirmed the purpose
of the *Glomar Explorer* project. Nor had it confirmed the project's yield or
a myriad of other facts. In affidavits submitted during the trial phase, officials insisted that there were still secrets—good secrets, national security
secrets—left to hide, so many that no one could count them all. "In international affairs," affirmed Cyrus Vance, Carter's secretary of state, "one
deals with intangibles and uncertainties." No one could predict what damage would ensue from additional disclosure of official information. But it
was his professional judgment, shared by other senior State Department
officials, that disclosure of the unreleased material could seriously damage
U.S. foreign relations. "Even to speculate publicly about specific consequences that might flow from such disclosures would, in all likelihood, be

damaging, as other governments might feel constrained to react to such speculation by comments or measures."[22]

On the intelligence side, CIA associate deputy director for science and technology Ernest Zellmer noted, the names of many present and/or former government officials and their employers remained secret. Reviewers, he wrote, had redacted from previously released documents the "identity of one government entity, the very existence of which is classified." Revealing "the names of those government officials, not associated with the CIA, who were involved in the *HGE* project, would signal to the world that these persons were and/or are engaged in highly sensitive intelligence activities and could lead to exposure of their cover and the cover used by a classified government entity."[23]

Certain disclosures could reverberate well beyond *Glomar* to harm America's ability to collect foreign intelligence. "The collection of foreign intelligence is increasingly dependent on sophisticated technology and the development of technological systems," Zellmer explained. U.S. intelligence agencies relied on private industry, signing black contracts with individual firms for the research, development, and production of these high-tech systems. Due to litigation, the government had been forced to acknowledge its contractual relationship with Hughes Tool, Summa Corporation, and Global Marine. But more corporations were reportedly involved in the *Glomar* enterprise. (Ten, according to a deposed Global Marine executive.) Many continued to partner with the U.S. intelligence community on ongoing projects. And Zellmer, a World War II submarine veteran involved with AZORIAN from the start, insisted that their official unmasking "would"—not *could*, but *would*—prevent the CIA from performing its core mission: collecting foreign intelligence.

If the CIA was precluded from entering or honoring confidential agreements for the production of covert nondomestic uses of technological intelligence gathering devices an extremely valuable means of gathering intelligence would be lost. The disclosure of the names of organizations and their employees who entered into such confidential agreements with the CIA, in connection with the *HGE* Project, would almost certainly impact negatively on the ability of the CIA to obtain the assistance of such entities and individuals in similar ventures in the future.[24]

When and how the CIA transferred money to those companies, what financial methods and procedures officials employed to obscure the transactions—that information, too, must be safeguarded, affirmed CIA finance director Thomas Yale, because the agency routinely employed many of those same methods and procedures in other instances, on clandestine projects whose success similarly depended on there being no attribution of U.S. government involvement. In order not to draw attention to the fact that something extraordinary was occurring, CIA financial officers followed normal commercial practice to the maximum extent possible. They did not follow security procedures normally associated with the handling of "classified" information, he explained, because doing so would only draw attention to the fact that they were attempting to effect "a Government transaction, which is obviously self-defeating." Instead, they secured CIA transactions by making them "indistinguishable from the thousands of ordinary transactions with which they are enmeshed. In effect, the sensitive transactions are lost against the background of normal commercial traffic, and the ability to follow the trail of these sensitive transactions is possessed by only a few witting individuals who participated in this process."

According to Yale, officials used intermediaries, both individual and institutional, "to break the payor-payee chain," that is, to conceal the true source of *Glomar* funds: the U.S. Treasury. Program records named a certain bank as the depository of the Hughes Tool Company. Were they disclosed, not only employees of that bank but bank regulatory agencies could then "identify the particular intermediary who effected the payment. Thus, in effect, a key to unlocking some very sensitive information would be placed in the hands of individuals not authorized to receive such information and over whom there is no control from a national security standpoint."

Armed with that data, unauthorized persons could then follow the "trail of financial transactions [that led to] other CIA-sponsored transactions, past or present. At this point the damage to operations of the Central Intelligence Agency would be difficult, or impossible, to contain," Yale averred, for these operating procedures were standard. They were not limited to the *Glomar Explorer.*[25]

Dollar amounts spent in connection with the *Glomar Explorer* project also merited protection, then CIA director Turner affirmed, because the annual CIA budget "is not now and never has been a matter of public knowledge. Neither have the details of that budget ever been matters of public knowledge." Nondisclosure of this information enjoyed a long record of approval in Congress. Both chambers had repeatedly rejected legislation that would have required publication of even aggregate figures. Information that disclosed detailed breakdowns of expenditures made in connection with any one intelligence operation required even greater protection in the interests of national security. "Release of this information," wrote Turner, echoing the late Richard Russell's warnings about telegraphing U.S. capabilities abroad,

> would be a valuable benefit to an intelligence service of a foreign country in that it would permit deductions to be made concerning the state of the art of intelligence collection in a certain area and the importance the United States attributed to particular collection activities. The existence of the technologies on which we depend, and to the level of their sophistication, could be compromised by such disclosure, and the risk of foreign countermeasures to nullify our advantage could be enhanced.[26]

* * *

On paper, the Freedom of Information Act gave federal courts full *de novo* review powers. In practice, judges gave "substantial weight" to affidavits filed by national security officials who, according to a key ruling, possessed "unique insights into what adverse effects might occur as a result of public disclosure of a particular classified record." Contrary evidence or evidence of bad faith on officials' part could counteract affidavits. Otherwise, judges deferred to executive affidavits—excessively so, scholars say—because they lacked the knowledge and expertise necessary to make disclosure decisions in national security cases.[27]

Each of the affidavits filed in the *Military Audit* case stated that disclosure could harm U.S. security. They effectively led the circuit court into the "wilderness of mirrors," a place, legendary CIA counterintelligence chief James J. Angleton once wrote, "where fact and illusion merge" and decision makers wander confused amid an array "of stratagems, deceptions, artifices and all the other devices of disinformation."[28] In its opinion, the court addressed the appellant's argument that *Glomar* data no longer qualified for national security exemption because the story had already been told. Knowledgeable persons, the court began, had offered two explanations for the vessel's existence: (1) that it was a commercial ship designed to mine the seabed for manganese nodules, and (2) that it was a spy ship used to salvage a sunken Soviet submarine. Both stories were plausible. It was equally "plausible that the *Glomar Explorer* was designed to perform yet some still-secret third function." Quoting *Time* magazine, the court noted that the world might someday discover "that raising a Soviet submarine was not (the *Glomar Explorer*'s) mission at all, but the supreme cover for a secret mission as yet safely secure."[29]

What might this still-secret third function be? The court did not know. But that did not prevent judges from speculating about other conceivable uses to which such a sophisticated ship could be put. American officials could use the *Explorer* to tap undersea communications cables. Or to install a submarine monitoring device. Or to construct an underwater missile silo. The possibilities were boundless.[30]

Even if the *Explorer*'s true purpose was to raise a submarine, there might be some advantage in leaving foreign security services guessing as to what really motivated the ship's mission or how many secrets it gleaned. After all, the court noted, again citing *Time* as an authority, some believed that the CIA only floated the partial success story to disguise the fact that it "wholly succeeded" in raising the entire submarine—missiles, codes, and all. "Whatever the truth may be," the court concluded, "it remains either unrevealed or unconfirmed. We cannot assume, as the appellants would have us, that the CIA has nothing left to hide. To the contrary, the record before us suggests either that the CIA still has something to hide or that it wishes to hide from our adversaries the fact that it has nothing to hide."[31]

In fact, U.S. intelligence officials designed the *Explorer* for one purpose and one purpose only: to retrieve a sunken Soviet Golf II–class submarine, which was raised only partially. But the court maintained that no one outside of a small circle of cleared officials knew the real truth. And some of them had stated, in affidavits carrying "substantial weight," that disclosure could— would, in some respects—harm the national interest. Since the full facts, for security reasons, were unknown, it was safest to protect the cover stories, the fake "fallback" cover stories, everything the government said needed protecting, because every public disclosure reduced the CIA's flexibility.

On May 4, 1981, the DC circuit court ruled that the affidavits provided a reasonable basis for the government's exemption 1 claim. Military Audit, the appellant, had not disproved that claim. The court thus affirmed the district court's judgment: all withheld information was properly exempt under FOIA.[32]

Weeks later, the court issued its final decision in *Phillippi v. CIA.* "We find the documents at issue in the present case to be exempt from disclosure under Exemption 3 of the Act for many of the same reasons which compelled our decision for the CIA in *Military Audit*," read the opinion, dated June 25. Wandering further into the wilderness, the opinion pointed once again to the text often cited by American security officials, Nikita Khrushchev's memoirs, where the former Soviet premier recalled that it was Dwight Eisenhower's public acknowledgement of Gary Powers's ill-fated U-2 mission, not the fact of the mission itself, that led him to scuttle the Paris Summit of 1960. "The parallel to the *Glomar Explorer* project is obvious," the court stated. "In the world of international diplomacy, where face-saving may often be as important as substance, official confirmation of the *Glomar Explorer* project through release of [the disputed material] could have an adverse effect on our relations with the Soviets." Therefore, the court affirmed the district court's grant of summary judgment for the CIA.[33]

* * *

Phillippi and *Military Audit* were not the last words. But they were the first judicial recognition of the principle that a federal agency can refuse, on security grounds, to confirm or deny the existence of records sought in a FOIA request. As such, they helped establish FOIA case law pertinent to national security. Thousands of cases (and counting) have since cited them, in proceedings pitting the public's right to know against the state's duty to protect. The state usually prevailed, in part because *Phillippi* and *Military Audit* established that official disclosure of information under the law could harm the public interest, even if the information was already public.[34]

Glomar quickly morphed into a verb, "to Glomar," to describe a federally recognized process, and its related noun, "Glomarization," in which agencies neither confirmed nor denied ("Glomared") public requests for government information. In a 1982 executive order (EO) governing national security data-handling procedures, President Reagan directed all applicable agencies to follow neither confirm nor deny (NCND) practice whenever possible. "An agency shall refuse to confirm or deny the existence or nonexistence of requested information whenever the fact of its existence or nonexistence is itself classifiable under this order."[35]

Subsequent presidents backpedaled somewhat, making Glomarization an option rather than a requirement. ("An agency may refuse to confirm or deny," President Bill Clinton's 1995 EO read.) But Reagan's order marked a departure from its predecessor, Carter's 1978 EO, which expressly recognized the public's right to know and remains the only such order in American history to limit NCNDs in any way. ("No agency in possession of a classified document may, in response to a request for the document made under [FOIA or Mandatory Declassification Review, another release route], refuse to confirm the existence of non-existence of the document, unless the fact of its existence or non-existence would itself be classifiable under this Order.")[36]

Glomarization crept horizontally across the federal FOIA exemption spectrum. Creep began in 1980, when the DC district court ruled that law enforcement agencies could NCND the existence of certain records in order to protect the privacy of persons not publicly known to have been the subject of a law enforcement investigation. Affirmed on appeal, that ruling grew to cover alleged government informants, trial witnesses, and individuals named in a law enforcement record, vastly expanding another FOIA exemption, exemption 7(C), shielding information compiled for law enforcement purposes.[37]

Glomarization reached into non-security areas in the 1990s, when courts endorsed NCND responses to FOIA requests seeking records that might reveal whether an individual government employee was investigated for misconduct or disciplined. Glomar responses were appropriate in these cases, courts ruled, because even to acknowledge the existence of such records would typically cause an unwarranted invasion of personal privacy. These rulings underwrote yet another FOIA exemption, exemption 6, sparing records from release on privacy grounds.[38]

***

Today, the *Glomar Explorer* no longer exists. It was scrapped in 2015 after serving as a commercial deep ocean drilling platform for two decades.[39] But the Glomar response—a product of extraordinary circumstances, an ad hoc solution particular to its historical moment—lives on to thwart calls for government transparency at every level.

It lives on at the state and local levels, where Glomarization has crept vertically. Police now routinely NCND the existence of records in response to requests filed under local access laws. State courts have endorsed this nonfederal use. And legislatures have amended state access statutes to permit Glomar denials. Such proliferation, scholar A. Jay Wagner writes, "threatens freedom of information laws at their most basic, grassroots level," where oversight may be limited, and citizens may have fewer legal options to challenge statutory access denials.[40]

It lives on at the international level, where Glomarization has crept into open records laws. Like other such statutes, Australia's Freedom of Information Act aims to enhance the accountability and transparency of governmental institutions in order to enable public debate on the performance of those institutions. Yet the act, as amended in 2020, contains a section allowing ministers to NCND the existence of records in response to access requests, in cases where revelation of information could harm the public interest. Canada's and the United Kingdom's freedom of information laws contain similar provisions.[41]

And it lives on at the federal level, in the aforementioned FOIA exemptions 1, 3, 6, and 7(C); in U.S. Department of Justice guidance, which directs federal agencies to Glomar requests for information whose disclosure could reasonably harm national security or personal privacy; in annual reports showing that those four exemptions, anchored by Glomar, account for the majority of all FOIA denials;[42] and in the letterheads on which denials are printed. Historically less secretive agencies such as U.S. Citizenship and Immigration Services, the Centers for Disease Control and Prevention, and the Census Bureau regularly Glomarize requests. Even the post office has gotten into the act.[43]

Mostly, it lives on in the national security realm—from the executive order currently governing the handling of classified national security information, President Barack Obama's EO 13526, issued in 2009, which states that an "agency may refuse to confirm or deny the existence or nonexistence of requested records whenever the fact of their existence or nonexistence is itself classified under this order or its predecessors,"[44] to the Glomar denials the CIA, the National Security Agency (NSA), and other intelligence agencies routinely issue.

How often do federal agencies Glomar requests? It is difficult to say with certainty, writes Nate Jones, the *Washington Post*'s FOIA director and a former FOIA specialist at the National Security Archive, a nongovernmental research center based in Washington, DC, because the Justice Department does not maintain a dedicated database. It annually tracks the final disposition of FOIA requests, which shows only that agencies Glomared some unknown portion of the hundreds of thousands of requests that are denied in full or in part each year, based on an exemption.

Journalists, watchdogs, and scholars who file records requests don't need a scorecard to know the chilling effect Glomarization has on public discourse. They see it written on the pages of FOIA logs that detail the disposition of each individual request. Only a fraction of the logs are readily searchable, but those that are tell the tale. "DENIAL/GLOMAR—0 pages released," entry after entry reports. "GLOMAR POSITION," report others. "The use of Glomar non-denial denials [is] rampant," Jones concludes.[45]

At fifty plus, FOIA remains, in the words of the *Washington Post*, "a vital tool for keeping government open and honest." Since its passage in 1966, the act, arguably the most significant access statute in American history, has worked to expose government waste and mismanagement, highlight threats to food and environmental safety, and even unmask some national security decisions.[46]

However, experts agree that FOIA's pro-disclosure intent remains unrealized for a number of reasons, not least of which is the Glomar response, a CIA invention that was neither included in the original act of Congress nor ever amended into the law. Unlike a "regular" FOIA denial, Jones explains, in which an agency states that it has responsive records but will not release them for certain reasons, the Glomar response ("We can neither confirm nor deny the existence of the information requested . . .") leaves a requestor in the dark, without sufficient information to challenge agency decisions. Do responsive records exist? Do they not? The response does not say. Either way, requestors are "screwed," as the legalese's originator Walter Lloyd explained, because the response stipulates that any surviving records would be unreleasable for security reasons.[47]

Requestors do sometimes win on appeal. In 2013, for example, the American Civil Liberties Union won a drone-related case when the DC circuit court ruled that the CIA's attempt to Glomarize the appellant's FOIA request was "neither logical nor plausible," since a wealth of information about the agency's use of unmanned aerial vehicles was already in the public domain.[48]

Appellants usually lose, though, because NCNDs leave judges in the dark too. Inexpert, unable to independently balance competing claims, they generally defer, giving "substantial weight" to agency affidavits claiming that disclosure can harm privacy or security interests. Fearful of releasing information that plausibly could cause harm, they rely on precedent, starting with *Phillippi* and *Military Audit*, cited in those thousands of cases (and counting) pitting the public's right to know against the state's duty to protect.

These are cited, for example, in cases involving electronic surveillance. Courts have consistently ruled that the NSA can Glomar requests for data about its activities, including its reported relationship with Google and other tech giants, because that information's official acknowledgment could cause harm cognizable under a FOIA exemption. These rulings, experts say, have effectively exempted the NSA from FOIA coverage, limiting the public's ability to judge whether the agency conducts surveillance in ethical, legal, and constitutional ways. And those rulings depend, in part, on legal decisions reached decades earlier, long before the advent of modern eavesdropping techniques. In that sense, *Phillippi, Military Audit*, and other cornerstone decisions have been used to build a structure of secrecy used by intelligence officials today. Or, as one expert puts it, "the legal victories achieved by old-school snoops have enabled new-school snoops."[49]

* * *

Government secrecy—that's the most durable by-product of the *Glomar Explorer* operation. More durable than the ship's technical achievement; more durable even than its intelligence take, the contribution it made to America's Cold War victory. Significant though both may have been, they cannot be evaluated properly, due to security restrictions that the Glomar response works to enforce. Yes, more data has entered the public domain since the circuit court's 1981 verdicts. In 2010, for example, the CIA released an internal history of AZORIAN in response to a FOIA request filed by the National Security Archive. Additional releases followed, including David Sharp's personal account and the official history documenting both AZORIAN and MATADOR that I researched and edited.[50] And those materials sourced another round of publications, this book among them.[51]

"Laymen," though, are hardly better positioned to judge the operation's outcome today than we were in 1975, when the *Washington Post* remarked that outsiders were ill-equipped "to say whether the findings are worth $350 million."[52] Too many unknowns still exist, because the vast majority of the

128,000 documents the CIA acknowledged possessing remain undisclosed, locked safely away in the agency's archive, impervious to open records laws, thanks in part to the Glomar response.

At every level: local and state, national and international. In every branch of government. In the courts. The Congress. The executive branch. Even the fourth estate. *Glomar*, a clandestine operation conceived in Cold War secrecy and dedicated to the proposition that plausible deniability matters, shielded CIA secrecy at a time when CIA secrecy needed shielding most: the sunshine era, which at its peak attempted to illuminate the darkest recesses of the intelligence community. Kick-started by revelations of past misdeeds, 1975, the Year of Intelligence, famously began with high-profile investigations—probes, many establishmentarians believed, that threatened to upset the prevailing equilibrium between national security and civil liberties, not to mention the very existence of the CIA itself. To be sure, those investigations unearthed a number of secrets, include some "bad" or "illegitimate" ones documenting domestic spying programs, covert actions to unseat democratically elected foreign governments, and plots to assassinate world leaders. Those findings led to the imposition of stronger oversight mechanisms. And they contributed to the new high standard set during the 1970s with regard to government transparency.

From the vantage point of the twenty-first century, however, when by all accounts national security secrecy remains expansive and the U.S. intelligence community grows with relatively little oversight, one would be hard-pressed to argue that the era marked a decisive break with the past. Arguably, the counterattack began with the March 1975 unmasking of the *Glomar Explorer*, which worked to "right the balance," in the words of Washington insider and columnist Joseph Kraft. *Glomar* did not operate alone, of course. But the unauthorized disclosure of the then still-active mission, widely portrayed as a technically wondrous and semi-successful effort to steal a nuclear-armed Soviet submarine out from under Americans' Cold War rivals, worked to raise the CIA's stature, rally supporters, and shield secrets—bad secrets pertaining to Watergate, if the CIA legislative liaison's account of his meeting with White House officials is to be believed, but "good" or "legitimate" ones, too, pertaining to foreign intelligence collection and analysis. Either way, the incident served to protect the agency and its ability to perform its core mission.[53]

And that was just the first step. The episode continued to resonate for months, even years afterwards, in the halls of Congress and in the courts, where the Glomar response sharply reduced the candlepower of FOIA, the sunshine era's showpiece legislation. "In my opinion," Lloyd wrote, "the Glomar Response was very effective in a very troubling time (mid-70s)."[54]

"Neither confirm nor deny." That clever evasion is not just for spies anymore. It is now part of the vernacular, standard operating procedure invoked by everyone from government officials and celebrity spokespeople working to stymie the efforts of official watchdogs or tenacious reporters, to furtive teens hoping to stonewall nosy parents. It is invoked so often, in fact, that it has become cliché, the source of a running joke. "We can neither confirm nor deny that this is our first tweet," @CIA deadpanned in a 2014 Twitter post since retweeted or liked almost half a million times.[55]

Shielding clandestine activity from view—for better or worse, that's why the portrait of the *Glomar Explorer* merits a place in the CIA's hall of fame, as it were. Because secrecy is what gave flight to the agency's imagination, pushing it to pour hundreds of millions of dollars into a "crazy" scheme to lift a waterlogged submarine from the bottom of the ocean, using a giant claw affixed to an experimental ship ostensibly owned by an eccentric billionaire—an impossible mission that stood only a 10 percent chance of success, according to the CIA's own reckoning. And because secrecy, preserved, is what gave the agency freedom to pursue other bold schemes, some now known, others undoubtedly still hidden.[56]

Titled *We Are Only Limited by Our Imagination*, *Glomar*'s portrait hangs inside the CIA's Langley headquarters today. Nestled between portraits depicting U-2 overflights of the Soviet Union in the 1950s and Stinger missiles targeting Soviet aircraft in Afghanistan in the 1980s, it is part of the agency's fine art collection celebrating great moments in American intelligence history. The collection exists to promote the past as prologue to the present, an important mission, curators say, given that most CIA employees entered service relatively recently, since the September 11, 2001, terrorist attacks. "Our workforce is a young workforce," a spokesperson explained, "and it's absolutely critical that they understand where we've come from as an agency so they can lead us to where we will go."[57]

You can visit the collection—online, at least. For security reasons, the physical collection is accessible only to CIA employees and cleared visitors.

ACKNOWLEDGMENTS

"Got anything on the *Glomar Explorer*?" Edward Keefer asked me in 2005 or so. At the time, Keefer was the (much-respected) general editor of the *Foreign Relations of the United States* (*FRUS*) series, the official documentary record of U.S. foreign policy published by the Department of State. He had seen a documentary on the sub-raising mission and wanted to know if it was documented in the *FRUS* volume I was then researching. No, I answered sheepishly. But his question sent me on a journey. Thanks, Ted.

That *FRUS* volume (volume 35 of the 1969–1976 *FRUS* subseries documenting the Nixon and Ford administrations) entered declassification review in 2007. It was published in 2014—with redactions, to be sure, but fewer than one would have guessed, given that major aspects of the *Glomar* mission remained unacknowledged by the U.S. government when the process began. This book relies heavily on that volume's contents. Neither would have been the same without the dedicated efforts of Susan Weetman, Carl Ashley, Erin Cozens, Dean Weatherhead, and especially Chris Tudda, who coordinated the volume's declassification review. Thank you.

The State Department's Office of the Historian is among the leading centers for the study of the history of U.S. foreign relations. I was privileged to work there for seven years among an extraordinary group of scholars, including Kristin Ahlberg, Josh Botts, Ambassador Edward Brynn, Myra Burton, Ambassador John Campbell, John Carland, Seth Center, Mandy Chalou, Elizabeth Charles, Bradley Coleman, Craig Daigle, Evan Dawley, Steven Galpern, Amy Garrett, David Geyer, Renée Goings, Paul Hibbeln, Adam Howard, Halbert Jones, Keri Lewis, Erin Mahan, Aaron Marrs, William McAllister, Michael McCoyer, Christopher Morrison, Richard Moss, David Nickles, Linda Qaimmaqami, Stephen Randolph, Kathleen Rasmussen, Doug Selvage, James Siekmeier, Nathaniel Smith, Melissa Jane Taylor, Jamie Van Hook, Laurie Van Hook, Joseph Wicentowski, Alexander Wieland, James

Wilson, Louise Woodroofe, David Zierler, and the late David Humphrey, Peter Kraemer, and Louis Smith.

My service in the Office of the Historian also enabled me to get to know members of the State Department's Advisory Committee on Historical Diplomatic Documentation, including Carol Anderson, Laura Belmonte, Richard Immerman, William Roger Louis, Robert McMahon, Edward Rhodes, Katie Sibley, and Tom Zeiler. Thanks for your support.

The CIA Office of Public Affairs provided illustrations, scheduled interviews with current employees, and arranged access to the agency's Langley, Virginia, headquarters. Chief Historian David Robarge helpfully corrected some misstatements of fact. I was required to submit the book manuscript to the CIA Prepublication Classification Review Board because I once had special access, in my State Department days, to CIA materials. The board demanded the removal of some classified material but did not otherwise object to the text's publication. The board also required the inclusion of the following disclaimer: "All statements of fact, opinion, or analysis expressed are those of the author and do not reflect the official positions or views of the U.S. Government. Nothing in the contents should be construed as asserting or implying U.S. Government authentication of information or endorsement of the author's views."

Many people who participated in the *Glomar* story graciously took time to speak with or assist me in some way. They ranged from Seymour Hersh and William Turner to Curtis Crooke, Ray Feldman, Admiral Bobby Ray Inman, David Sharp, Geary Yost, the late Walter Lloyd, and others who asked not to be named. They generously shared their memories, often over coffee, in their homes. They provided perspective I would not have otherwise had. And even if they don't agree with every word of this book, I hope they find it to be a respectable, well-researched, factually accurate account of an important episode in the nation's intelligence history. Miss you, Walt. Thanks, Montee, for the sandwiches!

I want to thank the librarians and archivists who assisted me at the Library of Congress, the University of Michigan's Bentley Historical Library, Southwestern University's A. Frank Smith Jr. Library Center, the LBJ Presidential Library, Texas Tech University's Southwest Collection/Special Collections Library, Arizona State University's Hayden Library, the Nixon Presidential Library, and the University of Nevada, Las Vegas's Lied Library. Special thanks to Aimee Miller of the Ronald Reagan Presidential Library; Alessandro Meregaglia of Boise State University's Albertsons Library; Ryan Semmes of Mississippi State University's Congressional and Political Research Center; Sheryl Vogt and Jill Severn of the University of Georgia's Richard B. Russell Library for Political Research and Studies; David Richards and Angie Stockwell of the Margaret Chase Smith Library; Stacy Davis, Mark Fisher, Geir Gundersen, Donna Lehman, William McNitt, Helmi Raaska, and the rest of the staff of the Gerald Ford Presidential Library; Susan McElrath, American University's former university archivist; Krista Peim of George Washington University's Gelman Library; and David Langbart, Don McIlwaine, John Powers, and their National Archives colleagues.

Financial support from the Association of Centers for the Study of Congress and the Margaret Chase Smith Foundation enabled me to research congressional records. A Public Scholar Award from the National Endowment for the Humanities (NEH) provided me with the precious gift of time: a year free of teaching and other university responsibilities to research and write. My employer, East Carolina University, provided generous support as well. A Grant-Seeking Reassignment Award from ECU's Thomas Harriot College of Arts and Sciences resulted in the proposal that won the NEH grant. A Brewster Scholar Award from ECU's Department of History underwrote a major research trip.

ACKNOWLEDGMENTS

I have enjoyed a rewarding experience since joining ECU's faculty in 2009 thanks to colleagues such as Charles Calhoun, David Dennard, Timothy Jenks, Jessica Kestler, Jennifer McKinnon, Ingrid Meyer, Christopher Oakley, Donald Parkerson, Kennetta Hammond Perry, Gerald Prokopowicz, Cindy Putnam-Evans, Jonathan Reid, Nathan Richards, Mona Russell, Carl Swanson, Karin Zipf, and the late Wade Dudley.

A number of colleagues made special contributions to this effort. Loch Johnson walked me through the realities of congressional oversight. Kathryn Olmsted shared copies of declassified files that should be readily available but are not. Cullen Nutt helped me find a needle in a haystack. Sarah Snyder discovered some *Glomar*-related material in an unexpected place. Jonathan Nashel talked me off the ledge. Chuck Grench broadened my thinking. Kelly McFarland, Mark Stout, Calder Walton, and David Oakley were among those who sharpened it during a North American Society for Intelligence History brown bag. William Imboden, Mark Lawrence, and Geoffrey Connor cohosted a stellar 2016 conference, "The Rise and Fall of Détente," at the University of Texas at Austin's Clements Center for National Security. Thanks to you all.

My aim was to write a history that would be respected by professional historians yet accessible to nonspecialists. That proved to be a difficult line to walk, and I don't know that I walked it well. But Stephen Wesley, my editor at Columbia University Press, shared that vision. Despite growing demands on his time, he never wavered in his support, demonstrating, through words and actions, his confidence in the project. And he applied his considerable editorial skills to the prose, which is crisper as a result. Thanks, too, to Marisa Lastres, Christian Winting, and the other members of the press's editorial and design staff, who expertly turned the raw manuscript into a completed book; to the anonymous peer reviewers who offered incredibly constructive feedback; and to copy editor Ryan Perks, who added considerable value to the final product. That said, all mistakes are mine, not theirs.

Last but not least, let me thank family and friends. The Bennetts. The Webbs. The Beebes. The Champions. The Rasmussens. All y'all. Special shoutouts to Robbie Marion and Basil, who were always there, even when I least expected it. (See chapter 9 for an example.) To UB, who served as my imaginary reader to whom I wrote much of the text. And of course, to Kathy and Zoë, who have to put up with me on a daily basis. Love you guys. You're the best. Thanks for giving me a home.

NOTES

ABBREVIATIONS IN THE NOTES

BSA	Donald L. Barlett and James B. Steele Archive
DoJ	Department of Justice
FRUS	*Foreign Relations of the United States*
GRFPL	Gerald R. Ford Presidential Library
JFK Collection	President John F. Kennedy Assassination Records Collection
LoC	Library of Congress
Memcons	Memoranda of Conversations
NARA	National Archives and Records Administration
NSAF	National Security Advisor's Files
OIP	Office of Information Policy
PPP	*Public Papers of the Presidents*
RNPLM	Richard Nixon Presidential Library and Museum
SMOF, WHSF	Staff Member and Office Files, White House Special Files
SSCPCA	Senate Select Committee on Presidential Campaign Activities
telcon	transcript of telephone conversation
WCPO	West Coast Program Office (CIA)
WSPF	Watergate Special Prosecution Force

INTRODUCTION

1. "The Great Submarine Snatch," *Time*, March 31, 1975, 20; "Project AZORIAN: The Story of the *Hughes Glomar Explorer*," *Studies in Intelligence* 22, no. 3 (1978): 4; David H. Sharp, *The CIA's Greatest Covert Operation: Inside the Daring Mission to Recover a Nuclear-Armed*

Soviet Sub (Lawrence: University Press of Kansas, 2012), 1. See also Jeffrey T. Richelson, *The Wizards of Langley: Inside the CIA's Directorate of Science and Technology* (Boulder, CO: Westview Press, 2002).

2. "Engineering for AZORIAN," *Studies in Intelligence* 24, no. 1 (1980): 1.

3. David S. Robarge, "Richard Helms: The Intelligence Professional Personified," *Studies in Intelligence* 46, no. 4 (2002): 35–43; Thomas Powers, *The Man Who Kept the Secrets: Richard Helms and the CIA* (New York: Knopf, 1979), 2, 93, 115 (emphasis in the original). Helms wrote not a word about AZORIAN in his memoirs, *A Look Over My Shoulder: A Life in the Central Intelligence Agency* (New York: Random House, 2003), published a decade after one of his successors, Robert Gates, publicly acknowledged the project's existence.

4. Walter T. Lloyd telephone interview with author, August 1, 2016. Lloyd permitted me, in writing, to use his actual name. He passed away in 2019.

5. "Project AZORIAN," 11; Helms to Henry Kissinger, memo, September 14, 1972, doc. 184 in *Foreign Relations of the United States* [hereafter *FRUS*], *1969–1976*, vol. 35, *National Security Policy, 1973–1976*, ed. M. Todd Bennett (Washington, DC: U.S. Government Printing Office, 2014).

6. "Project AZORIAN," 12. William Colby itemized the sub's contents in a memo to Kissinger, May 23, 1974, in *FRUS, 1969–1976*, vol. 35, doc. 185.

7. Sherry Sontag and Christopher Drew, *Blind Man's Bluff: The Untold Story of American Submarine Espionage* (New York: Harper, 1998), 91–92, 215.

8. Helms to Kissinger, memo, December 7, 1970, doc. 220 in *FRUS, 1969–1976*, vol. 2, *Organization and Management of U.S. Foreign Policy, 1969–1972*, ed. David Humphrey (Washington, DC: U.S. Government Printing Office, 2006). To succeed, U.S. intelligence agencies must have freedom of action, ex-CIA director Michael V. Hayden argues in *Playing to the Edge: American Intelligence in the Age of Terror* (New York: Penguin, 2016), xiv.

9. "Project AZORIAN," 1–2, 49–50.

10. Gareth Hector, *We Are Only Limited by Our Imagination*, 2013, in *The Art of Intelligence* (Washington, DC: CIA Museum and the Center for the Study of Intelligence, 2016), 42–43; "A Peek Into the CIA Art Gallery Reveals [REDACTED]," *Morning Edition*, National Public Radio, May 20, 2016, https://www.npr.org/2016/05/20/478706463/a-peek-into-the-cia-art-gallery-reveals-redacted.

11. Geary Yost (pseudonym) interview, August 4, 2016, suburban Washington, DC (a more precise location has been withheld to preserve source's anonymity).

12. Norman Polmar and Michael White, *Project AZORIAN: The CIA and the Raising of the K-129* (Annapolis, MD: Naval Institute Press, 2010); Sharp, *CIA's Greatest*; Josh Dean, *The Taking of K-129: How the CIA Used Howard Hughes to Steal a Russian Sub in the Most Daring Covert Operation in History* (New York: Dutton, 2017). Previous accounts include Clyde W. Burleson, *The Jennifer Project* (Englewood Cliffs, NJ: Prentice-Hall, 1977); Roy Varner and Wayne Collier, *A Matter of Risk: The Incredible Inside Story of the CIA's Hughes Glomar Explorer Mission to Raise a Russian Submarine* (New York: Random House, 1978).

13. Examples include Athan G. Theoharis, ed., *A Culture of Secrecy: The Government Versus the People's Right to Know* (Lawrence: University Press of Kansas, 1998); Robert Dean, K. A. Cuordileone, Janet Farrell Brodie, and Kathryn S. Olmsted, "Special Forum: Cultures of Secrecy in Postwar America," *Diplomatic History* 35, no. 4 (2011): 611–693; Christopher Moran, *Classified: Secrecy and the State in Modern Britain* (New York:

Cambridge University Press, 2013); Kaeten Mistry and Hannah Gurman, eds., *Whistle-blowing Nation: The History of National Security Disclosures and the Cult of State Secrecy* (New York: Columbia University Press, 2020); Alex Wellerstein, *Restricted Data: The History of Nuclear Secrecy in the United States* (Chicago: University of Chicago Press, 2021).

14. Loch K. Johnson, *America's Secret Power: The CIA in a Democratic Society* (New York: Oxford University Press, 1989), viii–ix, 10–11; Rhodri Jeffreys-Jones, *The CIA and American Democracy*, 3rd ed. (New Haven, CT: Yale University Press, 2003), 1–2. See also Gary Gerstle, *Liberty and Coercion: The Paradox of American Government from the Founding to the Present*, rev. ed. (Princeton, NJ: Princeton University Press, 2015).

15. Richard H. Immerman, *The Hidden Hand: A Brief History of the CIA* (Malden, MA: Wiley-Blackwell, 2014), 47; Loch K. Johnson, "Governing in the Absence of Angels: On the Practice of Intelligence Accountability in the United States," in *Who's Watching the Spies: Establishing Intelligence Service Accountability*, ed. Hans Born, Loch K. Johnson, and Ian Leigh (Washington, DC: Potomac Books, 2005), 58. John Stennis quoted in L. Britt Snider, *Congress and the CIA* (New York: Nova Science Publishers, 2009), 282. Historical studies of intelligence oversight include Frank J. Smist Jr., *Congress Oversees the United States Intelligence Community, 1947–1994* (Knoxville: University of Tennessee Press, 1994); David M. Barrett, *The CIA and Congress: The Untold Story from Truman to Kennedy* (Lawrence: University Press of Kansas, 2005); L. Britt Snider, *The Agency and the Hill: CIA's Relationship with Congress, 1946–2004* (Washington, DC: CIA Center for the Study of Intelligence, 2008); Loch K. Johnson, *Spy Watching: Intelligence Accountability in the United States* (New York: Oxford University Press, 2018). John Prados traces the agency's history of avoiding accountability in *The Ghosts of Langley: Into the CIA's Heart of Darkness* (New York: New Press, 2017).

16. Powers, *Man Who Kept the Secrets*, 319–320; Harry Howe Ransom, "Secret Intelligence in the United States, 1947–1982: The CIA's Search for Legitimacy," in *The Missing Dimension: Governments and Intelligence Communities in the Twentieth Century*, ed. Christopher Andrew and David Dilks (Urbana: University of Illinois Press, 1984), 199.

17. Sharp, *CIA's Greatest*, 271; Michael Drosnin, *Citizen Hughes* (New York: Holt, 1985), 390.

18. Mitchell B. Lerner, *The Pueblo Incident: A Spy Ship and the Failure of American Foreign Policy* (Lawrence: University Press of Kansas, 2002); Michael R. Beschloss, *Mayday: Eisenhower, Khrushchev and the U-2 Affair* (New York: Harper and Row, 1986).

19. Henry Kissinger, *Years of Renewal* (New York: Simon and Schuster, 1999), 38.

20. Andrew and Dilks, *Missing Dimension*; Hugh Wilford, "Still Missing: The Historiography of U.S. Intelligence," *Passport* 47, no. 2 (2016): 20–25. *Glomar* merits a footnote in Raymond L. Garthoff's definitive study, *Détente and Confrontation: American-Soviet Relations from Nixon to Reagan*, rev. ed. (Washington, DC: Brookings Institution, 2011), which limits discussion of intelligence matters, generally, to just seven of the book's twelve-hundred-plus pages. Anne Hessing Cahn's *Killing Détente: The Right Attacks the CIA* (University Park: Pennsylvania State University Press, 1998) stands out among détente-specific studies of intelligence matters.

21. See *FRUS, 1969–1976*, vol. 35. The volume entered declassification review in 2007.

22. Foreign Relations Authorization Act, Pub. L. 102-138, 105 Stat. 647 (1991).

23. The U-2 incident "dramatized the inherent incompatibility of diplomacy and espionage," Ransom noted in *The Intelligence Establishment* (Cambridge, MA: Harvard University Press, 1970), 239–240.

24. Garthoff, *Détente and Confrontation*, 4–5; John Lewis Gaddis, *Strategies of Containment: A Critical Appraisal of American National Security Policy During the Cold War*, rev. ed. (New York: Oxford University Press, 2005), 280, 287, 315.

25. Seymour M. Hersh, *The Price of Power: Kissinger in the Nixon White House* (New York: Summit, 1983), 39–41, 314–317; Walter Isaacson, *Kissinger: A Biography* (New York: Simon and Schuster, 1992), 209; William Bundy, *A Tangled Web: The Making of Foreign Policy in the Nixon Presidency* (New York: Hill and Wang, 1998); Jussi Hanhimäki, *The Flawed Architect: Henry Kissinger and American Foreign Policy* (New York: Oxford University Press, 2004), xvii, 44, 428, 450–451, 480; Robert Dallek, *Nixon and Kissinger: Partners in Power* (New York: HarperCollins, 2007), x, 111; Tim Weiner, *One Man Against the World: The Tragedy of Richard Nixon* (New York: Henry Holt, 2015), 261, 265.

26. William Colby and Peter Forbath, *Honorable Men: My Life in the CIA* (New York: Simon and Schuster, 1978), 417.

27. "Year of Intelligence," *New York Times*, February 8, 1975. On the causes and effects of adversarial journalism, see Michael Schudson, *Discovering the News: A Social History of American Newspapers* (New York: Basic Books, 1978), 176–183; Larry J. Sabato, *Feeding Frenzy: How Attack Journalism Has Transformed American Politics* (New York: Free Press, 1991); Thomas E. Patterson, *Out of Order* (New York: Knopf, 1993), 19, 79; Julian E. Zelizer, "Without Restraint: Scandal and Politics in America," in *The Columbia History of Post-World War II America*, ed. Mark C. Carnes (New York: Columbia University Press, 2007), 232–236; David Greenberg, *Republic of Spin: An Inside History of the American Presidency* (New York: Norton, 2016), 400–401.

28. Frank Church quoted in "CIA, Hughes Connection," *ABC Evening News*, March 19, 1975, clip #36304, https://tvnews.vanderbilt.edu (Vanderbilt Television News Archive, Special Collections, Heard Libraries, Vanderbilt University, Nashville, TN). On the reemergence of Congress, see David S. Broder, *Changing of the Guard: Power and Leadership in America* (New York: Simon and Schuster, 1980), 34–36; James L. Sundquist, *The Decline and Resurgence of Congress* (Washington, DC: Brookings Institution, 1981); Bruce J. Schulman, "Restraining the Imperial Presidency: Congress and Watergate," in *The American Congress: The Building of Democracy*, ed. Zelizer (Boston: Houghton Mifflin, 2004), 638–649; Julian E. Zelizer, *On Capitol Hill: The Struggle to Reform Congress and Its Consequences, 1948–2000* (New York: Cambridge University Press, 2004), 156–176; Robert David Johnson, *Congress and the Cold War* (New York: Cambridge University Press, 2006), 190–241.

29. Hugh Heclo, "The Sixties' False Dawn: Awakenings, Movements, and Postmodern Policy-Making," in *Integrating the Sixties: The Origins, Structures, and Legitimacy of Public Policy in a Turbulent Decade*, ed. Brian Balogh (University Park: Pennsylvania State University Press, 1996), 57. Journalist Meg Greenfield coined the "sunshine era" moniker in her memoir, *Washington* (New York: PublicAffairs, 2001), 94. See Jason Ross Arnold, *Secrecy in the Sunshine Era: The Promise and Failures of US Open Government Laws* (Lawrence: University Press of Kansas, 2014), xii; Katherine A. Scott, *Reining in the State: Civil Society and Congress in the Vietnam and Watergate Eras* (Lawrence: University Press of Kansas, 2013); Schudson, *The Rise of the Right to Know: Politics and the Culture of Transparency, 1945–1975* (Cambridge, MA: Belknap Press of Harvard University Press, 2015).

30. Bruce Schulman, *The Seventies: The Great Shift in American Culture, Society, and Politics* (New York: Free Press, 2001). See also David Frum, *How We Got Here: The 70's: The Decade that Brought You Modern Life (for Better or Worse)* (New York: Basic Books, 2000);

Edward D. Berkowitz, *Something Happened: A Political and Cultural Overview of the Seventies* (New York: Columbia University Press, 2006); Niall Ferguson, Charles S. Maier, Erez Manela, and Daniel J. Sargent, eds., *The Shock of the Global: The 1970s in Perspective* (Cambridge, MA: Belknap Press of Harvard University Press, 2010); Judith Stein, *Pivotal Decade: How the United States Traded Factories for Finance in the Seventies* (New Haven, CT: Yale University Press, 2010); Daniel J. Sargent, *A Superpower Transformed: The Remaking of American Foreign Relations in the 1970s* (New York: Oxford University Press, 2015). Despite appearances to the contrary, the seventies were eventful, argues Peter N. Carroll in *It Seemed Like Nothing Happened: America in the 1970s* (New York: Holt, 1982).

31. "Great Submarine Snatch." Continuity as well as change characterized the political culture of the 1970s, writes Kathryn S. Olmsted in *Challenging the Secret Government: The Post-Watergate Investigations of the CIA and FBI* (Chapel Hill: University of North Carolina Press, 1996), 5. On the rightward shift in the politics of national security, see Julian E. Zelizer, *Arsenal of Democracy: The Politics of National Security—From World War II to the War on Terrorism* (New York: Basic Books, 2010), 254–255, 262, 264; Bruce J. Schulman and Julian E. Zelizer, eds., *Rightward Bound: Making America Conservative in the 1970s* (Cambridge, MA: Harvard University Press, 2008); Jonathan M. Schoenwald, *A Time for Choosing: The Rise of Modern American Conservatism* (New York: Oxford University Press, 2001), 255–257.

32. "Stranger than Fiction," *New York Daily News*, March 20, 1975, in *Editorials on File 6*, no. 6 (March 16–31, 1975): 314; "The CIA Was Doing Its Job," *Washington Star*, March 21, 1975, in *Editorials on File 6*, no. 6 (March 16–31, 1975): 315. Discussions of the news media's constrained coverage of national security include Leon V. Sigal, *Reporters and Officials: The Organization and Politics of Newsmaking* (Lexington, MA: D. C. Heath, 1973), 84; David Halberstam, *The Powers that Be* (New York: Knopf, 1979), 578–579, 668; David S. Broder, *Behind the Front Page* (New York: Simon and Schuster, 1987), 149; William Greider, *Who Will Tell the People: The Betrayal of American Democracy* (New York: Simon and Schuster, 1992); Ted Galen Carpenter, *The Captive Press: Foreign Policy Crises and the First Amendment* (Washington, DC: Cato Institute, 1995); Bartholomew H. Sparrow, *Uncertain Guardians: The News Media as a Political Institution* (Baltimore, MD: Johns Hopkins University Press, 1999).

33. Joseph Kraft, "Lessons from the Soviet Submarine Incident," *Washington Post*, March 23, 1975.

1. THE OLD LINES

1. *Congressional Record*, 89th Cong., 2d sess., July 14, 1966, pp. 15676–15677; Gilbert C. Fite, *Richard B. Russell, Jr., Senator from Georgia* (Chapel Hill: University of North Carolina Press, 1991), 368, 463–466.

2. *Congressional Record*, 89th Cong., 2d sess., July 14, 1966, p. 15676.

3. Index cards, November 17, 1969, Intra Office [Memorandum, 1969], and January 30, 1970, Intra Office [Memorandum, 1970], both in box 7, Series V: United States Senatorial Years, Subgroup D: Winder Papers, Richard B. Russell Jr. Collection, Richard B. Russell Library for Political Research and Studies, University of Georgia Libraries, Athens, GA.

4. Thomas Powers, *The Man Who Kept the Secrets: Richard Helms and the CIA* (New York: Knopf, 1979).

5. National Security Act of 1947, Pub. L. 80-253, 61 Stat. 495 (1947).

6. Helms quoted in L. Britt Snider, *The Agency and the Hill: CIA's Relationship with Congress, 1946–2014* (Washington, DC: CIA Center for the Study of Intelligence, 2008), 232.

7. "Project AZORIAN: The Story of the *Hughes Glomar Explorer*," *Studies in Intelligence* 22, no. 3 (1978): 11; list attached to CIA to Dwight Ink, November 28, 1975, CIA, box 2, Series 1: Executive, John C. Stennis Collection, Congressional and Political Research Center, Mississippi State University Libraries, Starkville, Mississippi. Thomas Moorer quoted in Sherry Sontag and Christopher Drew, *Blind Man's Bluff: The Untold Story of American Submarine Espionage* (New York: Harper, 1998), 219.

8. Notecard, July 16, 1968, box 3, Series II: Intra-Office Communications, Subgroup C: United States Senatorial Papers, Russell Collection.

9. For details of the search, see memorandum to Henry Kissinger, May 28, 1974, doc. 186 in *Foreign Relations of the United States* [hereafter *FRUS*], *1969–1976*, vol. 35, *National Security Policy, 1973–1976*, ed. M. Todd Bennett (Washington, DC: U.S. Government Printing Office, 2014).

10. For speculation, see Sontag and Drew, *Blind Man's Bluff*, 87–88; David H. Sharp, *The CIA's Greatest Covert Operation: Inside the Daring Mission to Recover a Nuclear-Armed Soviet Sub* (Lawrence: University Press of Kansas, 2012), 2, 287–289; Norman Polmar and Michael White, *Project AZORIAN: The CIA and the Raising of the K-129* (Annapolis, MD: Naval Institute Press, 2010), 32–33, 148–167. Some have theorized that an explosion occurred when someone—the sub's rouge commander or a cabal of Soviet nationalists, depending on the telling—tried to launch an unauthorized nuclear strike on Hawaii. John Piña Craven, *The Silent War: The Cold War Battle Beneath the Sea* (New York: Simon and Schuster, 2001), 217–218; Kenneth Sewell with Clint Richmond, *Red Star Rogue: The Untold Story of a Soviet Submarine's Nuclear Strike Attempt on the U.S.* (New York: Simon and Schuster, 2005), xiii, 86, 89–92, 94.

11. Sontag and Drew, *Blind Man's Bluff*, 83–87; Sharp, *CIA's Greatest*, 3–4; Polmar and White, *Project AZORIAN*, 36–39, 43–46.

12. Sontag and Drew, *Blind Man's Bluff*, 87–89; Sharp, *CIA's Greatest*, 5. USS *Halibut* crewmember Roger C. Dunham recounts the activity of the "USS *Viperfish*" (navy censors required Dunham to make certain modifications prior to publication) in *Spy Sub: A Top Secret Mission to the Bottom of the Pacific* (Annapolis, MD: Naval Institute Press, 1996).

13. Index card, November 17, 1969, box 7, Intra Office [Memorandum, 1969], Subgroup D: Winder Papers, Russell Collection.

14. Sontag and Drew, *Blind Man's Bluff*, 87–89, 91; John T. Hughes to William Colby, memo, May 2, 1974, attachment to *FRUS, 1969–1976*, vol. 35, doc. 185.

15. For the USIB assessment, see Colby to Henry Kissinger, memo, May 23, 1974, and John T. Hughes to Colby, May 2, 1974, attachment, both in *FRUS, 1969–1976*, vol. 35, doc. 185. Emphasis in originals. Bobby Ray Inman, interview with author, November 16, 2016, Austin, TX.

16. For the underwater Cold War, see Craven, *Silent War*; Sontag and Drew, *Blind Man's Bluff*; W. Craig Reed, *Red November: Inside the Secret U.S.-Soviet Submarine War* (New York: Harper, 2011). For the Soviet buildup, see David F. Winkler, "An Overview of the Growth of the Soviet Navy," in *Soviet Navy: Intelligence and Analysis During the Cold War* (Washington, DC: CIA Historical Review Program, 2017), 25–26; Michael MccGwire,

"The Evolution of Soviet Naval Policy, 1960–74," in *Soviet Naval Policy: Objectives and Constraints*, ed. MccGwire, Ken Booth, and John McDonnell (New York: Praeger, 1975), 507–508; Robert W. Herrick, *Soviet Naval Strategy: Fifty Years of Theory and Practice* (Annapolis, MD: Naval Institute Press, 1968), 71–73.

17. Sontag and Drew, *Blind Man's Bluff*, 91; Sharp, *CIA's Greatest*, 5–6.

18. Craven, *Silent War*, 115–117, 119; William J. Broad, *The Universe Below: Discovering the Secrets of the Deep Sea* (New York: Simon and Schuster, 1997), 59–61.

19. Craven, *Silent War*, 110, 122, 130–131, 154; Sontag and Drew, *Blind Man's Bluff*, 55–57, 172–175. IVY BELLS remained active until American spy Ronald Pelton betrayed it to his Soviet handlers in the 1980s. See Michael J. Sulick, *American Spies: Espionage Against the United States from the Cold War to the Present*, paperback ed. (Washington, DC: Georgetown University Press, 2020), 112–114.

20. Sontag and Drew, *Blind Man's Bluff*, 356–357; Sharp, *CIA's Greatest*, 6.

21. "Project AZORIAN," 4.

22. See CIA, *The Office of Scientific Intelligence: The Original Wizards of Langley: A Symposium Commemorating 60 Years of S&T Intelligence Analysis* (Washington, DC: Center for the Study of Intelligence, 2013); Jeffrey T. Richelson, *The Wizards of Langley: Inside the CIA's Directorate of Science and Technology* (Boulder, CO: Westview Press, 2002).

23. "Engineering for AZORIAN," *Studies in Intelligence* 24, no. 1 (1980): 1; Sharp, *CIA's Greatest*, 6–11.

24. Powers, *Man Who Kept*, 2; Helms, *A Look Over My Shoulder: A Life in the Central Intelligence Agency* (New York: Random House, 2003), 184–185; unnamed CIA officer quoted in Loch K. Johnson, *America's Secret Power: The CIA in a Democratic Society* (New York: Oxford University Press, 1989), 8, 74.

25. "Engineering for AZORIAN," 1; Walter McDougall, *The Heavens and the Earth: A Political History of the Space Age* (Baltimore, MD: Johns Hopkins University Press, 1997).

26. Curtis Pebbles, *Guardians—Strategic Reconnaissance Satellites* (Novato, CA: Presidio Press, 1987), 43; Aaron Bateman, "Technological Wonder and Strategic Vulnerability: Satellite Reconnaissance and American National Security During the Cold War," *International Journal of Intelligence and Counterintelligence* 33, no. 2 (2020): 331–332. See also CIA, *Office of Scientific Intelligence*, 9; Walter T. Hitchcock, ed., *The Intelligence Revolution: A Historical Perspective* (Washington, DC: Office of Air Force History, 1991); Ingard Clausen, Edward A. Miller, Robert A. McDonald, and Courtney V. Hastings, eds., *Intelligence Revolution 1960: Retrieving the Corona Imagery That Helped Win the Cold War* (Chantilly, VA: Center for the Study of National Reconnaissance, 2012).

27. Sharp, *CIA's Greatest*, ix, 270. An exception to DS&T's record of success, the notorious mind-control Project MKULTRA led by DS&T chemist Sidney Gottlieb, was not yet widely known outside the agency. See Stephen Kinzer, *Poisoner in Chief: Sidney Gottlieb and the CIA Search for Mind Control* (New York: Henry Holt, 2019).

28. In 2013, the CIA released *An Underwater Ice Station Zebra*, a publication documenting the 1972 retrieval of the satellite capsule. For more on that publication, see "An Underwater Ice Station Zebra: Recovering a Secret Spy Satellite Capsule from 16,400 feet Below the Pacific Ocean," CIA Freedom of Information Act Electronic Reading Room, accessed May 13, 2022, https://www.cia.gov/readingroom/collection/underwater-ice-station-zebra-recovering-secret-spy-satellite-capsule-16400-feet-below.

29. "Engineering for AZORIAN," 1; "Project AZORIAN," 11.

30. Sontag and Drew, *Blind Man's Bluff*, 91–92, 215; Craven, *Silent War*, 257.

31. "The Great Submarine Snatch," *Time*, March 31, 1975, 20; memo for the record, July 1, 1974, *FRUS, 1969–1976*, vol. 35, doc. 188.

32. "Great Submarine Snatch," 20.

33. Quoted in John Ranelagh, *The Agency: The Rise and Decline of the CIA* (New York: Simon and Schuster, 1986), 546. See also Robert M. Hathaway and Russell Jack Smith, *Richard Helms as Director of Central Intelligence, 1966–1973* (Washington, DC: CIA Center for the Study of Intelligence, 1993), 62.

34. Sharp, *CIA's Greatest*, 25; Helms to Kissinger, memo, December 7, 1970, doc. 220, in *FRUS, 1969–1976*, vol. 2, *Organization and Management of U.S. Foreign Policy, 1969–1972*, ed. David Humphrey (Washington, DC: U.S. Government Printing Office, 2006).

35. Alice C. Maroni, *Special Access Programs and the Defense Budget: Understanding the "Black Budget,"* Congressional Research Service Issue Brief IB87201 (1989), 1–15.

36. "Security: Hidden Shield for Project AZORIAN," *Studies in Intelligence* 23, no. 4 (1979): 40; Clyde W. Burleson, *The Jennifer Project* (Englewood Cliffs, NJ: Prentice-Hall, 1977).

37. Office of Management and Budget (OMB), "A Review of the Intelligence Community," March 10, 1971, Defense Department—Intelligence & the Intelligence Community, box 54, James R. Schlesinger Papers, Manuscript Division, Library of Congress, Washington, DC.

38. "Project AZORIAN," 5; "Security: Hidden Shield," 39–51; Polmar and White, *Project AZORIAN*, 67–68.

39. William McAfee, interview by Charles Stuart Kennedy, September 9, 1997, Foreign Affairs Oral History Collection of the Association for Diplomatic Studies and Training, Library of Congress, Washington, DC.

40. Helms, *Look Over My Shoulder*, 184–185.

41. Helms to Kissinger, September 14, 1972, in *FRUS, 1969–1976*, vol. 35, doc. 184; "Project AZORIAN," 4–5.

42. Published accounts of the "new organization" include "Project AZORIAN," 4–5; Sontag and Drew, *Blind Man's Bluff*, 90; Richelson, *Wizards of Langley*, 135; Polmar and White, *Project AZORIAN*, 58–59; Josh Dean, *The Taking of K-129: How the CIA Used Howard Hughes to Steal a Russian Sub in the Most Daring Covert Operation in History* (New York: Dutton, 2017), 83–85. For the NRO, see Gerald K. Haines, *The National Reconnaissance Office: Its Origins, Creation, and Early Years* (Washington, DC: National Reconnaissance Office, 1997), 12–25.

43. For the USIB's 1970 decision, see "Project AZORIAN," 12; memo to Kissinger, May 28, 1974, in *FRUS, 1969–1976*, vol. 35, doc. 186.

44. OMB, "Review of the Intelligence Community."

45. Index card, January 30, 1970, Intra Office [Memorandum, 1970], Winder Papers, Russell Collection.

46. George L. Cary to Stennis, March 19, 1975, Central Intelligence, box 29, Series 43: Committees, Stennis Collection. Published estimates of the program's cost have risen from $350 million (Jack Anderson with Les Whitten, "Who Owns the News?" *Washington Merry-Go-Round*, March 25, 1975, box 96, Jack Anderson Papers, Special Collections Research Center, Gelman Library, George Washington University, Washington, DC) to $500 million (Seymour M. Hersh, "Participant Tells of CIA Ruses to Hide Glomar Project," *New York Times*, December 10, 1976, 18), to as much as $800 million (Chris Pleasance, "$800 Million Warship Built by the CIA During the Cold War Using Billionaire Howard Hughes as a Cover-up Is Due to Be Scrapped," *Daily Mail*, September 8, 2015,

http://www.dailymail.co.uk/news/article-3226440/The-800million-plot-steal-Russian
-nuclear-sub-Ship-built-CIA-Cold-War-using-billionaire-Howard-Hughes-cover
-scrapped.html). Price conversion is based on the U.S. Bureau of Labor Statistics' Consumer Price Index Inflation Calculator, available at https://www.bls.gov/data/inflation
_calculator.htm.

47. Central Intelligence Agency Act of 1949, Pub. L. 81-110, 63 Stat. 208 (1949); U.S. Senate,
Select Committee to Study Governmental Operations with Respect to Intelligence
Activities [hereafter Church Committee], 94th Cong., 2d sess., *Final Report* (No. 94-755),
book 1, *Foreign and Military Intelligence* (Washington, DC: U.S. Government Printing
Office, 1976), 492–494; L. Britt Snider, *Congress and the CIA* (New York: Nova Science
Publishers, 2009), 170. On the director's reserve fund and its uses, see also Victor Mar-
chetti and John D. Marks, *The CIA and the Cult of Intelligence* (New York: Knopf, 1974),
61–63.

48. Cary to Stennis, March 19, 1975.

49. U.S. Bureau of the Census, *Historical Statistics of the United States, Colonial Times to 1970*
(Washington, DC: U.S. Government Printing Office, 1975), pt. 1, pp. 135, 210, and 228,
and pt. 2, p. 1105; Allen J. Matusow, *Nixon's Economy: Booms, Busts, Dollars, and Votes*
(Lawrence: University Press of Kansas, 1998), 15, 29–30.

50. Record of President Nixon's meeting with the Foreign Intelligence Advisory Board,
July 18, 1970, doc. 344 in *FRUS, 1969–1976*, vol. 6, *Vietnam, January 1969–July 1970*, ed.
Edward C. Keefer and Carolyn Yee (Washington, DC: U.S. Government Printing
Office, 2006).

51. Church Committee, *Final Report*, bk. 1:28; Anne Daugherty Miles, *Intelligence Community Spending: Trends and Issues*, Congressional Research Service Report R44381 (2016), 8.

52. Clayton D. Laurie, *Congress and the National Reconnaissance Office* (Washington, DC:
NRO Office of the Historian, 2001), 4. As the Church Committee stated in *Final Report*,
bk. 1:41, "Intelligence has been the province of the President."

53. Laurie, *Congress and NRO*, 14; Joseph A. Fry, *Dixie Looks Abroad: The South and U.S. Foreign Relations, 1789–1973* (Baton Rouge: Louisiana State University Press, 2002), 269–
270. The exceptions proved the rule: Senate Appropriations chair Carl Hayden
(D-Arizona) announced his retirement on May 5, 1968, before the United States had
located the Golf. Representative Philip Philbin (D-Massachusetts) chaired the House
Armed Services Committee for three days following the death of Mendel Rivers on
December 28, 1970. Representative Melvin Price (D-Illinois) assumed the chairmanship
of the House Armed Service Committee in January 1975, years after most of the major
decisions had been made, and just months before the operation was terminated.

54. Ray S. Cline, *The CIA Under Reagan, Bush and Casey* (Washington, DC: Acropolis Books,
1981), 282.

55. Fite, *Richard B. Russell, Jr*, 462.

56. "The CIA: Maker of Policy, or Tool?" *New York Times*, April 25, 1966, 20; *Congressional
Record*, 89th Cong., 2d sess., July 14, 1966, p. 15673.

57. *Congressional Record*, 89th Cong., 2d sess., May 16, 1966, p. 10618; Russell to Mike Mansfield, May 26, 1966, CIA Committee Correspondence [1962–1967], box 125, Subgroup
C, Series IX: Legislative, Russell Collection.

58. *Congressional Record*, 89th Cong., 2d sess., July 14, 1966, pp. 15676–15677.

59. "The Senate: A Duel of Chairmen," *Time*, July 22, 1966, 21; Clayton Fritchey, "Who
Belongs to the Senate's Inner Club," *Harper's*, May 1967, 104.

60. *Congressional Record*, 92nd Cong., 1st sess., November 23, 1971, p. 42930; Church Committee, *Final Report*, bk. 1:150. Robert A. Caro, *Master of the Senate* (New York: Random House, 2002), 179.

61. Minutes, Senate Democratic Policy Committee Luncheon, April 28, 1969, box 1, Subgroup C, Series XVIII: Exhibit B, Russell Collection.

62. Snider, *Congress and CIA*, 180; Richard F. Fenno Jr., *The Power of the Purse: Appropriations Politics in Congress* (Boston: Little, Brown, 1966).

63. Ranelagh, *The Agency*, 480.

64. Frank J. Smist Jr., *Congress Oversees the United States Intelligence Community, 1947–1994* (Knoxville: University of Tennessee Press, 1994), 8; John Maury, "CIA and the Congress," *Studies in Intelligence* 18, no. 2 (1974): 2.

65. "Project AZORIAN," 2.

66. Milton Young quoted in "CIA's Mission Impossible," *Newsweek*, March 31, 1975, 31. Russell's name does not appear on a list of knowledgeable congresspeople compiled by the CIA in 1975, four years after his death. However, the list (attached to CIA to Ink, November 28, 1975, Stennis Collection) only sought to count sitting members of Congress and their staffs who had received classified briefings. The name of another deceased legislator, former House Armed Services chair Mendel Rivers, does not appear; Young's does. Young served in the Senate until 1981.

67. Maury, "CIA and the Congress," 11; Nicholas M. Horrock, "Most 'Oversight' May Have Been in the Other Direction: A Few in Congress Could See What the Spooks Were Doing," *New York Times*, February 1, 1976, E1.

68. Russell quoted in David M. Barrett, *The CIA and Congress: The Untold Story from Truman to Kennedy* (Lawrence: University Press of Kansas, 2005), 231. Powers, *Man Who Kept*, 319–320.

69. Helms, *Look Over My Shoulder*, 405; Snider, *Agency and Hill*, 232.

70. Cary to Stennis, March 20, 1975; Fite, *Russell*, 389. For descriptions of intelligence appropriations procedures, see Church Committee, *Final Report*, bk. 1:368–369, 499–500; David E. Rosenbaum, "CIA's Budget Is So Secret That Even Most Members of Congress Know Nothing About It," *New York Times*, December 27, 1974, 37.

71. *Congressional Record*, 84th Cong., 2d sess., April 11, 1956, p. 6048; Church Committee, *Final Report*, bk. 1:379.

72. *Congressional Record*, 84th Cong., 2d sess., April 11, 1956, p. 6048. Russell reiterated this argument a decade later. See *Congressional Record*, 89th Cong., 2d sess., July 14, 1966, p. 15676.

73. Dean Rusk quoted in Loch K. Johnson, *A Season of Inquiry Revisited: The Church Committee Confronts America's Spy Agencies* (Lawrence: University Press of Kansas, 2015), 2–3.

74. Maury quoted in Snider, *Congress and CIA*, 26.

2. THE HUGHES CONNECTION

1. For descriptions of Hughes's Desert Inn enclave, see James Phelan, *Howard Hughes: The Hidden Years* (New York: Random House, 1976), 67–69; Donald L. Barlett and James B. Steele, *Empire: The Life, Legend, and Madness of Howard Hughes* (New York: W. W. Norton, 1979), 324–327, 367–368. Karina Longworth demythologizes Hughes's womanizing

in *Seduction: Sex, Lies, and Stardom in Howard Hughes's Hollywood* (New York: Custom House, 2018).

2. Wallace Turner, "A Glimpse Into Hughes's Hidden Life," *New York Times*, December 10, 1970, 49, 54.

3. James Phelan, "The Secret Life of Howard Hughes," *Time*, December 13, 1976, 22–23; Phelan, *Howard Hughes*, 55, 59, 115; Barlett and Steele, *Empire*, 425; Dr. Jack L. Titus, final report, autopsy N-76-92, April 6, 1976, box 13, Series 3: Howard Hughes, Donald L. Barlett and James B. Steele Archive, University Archives and Special Collections, American University Library, Washington, DC.

4. For cover evaluations, see memo to Henry A. Kissinger, May 28, 1974, doc. 186 in *Foreign Relations of the United States* [hereafter *FRUS*], *1969–1976*, vol. 35, *National Security Policy, 1973–1976*, ed. M. Todd Bennett (Washington, DC: U.S. Government Printing Office, 2014); David H. Sharp, *The CIA's Greatest Covert Operation: Inside the Daring Mission to Recover a Nuclear-Armed Soviet Sub* (Lawrence: University Press of Kansas, 2012), 29–33.

5. Memo to Kissinger, May 28, 1974; Hank Greenspun, "Howard Hughes Vanishes!" *Las Vegas Sun*, December 2, 1970, 1; Donald L. Barlett and James B. Steele, "Secrecy Ethic Goes Through Organization," December 20, 1975, *Philadelphia Inquirer*, 1.

6. Memo to Kissinger, May 28, 1974; "The Secret World of Howard Hughes," *Newsweek*, April 19, 1976. William Colby quoted in "Submarines, Secrets, and Spies," *Nova*, transcript of PBS broadcast originally aired January 19, 1999: https://www.pbs.org/wgbh/nova/transcripts/2602subsecrets.html.

7. In response to a Freedom of Information Act request, the CIA declassified, in 2016, a fraction of a 1976 Office of Inspector General fact sheet reviewing the agency's ties with Hughes. The sanitized version of the original copy (John H. Waller, fact sheet, August 9, 1976, folder 2 [2 of 3], box 107, Segregated CIA Collection, JFK Task Force, Select Committee on Assassinations, Records of the U.S. House of Representatives, 95th Cong., President John F. Kennedy Assassination Records Collection [hereafter JFK Collection], National Archives and Records Administration [NARA], College Park, MD) is in the author's possession.

8. CIA memo for the record, "Meeting on Search for Watergate-Related Records," April 11, 1974, doc. CIA-RDP78-00300R000100090022-9, CIA Freedom of Information Act Electronic Reading Room, accessed August 28, 2000, https://www.cia.gov/readingroom/docs/CIA-RDP78-00300R000100090022-9.pdf.

9. Wallace Turner, "CIA Link Termed a Goal of Hughes," *New York Times*, March 20, 1975, 30, 38; John M. Crewdson, "CIA Covert Activities Abroad Shielded by Major US Companies," *New York Times*, May 11, 1975, 38; Leroy F. Aarons, "Hughes' Financial Umbrella," *Washington Post*, April 1, 1975, A8.

10. Walter T. Lloyd, telephone interview with author, August 4, 2016.

11. Sharp, *CIA's Greatest*, 35; Barlett and Steele, *Empire*, 434.

12. "Project AZORIAN: The Story of the *Hughes Glomar Explorer*," *Studies in Intelligence* 22, no. 3 (1978): 2. According to *FRUS, 1969–1976*, vol. 35, doc. 196, a version of Raymond M. Holliday's 1970 memo is in the CIA Executive Registry, Colby Files, Job 80M01009A, Box 16, MATADOR.

13. Holliday quoted in Mark Ashley, "Howard Hughes an Aloof Boss," *Milwaukee Journal*, March 5, 1975, 14. Hughes was aware of his firm's involvement in the CIA submarine

project, according to Frank William Gay, deposition, July 15, 1977, p. 346, Hughes Estate Lawsuits, Texas, Frank William Gay (3 of 3), box 10, Barlett and Steele Archive.

14. Global Marine Inc. (A. J. Field), Hughes Tool Co. (Holliday), U.S. Government (unnamed officer), letter agreement, November 13, 1970, *Glomar Explorer* Lawsuit Case Number 752752R, box 6, Barlett and Steele Archive; Sharp, *CIA's Greatest*, 36, 72.

15. Robert Maheu and Richard Hack, *Next to Hughes: Behind the Power and Tragic Downfall of Howard Hughes by His Closest Advisor* (New York: HarperCollins, 1992), 3.

16. Memo, "Robert Maheu" [n.d.], CIA record 104-10122-10141, and memo for CIA director of security, January 18, 1971, Senate Select Committee on Intelligence (Church Committee) record 157-10004-10274, both in JFK Collection.

17. Memo, "Robert Maheu" [n.d.], and memo, "Robert Maheu," October 4, 1973, CIA record 104-10121-10341, both in JFK Collection; Maheu and Hack, *Next to Hughes*, 40–41. The CIA released the 702-page "Family Jewels" collection in 2007, after years of Freedom of Information Act litigation. The document is available from the National Security Archive at https://nsarchive2.gwu.edu//NSAEBB/NSAEBB222/family_jewels_full_ocr.pdf.

18. Memo, "The Johnny Roselli Matter" [n.d.], CIA record 104-10121-10341, JFK Collection. For Roselli's stake in Hughes's Las Vegas properties, see Barlett and Steele, *Empire*, 295, 298. Maheu detailed the plot in *Next to Hughes*, 108–134.

19. Howard J. Osborn to Richard Helms, memo, January 20, 1971, CIA record 104-10122-10301, JFK Collection; Walter T. Lloyd, written statement provided to author, July 20, 2016. Helms was aware of a related 1960 incident in which Las Vegas police arrested a technician Maheu had hired to place a listening device in the hotel room of a man whom Giancana suspected of sleeping with his mistress. Federal prosecutors declined to pursue criminal charges after Maheu told the FBI that the CIA was behind the eavesdropping operation. But those in the know began to question Maheu's reliability. See Sheffield Edwards, memo for the record, May 14, 1962, doc. 337 in *FRUS, 1961–1963*, vol. 10, *Cuba, January 1961–September 1962*, ed. Louis J. Smith (Washington, DC: U.S. Government Printing Office, 1997).

20. Lloyd, written statement; memo for the record, July 1, 1974, *FRUS, 1969–1976*, vol. 35, doc. 188.

21. "The Case of the Invisible Billionaire," *Newsweek*, December 21, 1970, 75–76, 78.

22. Terry Lenzner, *The Investigator: Fifty Years of Uncovering the Truth* (New York: Blue Rider Press, 2013), 151; Charles G. Rebozo, testimony, March 20, 1974, U.S. Senate, Select Committee on Presidential Campaign Activities [hereafter SSCPCA], 93rd Cong., 2d sess., *Executive Session Hearings*, book 21, *The Hughes–Rebozo Investigation and Related Matters* (Washington, DC: U.S. Government Printing Office, 1974), 9987–9988.

23. Michael Drosnin, *Citizen Hughes* (New York: Holt, Rinehart and Winston, 1985), 390. The text of the November 14, 1970, proxy appeared on the front page of the *Las Vegas Sun* on December 12, 1970. According to a participant, the *Glomar* mission mistakenly relied "on the cover of an organization whose namesake and supposed absolute leader lay naked in a room, drapes taped shut, watching old movies over and over in drugged disregard for most of what went on beyond the room's walls." Roy Varner and Wayne Collier, *A Matter of Risk: The Incredible Inside Story of the CIA's Hughes Glomar Explorer Mission to Raise a Russian Submarine* (New York: Random House, 1978), 36.

24. Greenspun, "Howard Hughes Vanishes!;" "Shootout at the Hughes Corral," *Time*, December 21, 1970, 62–66.

25. Maheu and Hack, *Next to Hughes*, 233–234, 237, 264.

26. "The Hughes Caper," *Newsweek*, December 28, 1970, 56. See also Dial Torgerson, "Details of Hughes' Life Told," *Los Angeles Times*, December 15, 1970, 1.

27. Al Delugach, "Maheu Sues for Libel, Asks $17.5 Million," *Los Angeles Times*, February 11, 1972, A6. Published books included *Howard: The Amazing Mr. Hughes* (New York: Fawcett Publications, 1972), coauthored by Hughes's ex-lieutenant, Noah Dietrich, and a revised edition of John Keats's *Howard Hughes: The Biography of a Texas Billionaire* (New York: Random House, 1972). Hughes's camp staged the January 1972 press conference to disavow "The Autobiography of Howard Hughes," a fraud hatched by author Clifford Irving, reportedly after reading press coverage of Hughes's Las Vegas departure. Although withheld from publication, Irving's hoax attracted additional attention, including books detailing the scandal.

28. CIA officials recounted Maheu's December 1970 call to Deputy Director of Security James P. O'Connell in memo, n.d. [June 25, 1974?], CIA record 104-10122-10141, JFK Collection. Maheu quoted in Varner and Collier, *Matter of Risk*, 57. Cover stories included "Manganese Harvest: Hughes Tool Firm Launches Barge for Ocean Mining," *Los Angeles Times*, January 17, 1972, A3.

29. "One of Our Billionaires Is Missing," *60 Minutes*, transcript of Columbia Broadcasting System television broadcast, February 2, 1971, SSCPCA, *Executive Session Hearings*, bk. 21:9924; Jack Anderson, "6 Attempts to Kill Castro Laid to CIA," *Washington Post*, January 18, 1971, B7. Anderson's first column on the CIA-Mafia plot appeared on March 3, 1967.

30. Osborn to Helms, memo.

31. Jack Anderson, "Howard Hughes—Hidden Kingmaker," *Washington Post*, August 6, 1971, B11. Although the SSCPCA, chaired by Senator Sam Ervin, found no direct evidence of a quid pro quo, it reported that the facts surrounding the Dunes deal, in particular, showed "questionable conduct at high levels of the executive branch and raise[d] serious questions about the relation between campaign contributions by Hughes and Federal actions affecting Hughes." See SSCPCA, 93rd Cong., 2d sess., *Final Report* (Washington, DC: U.S. Government Printing Office, 1974), 981. Hughes never purchased the Dunes.

32. Federal Bureau of Investigation Las Vegas Field Office to FBI Director, telegram LV 80-77, August 7, 1971, Jack Anderson FBI File, FBI Freedom of Information Act Library, accessed March 31, 2022, https://vault.fbi.gov/jack-anderson/jack-anderson-part-08-of -11/view. Author Mark Feldstein identifies Maheu as a "longtime source" of Anderson's in *Poisoning the Press: Richard Nixon, Jack Anderson, and the Rise of Washington's Scandal Culture* (New York: Farrar, Straus and Giroux, 2010), 222. In his memoir, Maheu admits that he kept in contact with Anderson, whom he regarded as a "friend." Maheu and Hack, *Next to Hughes*, 132, 263.

33. H. R. Haldeman with Joseph DiMona, *The Ends of Power* (New York: Times Books, 1978), 20–21. The SSCPCA detailed the Hughes-Rebozo matter in its *Final Report*, 931–1079. Watergate special prosecutor Leon Jaworski dedicated a task force to the matter. For its report, see Paul R. Michel to Henry S. Ruth Jr., Closing Memo for Investigation of Hughes, Rebozo and Unreported Campaign Funds, October 16, 1975, box 117, Campaign Contributions Task Force #804—Hughes/Rebozo Investigation, Records of the Watergate Special Prosecution Force, Record Group 460, NARA. Nixon maintained

that the $100,000 was a campaign contribution, that Rebozo's acceptance of it was appropriate, and that any stories to the contrary were "untrue." See Nixon, *RN: The Memoirs of Richard Nixon* (New York: Grosset and Dunlap, 1978), 965–966.

34. Feldstein, *Poisoning*, 59–74; Donald A. Ritchie, *The Columnist: Leaks, Lies, and Libel in Drew Pearson's Washington* (New York: Oxford University Press, 2021), 209–210. For the Nixon administration review, see John Dean to John Ehrlichman, memo, February 3, 1972, box 42, Dean Subject File, Staff Member and Office Files (SMOF), White House Special Files (WHSF), Richard Nixon Presidential Library and Museum (RNPLM), Yorba Linda, CA.

35. Haldeman with DiMona, *Ends of Power*, 19.

36. Haldeman to Dean, memo, January 18, 1971, box 196, Haldeman Chronological Files, SMOF, WHSF, RNPLM.

37. Jack Caulfield to Dean, memos, January 22 and 25, 1971, SSCPCA, *Executive Session Hearings*, bk. 21:9748–9749.

38. Caulfield memo, "Operation Sandwedge" n.d., SSCPCA, *Executive Session Hearings*, bk. 21:9899.

39. Dean to Haldeman, memo, January 26, 1971, SSCPCA, *Executive Session Hearings*, bk. 21:9751–9753; Charles W. Colson to Roy Goodearle, memo, January 15, 1971, SSCPCA, *Executive Session Hearings*, bk. 21:9747.

40. Haldeman to Dean, memo, January 28, 1971, SSCPCA, *Executive Session Hearings*, bk. 21:9754.

41. Caulfield to Dean, memo, February 1, 1971, Caulfield memo, n.d. [1971?], and Caulfield testimony, March 16, 1974, SSCPCA, *Executive Session Hearings*, bk. 21:9715–9716, 9755, 9758.

42. Anderson, "Two Ghosts Haunt Nixon's Campaign," *Washington Post*, January 24, 1972, B11; Feldstein, *Poisoning*, 223.

43. Wallace Turner, "Hundreds of Copies of Hughes Memos Are Readily Available in Las Vegas," *New York Times*, February 3, 1972, 19. In 1972, White House Plumbers Liddy and Hunt made preparations, serious preparations, to assassinate Anderson by either poisoning him or staging an accident. See Feldstein, *Poisoning*, 282–285.

44. SSCPCA, *Final Report*, 22. Mitchell identified the material as being damaging to the candidacy of Senator Edmund Muskie, a contender for the Democratic Party's 1972 presidential nomination. As discussed below, however, attendees understood the primary target to be files documenting the Hughes payments.

45. E. Howard Hunt, testimony, September 25, 1973, SSCPCA, *Executive Session Hearings*, bk. 9:3686–3687.

46. SSCPCA, *Final Report*, 23–24. James H. Barron, in *The Greek Connection: The Life of Elias Demetracopoulos and the Untold Story of Watergate* (New York: Melville House, 2020), argues that O'Brien was targeted because he possessed proof that the Greek junta had funneled large amounts of illegal money to the 1968 Nixon campaign.

47. SSCPCA, *Final Report*, 29–30.

48. G. Gordon Liddy, *Will*, 3rd ed. (New York: St. Martin's, 1997), 237. Jeb Stuart Magruder quoted in J. Anthony Lukas, "Why the Watergate Break-in?" *New York Times*, November 30, 1987, A10. On the Hughes connection, see John M. Crewdson, "Report Links Watergate to Hughes-Rebozo Funds," *New York Times*, August 4, 1974, 34. Lenzner, *Investigator*, 145–185; J. Anthony Lukas, "The Hughes Connection," *New York Times Magazine*, January 4, 1976, 3; Lukas, *Nightmare: The Underside of the Nixon Years* (New York:

Viking, 1976; reprint, Athens: Ohio University Press, 1999), 179–182; Stanley I. Kutler, *The Wars of Watergate: The Last Crisis of Richard Nixon* (New York: Knopf, 1990), 202–205; David Greenberg, "The Unsolved Mysteries of Watergate," *New York Times*, June 5, 2005.

49. Lenzner, *Investigator*, 171.
50. "Animals in the Forest," *Time*, February 11, 1974, 26.
51. Nixon to Haldeman, memo, May 18, 1972, doc. 273 in *FRUS, 1969–1976*, vol. 2, *Organization and Management of U.S. Foreign Policy, 1969–1972*, ed. David C. Humphrey (Washington, DC: U.S. Government Printing Office, 2006).
52. Richard H. Immerman, *The Hidden Hand: A Brief History of the CIA* (Malden, MA: Wiley-Blackwell, 2014), 88; John Ranelagh, *The Agency: The Rise and Decline of the CIA* (New York: Simon and Schuster, 1986), 485.
53. Nixon, *RN*, 351; Jonathan Aitken, *Nixon: A Life* (Washington, DC: Regnery, 1993), 75–76; Evan Thomas, *Being Nixon: A Man Divided* (New York: Random House, 2015), 22–23.
54. Thomas Powers, *The Man Who Kept the Secrets: Richard Helms and the CIA* (New York: Knopf, 1979), 229; Henry Kissinger, *White House Years* (New York: Little, Brown and Co., 1979), 36. See Gregg Herken, *The Georgetown Set: Friends and Rivals in Cold War Washington* (New York: Knopf, 2014).
55. Kissinger, *White House Years*, 36; Richard Helms with William Hood, *A Look Over My Shoulder: A Life in the Central Intelligence Agency* (New York: Random House, 2003), 11–12, 382–383.
56. Kissinger, *White House Years*, 36; Helms with Hood, *Look Over My Shoulder*, 382; Robert M. Hathaway and Russell Jack Smith, *Richard Helms As Director of Central Intelligence, 1966–1973* (Washington, DC: CIA, 1993), 8–9.
57. Editorial note, doc. 35, *FRUS, 1969–1976*, vol. 34, *National Security Policy, 1969–1972*, ed. M. Todd Bennett (Washington, DC: U.S. Government Printing Office, 2011); Anne Hessing Cahn, *Killing Détente: The Right Attacks the CIA* (University Park: Pennsylvania State University Press, 1998), 93–99.
58. John W. Finney, "Administration Critics Say 'Intelligence Gap' Clouds ABM Issue," *New York Times*, June 1, 1969, p. 2; Kissinger to Nixon, memo, June 5, 1969, *FRUS, 1969–1976*, vol. 34, doc. 33n3. On Safeguard's use as a bargaining chip in strategic arms limitations talks with the Soviets, see Kissinger, *White House Years*, 204–210; Nixon, *RN*, 415–418.
59. Helms recounted the episode in *Look Over My Shoulder*, 384–388. See also Hathaway and Smith, *Richard Helms*, 12, 40–50; David Priess, *The President's Book of Secrets: The Untold Story of Intelligence Briefings to America's Presidents* (New York: PublicAffairs, 2016), 65–67.
60. Record of the President's Meeting with the Foreign Intelligence Advisory Board, July 18, 1970, doc. 344, *FRUS, 1969–1976*, vol. 6, *Vietnam, January 1969–July 1970*, ed. Edward C. Keefer and Carolyn Yee (Washington, DC: U.S. Government Printing Office, 2006); Nixon to Kissinger, memo, November 30, 1970, *FRUS, 1969–1976*, vol. 2, doc. 216; diary entry, July 23, 1971, Haldeman Diaries Collection, RNPLM.
61. Editorial note, *FRUS, 1969–1976*, vol. 2, doc. 224; Office of Management and Budget, "A Review of the Intelligence Community," March 10, 1971, Defense Department—Intelligence & the Intelligence Community, box 54, James R. Schlesinger Papers, Manuscript Division, Library of Congress, Washington, DC.

62. Hathaway and Smith, *Richard Helms*, 209–210.

63. "Project AZORIAN," 12–13, 16–18; Curtis Crooke, interview with author, July 15, 2016, Carmel, CA.

64. U.S. Senate, Select Committee to Study Governmental Operations with Respect to Intelligence Activities, 94th Cong., 2d sess., *Final Report*, book 1, *Foreign and Military Intelligence* (Washington, DC: U.S. Government Printing Office, 1976), 41, 65–69, 368; Peter Clapper to David Belin, May 2, 1975, National Security Archive Virtual Reading Room, accessed March 31, 2022, https://nsarchive.gwu.edu/dc.html?doc=2719471 -Document-11.

65. "Project AZORIAN," 13, 15.

66. Nixon to Secretary of State et al., memo, November 5, 1971, *FRUS, 1969–1976*, vol. 2, doc. 242. See chapter 1 for the USIB's 1970 decision.

67. Lee A. DuBridge to Nixon, memo, September 5, 1969, and DuBridge to Nixon, memo, September 13, 1969, both in White House–President Vol. II [1969] [2 of 2], box 26, Edward E. David, SMOF, White House Central Files, RNPLM; Presidential Daily Diary, September 16, 1969, SMOF, White House Central Files, RNPLM. https://www .nixonlibrary.gov/sites/default/files/virtuallibrary/documents/PDD/1969/015%20Sep-tember%201-30%201969.pdf.

68. Brent Scowcroft, affidavit, March 19, 1976, Military Audit Project v. William Casey, Director of Central Intelligence et al., 656 F.2d 724 (DC Cir. 1981) at 731.

69. Kissinger quoted in Colson to Des Barker, memo, May 12, 1972, Hughes [1 of 3], box 42, Dean Subject File, SMOF, WHSF.

3. THE RULES OF THE GAME

1. Memorandum for the record, July 1, 1974, doc. 188 in *Foreign Relations of the United States* [hereafter *FRUS*], *1969–1976*, vol. 35, *National Security Policy, 1973–1976*, ed. M. Todd Bennett (Washington, DC: U.S. Government Printing Office, 2014). Drafted after the fact, the memo recorded the 40 Committee's June 5 meeting.

2. "From Russia with Hope," *Newsweek*, June 5, 1972, 32; Richard Nixon, "Address to a Joint Session of the Congress on Return from Austria, the Soviet Union, Iran, and Poland," June 1, 1972, *Public Papers of the Presidents: Nixon, 1972* [hereafter *PPP: Nixon, 1972*] (Washington, DC: U.S. Government Printing Office, 1974), 660–666.

3. For the challenges détente posed to American intelligence, see Anne Hessing Cahn, *Killing Détente: The Right Attacks the CIA* (University Park: Pennsylvania State University Press, 1998), 70–85; Brent Durbin, *The CIA and the Politics of U.S. Intelligence Reform* (New York: Cambridge University Press, 2017), 108; Randall B. Woods, *Shadow Warrior: William Egan Colby and the CIA* (New York: Basic Books, 2013), 414.

4. Henry Kissinger, *Years of Renewal* (New York: Simon and Schuster, 1999), 38.

5. Richard Helms to Kissinger, memo, September 14, 1972, *FRUS, 1969–1976*, vol. 35, doc. 184; William Colby to Kissinger, memo, May 23, 1974, *FRUS, 1969–1976*, vol. 35, doc. 185. Emphasis in originals.

6. Richard Nixon, *RN: The Memoirs of Richard Nixon* (New York: Grosset and Dunlap, 1978), 618; Kissinger, statement before the Senate Committee on Foreign Relations, September 19, 1974, *Department of State Bulletin*, October 14, 1974, 505–519. For détente's

strategic purpose, see John Lewis Gaddis, *Strategies of Containment: A Critical Appraisal of American National Security Policy During the Cold War*, rev. ed. (New York: Oxford University Press, 2005), 280, 287, 289, 308–309; Jeremi Suri, *Power and Protest: Global Revolution and the Rise of Détente* (Cambridge, MA: Harvard University Press, 2003), 2.

7. Kissinger, *American Foreign Policy*, exp. ed. (New York: W. W. Norton, 1974), 94.

8. Nixon, annual foreign policy report to Congress, February 9, 1972, *PPP: Nixon, 1972*, 211.

9. Nixon, annual foreign policy report to Congress; Mike Bowker and Phil Williams, *Superpower Détente: A Reappraisal* (London: Royal Institute of International Affairs, 1988), 51.

10. "Basic Principles of Relations Between the United States of America and the Union of Soviet Socialist Republics," May 29, 1972, *PPP: Nixon, 1972*, 633.

11. Stanley Hoffmann, *Dead Ends: American Foreign Policy in the New Cold War* (Cambridge, MA: Ballinger, 1983), 90.

12. Harry Howe Ransom, "Secret Intelligence in the United States, 1947–1982: The CIA's Search for Legitimacy," in *The Missing Dimension: Governments and Intelligence Communities in the Twentieth Century*, ed. Christopher Andrew and David Dilks (Urbana: University of Illinois Press, 1984), 214; William Colby and Peter Forbath, *Honorable Men: My Life in the CIA* (New York: Simon and Schuster, 1978), 296.

13. "Project AZORIAN: The Story of the *Hughes Glomar Explorer*," *Studies in Intelligence* 22, no. 3 (1978): 16; National Security Decision Memorandum 40, February 17, 1970, National Security Council Institutional Files (hereafter NSC Files), Richard Nixon Presidential Library and Museum (RNPLM), Yorba Linda, CA.

14. Richard Kennedy to Kissinger, memo, August 18, 1972, box 994, Alexander Haig Chronological Files, NSC Files, RNPLM.

15. Department of the Navy, Office of the Judge Advocate General, memo for the file, August 21, 1970, quoted in "At Sea with the Law: Some Legal Aspects of the AZORIAN Program," *Studies in Intelligence* 23, no. 2 (1979): 2.

16. "At Sea with the Law," 1–2. Colby quoted in Jack Nelson, "Administration Won't Talk About Sub Raised by CIA," *Los Angeles Times*, March 20, 1975, A16.

17. Memo for the record, June 5, 1975, *FRUS, 1969–1976*, vol. 35, doc. 205; NSC staff paper [June 3, 1974?], attachment to *FRUS, 1969–1976*, vol. 35, doc. 187.

18. Memo to Kissinger, May 28, 1974, *FRUS, 1969–1976*, vol. 35, doc. 186; Rob Roy Ratliff, memo for the record, July 1, 1974, *FRUS, 1969–1976*, vol. 35, doc. 188.

19. Colby quoted in Sherry Sontag and Christopher Drew, *Blind Man's Bluff: The Untold Story of American Submarine Espionage* (New York: Harper, 1998), 369.

20. NSC staff paper [June 3, 1974?]; Michael R. Beschloss, *May-Day: Eisenhower, Khrushchev, and the U-2 Affair* (New York: Harper and Row, 1986).

21. Memo to Kissinger, May 28, 1974; CIA memo, April 30, 1975, *FRUS, 1969–1976*, vol. 35, doc. 202; CIA paper, "Vulnerability of *Hughes Glomar Explorer* to Physical Harassment" [April 30, 1975?], appendix B to *FRUS, 1969–1976*, vol. 35, doc. 202; Mitchell B. Lerner, *The Pueblo Incident: A Spy Ship and the Failure of American Foreign Policy* (Lawrence: University Press of Kansas, 2002).

22. Colby to Kissinger, memo, March 28, 1975, *FRUS, 1969–1976*, vol. 35, doc. 198; Sontag and Drew, *Blind Man's Bluff*, 369. *Explorer* crewmembers were painfully aware of the *Pueblo* analogy. "We knew that there was always the chance that [the *Explorer* would suffer the same fate as that which] befell the USS *Pueblo* . . . years earlier," deputy

mission director David H. Sharp recalls in *The CIA's Greatest Covert Operation: Inside the Daring Mission to Recover a Nuclear-Armed Soviet Sub* (Lawrence: University Press of Kansas, 2012), 159.

23. "Project AZORIAN," 16–17.

24. Helms to Kissinger, memo, September 14, 1972, *FRUS, 1969–1976*, vol. 35, doc. 184; "Project AZORIAN," 17.

25. Helms to Kissinger, memo, September 14, 1972, *FRUS, 1969–1976*, vol. 35, doc. 184.

26. "Project AZORIAN," 19.

27. "Hughes CIA Pact Is Put Month After Gift to Nixon," *New York Times*, August 4, 1975, 10; Sontag and Drew, *Blind Man's Bluff*, 92. See chapter 2 for discussions of the letter agreement and Hughes-Rebozo transactions.

28. James Phelan, "Howard Hughes, Beyond the Law," *New York Times*, September 14, 1975, 50.

29. "Project AZORIAN," 23–24. Cover stories include "Around the Shipyards," *Marine Engineering/Log*, December 1, 1972, 72.

30. "Project AZORIAN," 24–34.

31. Memo to Kissinger, May 28, 1974; Sharp, *CIA's Greatest*, 111–113.

32. Memo to Kissinger, May 28, 1974.

33. Kissinger, James Schlesinger, Colby, Thomas Moorer, and Brent Scowcroft, memo of conversation, January 22, 1974, National Security Advisor's Files, Gerald R. Ford Presidential Library, Ann Arbor, MI.

34. Jerry Greene, "How Colson Lifted Lid on Russian Sub Caper," *New York Daily News*, March 30, 1975, 3; Rudy Maxa, "Colson: Nixon Suspected CIA," *Washington Post*, June 24, 1974, A1.

35. Gene Blake, "Hughes 'Encouraged' Maheu in Projects for CIA, Court Told," *Los Angeles Times*, May 2, 1974, B1; Blake, "Hughes Wanted to 'Front' for CIA, Maheu Testifies," *Los Angeles Times*, May 16, 1974, B1.

36. CIA memo, "Special Projects Staff Matter" [June 25, 1974?], 104-10122-10141, President John F. Kennedy Assassination Records Collection, National Archives and Records Administration (NARA), College Park, MD.

37. Memo to Kissinger, May 28, 1974.

38. Sharp, *CIA's Greatest*, 126.

39. Quoted in memo to Kissinger, May 28, 1974. Emphasis and ellipsis in original.

40. NSC staff paper [June 3, 1974?].

41. Memo to Kissinger, May 28, 1974. Emphasis in original.

42. Memo to Kissinger, May 28, 1974. Emphasis in original.

43. Sergey Petrovich Bukan, *Po sledam podvodnykh katastrof* [On the trail of submarine disasters] (Moscow: Gildiya masterov Rus, 1992), 44, trans. Joint Publications Research Service, report JPRS-UMA-93-004-L, August 18, 1993, CIA Freedom of Information Act Electronic Reading Room, accessed April 4, 2022, https://www.cia.gov/readingroom/docs/DOC_0000078940.pdf. Anatoly Dobrynin also recalled receiving a tip from a "Well-wisher," but in late 1974 or early 1975. See Dobrynin, *In Confidence: Moscow's Ambassador to America's Six Cold War Presidents (1962–1986)* (New York: Times Books, 1995), 352.

44. Bukan, *Po sledam podvodnykh katastrof*, 83.

45. Bukan, 44–45.

46. Dobrynin, *In Confidence*, 352. Victor Dygalo quoted in Norman Polmar and Michael White, *Project AZORIAN: The CIA and the Raising of the K-129* (Annapolis, MD: Naval Institute Press, 2010), 68.

47. Leslie H. Gelb, "Nixon to Go to Moscow June 27," *New York Times*, June 1, 1974, 1. Détente "stalled" in 1973–1974, Raymond Garthoff reports in *Détente and Confrontation: American-Soviet Relations from Nixon to Reagan*, rev. ed. (Washington, DC: Brookings Institution, 1994), 458.

48. Moscow embassy to Department of State, telegram 3814, March 14, 1974, doc. 162 in *FRUS, 1969–1976*, vol. 15, *Soviet Union, June 1972–August 1974*, ed. Douglas E. Selvage and Melissa Jane Taylor (Washington, DC: U.S. Government Printing Office, 2011). Vladislav M. Zubok charts Kremlin opposition to Brezhnev's policy in *A Failed Empire: The Soviet Union in the Cold War from Stalin to Gorbachev* (Chapel Hill: University of North Carolina Press, 2007), 234.

49. Dobrynin, *In Confidence*, 310.

50. Yuri Andropov to Leonid Brezhnev, October 29, 1973, Cold War International History Project Digital Archive, Wilson Center, accessed April 4, 2022, https://digitalarchive .wilsoncenter.org/document/198187.

51. Memo to Kissinger, May 28, 1974. Emphasis in original.

52. Memo for the record, July 1, 1974.

53. U.S. Senate, Select Committee on Presidential Campaign Activities, 93rd Cong., 2d sess., *Executive Session Hearings, Watergate and Related Activities: The Hughes–Rebozo Investigation and Related Matters*, February 8–June 14, 1974, books 21–24 (Washington, DC: U.S. Government Printing Office, 1974); Paul R. Michel to Henry S. Ruth Jr., Closing Memo for Investigation of Hughes, Rebozo, and Unreported Campaign Funds, October 16, 1975, box 117, Campaign Contributions Task Force #804—Hughes/Rebozo Investigation, Records of the Watergate Special Prosecution Force, Record Group 460, NARA.

54. NSC staff paper [June 3, 1974?].

55. Memo for the record, July 1, 1974; Woods, *Shadow Warrior*, 375, 385.

56. Memo for the record, July 1, 1974; Colby to Kissinger, memo, May 23, 1974.

57. Memo for the record, July 1, 1974.

58. Kissinger and Scowcroft, October 11. 1973, 7:55 p.m., box 195, Telephone Conversation Transcript Copies, Henry A. Kissinger Papers, Part III (MS 2004), Yale University Library Digital Repository, accessed April 4, 2022, https://findit.library.yale.edu/catalog /digcoll:1192714; Thomas A. Schwartz, *Henry Kissinger and American Power: A Political Biography* (New York: Hill and Wang, 2020), 9, 241–242. In 1974, Kissinger exerted "virtually total control over the foreign policy making machinery," Jussi Hanhimäki agrees in *The Flawed Architect: Henry Kissinger and American Foreign Policy* (New York: Oxford University Press, 2004), xix.

59. Quoted in Robert D. Schulzinger, *Henry Kissinger: Doctor of Diplomacy* (New York: Columbia University Press, 1989), 170; Schwartz, *Henry Kissinger and American Power*, 228–229. Wiretapping features prominently in Seymour M. Hersh's critical biography, *The Price of Power: Kissinger in the Nixon White House* (New York: Summit Books, 1983).

60. Quoted in Schwartz, *Henry Kissinger*, 5–7, 211–212.

61. "It's Super K!" *Newsweek*, June 10, 1974.

62. Memo for the record, July 1, 1974.

63. Nixon, 1972 foreign policy report; Garthoff, *Détente and Confrontation*, 4. The Cold War "generated a gray area of superpower conflict not encompassed either in formal diplomacy nor by military action," remembered Kissinger in *Years of Renewal*, 338. Despite his emphasis on negotiation, Kissinger remained a dedicated cold warrior, according to Hanhimäki, *Flawed Architect*, xviii.

64. Helmut Sonnenfeldt quoted in NSC staff paper [June 3, 1974?].

65. "CIA's Mission Impossible," *Newsweek*, March 31, 1975, 24.

66. Kissinger to Nixon, memo, May 7, 1970, doc. 207 in *FRUS, 1969–1976*, vol. 2, *Organization and Management of U.S. Foreign Policy, 1969–1972*, ed. David C. Humphrey (Washington, DC: U.S. Government Printing Office, 2006); Haig to Kissinger, memo, December 3, 1970, *FRUS, 1969–1976*, vol. 2, doc. 218; Durbin, *CIA and Politics*, 108. On the transformational 1970s, see Niall Ferguson, Charles S. Maier, Erez Manela, and Daniel J. Sargent, eds., *The Shock of the Global: The 1970s in Perspective* (Cambridge, MA: Belknap Press of Harvard University Press, 2010); Daniel Sargent, *A Superpower Transformed: The Remaking of American Foreign Relations in the 1970s* (New York: Oxford University Press, 2015).

67. Nixon address, June 1, 1972; "What Nixon Brings Home from Moscow," *Time*, June 5, 1972, 15.

68. Bowker and Williams, *Superpower Détente*, 57; Gaddis, *Strategies*, 291–292.

69. National Intelligence Analytical Memorandum 11-9-74, "Soviet Détente Policy," May 23, 1974, *FRUS, 1969–1976*, vol. 15, doc. 181. Despite concerns, Kremlin leaders were determined "to proceed with the radical improvement of Soviet-American relations," recalled Dobrynin, *In Confidence*, 302–318.

70. Kissinger and *Washington Post* editors, memo of conversation, March 13, 1974, *FRUS, 1969–1976*, vol. 15, doc. 161.

71. ". . . And the Meaning for Détente," *Washington Post*, October 26, 1973, A26; Gaddis, *Strategies*, 314.

72. NSC staff paper, n.d., attachment to *FRUS, 1969–1976*, vol. 35, doc. 187.

73. Nixon, *RN*, 220; Kissinger, *White House Years* (Boston: Little, Brown and Co., 1979), 37–38; Richard H. Immerman, *The Hidden Hand: A Brief History of the CIA* (Malden, MA: Wiley-Blackwell, 2014), 89–90.

74. Durbin, *CIA and Politics*, 108; Andrew and Dilks, introduction to *Missing Dimension*, 11.

75. Nixon, *RN*, 390; Gaddis, *Strategies*, 301, 304. Critics of the administration's excessive secrecy include Hersh, *The Price of Power*, 39–41, 314–317; William Bundy, *A Tangled Web: The Making of Foreign Policy in the Nixon Presidency* (New York: Hill and Wang, 1998), xiii, 55, 519–520; Hanhimäki, *Flawed Architect*, xvii, 428, 450–451, 480; Robert Dallek, *Nixon and Kissinger: Partners in Power* (New York: HarperCollins, 2007), x, 111, 299–300. See also Arthur M. Schlesinger Jr., *The Imperial Presidency* (New York: Houghton Mifflin, 1973).

76. Dobrynin, *In Confidence*, 287; Craig Daigle, *The Limits of Détente: The United States, the Soviet Union, and the Arab-Israeli Conflict, 1969–1973* (New Haven, CT: Yale University Press, 2012), 298–299. See also Schulzinger, *Henry Kissinger*, 57–58; Jeremi Suri, *Henry Kissinger and the American Century* (Cambridge, MA: Harvard University Press, 2007), 222–226.

77. Dobrynin, *In Confidence*, 356–357. Dobrynin did not further identify the exchange. Kissinger does not mention it in his memoirs. According to official records, the two

met privately on December 22, 1970, to discuss a number of "irritants," including a confirmed espionage case. "Let us make an effort to begin shaping more constructive bilateral relations," proposed Kissinger, who suggested that "we both agree to use this channel whenever we see problems developing in our relations." Dobrynin reportedly agreed, recognizing that this proposed approach could prove "fruitful." Memo of conversation, December 22, 1970, doc. 105 in *Soviet-American Relations: The Détente Years, 1969–1972*, ed. David C. Geyer and Douglas E. Selvage (Washington, DC: U.S. Government Printing Office, 2007).

For Soviet intelligence activity during this period, see Christopher Andrew and Vasili Mitrokhin, *The Sword and the Shield: The Mitrokhin Archive and the Secret History of the KGB* (New York: Basic Books, 1999), 190–219, 228–240; Oleg Kalugin *The First Directorate: My 32 Years in Intelligence and Espionage Against the West* (New York: St. Martin's Press, 1994), 116, 151–152; Thomas Rid, *Active Measures: The Secret History of Disinformation and Political Warfare* (New York: Farrar, Straus and Giroux, 2020), 194–282.

78. Kissinger, *White House Years*, 139; Richard A. Moss, *Nixon's Back Channel to Moscow: Confidential Diplomacy and Détente* (Lexington: University Press of Kentucky, 2017), 9.

79. Memo for the record, July 1, 1974; Colby quoted in Sontag and Drew, *Blind Man's Bluff*, 369.

80. Memo for the record, July 1, 1974. Critiques of Kissinger's political acumen include David Allen, "Realism and Malarkey: Henry Kissinger's State Department, Détente, and Domestic Consensus," *Journal of Cold War Studies* 17 (Summer 2015): 184–219; Mario Del Pero, *The Eccentric Realist: Henry Kissinger and the Shaping of American Foreign Policy* (Ithaca, NY: Cornell University Press, 2010); Walter Isaacson, *Kissinger: A Biography* (New York: Simon and Schuster, 1992). Schwartz, though, is among those who see Kissinger as a shrewd "political actor . . . who understood that American foreign policy is fundamentally shaped and determined by the struggles and battles of American domestic politics." Schwartz, *Henry Kissinger*, 9. Barbara Keys disputes the portrait of Kissinger as coolheaded in "Henry Kissinger: The Emotional Statesman," *Diplomatic History* 35 (September 2011): 587–609.

81. Memo for the record, July 1, 1974.

82. Memo for the record, July 1, 1974.

83. Rob Roy Ratliff, memo for the record, June 10, 1974, *FRUS, 1969–1976*, vol. 35, doc. 188n3.

4. INSIDE JOB

1. "Project AZORIAN: The Story of the *Hughes Glomar Explorer*," *Studies in Intelligence* 22, no. 3 (1978): 37.

2. According to a summary of events compiled by the CIA, Summa's disclosures occurred on July 2–3, 1974, not June 6, as elsewhere reported. See CIA chronology, February 10, 1975, Summa Corporation General, box 22, Series 3: Howard Hughes, Donald L. Barlett and James B. Steele Archive (hereafter BSA), University Archives and Special Collections, American University Library, Washington, DC.

3. Michael E. Davis, transcript of Los Angeles County grand jury testimony, February 13, 1975, Woolbright, Donald Ray—Grand Jury—1975, box 24, BSA.

4. Edward L. Cline, transcript of Los Angeles County grand jury testimony, February 13, 1975, Woolbright, Donald Ray—Grand Jury—1975, box 24, BSA.

5. John Kendall, "Gang Flees with $60,000 After 4-Hour Raid on Hughes' Office," *Los Angeles Times*, June 6, 1974, C1; CIA West Coast Program Office (hereafter WCPO) tel. 1016, July 3, 1974, and CIA briefing note, "Project [AZORIAN]—Potential Compromise," July 6, 1974, both in Summa Corporation General, box 22, BSA.

6. Nadine Henley, transcript of Los Angeles County grand jury testimony, February 13, 1975, Woolbright, Donald Ray—Grand Jury—1975, box 24, BSA.

7. Grand Jury Exhibit No. 7 [June 20, 1974], Woolbright, Donald Ray—Grand Jury—1975, box 24, BSA; CIA briefing note, "Project [AZORIAN]—Potential Compromise."

8. Henley, grand jury testimony; David H. Sharp, *The CIA's Greatest Covert Operation: Inside the Daring Mission to Recover a Nuclear-Armed Soviet Sub* (Lawrence: University Press of Kansas, 2012), 153.

9. Raymond Holliday quoted in Mark Ashley, "Howard Hughes an Aloof Boss," *Milwaukee Journal*, March 5, 1975, 14.

10. Paul R. Michel, "Memoranda of Howard R. Hughes Relating to Political Campaign Contribution," memo to files, April 7, 1975, Hughes Memos re: Political Campaign Contributions, box 111, and Michel to Henry S. Ruth Jr., Closing Memo for Hughes-Rebozo and Unreported Campaign Funds Task Force, October 16, 1975, box 117, both in Campaign Contributions Task Force #804—Hughes/Rebozo Investigation, Records of the Watergate Special Prosecution Force (hereafter WSPF Records), 1971–1977, Record Group 460, NARA, College Park, MD. For the Romaine building's backstory, see Donald L. Barlett and James B. Steele, *Empire: The Life, Legend, and Madness of Howard Hughes* (New York: W. W. Norton, 1979), 212–215, and James Phelan, *Howard Hughes: The Hidden Years* (New York: Random House, 1976), 34–36.

11. WCPO tel. 1016, July 3, 1974.

12. Phelan, "Howard Hughes, Beyond the Law," *New York Times*, September 14, 1975, 50.

13. Sharp, *CIA's Greatest*, 135–136.

14. Michael E. Davis et al., transcript of tape-recorded conversation, April 3, 1975, Donald Ray Woolbright—Grand Jury—1975–1976, box 24, BSA. Davis also said that he flushed the memo down the toilet after finding it lying on the floor of the warehouse the night of the burglary. Detectives questioned the veracity of his claim. But his description of the memo's contents remained consistent. "I don't remember all the details," he told reporters, "but I recall that it said President Nixon knew about it and that the IRS would look the other way on how the money was being put in." William Farr, "Mystery of Hughes' Secret Memo Solved," *Los Angeles Times*, April 4, 1975, B1.

15. CIA briefing note, July 6, 1974.

16. Sharp, *CIA's Greatest*, 136.

17. CIA memo, "Summa Corporation Burglary," July [date illegible], 1974, Summa Corporation General, box 22, BSA; Barlett and Steele, *Empire*, 529–530n.

18. Stanton F. Ense (CIA deputy director of security), memo for the record, "Burglary of Summa Corporation Offices—Loss of Sensitive Document," July 5, 1974, CIA record 104-10122-10271, JFK Collection, NARA.

19. Cline, grand jury testimony.

20. Albert B. Gerber, *Bashful Billionaire: The Story of Howard Hughes* (New York: Lyle Stuart, 1967), 319.

21. Henley quoted in Barlett and Steele, *Empire*, 517. Robert Maheu quoted in Michael Drosnin, *Citizen Hughes* (New York: Holt, Rinehart and Winston, 1985), 466.

22. Quoted in Drosnin, *Citizen Hughes*, 3.

23. Michael Brenner, transcript of Los Angeles County grand jury testimony, February 13, 1975, Woolbright, Donald Ray—Grand Jury—1975–1976, box 24, BSA.

24. WCPO tel. [July 1974?], Summa Corporation General, box 22, BSA.

25. CIA memo, "Summa Corporation Burglary."

26. CIA memo, "Special Projects Staff Matter" [June 25, 1974?], CIA record 104-10122-10141, JFK Collection, NARA

27. Gene Blake, "Hughes Boasted He Could Buy Any Man, Maheu Testifies," *Los Angeles Times*, May 23, 1974, D1. On July 1, 1974, the jury decided the case in Maheu's favor, finding Hughes guilty of libel. A separate proceeding ended on December 4, 1974, and awarded Maheu over $2.8 million in compensatory damages. Summa appealed that decision, and the two parties eventually reached a settlement.

28. Kay Glenn statement, attached to Howard M. Jaffe to Judge Harry Pregerson, June 14, 1974, Theft of Hughes Memos—Documents Received from SEC (Turner) re: and Clips, box 18, WSPF Records.

29. CIA memo for the record, "Burglary of Summa Corporation Offices," July 8, 1974, Summa Corporation General, box 22, BSA.

30. CIA memo, "Summa Corporation Burglary."

31. CIA [author's name redacted] memo, "Summa Corporation Burglary," July [date illegible] 1974, Summa Corporation General, box 22, BSA.

32. Hughes to Nadine [Henley], Lee [Murrin], and Kay [Glenn], memo, "Romaine Robbery" [June 1974?], Hughes Estate Lawsuits, Texas—Nadine Henley (1 of 6), box 10, BSA; "Hughes's Office Ransacked on Coast," *New York Times*, June 6, 1974, 28.

33. Ense, memo for the record.

34. Notice of Motion and Second Motion for Pretrial Discovery, Points and Authorities in Support Thereof, filed October 12, 1976, California State Superior Court, Los Angeles County, California v. Donald Ray Woolbright, Woolbright, Donald Ray—Burglary, box 24, BSA. See chapter 2 for discussion of the planned Greenspun break-in.

35. Ense, memo for the record.

36. Affidavit of Richard H. Kirschner, filed September 30, 1976, U.S. District Court, Central District of California, Woolbright v. Securities and Exchange Commission, Woolbright, Donald Ray—Burglary, box 24, BSA.

37. Motion for Continuance of Trial, filed October 15, 1976, Woolbright v. Securities and Exchange Commission, Woolbright, Donald Ray—Burglary, box 24, BSA.

38. LAPD report, July 30, 1974, quoted in Kirschner affidavit.

39. Ense, memo for the record.

40. Motion for Continuance of Trial, Woolbright v. Securities and Exchange Commission.

41. WCPO, tel., n.d.; WCPO tel. 1812, September 19, 1974, Summa Corporation General, box 22, BSA.

42. LAPD detective quoted in Drosnin, *Citizen Hughes*, 22.

43. "Project AZORIAN," 37.

44. Sharp, *CIA's Greatest*, 174.

45. "Project AZORIAN," 39; Sergei Petrovich Bukan, *Po sledam podvodnykh katastrof* [On the trail of submarine disasters] (Moscow: Gildiya masterov Rus, 1992), 65, trans. Joint

Publications Research Service, report JPRS-UMA-93-004-L, August 18, 1993, CIA Freedom of Information Act Electronic Reading Room, accessed April 6, 2022, https:// www.cia.gov/readingroom/docs/DOC_0000078940.pdf.

46. "Project AZORIAN," 39–40.

47. Bukan, *Po sledam podvodnykh katastrof*, 65–67.

48. "Project AZORIAN," 40.

49. Sharp, *CIA's Greatest*, 186–187.

50. "Project AZORIAN," 40; Sharp, *CIA's Greatest*, 189–194.

51. Sharp, *CIA's Greatest*, 191.

52. "Project AZORIAN," 40–42; Sharp, *CIA's Greatest*, 194.

53. Sharp, *CIA's Greatest*, 194–195.

54. "Project AZORIAN," 44–45; Sharp, *CIA's Greatest*, 221–222.

55. "Project AZORIAN," 40; Sharp, *CIA's Greatest*, 192, 203.

56. "Project AZORIAN," 41.

57. Sharp, *CIA's Greatest*, 205.

58. Leo Gordon, transcript of Los Angeles County grand jury testimony, February 13, 1975, Woolbright, Donald Ray—Grand Jury—1975, box 24, Hughes Series, BSA. A senior document examiner with the LAPD verified that the typing on the white index card was done by an IBM typewriter that was located at the Romaine office at the time of the burglary, and later seized by police as evidence. Keith L. Woodward, transcript of Los Angeles County grand jury testimony, February 13, 1975, Woolbright, Donald Ray— Grand Jury—1975–1976, box 24, Hughes Series, BSA.

59. Gordon, grand jury testimony.

60. WCPO tel. 1433, August 10, 1974, Summa Corporation General, box 22, BSA.

61. CIA memo, "Summa Corporation Burglary."

62. Acting CIA Director of Security to FBI Director Clarence M. Kelley, memo, "Burglary of Summa Corporation Offices," August 5, 1974, Summa Corporation General, box 22, BSA.

63. William C. Turner, memo to files, n.d., Hughes—Theft of Hughes Memos—Documents Received from SEC (Turner) re: and Clips, box 18, WSPF Records.

64. Motion for Continuance of Trial, filed October 15, 1976, California v. Donald Ray Woolbright, Woolbright, Donald Ray—Burglary, box 24, BSA.

65. Steele, interview notes, March 10, 1975, *Glomar Explorer* General, box 5, BSA; David C. Martin, "Hughes–CIA," April 5, 1975, Howard Hughes, box 46, Obituary Files, Washington, DC, Bureau, Associated Press Corporate Archives, Associated Press Collections Online, accessed April 6, 2022, https://www.gale.com/c/associated-press-collections -online-washington-dc-bureau-part-i.

66. August Bequai, memo to files, February 11, 1975, Hughes—Theft of Hughes Memos— Documents Received from SEC (Turner) re: and Clips, box 18, WSPF Records.

67. Bob Woodward and Carl Bernstein, "The Plan: Use CIA to Block Probe," *Washington Post*, August 6, 1974, A1.

68. John M. Crewdson, "Report Links Watergate to Hughes-Rebozo Funds," *New York Times*, August 4, 1974, 1.

69. Michel, Closing Memo. Printed in June, the Ervin Committee's final report devoted an entire chapter to the Hughes-Rebozo investigation. See U.S. Senate, Select Committee on Presidential Campaign Activities, 93rd Cong., 2d sess., *Final Report* (Washington, DC: U.S. Government Printing Office, 1974), 931–1079.

70. Kirschner affidavit; CIA memo, "Summa Corporation Burglary."

71. Turner to Michel, February 3, 1975, Contacts with Bill Turner of Securities and Exchange Commission re: Theft of Hughes memos, box 5, WSPF Records.
72. Michel to Ruth, Closing Memo. LA prosecutor quoted in Drosnin, *Citizen Hughes*, 22.
73. Sharp, *CIA's Greatest*, 206–211; Ray Feldman, interview with author, August 13, 2016, Palo Alto, CA.
74. Ship's log, August 1, 1974, printed in Sharp, *CIA's Greatest*, 212.
75. Quoted in "Project AZORIAN," 45–46; Sharp, *CIA's Greatest*, 214–216.
76. Feldman interview; Sharp, *CIA's Greatest*, 217.

5. FISH OR CUT BAIT?

1. NSC meeting minutes, August 10, 1974, doc. 190 in *Foreign Relations of the United States* [hereafter *FRUS*], *1969–1976*, vol. 35, *National Security Policy, 1973–1976*, ed. M. Todd Bennett (Washington, DC: U.S. Government Printing Office, 2014). The cause of the failure was disputed. Some blamed the contractor, Lockheed, for manufacturing the capture vehicle's arms with Maraging 200, a relatively light steel that cracked under the extremely cold, high-pressure conditions on the ocean bottom. Others cited human error for repeatedly driving the vehicle into harder-than-expected soil and resting the claw on the seabed for hours while engineers repaired the heave compensator, whose manufacturer, Western Gear, also received criticism. See Seymour M. Hersh, "Human Error Is Cited in '74 Glomar Failure," *New York Times*, December 9, 1976, 1, 55; David H. Sharp, *The CIA's Greatest Covert Operation: Inside the Daring Mission to Recovery a Nuclear-Armed Soviet Sub* (Lawrence: University Press of Kansas, 2012), 236–244.
2. NSC meeting minutes; President Ford, Henry A. Kissinger, and Brent Scowcroft, September 25, 1974, 9:30 a.m., box 6, Memoranda of Conversations (hereafter Memcons), National Security Advisor's Files (NSAF), Gerald R. Ford Presidential Library (GRFPL), Ann Arbor, MI.
3. "Behind the Great Submarine Snatch," *Time*, December 6, 1976; Nicholas Wade, "*Glomar Explorer* Said Successful After All," *Science*, December 10, 1976, 1142. See also Thomas O'Toole, "A-Warheads Believed Recovered," *Washington Post*, March 21, 1975, A1; William J. Broad, "Russia Says U.S. Got Sub's Atom Arms," *New York Times*, June 20, 1993, 14; Clyde W. Burleson, *The Jennifer Project* (Englewood Cliffs, NJ: Prentice-Hall, 1977; College Station: Texas A&M University Press, 1997), 112–116.
4. Sharp, *CIA's Greatest*, 225–226.
5. William P. Clements Jr. to Kissinger, memo [November 14, 1974?], *FRUS, 1969–1976*, vol. 35, doc. 193; William Colby with Peter Forbath, *30 Ans de CIA*, trans. Jean-Pierre Carasso (Paris: Presses de la Renaissance, 1978), 331. My translation.
6. Jeffrey T. Richelson, *The Wizards of Langley: Inside the CIA's Directorate of Science and Technology* (Boulder, CO: Westview Press, 2002), 134.
7. Hersh, "Human Error." As sources, Hersh named brothers Wayne Collier, a former Global Marine executive in charge of AZORIAN recruiting, and Billy Collier, a cutting torch handler who the Colliers alleged was exposed to dangerous radioactivity from corroded nuclear warheads while working in close proximity to the sub. Wayne Collier coauthored (with Roy Varner), *A Matter of Risk: The Incredible Inside Story of the CIA's Hughes Glomar Explorer Mission to Raise a Russian Submarine* (New York: Random House, 1978), which details the mission's discoveries on pages 172–185.

8. Richelson, *Wizards*, 134.

9. John C. Stennis, notes [April 27, 1975?], Armed Services Committee (Chairman) (1975), box 31, series 43: Committees Series, John C. Stennis Papers, Congressional and Political Research Center, Mitchell Memorial Library, Mississippi State University, Starkville, MS.

10. Hersh, "Human Error"; "Finding of a Diary on Sub Reported," *New York Times*, April 8, 1975, 9.

11. Sharp, *CIA's Greatest*, 227–229.

12. CIA, Office of Public and Agency Information, "*Glomar Explorer*: Recovery and Burial of Soviet Sailors," press release, November 12, 1992, in author's possession. In 1992, CIA director Robert M. Gates presented the ensign and a videotape of the burial ceremony to Russian president Boris Yeltsin as a gesture of goodwill following the Soviet Union's collapse. See Gates, *From the Shadows: The Ultimate Insider's Story of Five Presidents and How They Won the Cold War* (New York: Simon and Schuster, 1996), 553–554. The video recording is widely available online.

13. Hersh, "Human Error."

14. George J. Keegan Jr. to Bobby Ray Inman, December 17, 1976, Missiles (2), box 12, Presidential Subject File, NSAF, GRFPL, available via the Clements National Security Papers Project, Clements Center for National Security, University of Texas at Austin, https://ns.clementspapers.org/clementsns/pdf/17752.

15. Geary Yost (pseudonym), interview with author, August 4, 2016, suburban Washington, DC.

16. Kissinger to Ford, memo, June 16, 1975, *FRUS, 1969–1976*, vol. 35, doc. 206.

17. Sherry Sontag and Christopher Drew, *Blind Man's Bluff: The Untold Story of American Submarine Espionage* (New York: Harper, 2000), 214; Sharp, *CIA's Greatest*, 244, 260.

18. Inman, interview with author, November 16, 2016, Austin, TX; John T. Hughes to Colby, memo, November 11. 1974, *FRUS, 1969–1976*, vol. 35, doc. 191.

19. Hughes to Colby, memo. See chapter 1 for a fuller discussion of the USIB's 1970 assessment.

20. William Hyland quoted in Bruce A. Lowe to Holders of USIB-D-72.1/17, November 14, 1974, *FRUS, 1969–1976*, vol. 35, doc. 192. Emphasis in the original.

21. Vincent de Poix paraphrased in Clements to Kissinger, memo.

22. Clements to Kissinger, memo.

23. Jacques Cousteau quoted in "The Great Submarine Snatch," *Time*, March 31, 1975, 20. See also Bayard Webster, "Sea-Mine Rivals Did Not Suspect Sub," *New York Times*, March 22, 1975, 38.

24. Clements to Kissinger, memo. Colby quoted in NSC meeting minutes.

25. Clements to Kissinger, memo. Sharp details the overhaul in *CIA's Greatest*, 245–247.

26. Colby to Kissinger, memo, November 23, 1974, *FRUS, 1969–1976*, vol. 35, doc. 193n4.

27. On the weakening of national security secrecy, see Kaeten Mistry, "The Rise and Fall of Anti-imperial Whistleblowing in the Long 1970s," in *Whistleblowing Nation: The History of National Security Disclosures and the Cult of State Secrecy*, ed. Kaeten Mistry and Hannah Gurman (New York: Columbia University Press, 2020), 130; Lloyd C. Gardner, *The War on Leakers: National Security and American Democracy, from Eugene V. Debs to Edward Snowden* (New York: New Press, 2016), 62–63. Historical examples include David Wise and Thomas B. Ross, *The Invisible Government* (New York: Random House, 1964); Victor Marchetti and John D. Marks, *The CIA and the Cult of Intelligence* (New York: Knopf, 1974); Philip Agee, *Inside the Company: CIA Diary* (London: Penguin, 1975).

28. Seymour Hersh, "Huge CIA Operation Reported in US Against Antiwar Forces, Other Dissident in Nixon Years," *New York Times*, December 12, 1974, 1.

29. Henry Kissinger, *Years of Renewal* (New York: Simon and Schuster, 1999), 320; William Colby and Peter Forbath, *Honorable Men: My Life in the CIA* (New York: Simon and Schuster, 1978), 391.

30. "The Democratic Caucus in Command," *Washington Post*, January 20, 1975, A18.

31. "Year of Intelligence," *New York Times*, February 8, 1975, 21.

32. CIA memo for the record, "Romaine Street Burglary," October 5, 1974, Summa Corporation General, box 22, Series 3: Howard Hughes, Donald L. Barlett and James B. Steele Archive (hereafter BSA), University Archives and Special Collections, American University Library, Washington, DC.

33. CIA West Coast Program Office (WCPO), tel. 1812, September 19, 1975, BSA.

34. CIA memo for the record, "Summa Corporation Burglary," October 7, 1974.

35. CIA memo for the record, "Romaine Street Burglary."

36. Leo Gordon, transcript of Los Angeles County grand jury testimony, February 13, 1975, Woolbright, Donald Ray—Grand Jury—1975, box 24, BSA.

37. James Phelan, "CIA Link to Hughes Reported Disclosed by Burglary," *New York Times*, March 14, 1975, 21.

38. CIA memo for the record, "Romaine Street Burglary."

39. CIA chronology, [n.d.], Summa Corporation General, box 22, BSA.

40. CIA memo for the record, "Summa Corporation Burglary," October 7, 1974.

41. WCPO tel. 2189, November 1, 1974, Summa Corporation General, box 22, BSA.

42. U.S. Senate, Select Committee to Study Governmental Operations with Respect to Intelligence Activities (hereafter Church Committee), 94th Cong., 2d sess., *Final Report* (No. 94-755), book 1, *Foreign and Military Intelligence* (Washington, DC: U.S. Government Printing Office, 1976), 427. Frank Church quoted in Loch K. Johnson, *A Season of Inquiry Revisited: The Church Committee Confronts America's Spy Agencies* (Lawrence: University Press of Kansas, 2015), 54.

43. Church Committee, *Final Report*, bk. 1:54–55, 59. Multiple searches of pre-1974 intelligence files in the NSC's physical custody revealed no *Glomar*-related items.

44. Brent Durbin evaluates 1970s-era reforms in *The CIA and the Politics of U.S. Intelligence Reform* (New York: Cambridge University Press, 2017), 105–162.

45. Rob Roy Ratliff to Scowcroft, memo, February 26, 1975, *FRUS, 1969–1976*, vol. 35, doc. 196. No evidence indicates that Kissinger was aware of the breach prior to February 1975.

46. CIA memo for the record, "Summa Corporation Burglary," November 25, 1974, Summa Corporation General, box 22, BSA.

47. CIA memo for the record, "Romaine Street Burglary"; CIA memo for the record, "Summa Corporation—Romaine Street Break and Entry—June 5—Donald Woolbright, Prosecution, LA County," November 24, 1975, Summa Corporation General, box 22, BSA.

48. Memo for the record, January 23, 1975, *FRUS, 1969–1976*, vol. 35, doc. 194.

49. Memo for the record, January 23, 1975. The Rockefeller Commission's final report dispensed with *Glomar* in a footnote stating that its inquiry "disclosed no improper activities by the agency." Commission on CIA Activities Within the United States, *Report to the President* (Washington, DC: U.S. Government Printing Office, June 1975), 216, available through Digital Collections, Intelligence Community Investigations and Reforms, GRFPL, at https://www.fordlibrarymuseum.gov/library/exhibits/intelligence/rcreport

.asp. The board reached that conclusion despite claims that CIA officers pressured local and federal officials to curb *Glomar*-related tax and securities investigations. See "CIA Asked Tax Assessor's Aid on Ship," *New York Times*, April 4, 1975, 3; Nicholas M. Horrock, "CIA Reported Pressing SEC to Curb Global Marine Inquiry," *New York Times*, April 27, 1975, 43; Joseph Volz, "CIA Probe Didn't Go Roamin' Near Glomar," *New York Daily News*, June 12, 1975.

50. Memo for the record, January 23, 1975, *FRUS, 1969–1976*, vol. 35, doc. 194; William Hyland and Richard W. Shryock, *The Fall of Khrushchev* (New York: Funk and Wagnalls, 1968).

51. On Kissinger's centrality, see Thomas A. Schwartz, *Henry Kissinger and American Power: A Political Biography* (New York: Hill and Wang, 2020), 270–275.

52. Memo for the record, January 23, 1975.

53. Ford, Kissinger, and Scowcroft, January 4, 1975, Memcons, NSAF, GRFPL; Thomas Powers, *The Man Who Kept the Secrets: Richard Helms and the CIA* (New York: Knopf, 1979), 13. Helms pled no contest to two misdemeanor counts of failing to testify "fully, completely and accurately" before a Senate committee.

54. Randall B. Woods, *Shadow Warrior: William Egan Colby and the CIA* (New York: Basic Books, 2013), 345; John Prados, *William Colby and the CIA: The Secret Wars of a Controversial Spymaster* (Lawrence: University Press of Kansas, 2009), 311.

55. Colby and Forbath, *Honorable Men*, 310.

56. Harold P. Ford, *William E. Colby as Director of Central Intelligence, 1973–1976* (Washington, DC: CIA Center for the Study of Intelligence, 1993), 141–142.

57. Ford, Kissinger, and Scowcroft, January 23, 1975, 9:35–10:18 a.m., Memcons, NSAF, GRFPL.

58. Kissinger to Ford, memo, February 5, 1975, *FRUS, 1969–1976*, vol. 35, doc. 195.

6. COLBY'S DIKE

1. Gerald Ford, Henry Kissinger, James Schlesinger, William Colby, David Jones, and Donald Rumsfeld, Memoranda of Conversations (Memcons), February 7, 1975, 5:22–5:50 p.m., National Security Advisor's Files (NSAF), Gerald R. Ford Presidential Library (GRFPL), Ann Arbor, MI; Carl Duckett and Colby, transcript of telephone conversation (hereafter telcon), February 7, 1975, 4:10 p.m., in author's possession. In response to litigation filed under the Freedom of Information Act, the CIA declassified, in 1977, records documenting contacts between agency officials and members of the media pertaining to publication of the *Glomar Explorer* story. The author thanks Kathryn Olmsted for providing copies of the published files.

2. Colby and Duckett, telcons, February 7, 1975, 4:50 p.m. and 5:45 p.m.; Colby and Peter Forbath, *Honorable Men: My Life in the CIA* (New York: Simon and Schuster, 1978), 414–415; William Farr and Jerry Cohen, "U.S. Reported After Russ Sub," *Los Angeles Times*, February 7, 1975, 1.

3. Farr and Cohen, "U.S. Reported After Russ Sub."

4. Rob Roy Ratliff to Brent Scowcroft, memo, February 26, 1975, doc. 196 in *Foreign Relations of the United States* [hereafter *FRUS*], *1969–1976*, vol. 35, *National Security Policy, 1973–1976*, ed. M. Todd Bennett (Washington, DC: U.S. Government Printing Office, 2014).

Emphasis in the original. "We briefed the Los Angeles Police Department," Colby recalled in a 1988 interview, "asking them to hold the line for us, but I think it was they who leaked the story to the *L.A. Times*." Harold P. Ford, *William E. Colby as Director of Central Intelligence* (Washington, DC: CIA Center for the Study of Intelligence, 1993), 186.

5. Ratliff to Scowcroft, memo. Emphasis in the original.

6. Ex-CIA officer, interview with the author, 2016. The officer requested anonymity in order to speak freely; for this reason, I've also withheld the exact date of our interview.

7. Colby and Forbath, *Honorable Men*, 415.

8. David H. Sharp, *The CIA's Greatest Covert Operation: Inside the Daring Mission to Recover a Nuclear-Armed Soviet Sub* (Lawrence: University Press of Kansas, 2012), 256, 268.

9. Colby and Forbath, *Honorable Men*, 415.

10. Sharp, *CIA's Greatest*, 253.

11. Loch K. Johnson, *America's Secret Power: The CIA in a Democratic Society* (New York: Oxford University Press, 1989), 184, 200–202, 249. For accounts of Colby's efforts at prior restraint, see Kathryn S. Olmsted, *Challenging the Secret Government: The Post-Watergate Investigations of the CIA and FBI* (Chapel Hill: University of North Carolina Press, 1996), 67–73; John Prados, *William Colby and the CIA: The Secret Wars of a Controversial Spymaster* (Lawrence: University Press of Kansas, 2009), 267–268.

12. New York Times Co. v. United States, 403 U.S. 713 (1971) at 730; Prados and Margaret Pratt Porter, eds., *Inside the Pentagon Papers* (Lawrence: University Press of Kansas, 2004), 199. On the distinction between necessary (sometimes defined as legitimate or "good") secrets, as opposed to unnecessary (illegitimate or "bad") secrets, see Johnson, *America's Secret Power*, 201–202; Jason Ross Arnold, *Secrecy in the Sunshine Era: The Promise and Failures of U.S. Open Government Laws* (Lawrence: University Press of Kansas, 2014), 14–23. For a defense of national security secrecy, see Gabriel Schoenfeld, *Necessary Secrets: National Security, the Media, and the Rule of Law* (New York: W.W. Norton, 2010).

13. Ben Bradlee, *A Good Life: Newspapering and Other Adventures* (New York: Simon and Schuster, 1995), 453; Stephen Isaacs, "Withholding of Story Defended," *Washington Post*, March 20, 1975, A15.

14. WCPO to CIA, telegram 2911, February 8, 1975; Colby and Forbath, *Honorable Men*, 414–415; Jack Nelson, "Administration Won't Talk About Sub Raised by CIA," *Los Angeles Times*, March 20, 1975, A1.

15. WCPO telegram 2911.

16. Farr and Cohen, "CIA Reportedly Contracted with Hughes in Effort to Raise Sunken Soviet A-Sub," *Los Angeles Times*, February 8, 1975, 18; Harrison E. Salisbury, *Without Fear or Favor: The New York Times and Its Times* (New York: Times Books, 1980), 544; WCPO telegram 2911.

17. Colby and Katharine Graham, telcon, February 13, 1975.

18. Colby and unnamed U.S. official, telcon, January 22, 1974; Seymour Hersh, telephone interview with author, June 22, 2016; Hersh, *Reporter: A Memoir* (New York: Knopf, 2018), 171. Former *New York Times* journalist David Halberstam spoke to Hersh's reputation in *The Powers That Be* (New York: Knopf, 1979), 679.

19. Sharp, *CIA's Greatest*, 114; Sherry Sontag and Christopher Drew, *Blind Man's Bluff: The Untold Story of American Submarine Espionage* (New York: PublicAffairs, 1998), 203. John Piña Craven addressed such speculation in his memoirs, *The Silent War: The Cold War Battle Beneath the Sea* (New York: Simon and Schuster, 2001), 199, 272–274.

20. Hersh, *Reporter*, 170–171; Sontag and Drew, *Blind Man's Bluff*, 200; Colby and unnamed U.S. official, telcon, February 4, 1974.

21. Colby and Hersh, telcon, January 30, 1974.

22. Kissinger, Schlesinger, Colby, and Thomas Moorer, Memcons, January 22, 1974, NSAF, GRFPL; Colby and unnamed U.S. official(s), telcons, January 22 and January 29, 1974; Colby and Forbath, *Honorable Men*, 416.

23. Colby and unnamed U.S. official, telcon, January 28, 1974; Colby and J. Fred Buzhardt, telcon, February 2, 1974.

24. Hersh interview; Hersh, *Reporter*, 173, 175, 227.

25. Colby and Scowcroft, telcon, February 2, 1974.

26. CIA, "Soviet Response to MATADOR Disclosures," paper [April 30, 1975?], *FRUS, 1969–1976*, vol. 35, doc. 202, appendix A; Colby and Scowcroft, telcon, February 14, 1975.

27. Hersh interview; Colby and Laurence Silberman, telcon, February 14, 1975; Salisbury, *Without Fear*, 545; Tom Wicker, *On Press* (New York: Viking, 1978), 217.

28. WCPO to CIA, telegram 3166, February 26, 1975; Colby and Silberman, telcon, February 14, 1975; Sontag and Drew, *Blind Man's Bluff*, 199–201.

29. WCPO to CIA, telegram 3166, February 26, 1975; Hersh, "CIA Salvage Ship Brought Up Part of Soviet Sub Lost in 1968, Failed to Raise Atom Missiles" *New York Times*, March 19, 1975, 52.

30. Colby and Forbath, *Honorable Men*, 416.

31. Schlesinger to All CIA Employees, memo, May 9, 1973, Central Intelligence Agency—General—1973, Subject File, Schlesinger Papers, Manuscript Division, Library of Congress (LoC), Washington, DC; Prados, *The Family Jewels: The CIA, Secrecy and Presidential Power* (Austin: University of Texas Press, 2013).

32. *New York Times* columnist Tom Wicker attended the luncheon. For his firsthand account, see Wicker, *On Press*, 188–196.

33. *CBS Evening News*, February 28, 1975, CBS—Washington, DC Bureau—Scripts, Broadcasts and Film, box 70, Daniel Schorr Papers, Manuscript Division, LoC; Schorr, *Clearing the Air* (Boston: Houghton Mifflin, 1977), 143–146.

34. Richard J. Aldrich, "Regulation by Revelation? Intelligence, the Media and Transparency," in *Spinning Intelligence: Why Intelligence Needs the Media, Why the Media Needs Intelligence*, ed. Robert Dover and Michael S. Goodman (New York: Columbia University Press, 2009), 13–36. On objective journalism, see Julian E. Zelizer, "Without Restraint: Scandal and Politics in America," in *The Columbia History of Post–World War II America*, ed. Mark C. Carnes (New York: Columbia University Press, 2007), 230–231; Katherine Fink and Michael Schudson, "The Rise of Contextual Journalism, 1950s–2000s," *Journalism* 15, no 1 (2014): 4; Thomas E. Patterson, *Out of Order* (New York: Knopf, 1993), 18–19. Former *Washington Post* reporter Carl Bernstein claimed that as many as four hundred American journalists had worked for the CIA since 1952 in "The CIA and the Media," *Rolling Stone*, October 20, 1977, 3. The CIA placed the figure at three dozen. See Hugh Wilford, *The Mighty Wurlitzer: How the CIA Played America* (Cambridge, MA: Harvard University Press, 2008), 225–248; Steven T. Usdin, *Bureau of Spies: The Secret Connections Between Espionage and Journalism in Washington* (Amherst, NY: Prometheus Books, 2018), 249, 258–259.

35. Richard Halloran, "Helms Defends the CIA as Vital to a Free Society," *New York Times*, April 15, 1971, 1; John Ranelagh, *The Agency: The Rise and Decline of the CIA* (New York: Simon and Schuster, 1986), 281.

36. Usdin, *Bureau of Spies*, 258. On the causes and effects of investigative journalism, see Halberstam, *Powers That Be*; Patterson, *Out of Order*, 19, 79; Zelizer, "Without Restraint," 232–236; David Greenberg, *Republic of Spin: An Inside History of the American Presidency* (New York: Norton, 2016), 400–401; Larry J. Sabato, *Feeding Frenzy: How Attack Journalism Has Transformed American Politics* (New York: Free Press, 1991); Michael Schudson, *Discovering the News: A Social History of American Newspapers* (New York: Basic Books, 1978), 176–183.

37. Fink and Schudson, "Rise of Contextual Journalism," 3–6.

38. Meg Greenfield, *Washington* (New York: PublicAffairs, 2001), 94. See also Arnold, *Secrecy in the Sunshine Era*, esp. xii, 2–3, 6, 375–376; Michael Schudson, *The Rise of the Right to Know: Politics and the Culture of Transparency, 1945–1975* (Cambridge, MA: Belknap Press of Harvard University Press, 2015), esp. 15–16, 18, 21, 24–25.

39. Colby and Forbath, *Honorable Men*, 402.

40. Hersh interview.

41. William P. Clements Jr. to Kissinger, memo [November 14, 1974?], *FRUS, 1969–1976*, vol. 35, doc. 193.

42. Sontag and Drew, *Blind Man's Bluff*, 213.

43. Halberstam, *Powers That Be*, 568; Wicker, *On Press*, 218–219, 238; Salisbury, *Without Fear*, 555; Olmsted, *Challenging*, 23, 33.

44. Hersh, *Reporter*, 227–228; Wicker, *On Press*, 218.

45. Wicker, *On Press*, 218; Salisbury, *Without Fear*, 550; Kathryn S. Olmsted, "'An American Conspiracy:' The Post-Watergate Press and the CIA," *Journalism History* 19, no. 2 (1993): 51.

46. Wicker, *On Press*, 192, 195.

47. CIA, memo for the record, February 27, 1975; Salisbury, *Without Fear*, 547–548.

48. Colby and Kissinger, telcon, February 27, 1975; Clifton Daniel and Kissinger, telcon, February 28, 1975, 12:03 p.m., Kissinger Telephone Transcripts, U.S. Department of State Freedom of Information Act Virtual Reading Room, available at https://foia.state.gov.

49. Daniel and Kissinger, telcon, February 28, 1975. The decision reached by *New York Times* executives "was anything but quick and easy," according to Morton Kondracke, "The CIA and 'Our Conspiracy,'" *(MORE): A Journalism Review*, May 1975, 11.

50. CIA, memo for the record, February 28, 1975; Howard Bray, *The Pillars of the Post: The Making of a News Empire in Washington* (New York: W. W. Norton, 1980), 151.

51. Colby and Angus Thuermer, telcon, March 13, 1975; Colby and Duckett, telcons, March 13, 1975, 3:00 and 4:58 p.m.

52. Colby, Les Whitten, and Jack Cloherty, telcon, March 18, 1975; Colby and Lloyd Shearer, telcon, March 13, 1975.

53. Colby and Scowcroft, telcons, February 25 and March 14, 1975.

54. Colby and Forbath, *Honorable Men*, 416; Colby and NBC executive, telcon, March 17, 1975.

55. Wicker, *On Press*, 217–218.

56. Colby and Forbath, *Honorable Men*, 416–417; Colby and Scowcroft, telcon, March 14, 1975.

57. Donald L. Barlett and James B. Steele, *Empire: The Life, Legend, and Madness of Howard Hughes* (New York: W. W. Norton, 1979), 536.

58. Hersh interview.

59. James Phelan, "CIA Link to Hughes Reported Disclosed by Burglary on Coast," *New York Times*, March 14, 1975, 21; Colby and William Thomas, telcon, March 18, 1975.

60. Marc Feldstein, *Poisoning the Press: Richard Nixon, Jack Anderson, and the Rise of Washington's Scandal Culture* (New York: Farrar, Straus and Giroux, 2010), 205–213.

61. Jack Anderson with Daryl Gibson, *Peace, War, and Politics: An Eyewitness Account* (New York: Forge, 1999), 277–278; script [1994?], Radio Scripts—Watch on Washington, box 234, Jack Anderson Papers, Special Collections Research Center, George Washington University, Washington, DC. See also Jack Anderson with James Boyd, *Confessions of a Muckraker: The Inside Story of Life in Washington During the Truman, Eisenhower, Kennedy and Johnson Years* (New York: Random House, 1979).

62. Colby, Whitten, and Cloherty, telcon, March 18, 1975, 5:25 p.m.; Anderson with Gibson, *Peace, War, and Politics*, 277–278.

63. Colby and Anderson, telcon, March 18, 1975, 6:52 p.m.

64. Colby and Scowcroft, telcon, March 18, 1975, 7:35 p.m.

65. Salisbury, *Without Fear*, 526

66. Colby and *Washington Post* representative, telcon, March 18, 1975, 7:16 p.m.; Colby and Forbath, *Honorable Men*, 416.

67. Thomas O'Toole summarized Anderson's broadcast in "CIA Recovered Part of Soviet A-Sub," *Washington Post*, March 19, 1975, A1, A10; Anderson with Gibson, *Peace, War, and Politics*, 277. Neither the script from which Anderson read nor an audio recording of his March 18 broadcast were found among the columnist's papers.

68. Anderson quoted in O'Toole, "CIA Recovered Part"; Martin Arnold, "CIA Tried to Get Press to Hold Up Salvage Story," *New York Times*, March 20, 1975, 31; Bill Boyarsky, "Why Editors Withheld Details on Sub," *Los Angeles Times*, March 20, 1975, A1, A18.

69. Hersh, *Reporter*, 228–229.

70. Hersh, "C.I.A. Salvage Ship."

7. NEITHER CONFIRM NOR DENY

1. Jerry Cohen and George Reasons, "CIA Recovers Part of Russian Sub," *Los Angeles Times*, March 19, 1975, A1; Thomas O'Toole, "CIA Recovered Part of Soviet A-Sub," *Washington Post*, March 19, 1975, A1; "Hughes, CIA Collaboration," *NBC Nightly News*, March 19, 1975, clip 481848, "CIA, Hughes Connection," *ABC Evening News*, March 19, 1975, clip 36304, and "CIA, Hughes Collaboration," *CBS Evening News*, March 19, 1975, clip 239116, all in Vanderbilt Television News Archive, (https://tvnews.vanderbilt.edu), Special Collections, Heard Libraries, Vanderbilt University, Nashville, TN.

2. Jeremiah O'Leary, "Silence Reigns on Sub Issue as US Awaits Détente Impact," *Washington Star*, March 20, 1975, A9; Jack Nelson, "Administration Won't Talk About Sub Raised by CIA," *Los Angeles Times*, March 20, 1975, A1; news conference transcript, March 19, 1975, box 7, Press Secretary's Press Briefing Transcripts, Ron Nessen Files, Gerald R. Ford Presidential Library (GRFPL), Ann Arbor, MI.

3. Ford, James Schlesinger, William Colby et al., March 19, 1975, Memoranda of Conversations (Memcons), National Security Advisor's Files (NSAF), GRFPL.

4. Ford, Schlesinger, Colby et al., March 19, 1975, Memcons, NSAF, GRFPL.

5. Henry Kissinger, *Years of Renewal* (New York: Simon and Schuster, 1999), 324–325. Richard Helms provided a scathing review of Colby's performance in *A Look Over My Shoulder: A Life in the Central Intelligence Agency* (New York: Random House, 2003), 431. See

John Prados, *William Colby and the CIA: The Secret Wars of a Controversial Spymaster* (Lawrence: University Press of Kansas, 2009); Randall B. Woods, *Shadow Warrior: William Egan Colby and the CIA* (New York: Basic Books, 2013).

6. Ford, Schlesinger, Colby et al., March 19, 1975, Memcons, NSAF, GRFPL; Colby and Peter Forbath, *Honorable Men: My Life in the CIA* (New York: Simon and Schuster, 1978), 417; Nikita S. Khrushchev, *Khrushchev Remembers: The Last Testament*, trans. and ed. Strobe Talbott (Boston: Little, Brown and Co., 1974), 443–456; Michael R. Beschloss, *May Day: Eisenhower, Khrushchev, and the U-2 Affair* (New York: Harper and Row, 1986), 61, 65, 372.

7. Ford, Schlesinger, Colby et al., March 19, 1975, Memcons, NSAF, GRFPL.

8. David H. Sharp, *The CIA's Greatest Covert Operation: Inside the Daring Mission to Recover a Nuclear-Armed Soviet Sub* (Lawrence: University Press of Kansas, 2012), 274.

9. CIA, President's Daily Brief (PDB), March 27, 1975, CIA Freedom of Information Act Electronic Reading Room, accessed April 12, 2022, https://www.cia.gov/readingroom /docs/DOC_0006014756.pdf; CIA memo, April 30, 1975, doc. 202 in *Foreign Relations of the United States* [hereafter *FRUS*], *1969–1976*, vol. 35, *National Security Policy, 1973– 1976*, ed. M. Todd Bennett (Washington, DC: U.S. Government Printing Office, 2014).

10. Donald Rumsfeld, April 2, 1975, Memos of Meetings with President Ford, Rumsfeld Papers, accessed April 12, 2022, http://library.rumsfeld.com/doclib/sp/2371/1975-04-02 .pdf.

11. Nelson, "Administration Won't Talk."

12. The expletives are omitted from the source text: Sergey Petrovich Bukan, *Po sledam podvodnykh katastrof* [On the trail of submarine disasters] (Moscow: Gildiya masterov Rus, 1992), 73–74, trans. Joint Publications Research Service, report JPRS-UMA-93-004-L, August 18, 1993, CIA Freedom of Information Act Electronic Reading Room, accessed April 12, 2022, https://www.cia.gov/readingroom/docs/DOC_0000078940 .pdf. For a profile of Gorshkov, see "Power Play on the Oceans," *Time*, February 23, 1968.

13. Nelson, "Administration Won't Talk."

14. PDB, March 27, 1975; CIA paper, "Soviet Response to MATADOR Disclosures" [April 30, 1975?], *FRUS, 1969–1976*, vol. 35, doc. 202, appendix A; Daniel F. Gilmore, "Soviet Seamen," United Press International wire report, April 24, 1975, *Glomar Explorer*, box 153, Daniel Schorr Papers, Manuscript Division, Library of Congress, Washington, DC.

15. According to U.S. diplomats, the Soviet press did not print the word "Glomar" until July. Moscow Embassy to Secretary of State, tel. Moscow 09563, July 9, 1975, Electronic Telegrams, Records of the Department of State, Record Group 59, Access to Archival Databases (https://aad.archives.gov/aad/), National Archives and Records Administration (NARA), College Park, MD.

16. Sharp, *CIA's Greatest*, 256.

17. CIA memo, April 30, 1975.

18. PDB, March 27, 1975. Emphasis in original.

19. PDB, March 27, 1975 (emphasis in original); Helmut Sonnenfeldt to Brent Scowcroft, March 22, 1975, USSR—"D" File, box 30, Kissinger-Scowcroft West Wing Office Files, NSAF, GRFPL.

20. PDB, March 27, 1975.

21. Colby to Kissinger, memo, March 28, 1975, *FRUS, 1969–1976*, vol. 35, doc. 198.

22. Colby to Kissinger, memo, March 28, 1975; President's Foreign Intelligence Advisory Board meeting, memo for the record, April 3, 1975, *FRUS, 1969–1976*, vol. 35, doc. 200.

23. Colby to Kissinger, memo, March 28, 1975; John T. Hughes to Colby, memo, Nov. 11, 1974, *FRUS, 1969–1976*, vol. 35, doc. 191.

24. Ad hoc 40 Committee meeting, memo for the record, April 4, 1975, *FRUS, 1969–1976*, vol. 35, doc. 201.

25. Soviet note [March 29, 1975?], *Glomar Explorer*, box 1, Peter Rodman Files, NSAF, GRFPL. Anatoly Dobrynin related his meeting with Kissinger in his memoirs, *In Confidence: Moscow's Ambassador to America's Six Cold War Presidents (1962–1986)* (New York: Times Books, 1995), 352–353. Though known to only a few, the classified contents of the review reportedly became "scandalous" within official circles because they documented navy inaction in the face of reports of the *Glomar Explorer*'s activity. Commander in Chief Gorshkov received "a good dressing-down," according to Bukan, *Po sledam podvodnykh katastrof*, 51–52, 73–75.

26. Soviet note; CIA, "*Glomar Explorer*: Recovery and Burial of Soviet Sailors" [November 12, 1992?], in author's collection; Robert M. Gates, *From the Shadows: The Ultimate Insider's Story of Five Presidents and How They Won the Cold War* (New York: Simon and Schuster, 1996), 553–554.

27. "Hooray for the CIA!," *Atlanta Constitution*, March 22, 1975, A4; "A Bold and Proper CIA Effort," *Chicago Tribune*, March 21, 1975, A2. See also *Anchorage Daily Times*, March 21, 1975, and *Washington Star*, March 21, 1975, printed in *Editorials on File* 6, no. 6 (March 16–31, 1975): 313, 315.

28. Sonnenfeldt and William G. Hyland to Kissinger, memo, March 28, 1975, Soviet Union, January–March 1975, box 5, Lot File 81D286 (Entry 5339), Records of the Office of the Counselor, Records of the U.S. Department of State, Record Group (RG) 59, NARA.

29. Dobrynin, *In Confidence*, 342, 352–359; Kissinger-Dobrynin, transcript of telephone conversation (telcon), December 23, 1975, Henry Kissinger Telephone Transcripts, U.S. Department of State Freedom of Information Act Electronic Reading Room, available at https://foia.state.gov.

30. CIA Interagency Intelligence Memo, NIO IIM 76-030J, "Implications for US-Soviet Relations of Certain Soviet Activities," June 1976, Records of the Central Intelligence Agency, RG 263, NARA.

31. Kissinger to Ford, memo, April 2, 1975, *Glomar Explorer*, box 1, Rodman Files.

32. Dobrynin–Kissinger, telcon, March 27, 1975, USSR—Dobrynin/Kissinger Exchanges—Telephone Conversations, box 34, Kissinger-Scowcroft West Wing Office Files.

33. Dobrynin–Kissinger, telcon, March 31, 1975, USSR—Dobrynin/Kissinger Exchanges—Telephone Conversations, box 34, Kissinger-Scowcroft West Wing Office Files.

34. CIA memo, April 30, 1975.

35. Gilmore, "Soviet Seamen."

36. O'Toole, "A-Warheads Believed Recovered," *Washington Post*, March 21, 1975, A1.

37. Thomas Powers, "The Sub Rosa Sub Affair," *New York Times Book Review*, October 9, 1977, 11.

38. Sharp, *CIA's Greatest*, 266.

39. Sharp, 266–267.

40. Kissinger, *The Necessity for Choice: Prospects of American Foreign Policy* (New York: Harper, 1961), 54.

41. Kissinger to Ford, memo, April 2, 1975.

42. Oral response [April 1975], *Glomar Explorer*, box 1, Rodman Files. Despite advising against a "quasi-confirmation," Kissinger also approved a paper identifying three of the six Soviet submariners whose remains were found aboard the sub. "It is the practice of the United States to treat bodies recovered at sea with complete dignity, including as appropriate burial with full military honors," stated the paper, delivered to Dobrynin on April 22. Scowcroft to Dobrynin, memo, April 22, 1975, USSR—"D" File, box 30, Kissinger-Scowcroft West Wing Office Files; Dobrynin, *In Confidence*, 352–353.

43. Non-denial denials were outgrowths of the Watergate era, according to Todd S. Purdum, "The Nondenial Denier," *New York Times*, February 16, 2003, WK5. In 1972, for example, Richard Nixon's domestic policy advisor, John Ehrlichman, refused to "affirm or deny" reports linking the White House to Watergate. Carl Bernstein and Bob Woodward, *All the President's Men* (New York: Simon and Schuster, 1974), 92, 161.

44. Critiques of the Dwight Eisenhower administration's handling of the U-2 affair include Beschloss, *May Day*, 372–374; David Wise and Thomas B. Ross, *The U-2 Affair* (New York: Random House, 1962); Lawrence W. Haapanen, "The Missed Opportunity: The U-2 and Paris," in *Eisenhower's War of Words: Rhetoric and Leadership*, ed. Martin J. Medhurst (East Lansing: Michigan State University Press, 1994), 251–272. See also Paul Kellogg, "U-2 Analogy Doesn't Work," letter to the editor, *International Herald Tribune*, April 11, 2001.

45. CIA memo, April 30, 1975. See chapter 3 for discussion of Kissinger and Dobrynin's non-disclosure efforts.

46. Kissinger to Ford, memo, June 16, 1975, *FRUS, 1969–1976*, vol. 35, doc. 206.

47. CIA paper, "Soviet Response to MATADOR Disclosures."

48. Bukan, *Po sledam podvodnykh katastrof*, 76; CIA paper, "Soviet Response to MATADOR Disclosures."

49. CIA memo, "Soviet Reaction to MATADOR Mission," April 30, 1975; CIA paper, "Vulnerability of *Hughes Glomar Explorer* to Physical Harassment," n.d. [April 30, 1975], *FRUS, 1969–1976*, vol. 35, doc. 202, appendix B.

50. CIA memo, April 30, 1975.

51. 40 Committee meeting, memo for the record, June 5, 1975, *FRUS, 1969–1976*, vol. 35, doc. 205.

52. 40 Committee meeting, memo for the record, June 5, 1975. See Robert J. Mahoney, *The Mayaguez Incident: Testing America's Resolve in the Post-Vietnam Era* (Lubbock: Texas Tech University Press, 2011).

53. 40 Committee meeting, memo for the record, June 5, 1975; Colby and Forbath, *Honorable Men*, 417.

54. Kissinger to Ford, memo, June 16, 1975.

55. PDB, April 8, 1975, CIA Freedom of Information Act Electronic Reading Room.

56. Leonid Brezhnev to Kissinger and Ford, oral message, April 10, 1975, USSR—"D" File, box 30, Kissinger-Scowcroft West Wing Office Files.

57. Dobrynin and Kissinger, telcon, April 10, 1975, USSR—Dobrynin/Kissinger Exchanges—Telephone Conversations, box 34, Kissinger-Scowcroft West Wing Office Files. Brezhnev and Ford held discussions in Helsinki from July 30 to August 2, 1975.

58. Kissinger and Andrei Gromyko, May 20, 1975, USSR Memcons and Reports, May 19–20, 1975—Kissinger/Gromyko Meetings in Vienna (2), box 1, Kissinger Reports on USSR, China, and Middle East Discussions, NSAF, GRFPL; Kissinger to Ford, memo, July 29,

1975, doc. 170 in *FRUS, 1969–1976*, vol. 16, *Soviet Union, August 1974–December 1976*, ed. David C. Geyer (Washington, DC: U.S. Government Printing Office, 2012).

59. Memo to the 40 Committee, May 19, 1975, *FRUS, 1969–1976*, vol. 35, doc. 203; Colby and Forbath, *Honorable Men*, 417.

60. Ford, Kissinger, and Scowcroft, September 25, 1975, Memcons, NSAF, GRFPL.

8. SHIVERING FROM OVEREXPOSURE

1. Seymour M. Hersh, "3 Panels in Congress Plan Inquiries Into Sub Salvage," *New York Times*, March 20, 1975, 30. Joshua Kurlantzick discusses Senator Symington's role in *A Great Place to Have a War: America in Laos and the Birth of a Military CIA* (New York: Simon and Schuster, 2016), 104–105, 182, 186–187.

2. Script, March 20, 1975, CBS Washington, DC, Bureau, box 70, Daniel Schorr Papers, Manuscript Division, Library of Congress, Washington, DC. Critiques of the mission's cost include Tom Wicker, "The Submarine Story," *New York Times*, March 21, 1975, 37; Alexander Cockburn and James Ridgeway, "The Great Submarine Caper," *Village Voice*, March 31, 1975; "National Insecurity," *The Progressive*, May 1975, 5.

3. "CIA, Hughes Connection," *ABC Evening News*, March 19, 1975, clip #36304, and "CIA, Hughes Collaboration," *CBS Evening News*, March 19, 1975, clip #239116, Vanderbilt Television News Archive (https://tvnews.vanderbilt.edu), Special Collections, Heard Libraries, Vanderbilt University, Nashville, TN.

4. KFWB radio news report, March 19, 1975, *Glomar Explorer—CIA*, box 35, Howard Hughes Public Relations Records (MS-00380), Special Collections, University Libraries, University of Nevada, Las Vegas.

5. "The CIA Was Doing Its Job," *Washington Star*, March 21, 1975.

6. Jack Nelson, "Administration Won't Talk About Sub Raised by CIA," *Los Angeles Times*, March 20, 1975, A15–A16; James R. Phelan, "Howard Hughes, Beyond the Law," *New York Times*, September 14, 1975, 14, 50, 54. Charles Colson reportedly made a similar statement before the Rockefeller Commission. See script, March 19, 1975, CBS Washington, DC, Bureau, box 70, Schorr Papers.

7. Gene Blake, "Hughes Wanted to 'Front' for CIA, Maheu Testifies," *Los Angeles Times*, May 16, 1974, B1.

8. "The Great Submarine Snatch," *Time*, March 31, 1975, 27. See chapters 3–4 for discussion of Maheu's suit.

9. "Senate CIA Investigation to Look for Hughes Links to Watergate," *New York Times*, March 26, 1975, 21.

10. "Animals in the Forest," *Time*, February 11, 1974, 26. "Conspiracy fever" gripped Americans in the 1970s, writes Kathryn S. Olmsted in *Real Enemies: Conspiracy Theories and American Democracy, World War I to 9/11*, 10th ann. ed. (New York: Oxford University Press, 2019), 168. See chapter 2 for discussion of Hughes's connection to Watergate.

11. Nicholas M. Horrock, "Files Said to Link Mafia to CIA in Plot on Castro," *New York Times*, May 20, 1975; George Lardner Jr., "Maheu Details Role," *Washington Post*, July 31, 1975, A1.

12. John M. Crewdson, "Church Doubts Plot Links to Presidents," *New York Times*, July 19, 1975, 1; Robert L. Jackson, "Capitol Leaders Promise Deeper CIA Investigation," *Los Angeles Times*, June 12, 1975, B1.

13. "'Recluse' Hughes Is Headliner," *Las Vegas Sun*, March 28, 1975, 4.

14. Robert Meyers, "Stolen Files Said to Link Hughes, CIA," *Los Angeles Times*, March 27, 1975, A1.

15. Crewdson, "CIA Covert Activities Abroad Shielded by Major U.S. Companies," *New York Times*, May 11, 1975, 38. See also Al Delugach, "Hughes Empire Suited to Be 'Front' for CIA," *Los Angeles Times*, March 21, 1975, A1.

16. Saul Friedman, "CIA Salvage Ship in Chile During Coup," *San Francisco Sunday Examiner and Chronicle*, March 23, 1975, A12. The *Explorer*'s weeklong stay in Chilean waters in September 1973 fueled speculation that the U.S. intelligence ship played some role in the coup. But a CIA history dismissed the timing of the vessel's visit on its journey to California as "a bizarre coincidence." "Project AZORIAN: The Story of the *Hughes Glomar Explorer*," *Studies in Intelligence* 22, no. 3 (1978): 22–24.

17. Felix Belair Jr., "SEC Staff Finds Data About *Glomar* Misleading," *New York Times*, April 1, 1975, 62; "CIA Asked Tax Assessor's Aid on Ship," *New York Times*, April 4, 1975, 3; Nicholas M. Horrock, "CIA Reported Pressing SEC to Curb Global Marine Inquiry," *New York Times*, April 27, 1975, 43.

18. Michael J. Harrington to Jack Brooks, May 8, 1975, Harrington—CIA—*Glomar Explorer* (1975), box 2, Michael Harrington Papers, Archives and Special Collections, Berry Library, Salem State University, Salem, MA.

19. William Colby and Peter Forbath, *Honorable Men: My Life in the CIA* (New York: Simon and Schuster, 1978), 402; Tom Braden, "What's Wrong with the CIA?" *Saturday Review*, April 5, 1975, 17–18; "Abolish the CIA!," *Newsweek*, April 7, 1975, 11. Public approval of the CIA dropped to a historic low in 1975 and 1976, notes Kathryn S. Olmsted in *Challenging the Secret Government: The Post-Watergate Investigations of the CIA and FBI* (Chapel Hill: University of North Carolina Press, 1996), 99.

20. Howard Flieger, "In from the Cold," *U.S. News and World Report*, March 31, 1975, 76.

21. "Shivering from Overexposure," *Time*, March 31, 1975, 29.

22. Colby and Forbath, *Honorable Men*, 402, 455–456.

23. Colby and Forbath, 15.

24. Colby and Forbath, 21; David Shamus McCarthy, *Selling the CIA: Public Relations and the Culture of Secrecy* (Lawrence: University Press of Kansas, 2018), 7–10, 21–23; Tricia Jenkins, *The CIA in Hollywood: How the Agency Shapes Film and Television* (Austin: University of Texas Press, 2012).

25. "The *Glomar Explorer*," *Washington Post*, March 23, 1975, 38.

26. Colby and Jack Anderson, telcon, March 18, 1975, 6:52 p.m.; Nelson, "Administration Won't Talk."

27. "Great Submarine Snatch," 26.

28. "CIA's Mission Impossible," *Newsweek*, March 31, 1975, 29.

29. Thomas O'Toole, "A-Warheads Believed Recovered," *Washington Post*, March 21, 1975, A1; "Behind the Great Submarine Snatch," *Time*, December 6, 1976; Nicholas Wade, "*Glomar Explorer* Said Successful After All," *Science*, December 10, 1976, 1142.

30. Hersh, "CIA Salvage Ship Brought Up Part of Soviet Sub Lost in 1968, Failed to Raise Atom Missiles," *New York Times*, March 19, 1975, 52; "Trying to 'Swipe' a Russian Sub Is Just Part of the CIA Saga," *U.S. News and World Report*, March 31, 1975, 17.

31. Colby paraphrased in Hersh, "CIA Salvage Ship," 1.

32. "Shivering from Overexposure."

33. Hersh, "3 Panels."

34. "Shivering from Overexposure"; script, *CBS Morning News*, March 26, 1975, CBS Washington, DC, Bureau, box 70, Schorr Papers; "CIA Officer Retires, Will Defend Agency," *Washington Post*, March 22, 1975, A4.

35. David Atlee Phillips, *The Night Watch* (New York: Atheneum, 1977), 269.

36. "Shivering from Overexposure."

37. "Shivering from Overexposure."

38. Belair Jr., "SEC Staff Finds."

39. Colby to Kissinger, memo, March 28, 1975, doc. 198 in *Foreign Relations of the United States, 1969–1976*, vol. 35, *National Security Policy, 1973–1976*, ed. M. Todd Bennett (Washington, DC: U.S. Government Printing Office, 2014). Public attacks left the CIA "naked and exposed," recalled former CIA deputy director for intelligence Ray S. Cline in *The CIA Under Reagan, Bush and Casey: The Evolution of the Agency from Roosevelt to Reagan* (Washington, DC: Acropolis Books, 1981), 260.

40. Roy Varner and Wayne Collier, *A Matter of Risk: The Incredible Inside Story of the CIA's Hughes Glomar Explorer Mission to Raise a Russian Submarine* (New York: Random House, 1978), 207–208. Emphasis in the original.

41. Colby, "Intelligence and the Press," address to Associated Press annual meeting, April 7, 1975, CIA (1974–76), box 31, series 43, John C. Stennis Collection, Congressional and Political Research Center, Mitchell Memorial Library, Mississippi State University, Starkville, MS; Martin Arnold, "Colby Tells Publishers That CIA Is Jeopardized by Sensational Headlines," *New York Times*, April 8, 1975, 10. Colby detailed the "devastating impact" media and congressional investigations of intelligence had on the inner workings of the CIA in *Honorable Men*, 411–412.

42. Center for the Study of Intelligence, "CIA Activities Contributing to Public Understanding of Intelligence and the CIA," April 1975, CIA Freedom of Information Act Electronic Reading Room, https://www.cia.gov/readingroom/docs/CIA-RDP80-00630A000300120001-4.pdf.

43. Thirteen of nineteen newspapers surveyed by *Editorials on File* (6, no. 6 [March 16–31, 1975]: 311–317) expressed support. See also "Great Submarine Snatch"; "Intelligence Coup," *Arizona Republic*, March 24, 1975.

44. *Nashville Tennessean*, March 20, 1975, and *Dayton Daily News*, March 21, 1975, both in *Editorials on File*, 317.

45. "The Spies in the Deep," *Los Angeles Times*, March 20, 1975.

46. "Great Submarine Snatch," 20; "Trying to 'Swipe,'" 16–17; Nicholas Wade, "Deep-Sea Salvage: Did CIA Use Mohole Techniques to Raise Sub?" *Science*, May 16, 1975, 710–713; "CIA Sub Caper: Effects on Research," *Science News*, March 29, 1975, 204–205.

47. "CIA's Mission Impossible," *Newsweek*, March 31, 1975, 32; "Stranger Than Fiction," *New York Daily News*, March 20, 1975, *Editorials on File*, 314; "A Bold and Proper CIA Effort," *Chicago Tribune*, March 21, 1975, A2.

48. "Project Jennifer," *New York Times*, March 20, 1975, 38.

49. "Bold and Proper."

50. "Something's Right with America," *Philadelphia Inquirer*, printed in the *Congressional Record*, 94 Cong., 1st sess., March 26, 1975, p. 8738.

51. James Reston, "Battle for the Oceans," *New York Times*, March 21, 1975, 37. At sea, the balance of power favored the United States, agreed the *Washington Post*'s editors in "*Glomar Explorer.*"

52. "CIA Was Doing Its Job."

53. "Hooray for the CIA!," *Atlanta Constitution*, March 22, 1975, and *Anchorage Daily Times*, March 21, 1975, both in *Editorials on File*, 313. See also *Houston Chronicle*, March 24, 1975, in *Editorials on File*, 313; "CIA's 'Project Jennifer' Was Worth Cost, Risk," *The State* (Columbia, SC), printed in the *Congressional Record*, 94th Cong., 1st sess., March 26, 1975, p. 8762.

54. Hanson W. Baldwin, "On U.S. Intelligence," *New York Times*, May 8, 1975, 39. Henry Kissinger bemoaned the press's actions in *Years of Renewal* (New York: Simon and Schuster, 1999), 338.

55. "Nuclear Torpedoes Believed Found," *New York Times*, March 21, 1975, 15. On the rightward shift in the politics of national security that took place in the mid-seventies, see Julian E. Zelizer, *Arsenal of Democracy: The Politics National Security—From World War II to the War on Terrorism* (New York: Basic Books, 2010), 254–255, 262, 264; Bruce J. Schulman and Zelizer, eds., *Rightward Bound: Making America Conservative in the 1970s* (Cambridge, MA: Harvard University Press, 2008); Jonathan M. Schoenwald, *A Time for Choosing: The Rise of Modern American Conservatism* (New York: Oxford University Press, 2001), 255–257.

56. Richard Bergholz, "US Has Right to Spy on Citizens, Reagan Asserts," *Los Angeles Times*, March 21, 1975, 9.

57. Ronald Reagan, "*Glomar Explorer*," November 1976, Hannaford/California Headquarters—Radio Commentaries/Broadcasts—Disc 76-1A thru 76-4 (1976), box 14, Ronald Reagan 1980 Presidential Campaign Papers, Ronald Reagan Presidential Library, Simi Valley, CA; "CIA Commission," August 1975, and "Intelligence," June 15, 1977, printed in *Reagan, In His Own Hand*, ed. Kiron K. Skinner, Annelise Anderson, and Martin Anderson (New York: Free Press, 2001), 121, 125.

58. Martin Arnold, "CIA Tried to Get Press to Hold Up Salvage Story," *New York Times*, March 20, 1975, 31.

59. Jack Anderson with Les Whitten, "Who Owns the News?," Washington Merry-Go-Round typescript, March 25, 1975, box 96, Jack Anderson Papers, Special Collections Research Center, Gelman Library, George Washington University, Washington, DC; Anderson and Whitten, "Press Forgets Prime Responsibility," Washington Merry-Go-Round, *Washington Post*, March 25, 1975, C21. Anderson also quoted in Stephen Isaacs, "Withholding of Story Defended," *Washington Post*, March 20, 1975, A15. Anderson continued to complain about the reemergence, in 1975, "of the pre-Watergate practice of cozy intimacy between press and government" in a memoir published over two decades later with Daryl Gibson, *Peace, War, and Politics: An Eyewitness Account* (New York: Forge, 1999), 278.

60. Isaacs, "Withholding of Story Defended."

61. Charles B. Seib, "The Confusing Coverage of the Submarine Story," *Washington Post*, March 27, 1975, A22; Seib, "Lessons from a Submerged CIA Story," *Washington Post*, October 28, 1977, A15. The *Boston Globe* (March 20, 1975) and the *St. Louis Post-Dispatch* (March 21, 1975) also approved the disclosure. See *Editorials on File*, 316.

62. Wicker, "Submarine Story." Wicker revisited the episode in his book *On Press* (New York: Viking, 1978), 198–202, 212–223.

63. "The Case of the Sunken Sub," *Columbia Journalism Review*, May/June 1975, 6.

64. Bill Boyarsky, "Why Editors Withheld Details on Sub," *Los Angeles Times*, March 20, 1975, A19.

65. Isaacs, "Withholding of Story Defended."
66. Isaacs; George Lardner Jr. and William Claiborne, "CIA's *Glomar* 'Game Plan,'" *Washington Post*, October 23, 1977, A10.
67. *"Glomar Explorer," Washington Post.*
68. *Detroit News*, March 20, 1975, in *Editorials on File*, 314.
69. *San Diego Union*, March 22, 1975, in *Editorials on File*, 314. The Louisville *Courier-Journal* took a similar position on March 23, 1975, in *Editorials on File*, 313.
70. "CIA Was Doing Its Job."
71. Paul A. McKalip, "There Has to Be Secrecy," *Tucson Daily Citizen*, April 2, 1975; "Shivering from Overexposure," 29.
72. "Spies in the Deep"; "Project Jennifer."
73. Joseph Kraft, "Lessons from the Soviet Submarine Incident," *Washington Post*, March 23, 1975, 39.
74. Daniel Schorr, *Clearing the Air* (Boston: Houghton Mifflin, 1977), 130–152. Roger Wilkins quoted in Howard Bray, *The Pillars of the Post: The Making of a News Empire in Washington* (New York: W. W. Norton, 1980), 154. "I won't tell if you won't" was the "clubby press establishment pact" news executives reached with Colby, Seib observed in "Lessons from a Submerged CIA Story."
75. Leslie H. Gelb, "The CIA and the Press," *New Republic*, March 22, 1975, 13–16; William Greider, "Aftergate," *Esquire*, September 1975, 102, 133. Discussions of the news media's constrained coverage of national security include Leon V. Sigal, *Reporters and Officials: The Organization and Politics of Newsmaking* (Lexington, MA: D.C. Heath, 1973), 84; David Halberstam, *The Powers That Be* (New York: Knopf, 1979), 578–579, 668; David Broder, *Behind the Front Page* (New York: Simon and Schuster, 1987), 149; William Greider, *Who Will Tell the People: The Betrayal of American Democracy* (New York: Simon and Schuster, 1992); Ted Galen Carpenter, *The Captive Press: Foreign Policy Crises and the First Amendment* (Washington, DC: Cato Institute, 1995); Bartholomew H. Sparrow, *Uncertain Guardians: The News Media as a Political Institution* (Baltimore, MD: Johns Hopkins University Press, 1999).
76. *"Glomar Explorer," Washington Post*; "CIA's Mission Impossible." *Glomar* was a "godsend to the beleaguered CIA," recalled journalists Donald L. Barlett and James B. Steele in *Empire: The Life, Legend, and Madness of Howard Hughes* (New York: W. W. Norton, 1979), 542. The news took a "lot of heat off the agency," an AZORIAN veteran told Hersh, "Participant Tells of CIA Ruses to Hide *Glomar* Project," *New York Times*, December 10, 1976, A18.
77. Script, *CBS Morning News*, March 26, 1975, Schorr Papers; "Salvaging the Sub Story," *Newsweek*, March 31, 1975, 66.
78. "Great Submarine Snatch," 20; Harriet Ann Phillippi v. Central Intelligence Agency, 655 F.2d 1325 (DC Cir. 1981) at 1330.
79. Colby, Whitten, and Jack Cloherty, telcon, March 18, 1975, 5:25 p.m.; Colby and Forbath, *Honorable Men*, 418.
80. Dated February 26, 1975, the memo was declassified in part in 1977. "CIA Plan Disclosed in Glomar Incident," *New York Times*, October 26, 1977, 23.
81. Seib, "Confusing Coverage." See also Morton Kondracke, "The CIA and 'Our Conspiracy,'" *(MORE): A Journalism Review*, May 1975, 11.
82. Harrison E. Salisbury, *Without Fear or Favor: The New York Times and Its Times* (New York: Times Books, 1980), 554. Howard Simons quoted in Bray, *Pillars of the Post*, 153.

83. Lloyd Shearer, "*Parade* and Project Jennifer," *Parade*, May 11, 1975, 6.
84. Colby and Forbath, *Honorable Men*, 449, 418.

9. HOLD THE LINE

1. George Cary, memo for the record, "Meeting with Jack Marsh and Phillip Buchen, of the White House Staff," March 7, 1975, quoted in Harold Ford, *William E. Colby as Director of Central Intelligence* (Washington, DC: CIA Center for the Study of Intelligence, 1993), 147. Declassified in 2011, Ford's biography quotes material redacted from a version of Cary's memo that was declassified in 2012 and is now accessible through the CIA Freedom of Information Act Electronic Reading Room at https://www.cia.gov/readingroom/docs/CIA-RDP77M00144R000500110068-4.pdf.

2. James Cannon, *Time and Chance: Gerald Ford's Appointment with History* (New York: HarperCollins, 1994), 358–359.

3. Hersh, "The Pardon," *The Atlantic*, August 1983, https://www.theatlantic.com/magazine/archive/1983/08/the-pardon/305571/; Larry DuBois and Laurence Gonzales, "The Puppet and the Puppetmasters: Uncovering the Secret World of Nixon, Hughes and the CIA," *Playboy*, September 1976, 182; David Greenberg, *Nixon's Shadow: The History of an Image* (New York: Norton, 2003), 215, 284.

4. John Maury quoted in L. Britt Snider, *The Agency and the Hill: CIA's Relationship with Congress, 1946–2014* (Washington, DC: CIA Center for the Study of Intelligence, 2008), 26.

5. Accounts of the 94th Congress's "revolution" include "The Democratic Caucus in Command," *Washington Post*, January 20, 1975, A18; John A. Lawrence, "The Revolution," in *The Class of '74: Congress After Watergate and the Roots of Partisanship* (Baltimore, MD: Johns Hopkins University Press, 2018), 93–116; Julian E. Zelizer, *On Capitol Hill: The Struggle to Reform Congress and Its Consequences, 1948–2000* (New York: Cambridge University Press, 2004), 168. On Congress's ascendancy, see James L. Sundquist, *The Decline and Resurgence of Congress* (Washington, DC: Brookings Institution, 1981), 275; Bruce J. Schulman, "Restraining the Imperial Presidency: Congress and Watergate," in *The American Congress: The Building of Democracy*, ed. Julian E. Zelizer (Boston: Houghton Mifflin, 2004), 638–649; Robert David Johnson, *Congress and the Cold War* (New York: Cambridge University Press, 2006), 190–241.

6. "The CIA Crisis," *Washington Post*, December 24, 1974, A10; Lawrence, *Class of '74*, 96–97.

7. U.S. Senate, Select Committee to Study Governmental Operations with Respect to Intelligence Activities [hereafter Church Committee], 94th Cong., 2d sess., *Final Report*, book 1, *Foreign and Military Intelligence* (Washington, DC: U.S. Government Printing Office, 1976), 424–425.

8. Loch K. Johnson, *A Season of Inquiry Revisited: The Church Committee Confronts America's Spy Agencies* (Lawrence: University Press of Kansas, 2015), 254. On the intelligence investigations and their contribution to the movement for more open government and executive branch accountability, see Paul Light, *Government by Investigation: Congress, Presidents, and the Search for Answers, 1945–2012* (Washington, DC: Brookings Institution Press, 2014), 193; Katherine A. Scott, *Reining in the State: Civil Society and Congress in the Vietnam and Watergate Eras* (Lawrence: University Press of Kansas, 2013), 178. Congress overstepped, according to some, dangerously limiting the ability of both the U.S.

intelligence community (Stephen F. Knott, *Secret and Sanctioned: Covert Operations and the American Presidency* [New York: Oxford University Press, 1996], 184–185) and the president (Thomas M. Franck, ed., *The Tethered Presidency: Congressional Restraints on Executive Power* [New York: New York University Press, 1981]; Gordon S. Jones and John A. Marini, eds., *The Imperial Congress: Crisis in the Separation of Powers* [New York: Pharos Books, 1988]) to act in the nation's interest.

9. Arthur Schlesinger Jr., "Reform of the CIA?" *Wall Street Journal*, February 25, 1976, 10; William Colby and Peter Forbath, *Honorable Men: My Life in the CIA* (New York: Simon and Schuster, 1978), 456; David H. Sharp, *The CIA's Greatest Covert Operation: Inside the Daring Mission to Recover a Nuclear-Armed Soviet Sub* (Lawrence: University Press of Kansas, 2012), 271.

10. Kathryn S. Olmsted, *Challenging the Secret Government: The Post-Watergate Investigations of the CIA and FBI* (Chapel Hill: University of North Carolina Press, 1996), 169. Skeptics include Richard H. Immerman, *The Hidden Hand: A Brief History of the CIA* (Malden, MA: Wiley, 2014), 98; Rhodri Jeffreys-Jones, *The CIA and American Democracy*, 3rd ed. (New Haven, CT: Yale University Press, 2003), 214–215. See also Jason Ross Arnold, *Secrecy in the Sunshine Era: The Promise and Failures of U.S. Open Government Laws* (Lawrence: University Press of Kansas, 2014).

11. "The CIA Was Doing Its Job," *Washington Star*, March 21, 1975, *Editorials on File* 6, no. 6 (March 16–31, 1975): 315.

12. *Congressional Record*, 94th Cong., 1st sess., March 20, 1975, p. 7883.

13. Seymour M. Hersh, "3 Panels in Congress Plan Inquiries into Sub Salvage," *New York Times*, March 20, 1975, p. 30; John C. Stennis, statement, March 20, 1975, Support of CIA Undertakings, box 25, series 51: Public/Press Releases, John C. Stennis Collection, Congressional and Political Research Center, Mississippi State University Library, Starkville, MS.

14. Hersh, "3 Panels."

15. John Tower quoted in *Anchorage Daily Times*, March 21, 1975, *Editorials on File*, 313.

16. "CIA, Hughes Connection," *ABC Evening News*, March 19, 1975, clip #36304, Vanderbilt Television News Archive (https://tvnews.vanderbilt.edu), Special Collections, Heard Libraries, Vanderbilt University, Nashville, TN.

17. Arthur Goldberger to Barry Goldwater, March 19, 1975, Select Committee on Intelligence—Central Intelligence Agency Investigations, Legislative Series, box 211, Barry M. Goldwater Papers (hereafter Goldwater Papers), Department of Archives and Special Collections, Arizona State University Libraries, Tempe, AZ.

18. Caroline McLaughlin to Goldwater, April 1975, and Paul A. McKalip, "There Has to Be Secrecy," *Tucson Daily Citizen*, April 2, 1975, both in Select Committee on Intelligence—Central Intelligence Agency Investigations, Legislative Series, box 211, Goldwater Papers.

19. Elbridge C. Bates to Goldwater, March 25, 1975, and "Intelligence Coup," *Arizona Republic*, March 24, 1975, both in Select Committee on Intelligence—Central Intelligence Agency (investigations), Legislative Series, box 212, Goldwater Papers.

20. John D. Royle to Goldwater, March 21, 1975, Select Committee on Intelligence—Central Intelligence Agency (investigations), Legislative Series, box 212, Goldwater Papers.

21. Percy E. Patrick to Gerald Ford, March 27, 1975, FG 6-2 CIA, White House Central Files, Gerald R. Ford Presidential Library (GRFPL), Ann Arbor, MI; Nancy Levy to Michael J. Harrington, telegram, March 31, 1975, CIA—*Glomar Explorer* (1975), box 2,

Michael Harrington Papers, Archives and Special Collections, Berry Library, Salem State University, Salem, MA.

22. Nicholas M. Horrock, "Intelligence Inquiries in Capitol Focus on Legitimacy of Covert Espionage," *New York Times*, May 18, 1975, 42.

23. Goldwater to Royle, April 4, 1975; Goldwater to McLaughlin, April 13, 1975; Goldwater to Bates, April 16, 1975, all in Select Committee on Intelligence—Central Intelligence Agency (investigations), Legislative Series, box 212, Goldwater Papers.

24. "CIA's Mission Impossible," *Newsweek*, March 31, 1975, 24, 32; scripts, March 21, 1975, CBS—Washington, DC Bureau—Scripts, box 70, Daniel Schorr Papers, Manuscript Division, Library of Congress, Washington, DC.

25. Henry Kissinger, *Years of Renewal* (New York: Simon and Schuster, 1999), 323–325; Ford, James Schlesinger, Donald Rumsfeld, et al., March 28, 1975, Memcons, National Security Advisor's Files (NSAF), GRFPL. Rumsfeld did not further elaborate in *Known and Unknown: A Memoir* (New York: Sentinel, 2011).

26. Ford, Kissinger, Brent Scowcroft, January 4, 1975, Memcons, NSAF, GRFPL; Colby and Forbath, *Honorable Men*, 406, 443–444; Randall B. Woods, *Shadow Warrior: William Egan Colby and the CIA* (New York: Basic Books, 2013), 417–419.

27. Kissinger, *Years of Renewal*, 325–326; Kissinger, James Schlesinger, Colby, et al., February 20, 1975, Memcons, NSAF, GRFPL.

28. Kissinger, James Schlesinger, Colby, et al., February 20, 1975, Memcons, NSAF, GRFPL; Kissinger, *Years of Renewal*, 342.

29. Nicholas M. Horrock, "Ford Likely to Name Aide in Spy Inquiries," *New York Times*, March 21, 1975, 77; scripts, March 21, 1975, Schorr Papers. Olmsted (*Challenging*, 145–167) and Johnson (*Season of Inquiry Revisited*, 32, 66–68, 96, 106–109) agree on the importance of White House resistance.

30. Church Committee, *Final Report*, bk. 1:427.

31. L. Britt Snider, *Congress and the CIA* (New York: Nova Science Publishers, 2009), 34.

32. Sherry Sontag and Christopher Drew, *Blind Man's Bluff: The Untold Story of American Submarine Espionage* (New York: PublicAffairs, 1988), 216–217.

33. Colby to Kissinger, March 28, 1975, doc. 198, in *Foreign Relations of the United States* [hereafter *FRUS*], *1969–1976*, vol. 35, *National Security Policy, 1973–1976*, ed. M. Todd Bennett (Washington, DC: U.S. Government Printing Office, 2014); Sontag and Drew, *Blind Man's Bluff*, 178, 233.

34. Hersh, "Submarines of US Stage Spy Missions Inside Soviet Waters," *New York Times*, May 25, 1975, 1.

35. William G. Miller to Frank Church, memo, "Outline of the Committee's Work through January," July 9, 1975, Senate Select Committee—Work Schedule, box 58, James E. Connor Files, GRFPL. See chapter 1 for a discussion of organizational matters.

36. Memo for the record of President's Foreign Intelligence Advisory Board meeting, April 3, 1975, *FRUS, 1969–1976*, vol. 35, doc. 200.

37. Bobby Ray Inman, interview with author, Austin, TX, November 16, 2016.

38. Sontag and Drew, *Blind Man's Bluff*, 221–222.

39. Colby, Les Whitten, and Jack Cloherty, telcon, March 18, 1975, transcript in author's possession.

40. Sontag and Drew, *Blind Man's Bluff*, 217–218. Aaron Donner quoted in Frank J. Smist Jr., *Congress Oversees the United States Intelligence Community*, 2nd ed. (Knoxville: University of Tennessee Press, 1994), 177.

41. Victor Marchetti and John D. Marks, *The CIA and the Cult of Intelligence* (New York: Knopf, 1974), 7; David Shamus McCarthy, *Selling the CIA: Public Relations and the Culture of Secrecy* (Lawrence: University Press of Kansas, 2018), 7, 10 123.

42. Marchetti and Marks, *Cult of Intelligence*, 345–346.

43. Smist, *Congress Oversees*, 176–177.

44. Smist, 177.

45. Sontag and Drew, *Blind Man's Bluff*, 218; Smist, *Congress Oversees*, 177.

46. Smist, *Congress Oversees*, 177.

47. Sontag and Drew, *Blind Man's Bluff*, 218.

48. "The CIA Report the President Doesn't Want You to Read," *Village Voice*, February 16, 1976, 88.

49. Sontag and Drew, *Blind Man's Bluff*, 223.

50. William S. White, "All Nice Guys Don't Finish Last," *Washington Star*, May 15, 1964, read into *Congressional Record*, 88th Cong., 2d sess., May 16, 1964, p. 10688.

51. Colby and Forbath, *Honorable Men*, 407; Janet M. Neugebauer, *A Witness to History: George H. Mahon, West Texas Congressman* (Lubbock: Texas Tech University Press, 2017), xxi, 5.

52. Mahon to R. D. Sawyer, December 16, 1975, Appropriations—Defense—CIA 1975, box 273, George H. Mahon Papers, Southwest Collection, Special Collections Library, Texas Tech University, Lubbock, TX; Neugebauer, *Witness to History*, 454.

53. Colby and Forbath, *Honorable Men*, 407–408; Walter Pincus, "Congressional Response to the CIA Budget," *Washington Post*, October 9, 1975, A10.

54. Marchetti and Marks, *Cult of Intelligence*, 58, 61.

55. *Congressional Record*, 94th Cong., 1st sess., September 30, 1975: p. 30987; Commission on CIA Activities within the United States, *Report to the President*, June 1975, 15, Digital Collections, Intelligence Community Investigations and Reforms, GRFPL, https://www.fordlibrarymuseum.gov/library/exhibits/intelligence/rcreport.asp. In 1976, the Church and Pike Committees also recommended greater budget transparency. Church Committee, *Final Report*, bk. 1:469–470; *The Unexpurgated Pike Report: Report of the House Select Committee on Intelligence, 1976*, ed. Gregory Andrade Diamond (New York: McGraw-Hill, 1992), 175–177.

56. *Congressional Record*, 94th Cong., 1st sess., September 30, 1975, pp. 30985–30986.

57. *Congressional Record*, 94th Cong., 1st sess., October 1, 1975, p. 31052.

58. "A Failure of Oversight," *Washington Post*, May 2, 1976, 34. Only two individuals affiliated with the House Appropriations Committee—Mahon and a senior staffer—had prior knowledge of *Glomar*'s classified role, according to CIA to Dwight Ink, November 28, 1975, CIA, box 2, series 1: Executive, Stennis Papers. That staffer kept Mahon apprised of the mission's progress. Ralph Preston to Mahon, memo, September 16, 1974, Appropriations—Defense: CIA, box 274, Mahon Papers.

59. *Congressional Record*, 94th Cong., 1st sess., October 1, 1975, p. 31039; Mahon memo, "CIA fight on Def. appro.," September 1975, Appropriations—Defense—CIA 1975, box 273, Mahon Papers.

60. Sam Attlesey, "Solon Foresees End of Concealed Budget," *Lubbock Avalanche-Journal*, July 3, 1975, A1.

61. Church Committee, *Final Report*, bk. 1:378–381; Frederick A. O. Schwarz Jr., *Democracy in the Dark: The Seduction of Government Secrecy* (New York: New Press, 2015), 98–99.

62. *Congressional Record*, 94th Cong., 1st sess., October 1, 1975, p. 31041.

63. *Congressional Record*, 94th Cong., 1st sess., October 1, 1975, p. 31047.

64. *Congressional Record*, 94th Cong., 1st sess., October 1, 1975, p. 31040; Mahon, Statement before the House Committee on Intelligence, January 24, 1978, Select Committee on Intelligence, box 246, Mahon Papers.

65. *Congressional Record*, 94th Cong., 1st sess., October 1, 1975, p. 31049.

66. Arthur Schlesinger Jr., "Reform of the CIA?"

67. *Congressional Record*, 94th Cong., 2nd sess., March 2, 1976, p. 4899; George Lardner Jr., "Helms Warns of Excessive Curbs on CIA," *Washington Post*, May 17, 1978, A24.

68. K. J. Kimbrough [1976], and Basil L. Webb [1976], both in Opinion Ballot CIA 1976, box 375, Mahon Papers. I was surprised to find my grandfather's letter among Mahon's papers. Prior to this happy discovery, I was unaware of any family connection to *Glomar*.

69. William R. Skirlock [1976], and Jimmy Cowan [1976], both in Opinion Ballot CIA 1976, box 375, Mahon Papers.

70. W. M. Bourland [1976], Opinion Ballot CIA 1976, box 375, Mahon Papers.

71. H. L. Hagler [1976], Opinion Ballot CIA 1976, box 375, Mahon Papers.

72. L. J. Walter [1976], Opinion Ballot CIA 1976, box 375, Mahon Papers. Of the fifty-eight ballots found in Mahon's files, forty-seven were marked no, ten were marked yes, and one registered no opinion.

73. Claude Byrd to Mahon, June 26, 1975, Select Committee on Intelligence, box 246, Mahon Papers; R. D. Sawyer to Mahon [December 1975], Appropriations—Defense—CIA 1975, box 273, Mahon Papers.

74. Mahon to Dorothy and Savannah, March 13, 1976, Policy Intelligence 1976, box 375, Mahon Papers.

75. Mahon to Webb, April 26, 1976, Opinion Ballot CIA 1976, box 375, Mahon Papers.

76. David E. Rosenbaum, "House Rejects, 267–147, Move to Disclose CIA Budget to the Public," *New York Times*, October 2, 1975, 26; "House Votes $132.8 Million for Navy F18," *Wall Street Journal*, October 2, 1975, 8. Only Montana's, Nevada's, and Rhode Island's delegations supported Giaimo's amendment or recorded no vote.

77. Holmes Alexander, "Mahon Reassures Allies by Defeating CIA Foes," *Lubbock Avalanche-Journal*, October 13, 1975.

78. Pincus, "Congressional Response."

79. Mary McGrory, "CIA Waits It Out—And Wins," *Chicago Tribune*, October 6, 1975, A4.

80. Mary Russell, "Retribution Not Mahon's Style," *Washington Post*, November 10, 1975, A4. See chapter 1 for discussion of AZORIAN funding procedures.

81. *Congressional Record*, 94th Cong., 1st sess., October 1, 1975, pp. 31041, 31044.

82. Taylor Branch, "The Trial of the CIA," *New York Times Magazine*, September 12, 1976, 118; Branch, *Parting the Waters: America in the King Years, 1954–63* (New York: Simon and Schuster, 1988).

83. Robert M. Gates, *From the Shadows: The Ultimate Insider's Story of Five Presidents and How They Won the Cold War* (New York: Simon and Schuster, 1996), 60. Anthony Lewis, "The Politics of Secrecy," *New York Times*, February 26, 1976, 30; Tom Wicker, "Protecting the Culprits, Punishing the Accusers," *New York Times*, February 22, 1976, E13. Church quoted in Laurence Stern and Pincus, "Hill Hurt by Leaks on CIA," *Washington Post*, February 9, 1976, A1.

CONCLUSION

1. Hank Phillippi to Angus Thuermer, March 21, 1975, quoted in Harriet Ann Phillippi v. Central Intelligence Agency, Stansfield Turner, Director Central Intelligence Agency, 655 F.2d 1325 (DC Cir. 1981) at 1327.

2. "Information: A Vital Gift," *Washington Post*, November 23, 1974, A14; Philip H. Melanson, *Secrecy Wars: National Security, Privacy, and the Public's Right to Know* (Washington, DC: Brassey's, 2001), 17–19.

3. "Opening Up Those Secrets," *Time*, April 14, 1975, 28–29. FOIA enjoyed "a brief heyday in the 1970s," writes Kate Doyle, "The End of Secrecy: U.S. National Security and the Imperative for Openness," *World Policy Journal* 16, no. 1 (1999): 37.

4. Walter T. Lloyd, written statement submitted to and cleared by the CIA Prepublication Classification Review Board in response to author's questions, July 20, 2016. Lloyd said he was unaware that Henry Kissinger had used similar language in April 1975 in response to Soviet ambassador Anatoly Dobrynin. See chapter 7 for details.

5. Robert S. Young to Mr. [*sic*] Hank Phillippi, April 4, 1975, *Phillippi*, 655 F.2d at 1333n7.

6. For CIA's May 21, 1975, reply, see Phillippi v. CIA 546 F.2d 1009 (DC Cir. 1976) at 1021n6.

7. "Report Says Ford Price to Go Down," *Huntington* (Indiana) *Herald*, July 31, 1916; Operations Coordinating Board, approved meeting minutes, January 8, 1958, quoted in Hans M. Kristensen, "The Neither Confirm nor Deny Policy: Nuclear Diplomacy at Work" (working paper, Federation of American Scientists, February 2006), https://nukestrat.com/pubs/NCND.pdf.

8. Nathan Freed Wessler, "'[We] Can Neither Confirm nor Deny the Existence or Non-existence of Records Responsive to Your Request:' Reforming the Glomar Response Under FOIA," *New York University Law Review* 85, no. 4 (2010): 1382.

9. Lloyd (pseudonym Logan) quoted in David H. Sharp, *The CIA's Greatest Covert Operation: Inside the Daring Mission to Recover a Nuclear-Armed Soviet Sub* (Lawrence: University Press of Kansas, 2012), 282. Lloyd permitted me, in writing, to use his actual name. Critics include Danae J. Aitchison, "Reining in the Glomar Response: Reducing CIA Abuse of the Freedom of Information Act," *UC Davis Law Review* 27, no. 1 (1993): 219–254.

10. In a public affidavit, Deputy Under Secretary of State for Management Lawrence Eagleburger affirmed "that the information relevant to the United States Government case has been classified . . . on the ground that public disclosure would damage the national security, including the foreign relations of the United States." *Phillippi*, 546 F.2d at 1012.

11. Taylor Branch, "The Trial of the CIA," *New York Times Magazine*, September 12, 1976, 35. William Colby once assured the 40 Committee that the ship would sell "for $40–50 million once [its spy] mission was complete." Memo for the record, January 23, 1975, doc. 194, in *Foreign Relations of the United States* [hereafter *FRUS*], *1969–1976*, vol. 35, *National Security Policy, 1973–1976*, ed. M. Todd Bennett (Washington, DC: U.S. Government Printing Office, 2014).

12. Thomas S. Martin et al., brief for appellee, February 1981, Phillippi v. CIA, box 1624, American Civil Liberties Union Papers, Seeley G. Mudd Manuscript Library, Princeton University, Princeton, NJ, Gale ACLU Database, accessed April 6, 2022, https://www.gale.com/c/making-of-modern-law-american-civil-liberties-union-papers-part-i. Published accounts included George Lardner Jr. and William Claiborne, "CIA's

Glomar 'Game Plan,'" *Washington Post*, October 23, 1977, A10; Charles B. Seib, "Lessons From a Submerged CIA Story," *Washington Post*, October 28, 1977, A15; Anthony Lewis, "The Secrecy Disease," *New York Times*, October 31, 1977, 31; Clyde W. Burleson, *The Jennifer Project* (Englewood Cliffs, NJ: Prentice-Hall, 1977); Roy Varner and Wayne Collier, *A Matter of Risk* (New York: Random House, 1978).

13. William S. Regan (contracting officer, CIA Directorate of Science and Technology), affidavit, September 28, 1977, Military Audit Project v. William Casey, Director of Central Intelligence, et al., 656 F.2d 724 (DC Cir. 1981) at n29.

14. Mark H. Lynch and Susan W. Shaffer, brief for the appellant, December 4, 1980, Phillippi v. CIA, box 1624, ACLU Papers; William Colby with Peter Forbath, *30 Ans de CIA*, trans. Jean-Pierre Carasso (Paris: Presses de la Renaissance, 1978), 331.

15. Lynch and Shaffer, brief for the appellant.

16. Dr. Jack L. Titus, preliminary notes, April 6, 1976; Titus, final report, autopsy N-76-92, April 6, 1976; Titus to Dr. Henry D. McIntosh, April 7, 1976, all in Autopsy, box 13, Series 3: Howard Hughes, Donald L. Barlett and James B. Steele Archive, University Archives and Special Collections, American University Library, Washington, DC.

17. Jack Anderson, "The Howard Hughes, Watergate Connection," Washington Merry-Go-Round, *Washington Post*, March 22, 1977. See also James R. Phelan, "Howard Hughes, Beyond the Law," *New York Times Magazine*, September 14, 1975, 14, 50, 54–58; Phelan, *Howard Hughes: The Hidden Years* (New York: Random House, 1976), xiii.

18. "Question and Answer Session with the President and the American Society of Newspaper Editors," April 13, 1976, p. 6, box 24, White House Press Releases, Gerald R. Ford Presidential Library, Ann Arbor, MI, https://www.fordlibrarymuseum.gov/library/document/0248/whpr19760413-026.pdf.

19. *Phillippi*, 655 F.2d at 1329.

20. Fritzi Cohen to Office of the Secretary of Defense, Public Affairs, Freedom of Information Directorate, April 3, 1975, *Military Audit*, 656 F.2d at 729.

21. *Military Audit*, 656 F.2d at 742–743.

22. Cyrus R. Vance, affidavit, February 2, 1978, *Military Audit*, 656 F.2d at 741–742.

23. Ernest J. Zellmer, affidavit, February 23, 1978, *Military Audit*, 656 F.2d at 748–749.

24. Zellmer affidavit, *Military Audit*, 656 F.2d at 739. The firms are identified at 739–740.

25. Thomas B. Yale, affidavit, March 4, 1978, *Military Audit*, 656 F.2d at 745–747.

26. Stansfield Turner, affidavit, March 3, 1978, *Military Audit*, 656 F.2d at 749.

27. Ray v. Turner, 587 F. 2d 1187, 1213 (DC Cir. 1978). For discussions of "excessive" judicial deference to state secrets claims, see Wessler, "[We] Can Neither Confirm nor Deny," 1407; Robert P. Deyling, "Judicial Deference and De Novo Review in Litigation Over National Security Information Under the Freedom of Information Act," *Villanova Law Review* 37 (1992): 67; Scott A. Faust, "National Security Information Disclosure under the FOIA: The Need for Effective Judicial Enforcement," *Boston College Law Review* 26 (1983): 611.

28. Jefferson Morley, "Wilderness of Mirrors: Documents Reveal the Complex Legacy of James Angleton," *The Intercept*, January 1, 2018, https://theintercept.com/2018/01/01/the-complex-legacy-of-cia-counterintelligence-chief-james-angleton/; Morley, *The Ghost: The Secret Life of CIA Spymaster James Jesus Angleton* (New York: St. Martin's Press, 2017).

29. *Military Audit*, 656 F.2d, quoting "The Great Submarine Snatch," *Time*, March 31, 1975, at 729.

30. *Military Audit*, 656 F.2d at 744.

31. "Great Submarine Snatch;" *Military Audit*, 656 F.2d at 745.

32. *Military Audit*, 656 F.2d at 754.

33. *Phillippi*, 655 F.2d at 1328, 1332–1333.

34. As of May 7, 2022, Google Scholar counted 808 case law citations for *Phillippi* and 1,824 for *Military Audit*. Citations included Wilner v. National Security Agency, 592 F.3d 60 (2nd Cir. 2009) affirming the NSA's Glomar denial of a FOIA request filed by representatives of individuals detained at Guantanamo Bay, Cuba; Electronic Privacy Information Center v. NSA, 798 F. Supp. 2d 26 (DC Cir. 2011) upholding the NSA's Glomarization of a request for records documenting the agency's relationship with Google; and Wilson v. CIA, 586 F.3d 171 (2nd Cir. 2009) ruling that the CIA could partially block publication of the memoir of Valerie Plame Wilson, a former CIA agent, even though the fact of her prior service had been widely reported.

35. Office of Information Policy (OIP), U.S. Department of Justice (DoJ), "Privacy: 'Glomarization,'" *FOIA Update*, January 1, 1986, https://www.justice.gov/oip/blog/foia-update -oip-guidance-privacy-glomarization; Executive Order (EO) 12356, "National Security Information," April 2, 1982, https://fas.org/irp/offdocs/eo12356.htm.

36. EO 12065, "National Security Information," June 28, 1978, https://fas.org/irp/offdocs/eo /eo-12065.htm; EO 12958, "Classified National Security Information," April 17, 1995, https://fas.org/sgp/clinton/eo12958.html.

37. According to OIP's 1986 guidance, "Privacy: 'Glomarization,'" key cases included Baez v. DoJ, 647 F.2d 1328, 1338 (DC Cir. 1980) ("There can be no clearer example of an unwarranted invasion of personal privacy than to release to the public that another individual was the subject of an FBI investigation."); Fund for Constitutional Government v. National Archives & Records Service, 656 F.2d 856, 865 (DC Cir. 1981) ("The disclosure of [the fact that specific individuals were the subjects of a criminal investigation] would produce the unwarranted result of placing the named individuals in the position of having to defend their conduct in the public forum outside of the procedural protections normally afforded the accused in criminal proceedings."); Miller v. Bell, 661 F.2d 623, 631 32 (7th Cir. 1981) (identities of individuals merely mentioned in law enforcement records should be protected). A. Jay Wagner maps Glomar's spread in "Controlling Discourse, Foreclosing Recourse: The Creep of the Glomar Response," *Communication Law and Policy* 21, no. 4 (2016): 552.

38. See "Exemption 6," *U.S. Department of Justice Guide to the Freedom of Information Act*, accessed April 21, 2022, https://www.justice.gov/oip/page/file/1207336/download#page =82. See Beck v. DoJ, 997 F.2d 1489 (DC Cir. 1993) (affirming Glomar response to request for records concerning misconduct by two Drug Enforcement Agency agents).

39. In 1997, Global Marine (later GlobalSantaFe after a merger) leased the *Explorer* for $1 million per year. Renamed, the *GSF Explorer* worked as a drill ship before being scrapped.

40. "State Police Win Right to 'Neither Confirm nor Deny' Records Exist," Reporters Committee for Freedom of the Press (RCFP), June 15, 2016, https://www.rcfp.org/state -police-win-right-neither-confirm-nor-deny-records-exist/; "Glomar Surfaces in State Courts," RCFP, n.d., https://www.rcfp.org/journals/news-media-and-law-winter-2015 /glomar-surfaces-state-court/; Wagner, "Controlling Discourse," 543–545.

41. See section 25(2) of the Australian Freedom of Information Act 1982, as amended in 2020, https://www.legislation.gov.au/Details/C2020C00246. For subsection 10(2) of Canada's

Access to Information Act, as amended in 2020, and sections 23 and 24 of the UK Freedom of Information Act of 2000, respectively, go to https://laws-lois.justice.gc.ca /eng/acts/a-1/page-2.html#h-259 and https://www.legislation.gov.uk/ukpga/2000/36 /contents.

42. "Glomar Response," *Department of Justice Guide to the Freedom of Information Act*, accessed April 21, 2022, https://www.justice.gov/oip/page/file/1197091/download#page=24. Exemptions 1, 3, 6, and 7(C) accounted for 62.95 percent of all denials in 2019. OIP, DoJ, *Summary of Annual FOIA Reports for Fiscal Year 2019*, accessed April 21, 2022, https:// www.justice.gov/oip/page/file/1282001/download.

43. Anais Vaillant and Shawn Musgrave, "Zen and the Art of the Glomar Rejection," *Muckrock*, February 13, 2014, https://www.muckrock.com/news/archives/2014/feb/13/glomar -neither-confirm-deny-bizarre/; Brian Sparks, "Census Bureau Can 'Neither Confirm nor Deny' That It Shared Info with Other Agencies," *Muckrock*, February 8, 2016, https:// www.muckrock.com/news/archives/2016/feb/08/Census-GLOMAR/. In 2014, the U.S. Postal Service Glomarized a FOIA request for information about its "mail covers" program, in which the service tracks the names and addresses on the mail of targeted individuals. Joshua Eaton and Alex Richardson, "Postal Service and the IRS Join the CIA in Handing Out Glomar Denials," *Muckrock*, March 17, 2015, https://www.muckrock .com/news/archives/2015/mar/17/postal-service-and-irs-join-cia-handing-out-glomar/.

44. EO 13526, "Classified National Security Information," December 26, 2009, https://www .archives.gov/isoo/policy-documents/cnsi-eo.html.

45. Nate Jones, " 'Neither Confirm nor Deny:' The History of the Glomar Response and the *Glomar Explorer*," *Unredacted: The National Security Archive Blog*, February 11, 2014, https:// unredacted.com/2014/02/11/neither-confirm-nor-deny-the-history-of-the-glomar-response -and-the-glomar-explorer/. In 2019, agencies denied 33,866 FOIA requests in full, based on exemptions. Agencies denied another 351,481 in part. OIP, DoJ, *Summary of Annual FOIA Reports for Fiscal Year 2019*. FOIA logs are searchable at https://foiamapper.com.

46. "FOIA at 50," *Washington Post*, July 3, 2016, https://www.washingtonpost.com/opinions /foia-at-50/2016/07/03/6283af88-3fb0-11e6-a66f-aa6c1883b6b1_story.html?utm_term= .5337e2232387.

47. Nate Jones, "FOIA Tip No. 7—The *Glomar* Response," *Unredacted*, January 7, 2010, https://unredacted.com/2010/01/07/foia-tip-7-glomar-response/. See also Vaillant and Musgrave, "Zen and the Art of the Glomar Rejection"; Brian Anderson, "Glomar: The Ship That Sinks FOIA Requests," *Vice*, June 20, 2012, https://www.vice.com/en/article /jppkyp/glomar. Kate Doyle discusses FOIA's dysfunctionality in "The End of Secrecy: U.S. National Security and the Imperative for Openness," *World Policy Journal* 16, no. 1 (1999): 37.

48. ACLU v. CIA, 710 F.3d 422 (DC Cir. 2013).

49. Benjamin W. Cramer, "Old Love for New Snoops: How Exemption 3 of the Freedom of Information Act Enables an Irrebuttable Presumption of Surveillance Secrecy," *Communication Law and Policy* 23, no. 2 (2018): 94. In addition to some of the decisions named above, the DoJ currently lists numerous rulings affirming government Glomar denials, including Carter v. NSA, No. 13-5322, 2014 WL 2178708, at *1 (DC Cir. Apr. 23, 2014); Moore v. Bush, 601 F. Supp. 2d 6 (DDC 2009). See "Exemption 1," *Department of Justice Guide to the Freedom of Information Act*, accessed April 21, 2022, https://www.justice.gov /oip/page/file/1197091/download#page=24.

50. Matthew Aid, William Burr, and Thomas Blanton, eds., "Project AZORIAN: The CIA's Declassified History of the *Glomar Explorer*," National Security Archive, George Washington University, February 12, 2010, https://nsarchive2.gwu.edu/nukevault/ebb305 /index.htm. Published by the State Department in 2014, my *FRUS* volume, *National Security Policy, 1973–1976*, was already in declassification review when the National Security Archive FOIAd the CIA in December 2007. Sharp's *CIA's Greatest* (2012) entered CIA prepublication review in 2008.

51. Norman Polmar and Michael White, *Project AZORIAN: The CIA and the Raising of the K-129* (Annapolis, MD: Naval Institute Press, 2010); *AZORIAN: The Raising of the K-129*, dir. White (Michael White Films, 2010); Josh Dean, *The Taking of K-129: How the CIA Used Howard Hughes to Steal a Russian Sub in the Most Daring Covert Operation in History* (New York: Dutton, 2017); "Neither Confirm nor Deny," *Radiolab*, podcast, June 4, 2019, https://www.wnycstudios.org/podcasts/radiolab/articles/confirm-nor-deny; *Neither Confirm nor Deny*, dir. Philip Carter (New Sparta, 2020).

52. "The Glomar Explorer," *Washington Post*, March 23, 1975, 38.

53. Joseph Kraft, "Lessons from the Soviet Submarine Incident," *Washington Post*, March 23, 1975. See Dana Priest and William M. Arkin, *Top Secret America: The Rise of the New American Security State* (New York: Little, Brown and Company, 2011).

54. Lloyd statement, 3.

55. CIA (@CIA), Twitter post, June 6, 2014, 1:49 p.m., https://twitter.com/cia/status /474971393852182528?lang=en. As of May 26, 2021, the CIA's first tweet had more than 270,000 retweets and 223,000 likes. See also Matt Mendelsohn, "The Spies Next Door," *Washingtonian*, August 2014, https://www.washingtonian.com/2014/08/04/the-spies -next-door/.

56. In 2020, the *Washington Post* reported that the CIA secretly co-owned Crypto AG, a Swiss firm that, for decades, supplied encryption technology to clients throughout the world. Greg Miller, "The Intelligence Coup of the Century," *Washington Post*, February 11, 2020, https://www.washingtonpost.com/graphics/2020/world/national-security /cia-crypto-encryption-machines-espionage/.

57. Gareth Hector, *We Are Only Limited by Our Imagination*, 2013, in *The Art of Intelligence* (Washington, DC: CIA Museum and the Center for the Study of Intelligence, 2016), 42–43; "A Peek Into the CIA Art Gallery Reveals [REDACTED]," *Morning Edition*, National Public Radio, May 20, 2016, https://www.npr.org/2016/05/20/478706463/a-peek -into-the-cia-art-gallery-reveals-redacted.

SELECTED BIBLIOGRAPHY

This book began as a volume of the *Foreign Relations of the United States* (*FRUS*) series, the official documentary history of U.S. foreign policy published by the Department of State. Major portions of the *Glomar* mission remained unacknowledged by the U.S. government when I started researching that *FRUS* volume in 2005 or so. True, the CIA had released, in response to a 1975 Freedom of Information Act (FOIA) request filed by journalist Harriet Ann Phillippi, some records documenting former director William Colby's attempts to prevent the story's publication. And in 1992, after the Cold War was over, then CIA director Robert Gates had given some material to Russian president Boris Yeltsin as a gesture of goodwill.

But that was about it. The private National Security Archive had yet to win release, under FOIA, of "Project AZORIAN: The Story of the *Hughes Glomar Explorer*," a fifty-page account originally published in the CIA's in-house journal *Studies in Intelligence*. The agency's Publications Review Board, as it was then known, had yet to clear former CIA officer David Sharp's insider account, *The CIA's Greatest Covert Operation: Inside the Daring Mission to Recover a Nuclear-Armed Soviet Sub*. Those texts would not see the light of day until 2010 and 2012, respectively.

Published since the Abraham Lincoln administration, the *FRUS* series is the gold standard in official documentary history because it is backed by the force of law. A 1991 statute requires the series to provide the public with a "thorough, accurate, and reliable" record of major U.S. foreign policy decisions and significant U.S. diplomatic activity.[1] Nevertheless, few in the State Department's Office of the Historian believed that my *FRUS* manuscript would emerge unscathed when it entered declassification review in 2007, full of Top Secret/Sensitive Compartmented Information concerning a Special Access Program whose identifying code words remained classified.

---

1. Section 198 of Foreign Relations Authorization Act, Pub. L. No. 102-138, signed by President George H. W. Bush on October 28, 1991.

It took years of effort by *FRUS*'s declassification and editing team. During that time, I left the State Department to return to academia. But I was pleased to discover in 2014 that the volume, *National Security Policy, 1973–1976*, volume 35 of the *FRUS, 1969–1976* subseries covering the Nixon and Ford administrations, had been published with its *Glomar* chapter relatively intact. It features copies of CIA records, National Security Council intelligence files, and other materials that are available nowhere else because the government archives from which they were drawn remained closed to the general public. As such, it serves as an important source for this book.

That and all other *FRUS* volumes are available electronically at https://history.state.gov /historicaldocuments, including the following in the *FRUS, 1969–1976* subseries:

Volume 2, *Organization and Management of U.S. Foreign Policy, 1969–1972*, edited by David Humphrey. Washington, DC: U.S. Government Printing Office, 2006.

Volume 15, *Soviet Union, June 1972–August 1974*, edited by Douglas E. Selvage and Melissa Jane Taylor. Washington, DC: U.S. Government Printing Office, 2011.

Volume 16, *Soviet Union, August 1974–December 1976*, edited by David C. Geyer. Washington, DC: U.S. Government Printing Office, 2012.

Volume 34, *National Security Policy, 1969–1972*, edited by M. Todd Bennett. Washington, DC: U.S. Government Printing Office, 2011.

PERSONAL INTERVIEWS

Henry Kissinger's staff did not make him available for interviews. Sadly, Brent Scowcroft passed away in 2020. But I did have the opportunity to speak with many individuals who participated in the *Glomar* venture. My talks with the late Walter Lloyd, originator of the Glomar response, were particularly instructive.

Curtis Crooke, July 15, 2016, Carmel, CA.

Ray Feldman, August 13, 2016, Palo Alto, CA.

Seymour Hersh, June 22, 2016, via telephone.

Bobby Ray Inman, November 16, 2016, Austin, TX.

Walter T. Lloyd, July 22, August 1 and 8, 2016, and January 22, 2018, via telephone; March 18–20, 2018, Green Valley, AZ.

William C. Tuner, August 8, 2016, Las Vegas, NV.

Geary Yost (pseudonym), August 4, 2016, suburban Washington, DC.

MEMOIRS

Anderson, Jack, with James Boyd. *Confessions of a Muckraker: The Inside Story of Life in Washington During the Truman, Eisenhower, Kennedy and Johnson Years.* New York: Random House, 1979.

Anderson, Jack, with Daryl Gibson. *Peace, War, and Politics: An Eyewitness Account.* New York: Forge, 1999.

Cannon, James. *Time and Chance: Gerald Ford's Appointment with History.* New York: Harper-Collins, 1994.

Colby, William, and Peter Forbath. *Honorable Men: My Life in the CIA*. New York: Simon and Schuster, 1978.

Colby, William, with Peter Forbath. *30 Ans de CIA*. Translated by Jean-Pierre Carasso. Paris: Presses de la Renaissance, 1978.

Craven, John Piña. *The Silent War: The Cold War Battle Beneath the Sea*. New York: Simon and Schuster, 2001.

Ford, Gerald. *A Time to Heal: The Autobiography of Gerald R. Ford*. New York: Harper and Row, 1979.

Gates, Robert M. *From the Shadows: The Ultimate Insider's Story of Five Presidents and How They Won the Cold War*. New York: Simon and Schuster, 1996.

Greenfield, Meg. *Washington*. New York: PublicAffairs, 2001.

Haldeman, H. R., with Joseph DiMona. *The Ends of Power*. New York: Times Books, 1978.

Helms, Richard. *A Look Over My Shoulder: A Life in the Central Intelligence Agency*. New York: Random House, 2003.

Hersh, Seymour M. *Reporter: A Memoir*. New York: Knopf, 2018.

Kissinger, Henry. *White House Years*. New York: Little, Brown and Co., 1979.

Kissinger, Henry. *Years of Renewal*. New York: Simon and Schuster, 1999.

Lenzner, Terry. *The Investigator: Fifty Years of Uncovering the Truth*. New York: Blue Rider Press, 2013.

Maheu, Robert, and Richard Hack. *Next to Hughes: Behind the Power and Tragic Downfall of Howard Hughes by His Closest Advisor*. New York: HarperCollins, 1992.

Nixon, Richard. *RN: The Memoirs of Richard Nixon*. New York: Grosset and Dunlap, 1978.

Phillips, David Atlee. *The Night Watch*. New York: Atheneum, 1977.

Rumsfeld, Donald. *Known and Unknown: A Memoir*. New York: Sentinel, 2011.

Schorr, Daniel. *Clearing the Air*. Boston: Houghton Mifflin, 1977.

Wicker, Tom. *On Press*. New York: Viking, 1978.

ARCHIVAL COLLECTIONS

Special Collections, University Libraries, University of Nevada, Las Vegas. Howard Hughes Public Relations Records

Despite my best efforts, Howard Hughes remains elusive. To my knowledge, neither his personal nor his business records are publicly available. Many official files documenting his ties to the CIA remain frustratingly out of reach as well. In 2016, for example, the CIA released a fact sheet the agency's Office of Inspector General had compiled in 1976 in response to press reports of "a long and close link between Howard Hughes and the CIA." Of the report's thirteen pages (including attachments), the agency released two in full. Two pages were released in part. Nine were denied in full.[2]

---

2. A copy of the released August 9, 1976, fact sheet, titled "September *Playboy* article, 'The Puppet and Puppet Master,' by Larry DuBois and Laurence Gonzales, and an August 9 *Playboy* press release stressing that 'CIA Funds Helped Elect President Ford to Congress in the 1968 Election,'" is in my possession. A sanitized version of the original document is located in folder 2 [of 3], box 107, Segregated CIA Collection, JFK Task Force, Select Committee on

That said, the University of Nevada, Las Vegas, holds collections relating to Hughes. These include the reference files of Hughes's longtime public representative, Richard Hannah.

University Archives and Special Collections, American University Library, Washington, DC. Donald L. Barlett and James B. Steele Archive. Series 3: Howard Hughes

Housed at American University in Washington, DC, the Donald L. Barlett and James B. Steele Archive includes a series of records the investigative journalists compiled while researching their 1979 biography of Hughes, *Empire: The Life, Legend, and Madness of Howard Hughes*. These remarkable records include not only Hughes papers and interview transcripts, but CIA files and grand jury testimony related to the 1974 burglary during which a memo outlining the CIA's submarine plan was reportedly stolen from the Hughes building located on Los Angeles's Romaine Street. They provide invaluable insight into Hughes and his affairs.

Archives and Records Center, Los Angeles County Superior Court, Los Angeles, CA

- Case No. A316449 (1975), People of the State of California v. Donald Ray Woolbright
- Case No. A804747 (1983), People of the State of California v. Jerry Wayne Woolbright (a.k.a. Donald Ray Woolbright)
- Case No. A464741 (1985), People of the State of California v. Jerry Wayne Woolbright

The Romaine case remains unsolved today. The Los Angeles Police Department, citing privacy concerns, denied my request, filed under the California Public Records Act, for materials concerning its criminal investigation. Neither the CIA nor the FBI had responded productively to my federal records requests by the time this book went to press.

The Los Angeles County Superior Court's case files did yield some information about Donald Ray Woolbright, the man charged with receipt of stolen property and attempted extortion in connection with the burglary. They showed that Woolbright had a lengthy criminal record, including a 1968 felony conviction for attempting to enter a premises with intent to commit larceny. Sentenced in 1970 to ten years in prison, he was paroled in 1972 after serving two years in the federal penitentiary in Leavenworth, Kansas. The files also revealed that Donald Ray was an alias. His actual name was Jerry Wayne Woolbright. Charges against him stemming from the Romaine Street theft were dismissed in 1978.

Assassinations, Records of the U.S. House of Representatives, 95th Cong., President John F. Kennedy Assassination Records Collection, National Archives and Records Administration, College Park, MD. Inspector General John H. Waller compiled the sheet in response to a report by journalists Larry DuBois and Laurence Gonzales, "The Puppet and the Puppetmasters: Uncovering the Secret World of Nixon, Hughes and the CIA," published in the September 1976 issue of *Playboy* magazine.

National Archives and Records Administration, College Park, MD

- Records of the Watergate Special Prosecution Force, Record Group 460. Campaign Contributions Task Force #804—Hughes/Rebozo Investigation
- President John F. Kennedy Assassination Records Collection
- Records of the Central Intelligence Agency, Record Group 263
- Records of the U.S. Department of State, Record Group 59. Electronic Telegrams, Access to Archival Databases (https://aad.archives.gov/aad/); Records of Joseph Sisco (Entry 5405); Records of the Office of the Counselor, Lot File 81D286 (Entry 5339).

The National Archives and Records Administration (NARA) holds many important sources. But two are particularly noteworthy. Record Group 460, the Records of the Watergate Special Prosecution Force, includes the Campaign Contributions Task Force Numerical File #804 relating to the Hughes/Rebozo investigation. Consisting of subpoenas, notes, memos, and reports, these records follow the trail of money that led from Howard Hughes's onetime aide, Robert Maheu, to Richard Nixon's friend, Charles "Bebe" Rebozo, and, finally, to Nixon himself. They also pursue (inconclusively) claims that the Romaine Street burglary was staged to remove incriminating Watergate-related files from Hughes's premises before investigators could obtain them.

NARA's President John F. Kennedy Assassination Records Collection is certainly unusual. But it is the product of a powerful transparency law, the JFK Assassination Records Collection Act of 1992, which mandated that all assassination-related material be housed in a single collection and opened within twenty-five years. There are exceptions, of course, and the collection is still not fully available. But it includes over three hundred thousand presidential commission, congressional committee, and federal agency records documenting figures such as Maheu, his involvement in various CIA plots, including the one to assassinate Fidel Castro in league with mobsters in the early 1960s, and subsequent claims that he was behind a security breach concerning "a sensitive SPS [Special Projects Staff] activity," as a 1974 memo cryptically called AZORIAN.

Other Useful Archival Collections

Department of Archives and Special Collections, Hayden Library, Arizona State University, Tempe, AZ. Barry M. Goldwater Papers.

Albertsons Library, Boise State University, Boise, ID. Frank Church Papers.

Gerald R. Ford Presidential Library, Ann Arbor, MI.

James E. Connor Files

Digital Collections (https://www.fordlibrarymuseum.gov/collections-digital.aspx). Foreign Affairs and National Security, Intelligence Community. Investigations and Reforms.

National Security Advisor's Files

- Kissinger Reports on USSR, China, and Middle East Discussions
- Kissinger-Scowcroft West Wing Office Files
- Memoranda of Conversations
- NSC Meeting Minutes
- Peter Rodman Files

Ron Nessen Files
President's Handwriting File
White House Central Files
- FG 6-2 CIA
- ND 6 Intelligence
- ND 15 Ships—Submarines

Special Collections Research Center, Gelman Library, George Washington University, Washington, DC. Jack Anderson Papers.

Lyndon Baines Johnson Presidential Library, Austin, TX. National Security File. Files of Walt W. Rostow.

Library of Congress, Washington, DC
  Foreign Affairs Oral History Collection of the Association for Diplomatic Studies and Training (https://www.loc.gov/collections/foreign-affairs-oral-history/)
  - William McAfee
  - Edward Peck
  - Ronald Spiers
  Daniel Schorr Papers
  James R. Schlesinger Papers

Congressional and Political Research Center, Mississippi State University Libraries, Starkville, MS. John C. Stennis Collection.

Richard Nixon Presidential Library and Museum, Yorba Linda, CA
  H. R. Haldeman Diaries Collection
  Henry A. Kissinger Office Files
  Kissinger Telephone Conversation Transcripts
  National Security Council Files
  - Country Files—Europe
  - Alexander M. Haig Chronological Files
  - Alexander M. Haig Special File
  - Name Files
  - Presidential/HAK Memcons
  - Subject Files
  National Security Council Institutional Files (H-Files)
  - Policy Papers
  - Intelligence Files
  White House Central Files, Staff Member and Office Files
  - Edward E. David Files
  White House Special Files, Staff Member and Office Files
  - John W. Dean III
  - H. R. Haldeman

Ronald Reagan Presidential Library, Simi Valley, CA. 1980 Presidential Campaign Papers.

Archives and Special Collections, Berry Library, Salem State University, Salem, MA. Michael Harrington Papers.

Margaret Chase Smith Library, Skowhegan, ME

Special Collections, A. Frank Smith Jr. Library Center, Southwestern University, Georgetown, TX. John G. Tower Papers.

Southwest Collection, Special Collections Library, Texas Tech University, Lubbock, TX. George H. Mahon Papers.

Richard B. Russell Library for Political Research and Studies, University of Georgia Libraries, Athens, GA. Richard B. Russell Jr. Collection.

Bentley Historical Library, University of Michigan, Ann Arbor, MI. Philip A. Hart Papers.

DECLASSIFIED MATERIALS

I filed dozens of FOIA or Mandatory Declassification Review requests starting in 2015. These requests went to the CIA, the FBI, the Joint Chiefs of Staff, the National Archives, the National Security Agency, the navy, the Office of the Secretary of Defense, and the Johnson, Nixon, and Ford libraries. Most cases remained open when this book went to press in 2022. But some declassified materials are available at the following:

Central Intelligence Agency Freedom of Information Act Electronic Reading Room. https://www.cia.gov/readingroom/.
Federal Bureau of Investigation Freedom of Information Act Library (https://vault.fbi.gov)
- Jack Anderson
- Howard Hughes
National Security Archive Virtual Reading Room. https://nsarchive.gwu.edu/virtual-reading-room.
U.S. Department of State FOIA Virtual Reading Room. https://www.foia.state.gov.
- Kissinger Telephone Transcripts

DIGITAL COLLECTIONS

American Civil Liberties Union Papers, Gale ACLU Database. https://www.gale.com/c/making-of-modern-law-american-civil-liberties-union-papers-part-i. Phillippi v. Central Intelligence Agency.
Associated Press Corporate Archives, Associated Press Collections Online. https://www.gale.com/c/associated-press-collections-online-washington-dc-bureau-part-i. Washington, DC, Bureau.
Clements National Security Papers Project, Clements Center for National Security, University of Texas at Austin. https://ns.clementspapers.org/.
Donald Rumsfeld Papers. https://papers.rumsfeld.com/.
Vanderbilt Television News Archive. https://tvnews.vanderbilt.edu.
Yale University Library Digital Collections. Henry A. Kissinger Papers. https://web.library.yale.edu/digital-collections/kissinger-collection.

SOVIET/RUSSIAN SOURCES

The last word on the Soviet side of the *Glomar* story remains unwritten. The COVID-19 pandemic, combined with Russia's invasion of Ukraine, limited my ability to travel to Moscow to conduct in-person research, including in two archives—the Archive of the Foreign Policy of the Russian Federation and the Russian State Archive of Contemporary History—that may hold *Glomar*-related materials. Soviet-era intelligence archives remain closed. However, I did attempt to gain the Soviet perspective with sources such as:

- Bukan, Sergey Petrovich. *Po sledam podvodnykh katastrof* [On the trail of submarine disasters]. Moscow: Gildiya masterov Rus, 1992. This is an account of Soviet submarine disasters that draws upon interviews with former Soviet naval officers to shed light on what they may have known about American efforts to recover the *K-129*. A translated version of the account is available in the CIA Freedom of Information Act Electronic Reading Room: https://www.cia.gov/library/readingroom/docs/DOC_0000078940.pdf.
- The Cold War International History Project, which publishes, via the Wilson Center's Digital Archive (http://digitalarchive.wilsoncenter.org), historical documentation from the former Soviet bloc.
- Dobrynin, Anatoly. *In Confidence: Moscow's Ambassador to America's Six Cold War Presidents (1962–1986)*. New York: Times Books, 1995. Dobrynin discusses the sub-raising mission within the context of détente-era Soviet-American "Intelligence Wars."
- Geyer, David C., and Douglas E. Selvidge, eds. *Soviet-American Relations: The Détente Years, 1969–1972*. Washington, DC: U.S. Government Printing Office, 2007. This joint documentary publication of the Russian Foreign Ministry and American State Department documents Dobrynin's back channel with Kissinger.

CONGRESSIONAL DOCUMENTS

U.S. Congress, *Congressional Record*. Washington, DC: U.S. Government Printing Office, 1966–75.

U.S. Congress. Senate. Select Committee on Presidential Campaign Activities. Executive Session Hearings, *Watergate and Related Activities: The Hughes–Rebozo Investigation, and Related Matters*, books 21–24. 93rd Cong., 2d sess., February 8–June 14, 1974. Washington, DC: U.S. Government Printing Office, 1974.

U.S. Congress. Senate. Select Committee on Presidential Campaign Activities. *Final Report*. 93rd Cong., 2d sess. Washington, DC: U.S. Government Printing Office, 1974.

U.S. Congress. Senate. Select Committee to Study Governmental Operations with Respect to Intelligence Activities. *Final Report*, book I, *Foreign and Military Intelligence*. 94th Cong., 2d sess. Washington, DC: U.S. Government Printing Office, 1976.

COURT CASES

Military Audit Project v. William Casey, Director of Central Intelligence, et al., 656 F.2d 724 (DC Cir. 1981).

Harriet Ann Phillippi v. Central Intelligence Agency, 546 F.2d 1009 (DC Cir. 1976).

Harriet Ann Phillippi v. Central Intelligence Agency, 655 F.2d 1325 (DC Cir. 1981).

OTHER PUBLISHED PRIMARY SOURCES

Diamond, Gregory Andrade. *The Unexpurgated Pike Report: Report of the House Select Committee on Intelligence, 1976.* New York: McGraw-Hill, 1992.

Skinner, Kiron K., Annelise Anderson, and Martin Anderson, eds. *Reagan, In His Own Hand.* New York: Free Press, 2001.

SECONDARY SOURCES

Articles, Chapters, and Reviews

Aitchison, Danae J. "Reining in the Glomar Response: Reducing CIA Abuse of the Freedom of Information Act." *UC Davis Law Review* 27, no. 1 (1993): 219–254.

Aldrich, Richard J. "Regulation by Revelation? Intelligence, the Media and Transparency." In *Spinning Intelligence: Why Intelligence Needs the Media, Why the Media Needs Intelligence*, edited by Robert Dover and Michael S. Goodman, 13–36. New York: Columbia University Press, 2009.

Doyle, Kate. "The End of Secrecy: U.S. National Security and the Imperative for Openness." *World Policy Journal* 16, no. 1 (1999): 34–51.

"Engineering for AZORIAN." *Studies in Intelligence* 24, no. 1 (Spring 1980): 1–45.

Fink, Katherine, and Michael Schudson. "The Rise of Contextual Journalism, 1950s–2000s." *Journalism* 15, no 1 (2014): 3–20.

Jones, Nate. " 'Neither Confirm nor Deny:' The History of the Glomar Response and the *Glomar Explorer*." *Unredacted: The National Security Archive Blog*, February 11, 2014. https://unredacted.com/2014/02/11/neither-confirm-nor-deny-the-history-of-the-glomar-response-and-the-glomar-explorer/.

Maury, John. "CIA and the Congress." *Studies in Intelligence* 18, no. 2 (Summer 1974): 1–14.

Olmsted, Kathryn S. "'An American Conspiracy:' The Post-Watergate Press and the CIA." *Journalism History* 19, no 2 (Summer 1993): 51–58.

Olmsted, Kathryn S. "Reclaiming Executive Power: The Ford Administration's Response to the Intelligence Investigations." *Presidential Studies Quarterly* 26, no. 3 (Summer 1996): 725–737.

"Project AZORIAN: The Story of the *Hughes Glomar Explorer*." *Studies in Intelligence* 22, no. 3 (Fall 1978): 1–50.

Schulman, Bruce J. "Restraining the Imperial Presidency: Congress and Watergate." In *The American Congress: The Building of Democracy*, edited by Julian E. Zelizer, 638–649. Boston: Houghton Mifflin, 2004.

"At Sea with the Law: Some Legal Aspects of the AZORIAN Program." *Studies in Intelligence* 23, no. 3 (Fall 1979): 1–18.

"Security: Hidden Shield for Project AZORIAN." *Studies in Intelligence* 23, no. 4 (Winter 1979): 39–51.

Wagner, A. Jay. "Controlling Discourse, Foreclosing Recourse: The Creep of the Glomar Response." *Communication Law and Policy* 21, no. 4 (2016): 539–567.

Wessler, Nathan Freed. " '[We] Can Neither Confirm nor Deny the Existence or Nonexistence of Records Responsive to Your Request:' Reforming the Glomar Response Under FOIA." *New York University Law Review* 85, no. 4 (2010): 1382.

Wilford, Hugh. "Still Missing: The Historiography of U.S. Intelligence." *Passport* 47, no. 2 (2016): 20–25.

Zelizer, Julian E. "Without Restraint: Scandal and Politics in America." In *The Columbia History of Post-World War II America*, edited by Mark C. Carnes, 226–254. New York: Columbia University Press, 2007.

Books

Andrew, Christopher, and David Dilks, eds. *The Missing Dimension: Governments and Intelligence Communities in the Twentieth Century.* Urbana: University of Illinois Press, 1984.

Andrew, Christopher, and Vasili Mitrokhin. *The Sword and the Shield: The Mitrokhin Archive and the Secret History of the KGB.* New York: Basic Books, 1999.

Arnold, Jason Ross. *Secrecy in the Sunshine Era: The Promise and Failures of U.S. Open Government Laws.* Lawrence: University Press of Kansas, 2014.

Barlett, Donald L., and James B. Steele. *Empire: The Life, Legend, and Madness of Howard Hughes.* New York: W. W. Norton, 1979.

Barrett, David M. *The CIA and Congress: The Untold Story from Truman to Kennedy.* Lawrence: University Press of Kansas, 2005.

Berkowitz, Edward D. *Something Happened: A Political and Cultural Overview of the Seventies.* New York: Columbia University Press, 2006.

Beschloss, Michael R. *Mayday: Eisenhower, Khrushchev and the U-2 Affair.* New York: Harper and Row, 1986.

Bowker, Mike, and Phil Williams. *Superpower Détente: A Reappraisal.* London: Royal Institute of International Affairs, 1988.

Bray, Howard. *The Pillars of the Post: The Making of a News Empire in Washington.* New York: W. W. Norton, 1980.

Broad, William J. *The Universe Below: Discovering the Secrets of the Deep Sea.* New York: Simon and Schuster, 1997.

Bundy, William. *A Tangled Web: The Making of Foreign Policy in the Nixon Presidency.* New York: Hill and Wang, 1998.

Burleson, Clyde W. *The Jennifer Project.* 1977; College Station: Texas A&M University Press, 1997.

Cahn, Anne Hessing. *Killing Détente: The Right Attacks the CIA.* University Park: Pennsylvania State University Press, 1998.

Carpenter, Ted Galen. *The Captive Press: Foreign Policy Crises and the First Amendment.* Washington, DC: Cato Institute, 1995.

Cline, Ray S. *The CIA Under Reagan, Bush and Casey: The Evolution of the Agency from Roosevelt to Reagan.* Washington, DC: Acropolis Books, 1981.

Daigle, Craig. *The Limits of Détente: The United States, the Soviet Union, and the Arab-Israeli Conflict, 1969–1973.* New Haven, CT: Yale University Press, 2012.

Dallek, Robert. *Nixon and Kissinger: Partners in Power.* New York: HarperCollins, 2007.

Dean, Josh. *The Taking of K-129: How the CIA Used Howard Hughes to Steal a Russian Sub in the Most Daring Covert Operation in History.* New York: Dutton, 2017.

Drosnin, Michael. *Citizen Hughes.* New York: Holt, 1985.

Durbin, Brent. *The CIA and the Politics of U.S. Intelligence Reform.* New York: Cambridge University Press, 2017.

Feldstein, Mark. *Poisoning the Press: Richard Nixon, Jack Anderson, and the Rise of Washington's Scandal Culture*. New York: Farrar, Straus and Giroux, 2010.

Fenno, Richard F., Jr. *The Power of the Purse: Appropriations Politics in Congress*. Boston: Little, Brown, 1966.

Ferguson, Niall, Charles S. Maier, Erez Manela, and Daniel J. Sargent, eds. *The Shock of the Global: The 1970s in Perspective*. Cambridge, MA: Belknap Press of Harvard University Press, 2010.

Fite, Gilbert C. *Richard B. Russell, Jr., Senator from Georgia*. Chapel Hill: University of North Carolina Press, 1991.

Ford, Harold P. *William E. Colby as Director of Central Intelligence, 1973–1976*. Washington, DC: CIA Center for the Study of Intelligence, 1993.

Gaddis, John Lewis. *Strategies of Containment: A Critical Appraisal of American National Security Policy During the Cold War*. Rev. ed. New York: Oxford University Press, 2005.

Garthoff, Raymond L. *Détente and Confrontation: American-Soviet Relations from Nixon to Reagan*. Rev. ed. Washington, DC: Brookings Institution, 2011.

Greenberg, David. *Nixon's Shadow: The History of an Image*. New York: W. W. Norton, 2003.

Greider, William. *Who Will Tell the People: The Betrayal of American Democracy*. New York: Simon and Schuster, 1992.

Halberstam, David. *The Powers That Be*. New York: Knopf, 1979.

Hanhimäki, Jussi. *The Flawed Architect: Henry Kissinger and American Foreign Policy*. New York: Oxford University Press, 2004.

Hathaway, Robert M., and Russell Jack Smith. *Richard Helms as Director of Central Intelligence, 1966–1973*. Washington, DC: CIA Center for the Study of Intelligence, 1993.

Hersh, Seymour M. *The Price of Power: Kissinger in the Nixon White House*. New York: Summit Books, 1983.

Hoffmann, Stanley. *Dead Ends: American Foreign Policy in the New Cold War*. Cambridge, MA: Ballinger, 1983.

Immerman, Richard H. *The Hidden Hand: A Brief History of the CIA*. Malden, MA: Wiley-Blackwell, 2014.

Isaacson, Walter. *Kissinger: A Biography*. New York: Simon and Schuster, 1992.

Jeffreys-Jones, Rhodri. *The CIA and American Democracy*. 3rd ed. New Haven, CT: Yale University Press, 2003.

Jenkins, Tricia. *The CIA in Hollywood: How the Agency Shapes Film and Television*. Austin: University of Texas Press, 2012.

Johnson, Loch K. *America's Secret Power: The CIA in a Democratic Society*. New York: Oxford University Press, 1989.

Johnson, Loch K. *A Season of Inquiry Revisited: The Church Committee Confronts America's Spy Agencies*. Lawrence: University Press of Kansas, 2015.

Johnson, Loch K. *Spy Watching: Intelligence Accountability in the United States*. New York: Oxford University Press, 2018.

Kutler, Stanley I. *The Wars of Watergate: The Last Crisis of Richard Nixon*. New York: Knopf, 1990.

Lawrence, John A. *The Class of '74: Congress After Watergate and the Roots of Partisanship*. Baltimore, MD: Johns Hopkins University Press, 2018.

Lukas, J. Anthony. *Nightmare: The Underside of the Nixon Years*. 1976; Athens: Ohio University Press, 1999.

Marchetti, Victor, and John D. Marks. *The CIA and the Cult of Intelligence*. New York: Knopf, 1974.

McCarthy, David Shamus. *Selling the CIA: Public Relations and the Culture of Secrecy*. Lawrence: University Press of Kansas, 2018.

Melanson, Philip H. *Secrecy Wars: National Security, Privacy, and the Public's Right to Know*. Washington, DC: Brassey's, 2001.

Mistry, Kaeten, and Hannah Gurman, eds. *Whistleblowing Nation: The History of National Security Disclosures and the Cult of State Secrecy*. New York: Columbia University Press, 2020.

Moss, Richard A. *Nixon's Back Channel to Moscow: Confidential Diplomacy and Détente*. Lexington: University Press of Kentucky, 2017.

Neugebauer, Janet M. *A Witness to History: George H. Mahon, West Texas Congressman*. Lubbock: Texas Tech University Press, 2017.

Olmsted, Kathryn S. *Challenging the Secret Government: The Post-Watergate Investigations of the CIA and FBI*. Chapel Hill: University of North Carolina Press, 1996.

Olmsted, Kathryn S. *Real Enemies: Conspiracy Theories and American Democracy, World War I to 9/11*. 10th ann. ed. New York: Oxford University Press, 2019.

Patterson, Thomas E. *Out of Order*. New York: Knopf, 1993.

Phelan, James. *Howard Hughes: The Hidden Years*. New York: Random House, 1976.

Polmar, Norman, and Michael White. *Project AZORIAN: The CIA and the Raising of the K-129*. Annapolis, MD: Naval Institute Press, 2010.

Powers, Thomas. *The Man Who Kept the Secrets: Richard Helms and the CIA*. New York: Knopf, 1979.

Prados, John. *The Ghosts of Langley: Into the CIA's Heart of Darkness*. New York: New Press, 2017.

Prados, John. *William Colby and the CIA: The Secret Wars of a Controversial Spymaster*. Lawrence: University Press of Kansas, 2009.

Ranelagh, John. *The Agency: The Rise and Decline of the CIA*. New York: Simon and Schuster, 1986.

Ransom, Harry Howe. *The Intelligence Establishment*. Cambridge, MA: Harvard University Press, 1970.

Richelson, Jeffrey T. *The Wizards of Langley: Inside the CIA's Directorate of Science and Technology*. Boulder, CO: Westview Press, 2002.

Salisbury, Harrison E. *Without Fear or Favor: The New York Times and Its Times*. New York: Times Books, 1980.

Sargent, Daniel J. *A Superpower Transformed: The Remaking of American Foreign Relations in the 1970s*. New York: Oxford University Press, 2015.

Schlesinger, Arthur M., Jr. *The Imperial Presidency*. New York: Houghton Mifflin, 1973.

Schudson, Michael. *Discovering the News: A Social History of American Newspapers*. New York: Basic Books, 1978.

Schudson, Michael. *The Rise of the Right to Know: Politics and the Culture of Transparency, 1945–1975*. Cambridge, MA: Belknap Press of Harvard University Press, 2015.

Schulman, Bruce J. *The Seventies: The Great Shift in American Culture, Society, and Politics*. New York: Free Press, 2001.

Schulman, Bruce J., and Julian E. Zelizer, eds. *Rightward Bound: Making America Conservative in the 1970s*. Cambridge, MA: Harvard University Press, 2008.

Schulzinger, Robert D. *Henry Kissinger: Doctor of Diplomacy.* New York: Columbia University Press, 1989.

Schwartz, Thomas A. *Henry Kissinger and American Power: A Political Biography.* New York: Hill and Wang, 2020.

Scott, Katherine A. *Reining in the State: Civil Society and Congress in the Vietnam and Watergate Eras.* Lawrence: University Press of Kansas, 2013.

Sharp, David H. *The CIA's Greatest Covert Operation: Inside the Daring Mission to Recover a Nuclear-Armed Soviet Sub.* Lawrence: University Press of Kansas, 2012.

Smist, Frank J., Jr. *Congress Oversees the United States Intelligence Community, 1947–1994.* Knoxville: University of Tennessee Press, 1994.

Snider, L. Britt. *The Agency and the Hill: CIA's Relationship with Congress, 1946–2004.* Washington, DC: CIA Center for the Study of Intelligence, 2008.

Snider, L. Britt. *Congress and the CIA.* New York: Nova Science Publishers, 2009.

Sontag, Sherry, and Christopher Drew. *Blind Man's Bluff: The Untold Story of American Submarine Espionage.* New York: Harper, 1998.

Sparrow, Bartholomew H. *Uncertain Guardians: The News Media as a Political Institution.* Baltimore, MD: Johns Hopkins University Press, 1999.

Suri, Jeremi. *Henry Kissinger and the American Century.* Cambridge, MA: Harvard University Press, 2007.

Suri, Jeremi. *Power and Protest: Global Revolution and the Rise of Détente.* Cambridge, MA: Harvard University Press, 2003.

Thomas, Evan. *Being Nixon: A Man Divided.* New York: Random House, 2015.

Usdin, Steven T. *Bureau of Spies: The Secret Connections Between Espionage and Journalism in Washington.* Amherst, NY: Prometheus Books, 2018.

Varner, Roy, and Wayne Collier. *A Matter of Risk: The Incredible Inside Story of the CIA's Hughes Glomar Explorer Mission to Raise a Russian Submarine.* New York: Random House, 1978.

Weiner, Tim. *One Man Against the World.* New York: Henry Holt and Co., 2015.

Wilford, Hugh. *The Mighty Wurlitzer: How the CIA Played America.* Cambridge, MA: Harvard University Press, 2008.

Woods, Randall B. *Shadow Warrior: William Egan Colby and the CIA.* New York: Basic Books, 2013.

Zelizer, Julian E. *Arsenal of Democracy: The Politics of National Security—From World War II to the War on Terrorism.* New York: Basic Books, 2010.

Zelizer, Julian E. *On Capitol Hill: The Struggle to Reform Congress and Its Consequences, 1948–2000.* New York: Cambridge University Press, 2004.

Zubok, Vladislav M. *A Failed Empire: The Soviet Union in the Cold War from Stalin to Gorbachev.* Chapel Hill: University of North Carolina Press, 2007.

INDEX

ABM. *See* antiballistic missile

accountability, 6–7, 15, 154, 220; Kissinger on, 250–251; lack of, 39, 260–261

advances: in intelligence tradecraft, 222–223; technological, 227, 228

affidavits, executive, 281–283, 287

AGI. *See* auxiliary, general intelligence

aircraft: TU-95, 191; U-2, 186, 188, 194–195, 227, 262, 290, 299n23

Air West, 115, 116, 127, 215

alidade, 120

Allende, Salvador, 80, 142, 218

ambiguity, intelligence, 201

ambition, 5, 223

American Civil Liberties Union, 274, 287

American Newspaper Publishers Association, 225

American Society of Newspaper Editors, 168

analysis: AZORIAN project risk/reward, 76–77, 92–93; cost-benefit, 252

Anchorage Daily Times, 229

Anderson, Jack, 54, 57, 176, 231–232, 335n59; Colby speaking with, 177–179; *Glomar* broadcast, 180–181; on Hughes, 178, 277; Maheu and, 52–53, 309n32; reputation, 180

Andrew, Christopher, 9, 99

Andropov, Yuri, 88–89, 152

Angleton, James J., 282

antiballistic missile (ABM), 63

Antitrust Division, Justice Department, 52

Appropriations Clause, U.S. Constitution, 34, 260, 269

Arizona Republic, 226, 247–248

Armed Services Committee, 17, 33, 213, 214, 247

artworks, CIA, 5, 290–291

assassinations, 47, 52, 167, 216, 217, 266, 270

Associated Press, 174

Association of Retired Intelligence Officers, 223

ATA *MB-11* (ship), 191–192, 204

ATF *MB-26* (ship), 205–207

Atlanta Constitution, 197, 229

Atomic Energy Commission, 123

auxiliary, general intelligence (AGI), 120

AZORIAN project, 4–5, 8, 26–28; "conspicuous bump" in budget for, 36–37, 262; cost, 29–30, 66–67, 183; delays, 82, 103; EXCOM guiding, 67, 73; 40 Committee on, 101–103; internal history of, 288; morality of, 74–75, 102; Nixon approving, 78–79; praise for, 222, 226–229; priority of, 70–71; responses to, 136–137, 191–194; risk/reward analysis, 76–77, 92–93; Sharp on, 82, 83, 128, 129, 133; success of, 133–134, 182; USIB on, 70–71. *See also* MATADOR project

back channels, 10, 99–100, 101, 207

Baker, Howard, 59–60, 216

balance: of power, 250; of secrecy, 13, 236, 237, 289

Baldwin, Hanson, 229–230

Barlett, Donald, 176

Basic Principles, of Soviet-American relations, 72, 200

Bennett, Robert, 55, 56, 58

Berlin Tunnel, 26, 227

Bernstein, Carl, 326n34

Black newspapers, 226

Blind Man's Bluff (Sontag and Drew), 19

Bowker, Mike, 72, 97

Bradlee, Ben, 161, 233

Bradley, James F., Jr., 21, 22, 24, 137, 163

bragging rights, 188–189

Branch, Taylor, 269, 270, 275

breach, of security, 111, 116, 243–244

break-ins: Romaine Street, 106, 126; Watergate, 58–59, 126

Brezhnev, Leonid, 69–70, 87, 89, 160, 189, 209–210

Brooks, Chester, 106, 107, 110, 124

Brzezinski, Zbigniew, 275

budget, intelligence, 29, 30–31, 34–35; "conspicuous bump" in, 36–37, 262; DS&T, 256; OMB and, 66; potential publication of, 262–263; reviews of, 259–262, 265; A. Schlesinger on, 264–265; S. Turner on, 281

bureaucracy, 251

burglary, 106–109, 111, 112, 114

burial, at sea, 135, 197, 322n12, 331n42

businesses, as CIA cover, 217–219, 269–270, 279, 280. *See also* nonofficial cover

Byrd, Robert, 246

Cahn, Anne Hessing, 70

California, 80, 141, *141*

camaraderie, of secrecy, 232

Cambodia, 208

cameras, closed-circuit television, 121, 129

Cannon, James, 243

Caro, Robert, 33

Carter, Jimmy, 275

Cary, George L., 241–244, 251, 337n1

Castro, Fidel, 47, 52, 216, 217

Caulfield, Jack, 54–57

caution, cramped, 251

cautiousness, intelligence, 230

censorship, 160–161, 234, 237

Central Committee of the Communist Party, Soviet Union, 196

Central Intelligence Agency (CIA): artworks, 5, 290–291; calls to abolish, 219; contracts, 46–47, 82–83, 218–219, 242, 252, 269; cutbacks, 64; damage to, 250; DCI, 17, 65; DS&T, 1, 2, 23, 24–25, 38, 224–225, 256; Nixon on, 60–61, 63–64, 99; nonofficial cover, 217–219, 269–270, 280; NURO, 28, 68, 253, 258; Office of General Counsel, 272; praise for, 246–248; subcommittees, 15–18, 31; transactions, 280–281; vulnerability of, 70. *See also specific topics*

Central Intelligence Agency Act (1949), 30, 36

ceremony, burial, 135, 197, 322n12, 331n42

Chancellor, John, 185

Chazhma (ship), 118–119

Chicago Tribune, 159, 197, 227, 228

Chile, 80, 99, 142, 218, 333n16

Church, Frank, 11, 143, 146, 214, 241, 244

Church Committee, 244–245, 247, 248, 251–252, 258, 268

CIA. *See* Central Intelligence Agency

CIA and the Cult of Intelligence, The (Marchetti and Marks), 260

Cincinnati Post, 226

cipher machine, 21

circuit courts, 275, 278, 282

civil liberty, 6

clandestine activity, 2, 22, 26, 73, 84–85; executive branch controlling, 146, 147; glorification of, 255–256; Kissinger favoring, 99; telegraphing, 262–263

claw, 119, 121, 128–129, 132

Clements, William, Jr., 90, 92, 94, 102, 139–142, 169

cliché, NCND as, 290

Cline, Ray S., 334n39

Clinton, Bill, 284

closed-circuit television cameras, 121, 129

codes, 21, 159, 183, 201

Cohen, Jerry, 158

Colby, William, 10–11, 43, 74, 75, 90, 92, 93; Anderson speaking with, 177–179; on AZORIAN success, 133–134; Ford, and J. Schlesinger with, *190*; Ford with, *187*; Hersh meeting, 164–165; Kissinger on, 250; on MATADOR project, 142, 149–150, 195; memoir of, 276; "no comment" policy of, 185, 188, 189; at NSC meeting, *132*; oversharing of, 186; Pike Committee and, 255–257; press leaks managed by, 174–176, 233, 238–239; on secrecy, 154, 169, 220, 223, 226; on sensationalism, 225; transparency of, 154, 220–221, 249

Cold War, underwater, 3, 21, 222, 258

collection, intelligence, 64–65, 96–97

Collier, Wayne, 321n7

collusion, 100, 101, 203

Colson, Charles, 58, 82–83, 215

Columbia Journalism Review, 234

commemorations, 194

commissions: Atomic Energy Commission, 123; Rockefeller Commission, 150, 167, 230, 260, 323n49; SEC, 115, 116, 127, 215

committees: Armed Services Committee, 17, 33, 213, 214, 247; Church Committee, 244–245, 247, 248, 251–252, 258, 268; Defense Appropriations Subcommittee, 258–260; DNC, 55, 58–59; EXCOM, 67, 73; House Appropriations, 17, 247, 258, 340n58; HSCI, 252–254; Pike Committee, 255–258; SSCI, 34, 214, 245; Watergate Committee, 57–60, 88, 90

communications: hub, 108; ship-to-shore, 117

communism, 7, 32, 168, 267

compartmentalization, 27, 28

competition: intelligence collection, 64–65; press, 238; superpower, 97–98

complex, corporate-intelligence, 219, 224

Conference on Security and Cooperation, 189, 210

confidentiality, 99–100

conflicts, of interest, 65

Congress, U.S., 17, 30; intelligence oversight, 11, 12, 31–32, 37–38, 214, 244–245, 265–267; obstructing, 242

Congressional Record, 265

"conspicuous bump," in intelligence budgets, 36–37, 262

Constitution, U.S.: Appropriations Clause, 34, 260, 269; First Amendment, 235

contracts: CIA, 46–47, 82–83, 218–219, 242, 252, 269; government, 38–39, 43, 45; Helms on, 77–78

corporate-intelligence complex, 219, 224. *See also* nonofficial cover

corruption, 49, 169, 177

cost: AZORIAN project, 29–30, 66–67, 183;
 benefit analysis, 252; MATADOR
 project, 152–153, 156; of openness, 229, 235;
 Schorr on, 213–214; of secrecy, 66; sunk, 77
courts, 160–161, 275, 278, 282
Cousteau, Jacques, 140
cover: nonofficial, 217–219, 269–270, 280;
 Zellmer on, 279
cramped caution, 251
Cranston, Alan, 214
Craven, John Piña, 21, 22, 24, 163
creativity, 250, 266
credibility, lost, 199
credulity, 231
Cregar, William O., 116
crime, organized, 47, 124
criticism, 184
Crooke, Curtis, 66
Crypto AG, 346n56
cryptography, 20–21, 71, 93, 134, 138, 139, 201
Cuba, 47, 52, 62, 216, 217, 244n34
Cuban Missile Crisis, 62
culture, of transparency, 12
cutbacks, CIA, 64
cutout, 46

Daigle, Craig, 100
damage: to CIA, 250; immediate, 160–161
Daniel, Clifton, 171–173
Daniel, Robert, 263
Davis, Chester, 48–50, 50
Davis, Ed, 145
Davis, Michael, 110, 115, 318n14
davits, claw, 128
Dayton Daily News, 226
DCI. See director of central intelligence
Dean, John, 54, 56
deception, strategic value of, 201
Deep Submergence Systems Project
 (DSSP), 21–22
Defense Appropriations Subcommittee,
 258–260

Defense Intelligence Agency (DIA), 138
delays, AZORIAN, 82, 103
deliberate ambiguity, 201
Dellums, Ronald, 254
demand, for transparency, 231
Democratic National Committee (DNC),
 55, 58–59
deniability, plausible, 6, 35, 68, 148, 188, 242
density, soil, 128
Desert Inn, Las Vegas, 41
Detroit News, 235
DIA. See Defense Intelligence Agency
diagram, Hughes Glomar Explorer, 25
diligence, due, 60, 204
diplomacy, 232; back channel, 100; of
 Glomar response, 211; intelligence
 coexisting with, 203
Directorate of Science and Technology, CIA
 (DS&T), 1, 2, 23–25, 38, 224–225, 256
director of central intelligence (DCI), 17, 65
disillusionment, 223, 224
district courts, 275
distrust, 62, 125
divers, 121
DNC. See Democratic National Committee
Dobrynin, Anatoly, 10, 87, 89, 99–101, 204,
 330n25; on Intelligence Wars, 198;
 Kissinger meeting, 199, 202, 202, 316n77;
 on maritime law, 196–197
documents, stolen, 106–110, 117, 144, 145,
 157–158
domain, public, 276
domestic intelligence, 246, 268, 269, 289
Donner, Aaron, 255–257
doublespeak, 203
Drew, Christopher, 19, 170, 252, 257, 258
drones, 287
DSSP. See Deep Submergence Systems Project
DS&T. See Directorate of Science and
 Technology
Duckett, Carl, 1, 2, 4, 23, 25, 26, 93; on FOIA
 request, 273–274; on sea tests, 206–207

due diligence, 60, 204

Dulles, Allen, 255

Dunham, Roger C., 302n12

Durbin, Brent, 99

Dygalo, Victor, 87

Eagleburger, Lawrence, 342n10

eccentricities, Hughes, 43

economy, 30, 66–67

Ehrlichman, John, 331n43

Eisenhower, Dwight, 8, 61, 186, 188, 274, 283

embargo, oil, 163

embarrassment, 199, 200, 234

engineering, 23, 66, 140–141, 321n1; claw, 119, 121, 128–129, 132; heave compensator system, 128

entrapment, 145

equilibrium, secrecy and openness, 236

Ervin, Sam, 309n31

etiquette, international, 231–232

EXCOM. *See* Executive Committee

executive affidavits, 281–283, 287

executive branch, intelligence oversight by, 31, 146, 147, 249–250, 251

Executive Committee (EXCOM), 67, 73

exemptions, FOIA, 271, 275, 283, 345n45

expectations, of transparency, 169

extortion, 109, 110, 115, 124, 127, 148, 158

failure, intelligence, 60, 181, 182

Family Jewels leak, 142–143, 167, 252, 308n17

Farr, William, 158

favors, government, 52

Federal Bureau of Investigation (FBI), 46, 52, 116–117, 125, 127, 144–146

federal level, Glomarization at, 286

Feldman, Ray, 128, 129

Fink, Katherine, 169

First Amendment, U.S. Constitution, 235

fiscal year (FY), 29–31, 36, 37, 259, 260

FOIA. *See* Freedom of Information Act

Ford, Gerald, 131, 143, 147, 150, 157, 167, 185; Brezhnev message to, 209–210; FOIA vetoed by, 272; on Hughes, 277; Kissinger and, 153–155, 208–209; MATADOR project approved by, 156, 242; MATADOR project ended by, 209; in meeting, *187*; Nixon pardoned by, 243; J. Schlesinger and Colby with, *190*

Ford Motor Company, 274

Foreign Assistance Act, U.S. (1974), 147

Foreign Relations of the United States (FRUS), 9–10

40 Committee, 69, 73, 78, 80, 83, 90; on AZORIAN project, 101–103; on MATADOR project, 149–153, 194–195, 208

freedom: preserving, 270; of press, 229, 230, 232, 234–235

Freedom of Information Act (FOIA), 9, 203, 272, 281, 307n7; case law, 284; exemptions, 271, 275, 283, 345n45; Glomar response and, 273, 274, 284–287, 290, 344n34; NSA and, 288

Freedom of Information Act, Australia, 285–286

freelance journalists, 174

FRUS. See Foreign Relations of the United States

Fulbright, J. William, 32, 33

fund, slush, 53

FY. *See* fiscal year

Gaddis, John Lewis, 98

gadgets, 256

GAMMA GUPPY, 227

Gates, Robert, 197, 270, 322n12

gates, well, 81

Gay, Frank William "Bill," 48, 49, 50, 56, 105–106, 110

Gelb, Leslie, 238

General Services Administration, 278

Geneva Conventions, 74

Georgetown Set, 61

Giaimo, Robert, 260–262, 264, 268, 269

Glenn, Kay, 106–110, 113–114

Global Marine Inc., 45, 77, 84, 183, 224, 279

Glomar II (ship), 84, 86, 87, 128

Glomarization, 284–287, 344n37, 345n43

Glomar response, 202–203, 210; diplomacy of, 211; FOIA and, 273, 274, 284–287, 290, 344n34

glorification, of clandestine activity, 255–256

Goldwater, Barry, 247–249, 265

Golf-class submarine, 1–3, 8, 18–21, 86–87, 121, 137, 204–205

Google, 288

Gordon, Leo, 122–124, 144–145, 320n58

Gorshkov, Sergey, 86, 191

government contracts, 38–39, 43, 45

government favors, 52

Graham, Katharine, 162, 234

Grechko, Andrey, 86, 88, 196

Greenspun, Hank, 48, 57, 58, 115

Greider, William, 238

Gromyko, Andrei, 210

Guantanamo Bay, Cuba, 344n34

H-4 Hercules, aka "Spruce Goose" (seaplane), 43, 80, 140, *141*

Hagler, H. L., 266

Haig, Alexander, 97

Halberstam, David, 170

Haldeman, H. R. "Bob," 53, 54, 56, 60, 126

Halibut, USS (submarine), 19, 21, 137, 302n12

Hall, Albert, 76, 92–93, 101, 151

hammer, 122

harassment tactics, 206

Harriman, W. Averell, 209

Harrington, Michael, 218–219, 224

Hayden, Carl, 305n53

heave compensator system, 128

Hébert, F. Edward, 244

Helms, Richard, 1–4, 7, 17, 168, 221; on contractor relations, 77–78; on Maheu,

47, 52, 308n19; Nixon and, 62, 63; NURO created by, 28; Russell and, *18*, 36; trust of, 26

Henley, Nadine, 106–107, 110, 112

Hersh, Seymour, 82, 154, 162–163; Colby meeting, 164–165; Family Jewels leak, 142–143, 167; *Glomar* article, 182, 184, 235; on HOLYSTONE, 253; reputation, 175; Rosenthal and, 171, 181–182; on U.S. intelligence, 166

history: of AZORIAN project, 288; intelligence, 6, 9

Hoffmann, Stanley, 72

Holliday, Raymond, 44–45, 49, 68, 106

Holloway, James L., III, 137

HOLYSTONE, 253

honey traps, 46–47

Hoover, J. Edgar, 52

House Appropriations, 17, 247, 258, 340n58

House Select Committee on Intelligence (HSCI), 252–254

Howard Hughes Medical Institute, 54

HSCI. *See* House Select Committee on Intelligence

hub, communications, 108

Hughes, Howard, 4, 7, 41–44, 57, 308n23; Anderson on, 178, 277; authority of, 107–108; death of, 277; Maheu working for, 46; Nixon and, 53–54, 59, 60, 68, 78, 80; physical health of, 42; problems with, 48–49; reputation, 214–215

Hughes Aircraft Company, 43, 217

Hughes Glomar Explorer (ship), 4–6, 9, 12, 13, 105; ATA *MB-26* surveilling, 205; conceivable uses for, 282; delays, 103; diagram, *25*; docked, *141*; as FOIA exempt, 283; improvements to, 140–142; *Los Angeles Times* leaks, 157–160; patch, *45*; sailing route, 80–81; scrapping of, 285; at sea, *81*; as unescorted, 75–76; USS *Pueblo* compared with, 313n22; vulnerability of, 205–206. *See also*

AZORIAN project; MATADOR project
Hughes Mining Barge-1, 141
Hughes Productions, 107
Hughes-Ryan Amendment, Foreign Assistance Act, 147
Hughes Tool Company, Inc., 41–45, 77, 105, 218, 279
human remains, 134–135, 197, 331n42
humiliation, 189, 200, 204
Hunt, E. Howard, 56, 58, 166, 216, 310n43
hurricane season, 149
hydraulics, 128, 129
Hyland, William, 139, 148, 151, 207

ICBM. *See* intercontinental ballistic missile
illness, mental, 41, 42
imagination, 4, 13, 227, 228, 250, 290
impeachment, 126
improvements, to *Hughes Glomar Explorer*, 140–142
inflation, 30, 67
information management, 203
ingenuity, 220
Inman, Bobby Ray, 138, 254
Inouye, Daniel, 34
intelligence, 3; ambiguity, 201; back channels, 10, 99–101, 207; briefings, 62; cautiousness, 230; collection, 64–65, 96–97; corporate-intelligence complex, 219, 224; diplomacy coexisting with, 203; domestic, 246, 268, 269, 289; failure, 60, 181, 182; Hersh on, 166; history, 6, 9; myths about, 256; operational methodology, 225; T. Powers on, 200; public faith in, 166; reforms, 147, 247; scrutiny of, 244; Sharp on protections for, 201; sources and methods protections, 243; Soviet, 84–87; superiority, 197; technical, 23–25, 64, 220, 236; tradecraft, 4–5, 222–223, 272; underwater, 19, 21–23, 28, 68, 253–254;

weaknesses, 193; Year of Intelligence, 11, 143, 150, 155, 170, 184, 215. *See also specific topics*
intelligence chief (*rezident*), 86
intelligence oversight, 7, 36; Congressional, 11, 12, 31–32, 37–38, 214, 244–245, 265–267; executive branch, 31, 146, 147, 249–251; minimal, 31; press, 167–169; SSCI, 34, 214, 245
intelligence value, 92, 101, 155; decreased, 76, 195; high, 13, 139, 229; unique, 20, 71
Intelligence Wars, 100, 198, 210
intercontinental ballistic missile (ICBM), 62–63
Internal Revenue Service (IRS), 54, 215
international etiquette, 231–232
international incidents, avoiding, 162, 165, 188, 208, 210
international law, 6, 73–74, 196–197
International Telephone and Telegraph, 218
inventory, document, 108–109
Iron Curtain, 189
IRS. *See* Internal Revenue Service
Irving, Clifford, 309n27
Isaacson, Walter, 317n80
IVY BELLS, 151, 303n19

Jackson, Henry "Scoop," 88
Jackson-Vanik Amendment, 151
Javits, Jacob, 214
Jaworski, Leon, 91
JENNIFER security system, 109, 182, 196
Johnson, Loch, 160, 245
Johnson, Lyndon B., 24, 55, 61
Jones, Nate, 286, 287
journal, submarine, 134
journalism: investigative, 169; sunshine-era, 142, 169, 203, 220, 289. *See also* press
Justice Department, U.S., 52, 286

Kalmbach, Herbert, 90, 91
Kamenev, Valentin, 192

Keegan, George, Jr., 136
Kelley, Clarence M., 124
Kemp, Jack, 262
Kennedy, John F., 24, 55, 61, 220
Kennedy, Robert, 55
Khrushchev, Nikita, 8, 75, 152, 188
Kimbrough, K. J., 265
King, Martin Luther, Jr., 269
Kirkpatrick, Lyman, 2
Kissinger, Henry, 9, 10, 61–63, 68, 69; on
     accountability, 250–251; on AZORIAN
     project morality, 74–75, 102; on Colby,
     250; Daniel speaking with, 172–173; on
     deception, 201; Dobrynin and, 99–101;
     Dobrynin meeting, 199, 202, 202, 316n77;
     on Family Jewels leak, 143; Ford and,
     153–155, 208–209; Gromyko meeting, 210;
     Isaacson on, 317n80; on MATADOR
     project, 149–151; Nixon and, 71–72, 79; at
     NSC meeting, 132; reputation of, 94;
     Schwartz on, 94–95; secrecy of, 98–100
Kostyushko, Vladimir, 135
Kosygin, Alexei, 193, 209
Kraft, Joseph, 13, 236–237, 289
Kremlin, 151–152, 189
Kremlinologists, CIA, 193

Laos, 213
LAPD. See Los Angeles Police Department
Las Vegas Sun, 43, 48, 49, 57, 115, 308n23
Laurie, Clayton, 31
law: international, 6, 73–74, 196–197;
     maritime, 196–197; salvage, 73–74, 151;
     secrecy, 239
Law of the Sea Conference, 192
lawsuits, by Maheu, 49–50, 113, 319n27
leaks, 33, 92, 93, 195, 266; Family Jewels,
     142–143, 167, 252, 308n17; Los Angeles
     Times, 157–160, 3254n4; by Maheu, 51;
     plugging, 56; possible, 92–94, 101, 102;
     press, 157–160, 174–176, 185–186, 257,
     3254n4; Village Voice, 257

Lenzner, Terry, 59
letters, of CIA praise, 247–248
Lewis, Anthony, 270
libel, 50
liberty, civil, 6
Liddy, G. Gordon, 58, 59, 88, 216, 310n43
Lloyd, Walter, 3, 44, 47–48, 272–274, 287
Lokhov, Victor, 135
Long Beach, California, 80, 140, 141
Long Island Press, 226
Los Angeles County District Attorney's
     Office, 110, 148, 158
Los Angeles Police Department (LAPD),
     110–112, 114–117
Los Angeles Times, 156–160, 162, 165, 324n4
loyalists, CIA, 246

Maheu, Robert, 44, 51, 55, 56, 83, 91;
     Anderson and, 52–53, 309n32; as burglary
     suspect, 114; Caulfield on, 57; as CIA
     contractor, 46–47, 242; lawsuits by,
     49–50, 113, 319n27; testimony, 215, 217;
     working for Hughes, 46
Mahon, George, 17, 34, 244, 247, 258–259,
     261–264, 267
Mandatory Declassification Review, 284
manganese nodules, 42
Manhattan Project, 178–179
Mansfield, Mike, 32, 33
Marchetti, Victor, 256, 260
maritime law, 196–197
Marks, John, 256, 260
Marsh, John O., Jr., 241–242, 249, 251
Maslov, Vladimir, 191
MATADOR project, 137, 140, 141, 146,
     170; active status of, 273; Colby on,
     142, 195; costs, 152–153, 156; Ford
     approving, 156, 242; Ford ending,
     209; 40 Committee on, 149–153,
     194–195, 208; J. Schlesinger on, 196;
     USIB on, 138–139
Maury, John, 35, 37–38

Mayaguez, USS, 208
Mayaguez incident, 208
McAfee, William, 27
McCarthy, Joseph, 250
McClellan, John, 246
McCone, John, 180
McCord, James, 58–59, 88
McGrory, Mary, 268
McKalip, Paul A., 247
memo, 103, 106–110, 158
memoir, of Colby, 276
mental illness, 41, 42
metallurgy, 133, 183
methodology, operational, 225
MHCHAOS, 261
Michel, Paul, 127
microwave radiation, 198
Military Audit Project, 277–278, 283
Military Audit Project v. William Casey,
    277–278, 282–284, 287, 288
mining, ocean, 42, 45, 118, 140, 153
missiles: ABM, 63; ICBM, 62–63;
    Safeguard, 63, 311n58; SS-9, 62–63;
    SS-N-5, 20, 92–93
Mitchell, John, 52
MKULTRA, 242
Model T automobile, 274
Moorer, Thomas H., 18, 34, 76, 93, 94, 102
morale, 223, 224, 250
morality, of AZORIAN project, 74–75, 102
Moscow Summit, 69–70, 72, 200
Moss, Richard, 101
Muskie, Edmund, 310n44
Mutual Radio Network, 180
mutual restraint, 200
My Lai Massacre, 163
myth, of intelligence, 256

naivety, 233
Nashville Tennessean, 226
National Reconnaissance Office (NRO), 28
National Science Foundation, 278

national security, 6, 12, 125, 126; press secrecy,
    162, 164, 165, 169–173; provisions, 221
National Security Act (1947), 31, 161, 271
National Security Agency (NSA), 242, 254,
    286, 288
National Security Archive, 286, 288
National Security Council (NSC), 4, 17, 62,
    131, *132,* 242–243, 251
National Security Policy, 1973–1976 (FRUS
    volume), 9
National Underwater Reconnaissance Office
    (NURO), 28, 68, 253, 258
National Write Your Congressman Club,
    264, 266
NATO. *See* North Atlantic Treaty
    Organization
Navy, U.S.: Office of the Judge Advocate
    General, 73–74; Pacific Fleet, 208
NCND. *See* neither confirm nor deny
Necessity for Choice, The (Kissinger), 201
Nedzi, Lucien, 214, 252
negligence, 252
neither confirm nor deny (NCND), 201–203,
    273, 274, 284, 285, 287
Nelson, Jack, 191
news cycle, 204
newspapers: American Newspaper
    Publishers Association, 225; American
    Society of Newspaper Editors, 168;
    Anchorage Daily Times, 229; *Arizona
    Republic,* 226, 247–248; *Atlanta
    Constitution,* 197, 229; Black, 226;
    Chicago Tribune, 159, 197, 227, 228;
    Cincinnati Post, 226; *Dayton Daily
    News,* 226; *Detroit News,* 235; *Long
    Island Press,* 226; *Los Angeles Times,*
    156–160, 162, 165, 324n4; *Nashville
    Tennessean,* 226; *Newsweek,* 95, 96,
    219, 227, 249; *New York Daily News,*
    227; *New York Times,* 142, 143, 162–165,
    176, 227–228; *Parade,* 240; *Philadelphia
    Inquirer,* 228; *Rolling Stone,* 271;

newspapers (*continued*)
San Diego Union, 235; *Time*, 49, 133, 192, 220, 223, 227, 282; *Tucson Daily Citizen*, 236, 247; *U.S. News and World Report*, 219, 223; *Village Voice*, 257; *Wall Street Journal*, 245, 264; *Washington Post*, 98, 161, 162, 165, 200, 233, 238; *Washington Star*, 13, *187*, 229, 235, 246
Newsweek, 95, 96, 219, 227, 249
New York Daily News, 227
New York Times, 142, 143, 162–165, 176, 227–228
Nixon, Richard, 8, 10, 48, 57, 88, 89; AZORIAN approval, 78–79; Brezhnev meeting, 69–70, 87; on CIA, 60–61, 63–64, 99; Ford pardoning, 243; Helms and, 62, 63; Hughes and, 53–54, 59, 60, 68, 78, 80; Kissinger and, 71–72, *79*; resignation, 131; Watergate tape, 126
Nixon Shock, 66–67
Nobel Peace Prize, 94
"no comment" policy, 185, 188, 189, 194, 201, 210
nodules, manganese, 42
nondisclosure, 11, 165, 203, 276, 281
nonofficial cover, 217–219, 269–270, 280
North Atlantic Treaty Organization (NATO), 119–120
Nosachev, Valentin, 135
note cards, of Russell, 16
NRO. *See* National Reconnaissance Office
NSA. *See* National Security Agency
NSC. *See* National Security Council
NURO. *See* National Underwater Reconnaissance Office

Obama, Barack, 286
O'Brien, Lawrence, 126, 310n46; career of, 55; discrediting, 56, 57; as lobbyist, 49; surveillance of, 58–59
ocean mining, 42, 45, 118, 140, 153
October War, 87, 95, 100

Office of General Counsel, CIA, 272
Office of Management and Budget (OMB), 27, 36, 64, 66
Office of Strategic Services, 255
Office of the Judge Advocate General, U.S. Navy, 73–74
oil, 119, 163
Olmsted, Kathryn, 171, 245, 324n1
OMB. *See* Office of Management and Budget
Onassis, Aristotle, 46
OPEC. *See* Organization of the Petroleum Exporting Countries
openness, 6, 7, 12, 13, 170, 203, 268; as abstract, 237; cost of, 229, 235; equilibrium of, 236. *See also* transparency
operational methodology, 225
operational records, 272
Operation Gemstone, 58
opinions, public, on Congressional oversight, 265–267
Organization of the Petroleum Exporting Countries (OPEC), 163
organized crime, 47, 124
Outfit, the, 47
oversight, intelligence. *See* intelligence oversight

Pacific Fleet, U.S. Navy, 208
Packard, David, 22, 67
pain, 42
Parade, 240
Parangosky, John, 27, 111, 188
Paris Peace Accords, 94
Paris Summit, 75, 100, 186
parsimony, of Mahon, 259
Parting the Waters (Branch), 269
patch, *Hughes Glomar Explorer*, *45*
patriotism, 165, 179, 237–238
PDB. *See* President's Daily Brief
peace, structured, 70, 71
Pearson, Drew, 53, 54

Pentagon Papers, 160, 162, 168, 170, 171

Phelan, James, 51, 174, 176

Philadelphia Inquirer, 228

Philbin, Philip, 305n53

Phillippi, Harriet Ann "Hank," 271–277

Phillippi v. CIA, 283–284, 287–288

Phillips, David Atlee, 223

photoreconnaissance satellites, 23, 24

Pike, Otis, 143, 244, 252, 254–255, 268

Pike Committee, 255–258

plausible deniability, 6, 35, 68, 148, 188, 242

plutonium, 85

poison, 256

Poix, Vincent de, 76, 139

polygraph examinations, 115

Postal Service, U.S., 286, 345n43

Potter, David S., 102, 137

power: abuses of, 269; balance of, 250

Powers, Francis Gary, 121, 152, 186, 188, 283

Powers, Thomas, 200

praise: for AZORIAN project, 222, 226–229; CIA, 246–248

precedent, 287

President's Daily Brief (PDB), 63, 191–193

President's Foreign Intelligence Advisory Board, 63, 195, 254

press: competition, 238; freedom of, 229, 230, 232, 234–235; intelligence oversight by, 167–169; leaks, 157–160, 174–176, 185–186, 257, 3254n4; national security and, 162, 164, 165, 169–173; reports, 276; responsibility, 232, 235; UPI, 174, 192, 200. *See also* newspapers

Price, Melvin, 305n53

priority, AZORIAN project, 70–71

prior restraint, 160–161, 167, 181

projects, CIA: GAMMA GUPPY, 227; MHCHAOS, 261; MKULTRA, 242

protections: Sharp on intelligence, 201; sources and methods, 243

protest, Kremlin, 194–196

provisions, national security, 221

publication: CIA, 303n28; intelligence budget, 262–263

Public Citizen Litigation Group, 274

public domain, 276

public interest, 179

public opinions, on Congressional oversight, 265–267

public relations, 221, 239–240

public safety, 231, 233

Pueblo, USS, 75, 252, 313n22

pushing tactics, ship, 206

radiation, microwave, 198

radio, 177, 180, 230

Ramparts (magazine), 168

Ranelagh, John, 34, 168

ransom, 123

Ransom, Harry Howe, 73

Reagan, Ronald, 230, 278, 284

realism, 71–72

Rebozo, Charles G. "Bebe," 48, 56, 80; Bennett and, 55; Capital Police with, 91; Hughes and, 52, 53; payments to, 52, 53, 90, 91

recession, 163

reconnaissance: aircraft, 186, 188, 191, 194–195, 227, 262, 290, 299n23; satellites, 23, 24; submarine, 253, 254

records, operational, 272

reflection, 258

reforms, intelligence, 147, 247

relations, public, 221, 239–240

remains, human, 134–135, 197, 331n42

repairs, 82, 128, 129

reports, press, 276

reputation, 78, 240; of Anderson, 180; of Hersh, 175; of Hughes, 214–215; of Kissinger, 94

resignation, Nixon, 131

response, to AZORIAN project, 136–137, 191–194. *See also* Glomar response

responsibility, press, 232, 235

Reston, James, 228

restraining order, 49

restraint, 72; mutual, 200; prior, 160–161, 167, 181

reviews, of intelligence budget, 259–262, 265

reward, risk and, 76–77, 92–93

rezident (intelligence chief), 86

Richelson, Jeffrey T., 134

right, to know, 172, 231–233, 267

risk, 2, 8, 67, 152; averseness, 250–251; reward analysis, 76–77, 92–93

Robert R. Mullen Company, 55–56, 216

Rockefeller, Nelson, 143

Rockefeller Commission, 150, 167, 230, 260, 323n49

Rogovin, Mitchell, 256

Rolling Stone, 271

Romaine Street break-in, 106, 126

Romanov, Valentin, 192

Rosenthal, A.M. "Abe," 164, 170, 171, 173, 181–182, 234

rumors, 125–126

Rumsfeld, Donald, 152, *187*, 250

Rush, Kenneth, 73, 76–77

Rusk, Dean, 37

Russell, Richard, 7, 29; Helms and, *18*, 36; note cards of, 16; on secrecy, 15, 16, 32–33

safe, 111

Safeguard missile, 63, 311n58

safety, public, 231, 233

Salisbury, Harrison, 171

salvage laws, 73–74, 151

San Diego Union, 235

SAP. *See* Special Access Programs

satellites, photoreconnaissance, 23, 24

Saturday Night Massacre, 88

SB-10 (ship), 119–121, *121*, 129, 140

Schlesinger, Arthur, Jr., 245, 264–265

Schlesinger, James R., 156, 166–167; Ford and Colby with, *190*; on MATADOR

project, 196; at NSC meeting, *132*; on press leak, 185–186; report, 64, 65

Schorr, Daniel, 167, 213–214, 237, 238

Schudson, Michael, 169

Schwartz, Thomas, 94–95

Scowcroft, Brent, 132, 148, 152–153, 158, 180

scrutiny, intelligence, 244

SEALAB, 22

SEC. *See* Securities and Exchange Commission

secrecy, 6, 7, 10, 211, 288–290; balance of, 13, 236, 237, 289; camaraderie of, 232; Colby on, 154, 169, 220, 223, 226; diminution of, 194; equilibrium of, 236; Goldwater on, 248–249; of Kissinger, 98–100; Kraft on, 236–237; laws, 239; Mahon on, 259; McKalip on, 247; press, 162, 164, 165, 169–173; Reagan on, 230; Russell on, 15, 16, 32–33; *Tucson Daily Citizen* on, 236

Securities and Exchange Commission (SEC), 115, 116, 127, 215

security, 27, 41–42; breach, 111, 118, 243–244; heavy, 112. *See also* national security

Seib, Charles, 233, 239, 336n74

self-containment, 72

Senate Select Committee on Intelligence (SSCI), 34, 214, 245

sensationalism, 225

September 11 attacks, 291

sextant, 120

SHAMROCK, 242

Sharp, David, 160; on AZORIAN project, 82, 83, 128, 129, 133; on bragging rights, 188–189; on human remains, 135; on intelligence protection, 201; recalling *SB-10*, 120

Shearer, Lloyd, 240

ships: ATA *MB-11*, 191–192, 204; ATF *MB-26*, 205–206, 207; *Chazhma*, 118–119; *Glomar II*, 84, 86, 87, 128; *Hughes Mining Barge-1*, 141; pushing tactics, 206; *SB-10*, 119–121, *121*, 129, 140; USS *Halibut*, 19, 21,

137, 302n12; USS *Mayaguez*, 208; USS *Pueblo*, 75, 252, 313n22; USS *Thresher*, 22. See also *Hughes Glomar Explorer*
ship-to-shore communications, 117
Simons, Howard, 239–240
Sisco, Joseph, 90, 92–94, 101–102, 151, 156
slander, 50
slush fund, 53
Snider, L. Britt, 252
soil density, 128
Sonnenfeldt, Helmut, 96, 194, 198
Sontag, Sherry, 19, 170, 252, 257, 258
sources: journalist, 163–164; protections for methods and, 243
Soviet Union, 1–2, 15, 69, 70–72; AZORIAN project response, 191–194; intelligence, 84–87; Kremlin, 151–152, 189
Special Access Programs (SAP), 26
Special Projects Staff, DS&T, 38
SS-9 missile, 62–63
SSCI. *See* Senate Select Committee on Intelligence
SS-N-5 missile, 20, 92–93
status quo, 97
steel, 141
Steele, James, 176
Stennis, John, 7, 246, 247
sting operation, 143–145
stock, 115
Stoessel, Walter, 88, 89, 198, 209
stolen documents, 106–110, 117, 144, 145, 157–158
Strategic Arms Limitation Talks (SALT), 88, 151
subcommittees, CIA, 15–18, 31
submarine, Golf-class, 1–3, 8, 18–21, 86–87, 121, 137, 204–205
subpoena, 115, 116
success: of AZORIAN project, 133–134, 182; MATADOR project chances of, 207
Sulzberger, Arthur Hays, 168
Sulzberger, Arthur Ochs "Punch," 164, 165

Summa Corporation, 82, 105–106, 114–115, 124, 279; disclosures of, 317n2; nonofficial cover provided by, 217
sunk costs, 77
sunshine-era journalism, 142, 169, 203, 220, 289
superiority, intelligence, 197
superpower competition, 97–98
Supreme Court, U.S., 160–161
surveillance, 58–59, 84, 85, 137, 205–206, 207, 288
Symington, Stuart, 213, 214

tactics, ship harassment, 206
Talbott, Strobe, 192, 223
tape, of Nixon, 126
technical intelligence, 23–25, 64, 220, 236
technology: advances in, 227, 228; development of, 279
testimony: of Inman, 254; of Maheu, 215, 217
tests: deepwater, 149; *Hughes Glomar Explorer*, 80, 81, 83, 206–207
Thomas, William, 161, 162, 173–174, 234
Thresher, USS, 22
Thurmond, Strom, 246
Time, 49, 133, 192, 220, 223, 227, 282
torch, 111
torpedoes, 134
Tower, John, 247
tradecraft, 4–5, 222–223, 272
Trade Reform Act, U.S., 88
transactions, CIA, 280–281
transcript, 172–173
transparency, 229; CIA shielded from, 270; of Colby, 154, 220–221, 249; culture of, 12; demand for, 231; expectations of, 169. *See also* openness
Treasury, U.S., 280
triumphalism, 197–199
trust, 7, 168, 237; distrust, 62, 125; of Helms, 26
TU-95 (reconnaissance aircraft), 191
Tucson Daily Citizen, 236, 247

Turner, Stansfield, 275, 281
Turner, William, 127
Twitter, 290, 346n55
typewriter, 320n58
typhoon, 117–118

U-2 (reconnaissance aircraft), 186, 188,
194–195, 227, 262, 290, 299n23
underwater Cold War, 3, 21, 222, 258
Underwater Ice Station Zebra, An (CIA
publication), 303n28
underwater intelligence, 19, 21–23, 28, 68,
253–254
unemployment, 67
United Press International (UPI), 174, 192, 200
United States (U.S.): Foreign Assistance
Act, 147; Justice Department, 52, 286;
Postal Service, 286, 345n43; Supreme
Court, 160–161; Trade Reform Act, 88;
Treasury, 280. *See also specific topics*
United States Intelligence Board (USIB),
20, 21, 28–29, 65; on AZORIAN
priority, 70–71; on MATADOR project,
138–139
UPI. *See* United Press International
U.S. *See* United States
Usdin, Steven, 168
USIB. *See* United States Intelligence Board
U.S. News and World Report, 219, 223

value. *See* intelligence value
Vance, Cyrus, 278–279
Victory in Europe Day, 194, 209
Vietnam, 11, 31, 37, 99, 163, 168, 203
Village Voice, 257
Vorontsov, Yuli, 192
vulnerability: of CIA, 70; *Hughes Glomar
Explorer*, 205–206

Wagner, A. Jay, 285
Walker, John Anthony, Jr., 27

Wall Street Journal, 245, 264
"Washington Merry-Go-Round"
(column), 231
Washington Post, 98, 161, 162, 165, 200,
233, 238
Washington Star, 13, 187, 229, 235, 246
watchdogs, 244
Watergate break-in, 58–59, 126
Watergate Committee, 57–60, 88, 90
Watergate investigation, 126, 127, 168–169
Watergate Office Building, 58–59
Watergate Special Prosecution Force,
215, 277
weaknesses, intelligence, 193
We Are Only Limited by Our Imagination
(artworks), 5, 290–291
Webb, Basil L., 265, 267
Webb, Robbie Marion, 265
Welch, Richard, 245, 266
well, ship, 81, 117, 118
White Paper, 180
Whitten, Les, 177
Wicker, Tom, 172, 175, 233–234
Wilkins, Roger, 237
Williams, Phil, 72, 97
Wilson, Valerie Plame, 344n34
Winte, Ralph, 58, 115
wiretap, 59
Woods, Rose Mary, 53, 90
Woolbright, Donald, 122–124, 143–146, 148,
318n14. *See also* Brooks, Chester

Yale, Thomas, 280–281
Year of Intelligence, 11, 143, 150, 155, 170,
184, 215
Yeltsin, Boris, 197, 322n12
Yermishkin, Oleg, 192
Young, Milton, 35, 306n66

Zellmer, Ernest, 279–280
Zumwalt, Elmo, Jr., 76